Instructor's Annotated Edition

THE WORLD OF WORDS

As part of Houghton Mifflin's ongoing
commitment to the environment, this text
has been printed on recycled paper.

Instructor's Annotated Edition

THE World OF Words

Vocabulary for College Students

FIFTH EDITION

Margaret Ann Richek
Northeastern Illinois University

HOUGHTON MIFFLIN COMPANY   Boston   New York

Senior Sponsoring Editor: Mary Jo Southern
Senior Associate Editor: Ellen Darion
Editorial Assistant: Danielle Richardson
Project Editor: Tracy Patruno
Senior Manufacturing Coordinator: Sally Culler
Senior Marketing Manager: Nancy Lyman

Cover design: Harold Burch, Harold Burch Design, New York City

Printed in the U.S.A.

Library of Congress Catalog Card Number: 99-71923

ISBN: 0-395-95829-6

123456789-CS-03 02 01 00 99

Dedicated to the memories of my father, Seymour Richek, and my stepfather, Milton Markman; and to my husband Perry Goldberg

Contents

Teaching with *The World of Words*

Resources for Teaching

In addition to the **student book** for *The World of Words,* there are three resources for teaching. (1) The **Instructor's Annotated Edition,** which you are now reading, contains suggestions for teaching and answers to exercises. (2) The **Test Package,** available upon adoption, gives a series of tests for students and supplementary exercises to reinforce learning. (3) Finally, additional exercises, also available upon adoption, may be accessed through the Internet through the Houghton Mifflin College Division website, Developmental English location. The address for the main website is http://www.hmco.com/college. To obtain more information for faculty support, call 1-800-733-1717 or fax your request to 1-800-733-1810.

Philosophy and Purposes of Text

The World of Words, Fifth Edition, is designed to teach independent learning strategies in a systematic way, to encourage a continuing interest in words, and to develop mastery of a specific set of useful words. Each chapter presents a number of words to be mastered, teaches a learning strategy (dictionary use, context clues, or word elements), and presents interesting features about words.

Mastering Words

Consistent student reaction over several years has convinced me that students want to master specific words in a vocabulary course or in the vocabulary component of a reading or English course. This word learning gives them a sense of concrete accomplishment. In addition, the words serve as vehicles for learning independent strategies, for becoming interested in and excited about language, and for understanding the world around them.

These words are presented in the two Words to Learn sections of each chapter. Treatment is detailed enough to encourage in-depth mastery. Often several illustrative sentences or a usage note is given. Words are fully defined; if a word has two common meanings, both are given so that students will not be confused when they meet the word in different contexts.

The word list and its treatment grew from several years of experience at Northeastern Illinois University with students of many different backgrounds and reading levels. Three years of piloting and use enabled me to refine the list and to keep only the words that students found most useful. Ten additional years of using the first four editions inspired the changes and revised Related Words included in the Fifth Edition. The number of definitions, depth of word treatment, and accompanying notes have all benefited from student feedback.

The Words to Learn sections are designed to hold student interest rather than simply to be a dull list of definitions. Hence, the reader will notice lively example sentences and frequent interspersed boxes that expand on common associations of words or present their unique histories.

Learning Strategies

Each chapter contains a portion devoted to teaching independent learning strategies. These strategies are integrated with the words in the chapter.

Dictionary use   Since most developmental students are familiar but not proficient with a dictionary, Chapter 1 is devoted to efficient dictionary use. Additional dictionary exercises are given in Chapters 3, 5, 7, 9, and 11. Examples and instruction are based on the *American Heritage College Dictionary,* Third Edition (1993). In addition, a pronunciation guide is found inside the front cover of *The World of Words.*

Context clues   Context clues follow in Chapters 2 through 4. They are easily paired with dictionary use and are fundamental to independent vocabulary learning. The three context strategies presented (clues of substitution, definition, and opposition) are the ones students find easiest and most natural to use.

Word elements   Greek and Latin word elements are often found in college-level words and form an indispensable tool for independent vocabulary learning. Therefore, two-thirds of the book, Chapters 5 through 12, is devoted to the study of word elements. Exercises combining the use of context clues with word elements are included in each chapter to ensure that students integrate and internalize their learning.

The word elements that have been included occur in a number of high-level English words and were selected through a survey of college textbooks. The results of this survey were refined using several published studies and student feedback.

The study of word elements has many advantages for college students. It provides an excellent way of determining the meaning of many higher-level words, especially those in specialized fields. The use of such words requires a type of higher-level thinking and generalization that improves reasoning skills and reading comprehension, as well as vocabulary. Finally, because most word elements are drawn from Latin and ancient Greek, a study of such word elements gives an opportunity to acquaint students with these civilizations and their many valuable contributions to our present culture. This discussion fascinates my students and helps broaden their background knowledge.

Care has been taken in this book to ensure thorough learning of word elements and the ability to apply them in unknown words. First, the instruction in the Introduction to Part Two and in Chapters 5 and 6 has been carefully sequenced. The Introduction describes prefixes, roots, and suffixes and shows students that word elements often present figurative meanings of words. For example, the word *reject,* which according to word elements would mean "to throw back," has a different meaning in English; students are then shown how to use the literal meaning of "to throw back" as a clue to the current English meaning of *reject.* Following the Introduction, prefixes are treated first and explained through familiar examples: Chapter 5 concentrates entirely upon prefixes. Chapter 6 introduces word roots.

Extensive checks of word frequency were done using a full-text search of the *Chicago Tribune.* This rich data base enabled me to determine word frequency in contemporary usage, resulting in several revisions in the Related Words for the Fifth Edition.

The words presented are, on average, at the twelfth-grade level (known by 50 percent or more of high school seniors). I have found that these words are unknown, or only very indistinctly known, by developmental freshmen and sophomore college students. My teaching experience suggests that students who do not speak English as a native language can profit from learning these words.

A second provision to encourage word element learning is the use of a unifying theme for the word elements in each chapter. Chapter 7, for example, presents the theme of "movement," and Chapter 8 presents the theme of "together and apart." These themes encourage more coherent learning by helping students to connect words.

Third, word elements are presented in a way that helps students recognize and use them in modern English words. Students are not given a detailed discussion of precise classical infinitive forms, past participles, present participles, and stems. Rather, they are given the word-element spellings most frequently seen in English words. More detailed etymological information is, however, given in the "Notes and Comments on Each Chapter," on pages IAE24–IAE46.

Student Interest and Background

This book is based on the premise that vocabulary learning must be interesting; if students are motivated, learning will be lasting. It is my contention that vocabulary must be integrated into background experiences for words to be fully learned (Richek, 1988). Hence, this book contains features that link student knowledge to vocabulary learning and that cover such subjects as naming customs, car names, and sports headlines. Students enjoy these features and start to see vocabulary learning as an activity that is relevant to their everyday lives. While reinforcing these links, the book also seeks to supply more sophisticated background information. Thus, as the book progresses, information is provided on ancient Greek and Roman culture, famous figures in literature, and scientific advances. All Related Words exercises now contain useful information in paragraph form. Finally, a Passage in each chapter provides an interesting or informative essay that shows the chapter's words in extended contextual use.

Our college population is increasingly cosmopolitan. Because of this, several features in this book stress contributions to English from other languages, information about other cultures, and links between Spanish and English. The teacher will also note that a wide variety of names have been used throughout the text.

Geographical knowledge is key to information about the world. For this reason, several maps included in the Fifth Edition illuminate concepts discussed in the text. In addition, a world map given on the very first page of the book makes it more truly the *"World" of Words*.

In other words, this book is intended to broaden students' backgrounds as well as to teach vocabulary words and strategies. Research over several years has substantiated the importance of vocabulary in adult IQ (Stahl, 1999; Weschler, 1981) and reading comprehension (Botzum, 1951; Daneman, 1991; Davis, 1944, 1968; Thorndike, 1973). Vocabulary is also an important component in the ACT and the verbal portion of the SAT, both significant predictors of college success (Aleamoni and Oboler, 1978; Houston, 1980; Malloch and Michael, 1981; Mathiasen, 1984; Weitzman, 1982). Many researchers postulate that vocabulary can be correlated with college success because words are the representatives of concepts and knowledge (Adams and Collins, 1979; Lesgold and Perfetti, 1978; Spiro, 1980). Thus, to teach vocabulary effectively, background and concepts must be connected to words. Placing words in such context provides enrichment for the student, makes words easier to learn, and facilitates the extension of vocabulary learning beyond the classroom. Research suggests knowledge is stored in organized schemata in the mind (Spiro, 1980). To be learned thoroughly, the subject at hand must be connected to one's life and experience (Readence, Bean, and Baldwin, 1998). This book provides a natural and interesting way to make such connections while enriching the student's fund of knowledge.

Ensuring Effective Vocabulary Learning

Recent research in vocabulary learning has shown the importance of two different activities for vocabulary growth. First, a meta-analysis of many studies (Stahl and Fairbanks, 1986) as well as an extensive review of research (Beck and McKeown, 1991) showed that direct instruction of vocabulary has a substantial positive effect on vocabulary growth. Well-formed definitions and examples facilitate the learning of word meanings (Nist and Olejnik, 1995). *The World of Words* provides helpful direct instruction in vocabulary.

In addition, recent research indicates that students learn a certain amount of words incidentally, simply through reading (Jenkins, Stein, and Wysocki, 1984; Nagy, Anderson, and Herman, 1987; Beck and McKeown, 1991). West, Stanovich, and Mitchell (1993) have found that reading is a particularly rich source of vocabulary growth and world knowledge. Thus it is important to encourage students to read as much material as possible. Suggestions for encouraging reading are given in the following section.

Listening has also been shown to be an effective method for vocabulary growth (Stahl, Richek, and Vandiver, 1991). Suggestions for using this mode are also included.

Organizing Instruction

Student Level Appropriate for Book

Results of a three-year pilot study and ten years of using the text at Northeastern Illinois University show that this book may be used successfully with students reading from the seventh-grade to the eleventh-grade level. In addition, some students reading at the sixth-grade level have used it; those students have had to work hard, but they have succeeded. The book has also been used by students reading at the twelfth-grade level or at college levels.

The book is appropriate for students from many different backgrounds. The student population at Northeastern Illinois University is cosmopolitan, and the book has been used by students from more than fifty different language backgrounds. It has proven eminently suitable for those whose native language is not English. Features on such topics as the Dalai Lama, Jackie Robinson, Samuel Maverick, and Spanish words in English ensure wide and varied student appeal.

Planning the Course

The World of Words can be used as a basic text in a vocabulary course or as a supplementary text in a reading, study skills, or English course. I suggest that it be used at the rate of one chapter per week or half a chapter per week. If used in half-chapter segments, each chapter might be divided as follows:

First week
    Quiz Yourself
    Did You Know?
    Learning Strategy
    Words to Learn, Part 1
    Exercises, Part 1
    Mastery Test from the **Test Package** for first part of chapter

Second week
    Words to Learn, Part 2
    Exercises, Part 2
    Chapter Exercises
    Passage
    Quiz Again
    Mastery Test from the **Test Package** for second part of chapter

This organization encourages consistent learning by breaking up the coverage of the Learning Strategy over two weeks. In the first week, the strategy is introduced and reinforced by the words; in the second week, the Chapter Exercises reinforce the strategy.

Some instructors may not wish to give chapter or half-chapter Mastery Tests but would prefer to test several chapters at one time. They can simply use the Review Tests, each of which covers four, six, or twelve chapters.

Each four-chapter Review Test (Chapters 1 through 4, 5 through 8, and 9 through 12) contains twenty-five items. Like the chapter Mastery Tests, each is divided into a matching segment and a sentence-completion segment. The matching segments for Chapters 5 through 8 and 9 through 12 do not, however, include word elements.

Each six-chapter Review Test (Chapters 1 through 6 and 7 through 12) contains thirty-three items. Thirteen of these items cover learning strategies (including word elements), and twenty cover vocabulary words.

The Review Test for the entire book contains fifty items. Seventeen items cover the learning strategies (including word elements), and thirty-three cover vocabulary. This test may be used as a final.

If time demands in the course allow, I strongly recommend that students use the Review Exercises provided in the student text and the **Test Package.** These exercises help consolidate learning. Students may feel apprehensive about reviewing a hundred or so words (one wise guy in my class cried out, "Hey, I thought this was an *easy* course!"), but they also appreciate the time to rest and review. Each Review Test has a set of related exercises. Review Exercises for Chapters 1 through 4, 5 through 8, and 9 through 12 are presented in the student text. Review Exercises for Chapters 1 through 6, Chapters 7 through 12, and the entire book are in the **Test Package.**

In my course, which lasts fifteen weeks plus one finals week, students review Chapters 1 through 4 during the fifth week, Chapters 5 through 8 during the tenth week, and Chapters 9 through 12 during the fifteenth week. Finals week contains a review and test of the entire book.

Organizing tests and keeping them confidential   With so many tests to give, we have to devise a system to organize them. We developed a color-coded system, printing the tests in cycles of five colors. The use of colors helps us to sort our tests easily and to find them quickly.

We maintain test security by not allowing students to take tests from the instructional room. We also ask students to clear their desks while taking tests. The colors help us to notice when the occasional test is inadvertently about to be removed. In addition, after I have graded and given back tests for discussion, I collect them again. Only after they are in my permanent possession is the grade recorded. This ensures that students will not keep their tests and circulate them. This system also provides that, in case of a query, we can easily locate the completed tests.

An excellent idea for checking exercises was provided by a fellow instructor, who reviewed the book manuscript. This instructor requires students to complete all exercises, but collects and grades only a few each week. Since students do not know which exercises will be collected, they must complete all. However, the grading burden is not overwhelming for the instructor.

Chapter Format and Exercises

A consistent format for each chapter encourages systematic student learning:

Quiz Yourself—a true-false pretest on four words.

Did You Know?—highlighting an interesting fact about everyday words.

Learning Strategy—a systematic introduction to the use of the dictionary, context clues, or word elements.

Words to Learn—Part 1—twelve words and accompanying exercises.

Words to Learn—Part 2—twelve words and accompanying exercises.

Chapter Exercises—a review of learning strategies, word usage, and a writing exercise using the words that have been learned.

Passage—an informative or inspiring passage using at least fourteen of the chapter's twenty-four words. Knowledge of these words is tested in an accompanying exercise and in discussion questions.

Idioms—a presentation of several common English idioms, focused around a chapter-related theme.

Quiz Again—a repeat of the quiz given at the beginning of the chapter.

Numerous and varied exercises in *The World of Words* assure mastery of words and learning strategies. The exercises in the Words to Learn section have these purposes:

1. A matching exercise provides immediate reinforcement of learning by asking students to match a word (or phrase containing a word) to its definition.

2. Words in Context, a sentence-completion exercise that requires students to write out the words, gives practice in using words in context.

3. Using Related Words gives students practice with derived forms. A few sentences on a single informative topic contain two to four cloze blanks. The student fills in various forms of a single word to complete the passage. The alternatives are presented (e.g., *exuberance, exuberant*). In this exercise students are sometimes required to write out the past-tense and third-person-singular forms of verbs as well as noun inflections. This gives them practice in working with forms that are often used incorrectly in writing. Teachers also may wish students to write down the part of speech of each word that they use to fill a blank. The exercise presents continuous dis-

course (rather than discrete sentences). This provides more contextual reading and gives students additional opportunities to acquire background information. The Fifth Edition increases the amount of informational material in this exercise and, in addition, provides some exercises that form one continuous narrative.

4. Which Should It Be?, True or False?, and Reading the Headlines are application exercises that require students to apply their knowledge to more difficult language. One of these exercises appears for each group of twelve words. These more challenging tasks help students to consolidate their mastery over words.

The Chapter Exercises have the following purposes:

1. Writing with Your Words contains ten "sentence starters" that must be continued by students to form complete sentences. The following items are examples:

    Only a *gullible* person would believe that _____ .

    When I am *affluent*, I will _____ .

    This exercise gives students an opportunity to practice writing in a controlled situation and to use newly learned words creatively. I find that students express themselves in personal ways that deepen vocabulary learning and camaraderie. Students should be encouraged to write longer phrases and to avoid one-word answers. Some will find this exercise quite challenging and may want to complete it orally rather than in writing. Other students may be encouraged to form pairs to compose one set of written responses. The creative aspect of this exercise makes it a favorite with my students.

2. Companion Words has students choose the preposition (or other small word) that follows a Word to Learn. This gives students the practice that enables them to use words comfortably.

3. A set of Practicing Strategies exercises in Chapter 1 encourages students to consolidate dictionary skills by interpreting dictionary entries, using a pronunciation key, and doing independent dictionary research. Since dictionary use is a skill that is often learned slowly, additional exercises for reinforcing dictionary skills by interpreting dictionary entries are found in Chapters 3, 5, 7, 9, and 11. *The American Heritage College Dictionary,* Third Edition, is the source of the exercises.

4. The sets of Practicing Strategies exercises in Chapters 2 through 4 encourage students to apply context clues. They must read sentences that contain such clues and then make a hypothesis of a probable meaning for a difficult word. Instructors may integrate dictionary use with this exercise by having students check their answers with the dictionary. A particularly valuable exercise in Chapter 2 has students infer new meanings for common words like *air, stormed,* and *shy.*

5. In Chapters 5 through 12, three exercises reinforce word element learning:

   a. Immediately after the student learns the elements and words that use them, a reinforcing exercise has the student match word elements to their meanings.

   b. In the Chapter Exercises section, students apply their knowledge of word elements by identifying other words formed from these word elements. Using the chapter's word elements, students choose words that are not presented in the chapter and insert them into defining sentences.

   c. In the exercise Combining Context Clues and Word Elements, students read sentences in which one difficult word contains a word element they have been studying. The student then uses both context clues and word elements to work out the meaning of the word. An example is

   Using the *autofocus* feature of a camera, even an amateur can take a clear picture.

   Autofocus means _____ .

The Passage in each chapter is accompanied by a short, multiple-choice exercise that checks that students have read the passage and can show an understanding of words in extended contextual use. Three comprehension questions are also included to spark class discussion. One instructor, Joyce Jennings, uses the Passage to *introduce* each chapter. As the Passage is read, students hypothesize the meanings of the chapter words.

Supplementary Exercises in the Instructor's Test Package

It has been my experience that students need many opportunities to use a word in context before they can fully understand and use it. Two supplementary sets of exercises are provided in the Instructor's Test Package to further aid students.

1. For students at a lower level, there are sets of Multiple-Choice Sentences. Each sentence contains a blank followed by three words from which the student must choose the correct one. This exercise provides easy practice in context and helps students develop strategies for taking multiple-choice tests. The exercise also gives students experience in choosing the *best* of three alternatives. There are twenty-four of these exercises, one for each half-chapter.

2. For more advanced students, twenty-four Passage exercises have been written. Each one is a passage on a single topic and contains ten blanks that students must fill in from twelve alternatives. These include derived forms of chapter words.

Website Exercises

A set of exercises on the Internet, available upon adoption of the text, provides additional student practice. There are five exercises for each chapter: (1) filling a word into a sentence from ten choices, which diminish as they are used, (2) filling a word into a sentence from two choices, (3) judging statements as true or false, (4) filling a word into a blank from four alternatives, and (5) filling words into a continuous passage. The website can be accessed through *http://www.hmco.com/college*. Once there, choose the Developmental English section.

Review Sections

After each four-chapter segment, a review section is presented in the text. Each of these sections contains several types of exercises.

1. Words in Context, for filling words into sentences.

2. Passage for Word Review, for filling words into a connected passage.

3. Reviewing Learning Strategies, for practice in strategies (dictionary use, using context, and using word elements) that have been covered in the four previous chapters.

Several of the Words in Context and Passage exercises are based on the writing of my developmental students.

Supplementary Review Exercises in the Instructor's Test Package

Additional Review Exercises for Chapters 1 through 6, 7 through 12, and the entire book are found in the Test Package.

Additional Ideas for Fostering Student Learning

Supplementary Reading

In recent years, I have been encouraging students to foster their own vocabulary learning by reading as much as possible on their own. To do this, I ask them to bring in interesting things that they have read. I assure them that such sources as the daily newspaper or *Reader's Digest* are perfectly acceptable. In addition, I require students to read at least one book during the semester.

In one format, each student reads the same book, and we have group discussions as the students finish selected chapters. For several semesters,

I assigned Farley Mowat's *Never Cry Wolf* (available in paperback). This book is read during the last five weeks of the class. Since the passage in *The World of Words* focuses on Mowat and his work with wolves, the free-reading assignment is correlated with the last chapter of the text. Several words that have been taught, or that contain word elements that have been taught, are found in *Never Cry Wolf*. A colleague reports that her developmental students have profited from writing individual book reports. More recently I have used the nonfiction book *How to Win Friends and Influence People* by Dale Carnegie. Although not new, the book inspired much discussion and some changes in behavior.

In another collaborative group format, I briefly describe three (or four) books, and students write out their first and second choices. Based on these, I assign the students books to read with small groups. Generally, each book is read by two small groups. Each time they meet, the group discusses the chapters they have read and each member prepares an assigned job. The jobs, which rotate, are:

Discussion Leader and "Hot Spot" Locater
> Lead the discussion, making sure that everyone does his or her job. At the end of the discussion, present at least one spot that was difficult to comprehend.

Vocabulary Finder
> Locate five difficult vocabulary words and determine definitions. Other members in your group will check them with you.

Summarizer and Reactor
> Briefly summarize the article (in two or three sentences) and write a personal reaction.

Books suitable to this collaborative format include *The Water Is Wide* by Conroy, *The Color Purple* by Walker, *Kramer versus Kramer* by Corman, *I Heard the Owl Call My Name* by Craven, *Like Water for Chocolate* by Esquivel, and *Dances with Wolves* by Blake.

I also encourage students to take home and read young-adult novels, such as *Pigman* by Zindel, *The Great Gilly Hopkins* by Patterson, *Where the Red Fern Grows* by Rawls, *Roll of Thunder, Hear My Cry* by Taylor, and *The Outsiders* by Hinton. An occasional student has also read children's books such as *Charlotte's Web* by White or *Roosevelt Grady* by Shotwell. Sports biographies are also popular with many of my students. I often just bring a variety of books to class and pass them out to encourage reading.

I have also asked students to read interesting newspaper editorials aloud in class. The practice in oral reading is beneficial, and the class enjoys discussing the editorials. One student has even braved the *New York Times* op-ed page.

One instructor, Phyllis Glorioso, helps students to familiarize themselves with computer-based library searches by giving them a "media assignment." In this, they choose terms such as *family business* or *Russian bilingual educa-*

tion and find (1) a newspaper article, (2) a popular journal article (such as from *American Psychologist* or *The Reading Teacher*), and (3) a magazine article (such as from *Time* or *Business Week*) that deal with this topic. They summarize each article and locate and define at least five words that seem to be used in their chosen field. Finally, each student makes a five- to ten-minute presentation in class, which summarizes what he or she learned and presents and defines the five (or more) chosen words. This assignment sharpens research skills, encourages independent word learning in an area of interest, and builds oral presentation abilities.

Personal Word Cards

Making word cards is one way to encourage systematic study habits in developmental students. Word cards can be constructed from 3″ by 5″ index cards. The front of the card gives the word and, in the upper right-hand corner, the chapter of the book in which the word was found. The back of the card might have the pronunciation of the word, a definition (formulated by the student), and an example sentence. If the student is ambitious, two sentences might be included, one from the book and one by the student.

Students can quiz themselves or each other on word meanings and pronunciations using these word cards. They can be encouraged to form three piles of words: words well known, words known but needing further work, and unknown words.

Students can also incorporate words found outside of the text into their word cards. If the word comes from another text, the card should contain an abbreviation for the book on the front right-hand corner. If found in general reading, the source should be abbreviated as "G."

Expert Word Cards

In another adaptation of vocabulary cards, Sharon Lansdown (1991) had students share their word learning by each becoming an "expert" in a subsection of words to be learned. I have used this strategy very successfully in my class; I find it encourages enthusiasm, active learning, and a sense of mastery. The words may be taken from a text chapter or from a book that students are reading. If taken from a book, they may be chosen by the students (before reading) or identified by the instructor. In the strategy, each student is responsible for a few words.

To become an "expert," the student constructs a card for each word. The card is simply a half piece of construction paper, folded over, that opens vertically. On the outside, the student writes the word. Next, the student writes the definition and a sentence on the inside. (Often students need instructor input to make these accurate and interpretable.) Finally, on the outside, below the word, the student draws a picture that serves as a reminder of the word. Thus, the word *crimson* may have a picture in red magic marker of blood running from a wound. To summarize

Outside of card: Word and picture
Inside of card: Definition and sentence

The students then are paired with partners. Each partner teaches his or her partner the words. After about ten minutes the partners rotate, and each person gets a new partner.

I have had much success with this strategy, which, among other things, allows students to personally and visually interpret words (Readence, Bean, and Baldwin, 1998). My students become active word learners and often ask, "Is class over so soon?" It also fosters the ease and conversational tone that is essential to successful developmental learning. When they leave class, the students leave their word cards with me, so that I am certain they will be available for the next review.

Bringing in Words

I encourage students to bring to class examples of chapter words that they come across in other texts or in general reading. This helps them to integrate vocabulary learning. In addition, when we are studying context clues, I ask students to bring in a paragraph that contains a very difficult word. The student reads the paragraph, highlighting the difficult word, and the class tries to infer the meaning of the word from the context. The magazine or text in which the word was found should also be identified as another context clue.

The Words-in-a-Sentence Game

Like swimming, playing the piano, and pitching on a softball team, vocabulary is a skill that benefits from use. The following game, which I stumbled on accidentally, is guaranteed to involve even the most recalcitrant student. The game takes about twenty minutes for thirty students to play.

Students are separated into permanent teams of three or four people. Each team gives itself a name, which is written on the board. (Names seem to generate considerable enthusiasm.) Then each team takes five words (from the week's work, or a list) and writes them on a slip of paper. Each team then gives its list of words to another team.

Once a team has received a list, its job is to use all of the words in as few sentences as possible. Students must write the sentence(s) down. Related words may be used (e.g., *adroitness* for *adroit*), and the teacher may assist with spelling or grammar.

Finally, each team reads its sentence(s) orally. Assuming the words are used correctly in the sentence, the following point system is used:

A sentence with one word—one point
A sentence with two words—three points
A sentence with three words—five points

A sentence with four words—seven points
A sentence with five words—ten points

Thus, if a team produces one sentence with three words (five points) and two sentences with one word (two points), its total is seven points. Of course, the total points are added and compared. The students may wish to keep a running total of points.

This simple game is always received enthusiastically by students. Sometimes even students who have lacked motivation will take the words home and try to get them into one sentence. The instructor may assign one member of the team the task of reading the sentences orally, ensuring that quiet students or students who speak English as a nonnative language receive some oral practice.

The Two-Team Game

This game is excellent for giving continued practice. The class is divided into two permanent teams. The words to be studied are written on slips of paper and put in a paper bag, and then a word is pulled from the bag. A student on one team must pronounce it (for one point), define it (for one point, or two points if there is more than one definition), and use it in a sentence (for one point). If the student can do these three things, the team gets three (or perhaps four) points. A member of the other team then gets a turn. Teams may challenge the pronunciation, definition, or sentence of their opponents.

This game is valuable because it systematically gives each member of the class a chance to participate. It also builds relationships among members of the class: team members with a good mastery of the words often start to tutor members who are experiencing more difficulty.

The Automaticity Game

Beck and McKeown (1984) stress that to be learned well, vocabulary must become automatic. To this end, I have adapted a game they devised with great success. I compose a series of statements to which students must quickly answer "yes" or "no" as a group, or individually by holding up cards. Examples from words in the first chapter might include

Is an *affluent* person rich?
Does a *stoic* person complain?
Is a *novice* experienced?

I find this game supplies the practice needed to learn words well. In addition, it is fast-paced and enjoyable.

Words in Conversation

Some instructors conduct a conversation once per week on a previously announced topic. During conversation time, require each student to use at least one of the words in the vocabulary chapter being studied.

Listening

I often duplicate difficult but short selections and then read them to my students. Poe's *Cask of Amontillado* and Dickens's *A Christmas Carol* (where Scrooge meets Marley's ghost) are both valuable—and out of copyright. With the former, I challenge students to translate the complex sentences into simple English. We act out the Dickens selection, including sound effects. I have also used excerpts from collections like *Eyewitness to History* (Carey, 1987), which consists of reports of historical events from antiquity to the present.

Student-Generated Passages and Journals

I encourage my students to compose passages containing words they have learned in class. In some classes, they get a few "extra credit" points. Fellow students are invited to fill in the cloze blanks. Students have written about the homeless, the fact that the Chicago Cubs needed a mascot, and experiences during the Gulf War.

In other classes, I require students to write a passage containing five words from Chapters 1–4, 5–8, and 9–12 when they finish these chapters. Students explore various topics in their essays, including their pet cats, their best friends, their used (but beloved) cars, the nicknames they had in high school, and descriptions of native countries. The student essays featured in the review chapters of the book all originated from this assignment.

A final suggestion for a writing assignment is to ask students to write about something they have done successfully. Students enjoy this assignment, and have reported on topics ranging from learning English to playing football to making good coffee.

In addition, I may ask students to correspond with me by keeping a journal. Two times per semester, each student writes to me (about anything he or she wishes) and I answer back in the journal. Two students recently told me that this was their first "free writing" experience in English and that it had fostered several other writing activities.

Culminating Assignments

For several semesters, I have required students to do a culminating assignment that uses the words they have learned. They may choose from a variety of options, including writing a passage using ten words, creating a crossword puzzle for fifteen words, highlighting fifty occurrences of learned words in a newspaper, finding or creating pictures to represent ten words (e.g., a picture of a Rolex watch to represent "exorbitant"), and writing poetry or song lyrics. My students enjoy the creativity of this project, which, on the last day of class, they present to their peers.

Notes and Comments on Each Chapter

Introduction to Part One

The Introduction is a guide to the plan of the book and a reference section for future use, covering the parts of speech, the use of inflectional and derivational suffixes, and pronunciation changes. I find that developmental students' lack of knowledge about the parts of speech makes vocabulary books, grammar books, and writing books difficult to comprehend. The explanation in this section gives students a basis for further learning and prepares them for an in-depth discussion of the dictionary in Chapter 1. In addition, it deals with some troublesome usage points (such as the past-tense suffix).

The discussion of suffixes and pronunciation prepares students to work with the Related Words throughout the book. To point out the importance of suffixes, I often have one student choose a passage from a magazine or newspaper to read orally. The other students count the number of suffixes used. Generally, we count six or seven suffixes in each *line* of text.

Chapter 1

Did You Know?

Most students are fascinated and amused by the meanings of their names. In fact, a standard instructional tool of mine is a paperback book called *Name Your Baby*. I pass it around in class, so that students can try to find their own names. (Books like this are available in most bookstores.)

My school has a varied student population, and we cannot always find names such as Su (a Korean name), Minh (a Vietnamese name), or Ahmed (an Arabic and Egyptian name). I ask these students to investigate the meanings of their names, and they usually come up with answers. Students with Spanish names can often use English cognates (such as *Oswaldo/Oswald*, "divinely powerful"). In this context, I usually ask my students to list all the languages that they speak. I often find I have a number who speak two languages, a few who speak three, and an occasional student who speaks four. This activity engenders great respect for the capabilities of students who speak English as a nonnative language.

As stated in the textbook, names most frequently chosen for girls seem to change more than those chosen for boys. Michael and James, for example, have been among the top ten names since the 1930s. In fact, only two boy's names, Andrew and Daniel, are new to the ten most frequently chosen names list in the 1990s. But seven of the most popular girl's names make their first appearance in the 1990s: Ashley, Brittany, Amanda, Stephanie, Samantha, Megan, and Lauren. Recently a trend toward non-Anglicized names has been noted for boys; in 1998, José led the list of popular boy's names in New York and Texas. (All facts are reported by the Social Security Administration.)

With the advent of the Internet, the meanings, origins, and popularity of names can be easily researched. Two sample sites containing all this information are *babycenter.com.* and *electricalsocket.com/BabyNames*.

Hook (1983) finds that names can affect people's perceptions. In a study conducted in California, essays identical in quality were submitted under common names (Michael, David) and uncommon ones (Elmer, Hubert). Teachers graded boys' essays submitted with uncommon names lower than those with common names; for girls, however, there was no grade difference.

Learning Strategy

Although most developmental students have been repeatedly admonished to use the dictionary, few have mastered this tool. The instruction in the text leads them through two entries, a simple one (*amicable*) and a complex one (*key*). Many students will actually be surprised that there are different types of dictionaries. With this instruction, students should become familiar with the level of detail typical of a college dictionary.

My students seem to have considerable difficulty with identifying the number of parts of speech functions in dictionary entries, using the various forms of nouns and verbs (plural form, past-tense form, etc.), and ordering etymologies in a correct (not backwards) fashion. In addition, finding the best definition for a word in context is a perennial problem.

In *The World of Words,* dictionary instruction teaches students how to use a pronunciation key, which is given inside the front cover of the book. To facilitate integration of dictionary use with vocabulary instruction, the book uses the same pronunciation system as the *American Heritage Dictionary*. A special pronunciation exercise in the Chapter Exercises section helps students to understand this key. You may also wish to have students use the key to pronounce some of the words in the Words to Learn section.

An important dictionary exercise in the Chapter Exercises lets students do some independent work in any college-level or unabridged dictionary. This acquaints them with a more detailed dictionary than the pocket ones they are likely to purchase.

Words to Learn

I find that the format of the Words to Learn section is usually clear to students; however, you might want to explain it. For Part 1, students might want to think of *intrepid, hypocritical, ascetic,* or *altruistic* people that they know.

For Part 2, *candid* comes from the Latin verb *candēre,* "to be shining white." This reflects the spotless purity of one who is always truthful. The word *candle* and *candidate* also come from this source. In ancient Rome, a *candidate* for high office suggested his purity by wearing a pure white toga, the color of which had been intensified by rubbing in chalk. Thus the candidate was clothed in "shining whiteness."

Stoic is one of many English words that derive from Greek philosophy. *Epicure*, a person with refined tastes, derives from Epicurus (341–270 B.C.E.), who advised avoiding superstitions and pursuing pleasures. Although Epicurus believed in simple pleasures that led to peace of mind, the meaning of *epicurian* has changed to pursuing the pleasures of the senses. The word *cynic* came from an ancient Greek philosopher who taught in a gymnasium called "Cynosarges," a word that resembled the ancient Greek word for *doglike* (*cynikos*). Thus *cynic* (doglike) was an expression of contempt for this school of philosophy, whose members had little interest in material possessions or cleanliness. *Skeptic*, another word from Greek philosophy, is presented in Chapter 3.

My students enjoy discussing *aliens* that appear in current TV shows and movies.

Passage

In addition to Ben & Jerry's Homemade Inc., other companies have shown altruism, social concern, and concern for the environment. Benetton, a clothing manufacturer, has run ads promoting AIDS awareness, tolerance, and (in conjunction with Amnesty International) awareness of human-rights violations.

Ben & Jerry's flavors often have allusive names. Your students might enjoy discussing associations to *White Russian, Aztec Harvest Coffee, Rainforest Crunch* (with Brazil nuts and cashews), and *Chubby Hubby*. Be sure to have your students visit the website *www.benjerry.com*. My favorite place is the "Flavor Graveyard."

Idioms

The color (and substance) gold is used in many idioms. Your students might be interested in *golden handshake, golden parachute, gold mine, golden oldie, golden years, golden age,* and *goldbrick*.

Chapter 2

Did You Know?

Sports headlines can be used to teach connotation and the figurative use of language in a colloquial context. In class I usually ask someone to read me that day's sports headlines and to find synonyms for *win* and *lose*. (Somebody always brings the paper to class.) Sometimes I ask students to bring in sports headlines with these synonyms underlined. Here are a few more samples of the several hundred I have collected:

Cold-shooting Loyola falls short
49ers run over Lions
Bills crush Raiders, keep rolling
Bearcats struggle, then cruise
Rocky start, Tee-rrific finish as Tennessee winds up on top
Pitt purrs past Army
Ohio State surprises Rutgers

Learning Strategy

Surprisingly, many students are unfamiliar with the use of context and are very excited to discover this strategy. Clues of substitution are presented first because they seem to be the clues that students use most naturally. Often college students find it hard even to identify the words they do not know. To help them use context, I ask them to bring in something they have read that contains one unknown word, which they must underline. (I often suggest they use *Reader's Digest.*) I pronounce the word for them in class. Then they read aloud the paragraph that contains the word, and the class must guess the meaning of the word from context. We check this meaning with a college dictionary.

Words to Learn

Every student who has attended college is familiar with the concept of, if not the word, *bureaucracy.* The word *catastrophe* lends itself to a discussion of news events such as the 1998 hurricanes Georges and Mitch, which tore through the Gulf states, the Caribbean, and Central America. Mitch killed more than 10,000 people and caused untold damage in Nicaragua, Honduras, Guatemala, El Salvador, and nearby countries. Less publicized was the *catastrophic* earthquake in the spring of 1999 in the Himalayan foothills, near the Indian border with China. The strongest earthquake of the century, it killed more than 100 people in the village of Biyasi. Students can also discuss the *diplomatic* efforts that have been made to settle problems in Iraq, Kosovo, and other parts of the world.

In Part 2, students enjoy discussing their ideas of the *epitome* of a great football star, a movie star, or evil. A copy of the *National Enquirer* can sometimes be used to locate a *ludicrous* story. Students may also be asked to identify *reactionary, conservative, liberal,* and *radical* politicians. Although most students have heard these four words, they often have difficulty using them with precision.

Passage

This passage focuses on the role of dogs as companions, coworkers, and symbols. Each breed of dog seems to have a well-developed website. Your students might want to check the Chihuahua links website at *www.iolinc.net/mlake/chilinks.htm.* How do your students feel about the Taco Bell Chihuahua? Do they feel he is an appealing and clever symbol, or do they feel that he perpetuates stereotypes or, as one writer opined, takes advertising jobs away from real people?

In 1998 the *Boston Globe* reported that software billionaire David Duffield pledged $200 million to find a home for every healthy cat and dog in the United States. The gift honors Maddiek, a schnauzer that "gave him unconditional love when he was a struggling entrepreneur." How do your students feel about this gift?

Idioms

In a provocative comment, now deceased pop artist Andy Warhol predicted that every person would be famous for fifteen minutes. Thus, through media hype, each of us, regardless of merit, could be made, at least briefly, into a celebrity. To underline the fact that people of little talent were being made into celebrities simply by having their name and image repeatedly exposed, Warhol featured unknown actors as "superstars" in his often outrageous movies. The phrase "fifteen minutes of fame" is now widely used. Do your students feel that Warhol was an accurate social commentator?

Chapter 3

Did You Know?

These are some car names you might want to discuss. Students can add the names of their own cars.

> Mustang, Pinto (wild horses)
> Pontiac (a famous Native American warrior)
> Century (a car built to go one hundred miles per hour)
> Impala (a fast-running African animal)
> Aurora (dawn)
> Avalon (an island paradise to which legendary King Arthur went after death)
> Eagle, Ram, Lynx, Stanza, Sunbird, Citation, Reliant, Tempo, Omni, Sentra, Blazer, Breeze, Lumina, and Avenger

The fascinating history of the automotive industry is a worthy research topic. Early innovators such as Henry M. Leland, Ransom E. Olds, David D. Buick, the Studebakers, and the Dodge brothers both cooperated and fought bitterly as they created a product that revolutionized our lives. Leland, for example, improved the Olds engine, but Olds rejected the improvement. Leland then took the engine to Henry Ford and associates, but Ford quit the gathering, leaving to form the Ford Motor Company. With the remaining participants, Leland invented the Cadillac, which was sold to General Motors in 1908. But, after yet another disagreement, Leland quit GM and organized the Lincoln Motor Company. Leland sold his company to Ford in 1920.

Learning Strategy

The defining context clues are generally straightforward. If students have trouble with appositives, these additional sentences may be used for practice.

Some ants use a *formicary,* an ant's nest.
Druids, members of the ancient Celtic priesthood, once were common in Ireland.
She wore *frangipani,* a red-jasmine perfume.

Students may also enjoy looking in other texts to see how technical words are defined there. Texts use all of these devices plus some others, such as printing a word in boldface type or supplying a glossary.

Words to Learn

Enigma is derived from the ancient Greek verb *ainissesthai* (to speak in riddles). There remain many enigmas, which can be discussed in class. For example, several South American cities (including Vaxactun) were mysteriously abandoned over a thousand years ago, apparently at the height of their prosperity. The plain of Nazca, on a Peruvian hillside, contains markings that resemble an airplane landing field. These were built centuries before humans could fly, and some hypothesize that they were intended for aliens.

In Part 2, students may enjoy considering the word *antebellum* in relation to *bellum* (for belligerent). Most students have seen the movie *Gone with the Wind* and remember its depiction of the antebellum South. Was this an accurate depiction?

Passage

There are stories similar to that of Jackie Robinson's that students may find informative. Perhaps they could be told about Marian Anderson, the famous contralto who was prohibited from singing at Constitution Hall in 1939 because she was African American. In protest, a group of citizens, including First Lady Eleanor Roosevelt, arranged a concert at Lincoln Memorial that drew 75,000 people. Miss Anderson was the first African American to sing at the Metropolitan Opera in New York.

The fascinating history of African-American baseball has been featured in recent years and can be found in such books as William Brashler's *The Story of Negro League Baseball* (1994, Ticknor & Fields) and John B. Holway's *Blackball Stars: Negro League Pioneers* (1988, Meckler). The video set *Baseball: A Film by Ken Burns* (1994) also honors Negro League players.

The contributions of African Americans are shown in every field of endeavor. In invention, to give a few examples, Dr. Charles Drew invented a way to preserve blood plasma. Otis Boykin originated the control unit used in pacemakers and many other electronic devices. Frederick Jones gave us the portable X-ray machine and the self-starting gasoline motor. Granville

T. Woods initiated the automatic air brake and the telephone receiver. The almost innumerable inventions of George Washington Carver include even peanut butter.

Chapter 4

Did You Know?

The size and international nature of English always fascinates students. Here are a few more of our foreign borrowings: *apricot* from Arabic; *yogurt* from Turkish; *orange* from Arabic, Persian, and Sanskrit. The word *salt* comes from ancient Greek, meaning both "sea" and "salt." The word *salary* (from Latin *salarium,* meaning "salt money") is derived from *salt,* since in ancient Rome workers often received a ration of salt for their work. Looking up the origin of one's favorite food is a painless way to practice dictionary usage.

In the closing days of 1998, the New Words Team of the Oxford English dictionary selected sixty-two words that "offer a fascinating snapshot of the past twelve months." These include *ego-surfing*—searching the Internet for your own name; *uplift anxiety*—a term to describe psychological problems that arise from being cured of depression; *web rage*—(from *road rage*), anger due to slow Internet access; *waitress mom*—a parent of low income; and *microphobes*—opponents of Microsoft Corporation. The comeback of yo-yos has repopularized *walk the dog, milk the cow,* and *reach for the moon* as yo-yo routines.

The *Los Angeles Times* has reported, from business, new words such as *cube farm*—offices made of rows of cubicles, and *to prairie dog*—to pop up over the side of your cubicle when you need a little break and just want to have a look around. Internet coinings include *404*—formerly known as *airhead*, from a "404" web message stating that the document cannot be found. Internet acronyms include FWIW—for what it's worth, and RTM—read the manual. Both the Oxford group and the *Los Angeles Times* agree that a word based on *Watergate* has entered the language. It is *Zippergate,* in testament to President Clinton's impeachment process.

The *Atlantic Monthly* sometimes contains a "Word Watch" feature by Anne Soukhanov, editor of the *American Heritage Dictionary.* In this she discusses new words being considered for dictionary inclusion. Back columns are available on the Internet through *theatlantic.com.*

Learning Strategy

The first two opposing structures are the easiest for students to recognize because they contain words that clearly signal the opposition. The following sentences will provide students with additional practice in recognizing the last two opposing structures.

Sam is complacent and *hardly ever* feels uncertain about his actions.

That typewriter is obsolete and has been *unused* for many years.

Words to Learn

Students enjoy seeing if they know the answers to the following questions about rock stars who, in years past, have been *adulated* by the public.

1. What is the first line of the Elvis song containing the word *hound*?
   ("You Ain't Nothing but a Hound Dog")

2. Who were the four Beatles?
   (John Lennon, Paul McCartney, George Harrison, Ringo Starr)

3. What type of glove does Michael Jackson wear?
   (One white glove)

Have today's students lost interest in these groups and their contemporaries? The sales of merchandise licensed to the Grateful Dead topped $8 million in 1998. That's a lot of Deadheads still *adulating* a now-disbanded group!

Students can compose questions or trivia facts about more current music groups.

The many senses of *cultivate* are often difficult for students. You might ask them if they know anyone who is cultivated or if they have ever tried to cultivate a friend.

Military jargon is a rich source of euphemisms. These include *friendly fire*, *neutralize a target* (kill the enemy), and *collateral damage* (the hitting of unintended targets, such as hospitals and schools).

Mammoth gets its current meaning of "enormous" from the large size of the extinct mammoth, a hairy type of elephant. *Chivalrous* derives from the Latin word for horse (*caballus*). *Chivalry* was first used to refer to nobles, who were rich enough to afford horses. Later the word came to mean a code of honorable conduct supposedly characterizing the nobility. My class enjoys making lists of other animal words and phrases. One group came up with these:

loan shark	to hound
sing like a canary	lounge lizard
snake in the grass	turkey
hogwash	rat
lionize	catty
horse around	chicken
foxy	a wolf
to parrot	to carp
old goat	

Cryptic derives from the ancient Greek verb *kruptein*, "to hide." Similar words use the concept of hidden in different ways. A *crypt* is an underground hidden chamber, often carrying the meaning of burial place. The cracking of codes or hidden messages is called *cryptanalysis*, and a code breaker is called a *cryptographer*. *Cryptic coloration* in an animal is used to camouflage, or hide appearance.

Exercises

The Related Words exercises in Chapter 6 present the life stories, in continuous narrative form, of Eleanor of Aquitaine and Elvis Presley.

Passage

The history of Australia has many modern-day echoes that are not lost on my students. They debate our current penal system and whether crime is caused by environment. The source for this article is Robert Hughes's *The Fatal Shore* (Vintage Books, 1986).

Review: Chapters 1–4

Students Rocio and Sophia Ruiz wrote the essay that formed the basis of the "Trouble Twins" sentence exercise. Student Ashanti Roberts wrote the essay for "My Job in Telemarketing." Both pieces were completed as class exercises in the fall semester of 1998 and read to class members. I feel that both speak, with humor, straight from the heart, and show the high quality of the developmental students I am privileged to teach.

Introduction to Part Two

This Introduction establishes the groundwork for the study of word elements by guiding students from the analysis of words that are relatively straightforward (e.g., *impolitely*) to more metaphorical analyses (such as *reject*). Prefixes, roots, and suffixes are distinguished. In addition, root words are divided into base words and combining roots, the latter being more important for the development of higher-level vocabulary skills. Many prefixes and roots will be covered in Chapters 5 through 12. Since most suffixes are derivational (in that they change the part of speech rather than adding lexical meaning), they receive less emphasis. Lexical suffixes such as *-meter* and *-logy* are included. Remind students that a hyphen after an element indicates a prefix; a hyphen before indicates a suffix. In other words, a hyphen is provided where a base word or combining root would be joined.

Chapter 5

Did You Know?

Since a knowledge of classical cultures is important to an educated person, you might want to spend a few minutes discussing the ancient Greeks and Romans. My students generally enjoy hearing about Plato's *Republic* and the *academy* at which he taught. (This was named for the mythical hero-student Akadēmos. From his name, we also derive *academic*.) The unexpected victory of the small city of Athens over the mighty Persian empire on the plain of

Marathon in 490 B.C.E. also interests students. A messenger ran back to Athens to report on the victory, and from that run *marathon* has come to mean "long-distance run." The Romans are remembered for their excellent administrative skills and the oratory of speakers such as Cicero. *Oration* comes from the Latin verb *orāre*, which means "to plead, speak, pray." Our word *senate* comes from the Latin *senatus*, which means "council of elders." *Senex* is Latin for "old man" and *senile* derives from the same source. Those students with some knowledge of the Renaissance should be reminded of the importance of classical studies in that period of history.

The Related Words exercise of this chapter expands on knowledge about the ancient Greeks and Romans.

Learning Strategy

This first lesson in word elements concentrates entirely on prefixes. Each of them is free-forming and can be used with base words. Examples are *anti-nuclear, equidistant, retry, subcontract, ex-president,* and *invalid.* Caution students, however, that *re-* and *ex-* have two very distinct meanings. Instructors with a background in classical languages will already know that many prefixes were derived from Greek or Latin prepositions. Further etymological information is given below.

Part 1

Anti- comes from a Greek preposition and prefix of the same spelling. The prefix is spelled *ant-* before vowels.

Equi- is from the Latin adjective *aequus,* meaning "equal." The spelling change took place when the word was used in Old French. The prefix is spelled *equ-* before vowels.

Re- is from a Latin prefix of the same spelling.

Sub- is a Latin preposition meaning both "under" and "below."

Part 2

Auto- is from the Greek word for "self," *autos.*

In-: This set of prefixes is complex. The "not" meaning comes from the Latin prefix *in-,* similar to the Germanic prefix *un-.* The other meaning, "in," is from a Latin preposition and prefix *in,* meaning "in, into, toward, against." The spelling *im-* is used before *p, m,* and *b* (these are all labial consonants), as in *impartial, immodest,* and *imbibe. Il-* is used before *l* (*illogical*), and *ir-* is used before *r* (*irrational*). The *ir-* and *il-* spellings always indicate "not."

Ex-: Both Latin and Greek had prepositions, *ex* and *ek,* that meant "out of." When used as prefixes, they changed to *e-, ec-,* or *ef-,* depending on the first letter of the root. Currently, *ec-* is used before *c* (*eccentric*), and *ef-* is used before *f* (*effervescent*).

Words to Learn

It is particularly important to relate each word to its word elements in this lesson. An additional discussion topic for Part 1 might be the accusation that the livestock industries have been feeding animals too many *antibiotics*. (This word is included in a note under *antidote*.) Antibiotics enable the animals to live in suboptimal conditions, making care less expensive, but both the animals and humans (through eating their meat) may be overexposed to such medicines. In addition, strains of bacteria may mutate so that they are not killed off by the antibiotics. Recently, this practice has been thought to be the root of outbreaks of salmonella poisoning. *Equilibrium* comes from the same root as *Libra*, a sign of the zodiac symbolized by balance scales. Libras are said to be even tempered, and thus possess *equilibrium*.

For Part 2, undoubtedly somebody's *autobiography* will be found on the best-seller list and can be discussed. The two meanings and pronunciations of *exploit* are difficult for students to distinguish. You might discuss child labor in the early 1900s to give a sense of one meaning, and some current adventure stories for the other.

Exercises

The two Related Words exercises in this chapter are each related within their sets. The first gives a continuous, if very abbreviated, narrative of the history of the Roman Empire. This topic will be revisited, with the life history of Julius Caesar, in the Passage of Chapter 9. In the second Related Words exercise all topics center around Ancient Greece. I felt that these topics would enrich students' knowledge of ancient Greece and Rome, and hence enhance the appreciation of the role of their languages in modern English.

Passage

My students enjoyed the topic of SPAM® immensely. A few even volunteered the fact that it was a relative's favorite food. Of course, in the modern world, *spam* has taken on the meaning of unwanted e-mail. A debate currently rages on whether the outlawing of spam would be wise, and whether such a prohibition would violate the First Amendment, which guarantees freedom of expression. On a lighter note, Hormel's SPAM® website, *www.spam.com*, is the best I have ever seen. It features outstanding music and seven decades of Spam history. Your students can also search the Internet for interesting Spam recipes and uses. Note that, like *motel* and *smog*, *spam* is a portmanteau word.

Chapter 6

Did You Know?

Other words taken from names include: *guy* from Guy Fawkes, who was hanged for conspiring in the English Gunpowder Plot of 1605; *mausoleum*, from Mausolus, a king of Asia Minor whose wife built a beautiful tomb for him; *sadistic* from the Marquis de Sade (1740–1814), whose writings described people who liked to torment those they loved. Similar words that you might want to discuss with all of your students are *gerrymander, laconic, ostracize, sisyphean, vandalize, tantalize, thespian, zinnia, Barcelona, Boolean algebra, Cincinnati, bloomers, America, ampere, Bakelite, batty, bowdlerize, camellia, cardigan, derby, diesel, draconian, Geiger counter, leotard, mesmerize, Morse code, nicotine, pasteurize, Richter scale, saxophone, silhouette,* and *volt.*

Learning Strategy

This important section introduces root words and shows how they are used. Students should be encouraged to read it carefully. Part 1 word elements are all roots; the elements in Part 2 are two prefixes (although both are occasionally used as roots) that relate to mythical figures. The etymological information follows.

Part 1

Anthrop(o): The word *anthrōpos* meant "human" in ancient Greek. Although sometimes it is given as *anthropo,* many words simply employ *anthrop,* so the latter form is used.

Gen: In Greek, *genos* means "birth, race, kind." In Latin, *gignere* is the verb for "to bring forth," and *genitus* is its past participle.

Nom and *nym:* The Latin word for "name" was *nōmen.* The Greek word was *onoma,* later *onyma.*

Viv and *vit:* In Latin, *vīta* means "life" and *vīvere* is "to live."

Part 2

Pan-: As stated in the text, Pan, the god of woods, delighted all. However, the meaning of *pan* as "all" predates the Greek myth, which merely personifies the word. *Pan* is the neuter form of the Greek *pas* (stem, *pant-*) meaning "all, every."

Psych-: Again, the mythology personified a term, *Psukhē,* later spelled *psychē,* as the ancient Greek term for "breath, spirit, life, soul." The spelling *psycho-* is also used in English.

Words to Learn

Wars seem to spark genocide. Are the students familiar with the genocide attempts directed at Jews and Gypsies (World War II) and the Armenians (World War I)? Would the murders of fellow Cambodians by Pol Pot in the 1970s be considered *genocide*? How about the 1990s "ethnic cleansing" in the Balkans and in Rwanda? The well-known character Scrooge is used to exemplify a *misanthrope.* For students who wish to explore the world of Charles Dickens further, Norie Epstein's *Being a Good-Natured Guide to the Art and Adventures of the Man Who Invented Scrooge* (1998, Viking) provides much information. An entire chapter is devoted to Dickens's use of names. The *viv-* words give students a chance to discuss musical terms, most of which are Italian and thus directly descended from Latin. Do students know the meanings of *vivace, moderato, largo, piano, forte*?

Part 2 words should interest students and spark much conversation. Students may know the musical or movie *Man of La Mancha.* Spanish-speaking students are usually familiar with *Don Quixote.* Famous phrases (other than those cited in the text) found in *Don Quixote* include "give the devil his due," "the pot calls the kettle black," and "the pink of courtesy." These and others can be found in books of quotations. The author of *Don Quixote,* Miguel de Cervantes (1547–1616), was the son of a traveling apothecary-surgeon. As a boy he developed a passion for reading. He fought on a Spanish ship against the Turks and was injured. Later, he was captured and taken into slavery in Algiers. He escaped, but was later recaptured, and this escape attempt was followed by another unsuccessful escape attempt. Finally the 500 gold ducats needed for his release were raised, and he returned to Spain.

Many English words and expressions come from Homer's *Iliad* and *Odyssey.* These include the expressions *bite the dust* ("fall headlong in the dust and bite the earth") and *eat your heart out.* A *siren* has come to mean a seductive and beautiful woman. *Mentor,* a trusted counselor of Odysseus, was left in charge of Odysseus's son when the hero left for war. In Odysseus' absence, Mentor advised the hero's wife not to remarry. Finally, in honor of his great strength, *Ajax,* a Greek hero of the *Iliad,* has had a modern-day cleanser named for him.

Exercises

Continuing with an emphasis on ancient Greece, the first Related Words exercise features this civilization. The first four paragraphs are about Greek myths, a topic that will be echoed in the story of Persephone in the chapter Passage.

Passage

The myth of Persephone captures students' imagination. Have students heard any other myths? Myths can now be explored through the Internet on such sites as *www.loggia.com/myth/myth.html* and *www.exotique.com/fringe/ Mythology.htm.*

Chapter 7

Did You Know?

This section acquaints students with inventions with names that have been derived from Latin or Greek word elements. I ask students to list other inventions such as the microphone, typewriter, computer, or video recorder, and we then see what word roots they contain. To further emphasize the importance of classical word elements, I often have students note the large number of derivations from classical roots found in modern scientific words. In chemistry, for example, *atom* comes from *a-* (without) and *temnein* (to cut), both from Greek. *Nucleus* means "kernel" in Latin and is derived from *nux* (nut). *Oxygen* comes from word elements meaning "giving birth to acid" in ancient Greek; *hydrogen* means "giving birth to water."

Learning Strategy

The word elements in this chapter all deal with movement. This theme facilitates student concept formation but also can cause some confusion. Words formed from these word elements require imaginative, metaphorical thinking. The following are the etymologies of the word elements.

Part 1

> *Duct* comes from Latin *ducere*, meaning "to lead" (past participle, *ductus*).
>
> *Ject* from Latin *jacere*, meaning "to throw," also appears as *jactus* (past participle) and *-jectus* (past participle of the form combining with prefixes).
>
> *Stans* and *stat* are from the Latin and Greek verbs *stāre* and *histasthai* (to stand). *Stans* is the Latin present participle form; *statos* means "standing" or "placed" in ancient Greek.
>
> *Ten* and *tain* are from the Latin verb *tenēre* (to hold), with the past participle *tentus*. The *tain* form (in *contain, obtain*) reveals an ancestry through Old French, in which a spelling change took place.

Part 2

> *Tract* is from the Latin verb *trahere* (to draw, pull) and its past participle *tractus*. The spelling in *distraught* reveals a Middle English change.
>
> *Vers* and *vert* come from the Latin verb *vertere* (to turn) and its past participle *versus*.
>
> *Circum-* is from the Latin preposition and prefix of the same spelling, meaning "around." *Circus* means "circle."
>
> *Trans-* is from the Latin preposition and prefix of the same spelling, meaning "across, over, beyond, through."

Words to Learn

Perhaps because of the abstractness of the word elements or the similarity of the words, I often find that students confuse many of the words in this chapter. For this reason, you might want to devote additional time to the words in Chapter 7.

Students often enjoy discussing Sherlock Holmes and his many *deductions*. They are sometimes inspired to listen to CDs, see movies, or even read stories about him. Some scientists now consider the following theory *tenable* although not proven, of course. Once every twenty-six million years, a star called Nemesis comes close to the earth and sprays it with destructive meteorites. The extinction of the dinosaurs may be linked to the passing of Nemesis or another celestial body near the earth.

In Part 2, the concept of *perverse* may need some explanation. Some students may have perverse brothers, sisters, or children, who do exactly the opposite of what they are told even if it harms them. Several public officials are *circumspect,* but others are not. You might discuss current scandals of people who did not demonstrate this characteristic. Burmese Aung San, featured in a box, gives new meaning to the word *tenacious.* Recently, the Burmese government refused to let her see her dying husband! Yet she continues to fight for her cause. The latest events in the life of this heroic woman are a worthy topic for discussion.

Passage

Students find the analysis of body language amusing and informative. I demonstrate some poses or let a willing student try a few. With a good-humored class, common postures of students and the instructor might be discussed.

Chapter 8

Did You Know?

The fusion of Old French and Old English is a topic of great interest to speakers of all Romance languages. Since many of my Romance-language-speaking students speak Spanish, I often follow up by having them use an English or Spanish dictionary to list fifty English-Spanish cognates (a small fraction of the total). This topic also helps students to see why speaking a language other than English can help one's English. Of course, Romance languages did not make the only contribution to English (although theirs is the largest). The words *pajamas, bungalow, thug, punch* (the drink), and *shawl* all come from the languages of India and Pakistan. Finally, although most students have heard of Shakespeare, few know of his role in the growth of English.

Learning Strategy

The theme of together-and-apart concentrates on prefixes in Part 1 and roots in Part 2.

Part 1

> *Com-:* From the Latin preposition and prefix *cum,* meaning "with," this prefix has many variations: *col-* (joined to *l*), *com-* (joined to the labials *p, m,* and *b*), *con-,* and *cor-* (joined to *r*).

Dis-, from the Latin prefix of the same spelling meaning "apart," often means "not" in current usage.

Syn- is from the Greek preposition *sun* (which became *syn* in Latin), meaning "together, alike." Variants are *syl-* (before *l*), *sys-* (before *s*), and *sym-* (before labials *b, p,* and *m*).

Part 2

Greg: The Latin *grex,* with the stem *greg-,* means "flock of sheep, herd of cattle."

Spers is from the Latin verb *spargere* (to scatter, distribute). Other forms include *sparsus* (past participle) and *-spersus* (combining form of the past participle).

Words to Learn

For Part 1, students may enjoy discussing some of the *communes* that were formed during the 1960s. The word *contemporary* should be stressed in both its senses. Students like to discuss whether their parents have contemporary values, as well as the contemporaries of their parents. (Older students often discuss their children in these same contexts.) How many *synthetic* fibers can students name? A few are *rayon, nylon, polyester*. What are microfibers? Can they name any natural fibers? *Syndromes* such as *carpal tunnel syndrome, toxic shock, Gulf War,* and *attention deficit disorder* are often in the news. Can students think of others?

In Part 2, students might want to spend a few days listening for clichés and reporting the ones that are most common. This is particularly profitable for students who do not speak English as a native language.

Passage

The inspiring story of the role of the Navajos in World War II is now becoming well known. The History Channel, a part of A & E Television Networks, published an excellent 50-minute video titled *Navajo Code Talkers*. It is available through New Video Group, 126 Fifth Avenue, NY, 10011. In addition, the Choctaw Code Talkers, who operated in both world wars in the European theater, received recognition only in 1986. Similarly, seventeen Comanche men operated in the European theater in World War II. Among their codes was "crazy white man" for Hitler and "pregnant airplane" for bomber. Both nations were honored in 1989, when France bestowed its highest national honor on the heroes, naming them Chevaliers de l'Ordre National du Mérite.

Review: Chapters 5–8

Two review exercises are based upon the writings of students in my fall 1998 class. Both are stories of triumph over adversity. First, student Viem Nguyen tells of his difficult escape from his native Vietnam in the late 1980s. Then, William Mojica relates how he overcame shyness and slight stature to become a champion runner, only to be brought down by injuries.

Chapter 9

Did You Know?

This section gives further background knowledge on the Romans and may interest students in everyday words. You might like to discuss the origins of the days of the week. *Sunday* and *Monday* are Old English translations of the Latin "day of the sun" and "day of the moon," respectively. *Tuesday* has a Germanic origin and means "day of Tiu," who was the god of war and sky. *Wednesday* has a Germanic origin and means "day of Woden," who was the chief god. *Thursday* has a Germanic origin and means "day of Thor," who was the god of thunder. *Friday* also has a Germanic origin and means "day of Freya," the goddess of beauty. Finally, *Saturday* comes from the Latin for "day of Saturn." Originally all the days of the week were named after Latin gods, but six were changed to honor Germanic (often Norse) gods. Latin derivatives for days of the week can be seen in the French *lundi* and Spanish *martes*. Bilingual students can list them and relate them to the Roman gods introduced in Chapters 5 and 6.

Learning Strategy

Twelve word elements are given for numbers and quantities. Since many follow a pattern, my students find them easy to learn.

Part 1

Uni- is from Latin *ūnus* (one).

Mono- is from ancient Greek *monos* (alone, single).

Bi- is from Latin *bis* (twice).

Di- and *du-* are from *dis,* meaning "twice" in ancient Greek, and *duo,* meaning "two" in Latin and ancient Greek.

Tri- is from ancient Greek *treis* and Latin *trēs,* both meaning "three."

Dec- is from ancient Greek *deka* and Latin *decem,* both meaning "ten."

Part 2

Cent- comes from Latin *centum,* meaning "hundred."

Ambi- and *amphi-* derive from Latin *ambi* and ancient Greek *amphi,* both meaning "both."

Ann- is from Latin *annus,* meaning "year."

Integer- is from the Latin adjective of the same spelling, meaning "whole, entire."

Magn- and *mega-* derive from Latin *magnus* and ancient Greek *megas,* meaning "large."

Meter is from ancient Greek *metron* (measure).

Words to Learn

In Part 1, students might be asked to think of *dilemmas* that have confronted them. The word element *arch* (leader, ruler) might be discussed in relation to such words as *archenemy, archbishop,* and *matriarch.* The word *anarchy* will be learned in Chapter 11.

In Part 2, *ambivalent* might be discussed. Perhaps some students have had ambivalent feelings toward a course that was difficult but valuable, or they may have ambivalent feelings about other people. The students might be able to think of athletes who have exhibited *magnanimous* behavior in victory and others who were not so gracious. What would a magnanimous victor say? They can also look for *symmetrical* objects.

Passage

Although not new, Caesar is a perennially interesting topic. My class enjoys pantomiming the life of Caesar as one student reads the passage. Last time, one of the male students made a very effective Cleopatra. Caesar's continuing fame and contributions are attested to by the fact that the words *czar* and *kaiser* derive from his name. In addition to the many contributions to our calendar, Julius Caesar also originated our modern system of numbering even and odd addresses on opposite sides of a street. Note the relationship of this passage to the first related exercise in Chapter 5.

Chapter 10

Did You Know? and Idioms

Idioms using animal words are so plentiful that a number can be given just for birds. These include *featherweight, a feather in one's cap, featherbedding, ruffled feathers, soar like an eagle, talk turkey, stool pigeon, to sing like a canary, goosebumps, silly goose, mother hen, bill and coo,* and *as the crow flies.* Can students think of more?

Learning Strategy

The word elements in this chapter center on faith and belief. The etymological information follows.

Part 1

> *Cred* comes from the Latin verb *crēdere,* meaning "to believe"; its past participle is *creditus.*
>
> *Fid* is from the Latin *fidēs,* meaning "faith."
>
> *Ver* is from *vērus,* the Latin adjective "true," and *vērum,* the Latin noun for "truth."
>
> *-Phobia* comes from the Greek word *phobos* (fear, terror).

Part 2

> *De-:* The Latin preposition of the same spelling means "down from" or "away from." As a prefix in English, the meanings of *de-* include a pejorative sense, which occurs in *delude,* one of the chapter words.
>
> *Non-* is from the Latin *nōn,* meaning "not."

Words to Learn

The modern sense of *credit,* derived from the Latin sense of belief, might be discussed. Students are always interested in *phobias.* Phobos, the Greek deity personifying fear and terror, was often painted on shields to frighten enemies. Here are a few more phobias to inspire students: *glossophobia,* fear of speaking in public; *ochlophobia,* fear of crowds; *triskaidekaphobia,* fear of the number thirteen (note the derivation from the Greek three and ten).

In Part 2, students might enjoy learning about the Old *Deluder* Satan Bill of 1647. This was the first comprehensive act for public education, passed in Massachusetts. The strict Protestants felt that unless children could read the Bible, they would be deluded by Satan: ". . . it being one chief project of that ould deluder Satan to keep men from the knowledge of the Scriptures." Therefore, they mandated education. The term *nonchalant* might be related to the figure of speech "hot under the collar."

The figures of speech are particularly valuable to students who speak English as a nonnative language. *Star-crossed* makes reference to astrology. Do your students read their horoscopes?

You might want to supplement the figures of speech presented by mentioning *left-handed compliment, play a trump card, red-letter day, between the devil and the deep blue sea,* and *leave no stone unturned.* Some of these have interesting histories, which students may want to explore.

The website *www.facstaff.bycknell.edu/beard/diction.html* now contains an excellent etymological phrase dictionary that includes origins.

Passage

Superstitions fascinate all of us, and many people feel just a little uncomfortable sitting in the thirteenth row of an airplane. The origins of superstitions about thirteen and Friday can be found in the Christian religion. Jesus and his twelve disciples formed a group of thirteen. Judas, who betrayed Jesus, was perhaps the first unlucky thirteenth. Many people will not seat thirteen people around a table in an unconscious reminder of the Last Supper. Similarly, Friday was the day Christ was crucified. My students often ask me whether certain superstitions are true. One wanted to know whether, if you dream you are dying, you will actually die.

In this context, you may hesitate to recommend websites, but there are many to be found. An excellent book on follies, many of which served as the bases of passages for previous editions, is Charles Mackay's *Extraordinary Popular Delusions and the Madness of Crowds* (1841; 1980, Crown Publishers).

Chapter 11

Did You Know?

Students may think of other vivid junk food names such as *Twinkies* and *Jolt*. On the other hand, other food names, including *Lite, Fiber One,* and *Total,* suggest health. An excellent book on the history of junk food and food in general is Carolyn Wyman's *I'm a Spam Fan* (1993, Longmeadow Press).

Learning Strategy

These word elements deal with the body and health. The etymological information follows.

Part 1

> *Audi:* The Latin verb *audīre* (to hear) has the past participle *audītus.*
>
> *Patho* and *-pathy* come from ancient Greek *pathos,* meaning "suffering."
>
> *Ped:* The Latin *pēs,* with the stem *ped-* means "foot."
>
> *Spec* comes from the Latin *specere,* meaning "to look" (past participle, *spectus*).

Part 2

> *A-:* The Greek prefix *a-* means "not," with the particular sense of "without." The *an-* variant is used before vowels.
>
> *Bene-* is from the Latin verb *bene* (well).
>
> *Bio-* and *bio* come from ancient Greek *bios* (life).
>
> *Mal-* is from the Latin adverb *male* (ill, badly).

Words to Learn

The importance of *pedigree* in former times often amuses students. Until the twentieth century, nobles often ordered elaborate studies of their ancestries. Since members of the nobility commonly married each other, most were related. Students can be asked to identify the family ancestry of the late Diana, Princess of Wales. Pedigrees are still very important in the breeding of racehorses.

In Part 2, the students might consider the relationship of *biopsy, benign,* and *pathologist* in relation to the diagnosis of cancer. You might also discuss the word *malignant*. Do students feel there should be limits to *malpractice* suits?

Passage

The story of Jenner's smallpox vaccination is one of the great triumphs of medical science. Many vaccinations for diseases have been developed to protect against polio, whooping cough, tetanus, measles, and (recently) chicken pox. Nevertheless, diseases remain, such as AIDS and ebola, which can be neither prevented nor cured.

Idioms

Other idioms containing food include:

in a pickle	apple of my eye
drive me nuts	act like a nut
egghead	nuts about you
butter me up	top banana
take the cake	cool as a cucumber
you're a honey	clam up
bread (money)	peachy
juicy story	wet noodle
got a beef	dough (money)
hot dog	something's fishy
macaroni (fashionable)	a meaty issue
use your noodle	say "cheese"
cut the mustard	you don't know beans
alphabet soup	peachy keen
cheesecake	spill the beans
corny	out to lunch

Chapter 12

Did You Know?

Other clipped words include *e-mail, mob* (from Latin *mobile vulgus,* "unstable crowd"), *fan* (from *fanatic*), and *piano* (from *pianoforte*). Acronyms include A.M. and P.M. (ante and post meridian), C.E. (of the common era) and B.C.E. (before the common era).

Learning Strategy

Although word elements comprise an important part of this lesson, the confusable word pairs are also important. Etymological information for the word elements follows. *Dict, log,* and *voc* can be confusing, so warn students to study them carefully. They do not have as much difficulty with *graph* and *script.*

Part 1

> *Dict* is from the Latin verb *dīcere* (to say). The *dict* spelling is derived from the past participle *dictus.*

> *Voc* comes from the Latin noun *vōx,* meaning "voice"; its stem is *voc-.* The Latin verb *vocāre* (to call) and its past participle, *vocātus,* are other sources of words with the roots *voc* and *vok.*

> *Loq* comes from the Latin verb *loquī* and its past participle *locūtus,* meaning "to speak." The ancient Greek word *logos,* meaning "word, speech," gives the *log* and *-logy* forms.

Part 2

> *Graph* had its source in the Greek verb *graphein,* meaning "to write," and the related words *graphos* (written) and *gramma* (letter).

> *Scrib* and *script* come from the Latin verb *scrībere,* meaning "to write," and its past participle, *scriptus.*

Words to Learn

For Part 1, students may discuss recent events related to *ecology,* since this is a subject of continuing interest in the news.

In Part 2, students may want to know that the word *paragraph,* containing the word element *graph,* originally meant "beside (*para*) the writing." A paragraph was a mark made by the side of writing to show that a topic or speaker had changed. Students might cogitate over the meaning of the epigram "Man proposes, God disposes" found in an exercise in the chapter. The confusable words are very important for correct writing. For extra practice, students might try filling word pairs into these frames:

affect, effect

> The _____ of the snowstorm was to paralyze the city.

> The snowstorm had a terrible _____ on the city.

> The snowstorm will never _____ the city.

> The _____ of the snowstorm will not _____ the election.

conscience, conscious

My _____ would never let me do that.

I am not _____ of a desire to steal.

A good _____ is valuable.

I am _____ that my _____ guides me.

imply, infer

By your actions, you _____ that you are pleased.

We _____ from your actions that you are pleased.

I would never _____ such a thing in my speech.

If you _____ things, people will _____ them.

Passage

Most of my students are aware of the danger to wildlife caused by human activities. Mowat's adventures make these come alive and provoke considerable discussion. Since articles of wolf preservation appear frequently in newspapers and other periodicals, several students have practiced using the *Reader's Guide to Periodical Literature* to locate information on wolves. This increases their skills while satisfying their curiosity on this topic. One interesting article on wolves is found in the May 1987 issue of *National Geographic:* "At Home with the Arctic Wolves," by L. D. Mech.

Review: Chapters 9–12

In the final student contribution in this book, Semir Mohammed details his family's journey from their native Ethiopia to Saudi Arabia and then to the United States. His story is a reminder that many students are learning English as a third or even fourth language. His ever positive attitude is a tribute to the human spirit.

The passage "Why My Stepfather Was Court-Martialed" is based upon the World War II experiences of my own stepfather, Milton Markman, who came to class to share memories with my students. *The World of Words* is, in part, dedicated to his memory.

References

Adams, M. J., and A. C. Collins. (1979). A schema-theoretic view of reading. In *New directions in discourse processing,* edited by R. Freedle. Norwood, N.J.: Ablex.

Aleamoni, L. M., and L. Oboler. (1978). ACT versus SAT in predicting first semester GPA. *Educational and Psychological Measurement, 38,* 393–399.

Botzum, W. A. (1951). A factorial study of reasoning and closure factors. *Psychometrica, 16,* 361–386.

Carey, J. (1987). *Eyewitness to history.* Cambridge, Mass.: Harvard University Press.

Davis, F. B. (1944). Fundamental factors of comprehension in reading. *Psychometrica, 9,* 185–197.

Davis, F. B. (1968). Research in comprehension in reading. *Reading Research Quarterly, 3,* 499–545.

Beck, I. L., and McKeown, M. G. (1991). Conditions of vocabulary learning. In R. Barr, M. L. Kamil, P. Mosenthal, and P. D. Pearson (Eds.), *Handbook of reading research* (Vol. 2, pp. 789–814). White Plains, N.Y.: Longman.

Daneman, M. (1991). Individual differences in reading skills. In R. Barr, M. L. Kamil, P. Mosenthal, and P. D. Pearson (Eds.), *Handbook of reading research* (Vol. 2, pp. 512–538). White Plains, N.Y.: Longman.

Hook, J. N. (1983). *The book of names.* New York: Franklin Watts.

Houston, L. N. (1980). Predicting academic achievement among specially admitted black female college students. *Educational and Psychological Measurement, 40,* 1189–1195.

Jenkins, J. R., M. L. Stein, and K. A. Wysocki. (1984). Learning vocabulary through reading. *American Educational Research Journal, 21,* 767–787.

Lansdown, S. (1991). Increasing vocabulary knowledge using direct instruction, cooperative grouping, and reading in junior high school. *Illinois Reading Council Journal, 19,* 15–21.

Lesgold, A. M., and C. A. Perfetti. (1978). Interactive processes in reading comprehension. *Discourse Processes, 1,* 323–326.

Malloch, D. C., and W. B. Michael. (1981). Predicting student grade point average at a community college: SAT, ACT scores, and measures of motivation. *Educational and Psychological Measurement, 41,* 1127–1135.

Mathiasen, R. E. (1984). Predicting college academic achievement: A research view. *College Student Learning, 18,* 380–386.

Nagy, W. E., R. C. Anderson, and P. A. Herman. (1987). Learning word meanings from context during normal reading. *American Educational Research Journal, 24,* 237–270.

Nist, S. L., and S. Olejnik. (1995). The role of context and dictionary definitions on varying levels of word knowledge. *Reading Research Quarterly, 30,* 172–193.

Readence, J. E., T. W. Bean, and R. S. Baldwin. (1998). *Content area literacy: An integrated approach* (6th ed.). Dubuque, Iowa: Kendall/Hunt.

Richek, M. A. (1988). Relating vocabulary learning to world knowledge. *Journal of Reading, 32,* 262–267.

Spiro, R. J. (1980). Constructive processes in prose comprehension and recall. In *Theoretical issues in reading comprehension,* edited by R. J. Spiro, B. C. Broce, and W. F. Brewer. Hillsdale, N.J.: Erlbaum.

Stahl, S. A. (1999). Vocabulary development. From *Reading research to practice,* Vol. 2 (Series editor J. Chall). Cambridge, Mass.: Brookline Books.

Stahl, S. A., and M. A. Fairbanks. (1986). The effects of vocabulary instruction: A model-based meta-analysis. *Review of Educational Research, 56,* 72–110.

Stahl, S. A., Richek, M. A., and Vandiver, R. J. (1991). Learning meaning through listening: A sixth-grade replication. In J. Zutell and S. McCormick (Eds.), *Learner factors/teacher factors: Issues in literacy research and instruction* (pp. 185–192). Chicago, Ill.: National Reading Conference.

Thorndike, R. L. (1973). Reading as reasoning. *Reading Research Quarterly, 9,* 135–147.

Weschler, D. (1981). *Weschler Adult Intelligence Scale.* New York: The Psychological Corporation.

Weitzman, R. A. (1982). The prediction of college achievement by the SAT and the high school record. *Journal of Educational Measurement, 19,* 179–191.

West, R. F., Stanovich, K. E., and Mitchell, H. R. (1993). Reading in the real world and its correlates. *Reading Research Quarterly, 28,* 35–50.

THE WORLD OF WORDS

NORTH
AMERICA

EUROPE

ASIA

PACIFIC
OCEAN

AFRICA

SOUTH
AMERICA

ATLANTIC
OCEAN

INDIAN
OCEAN

PACIFIC OCEAN

AUSTRALIA

THE World OF Words

Vocabulary for College Students

FIFTH EDITION

Margaret Ann Richek
Northeastern Illinois University

HOUGHTON MIFFLIN COMPANY   Boston   New York

Dedicated to the memories of my father, Seymour Richek, and my stepfather, Milton Markman; and to my husband Perry Goldberg

Senior Sponsoring Editor: Mary Jo Southern
Senior Associate Editor: Ellen Darion
Editorial Assistant: Danielle Richardson
Project Editor: Tracy Patruno
Senior Manufacturing Coordinator: Sally Culler
Senior Marketing Manager: Nancy Lyman

Cover design: Harold Burch, Harold Burch Design, New York City

Printed in the U.S.A.

Library of Congress Catalog Card Number: 99-71923

ISBN: 0-395-95828-8

123456789-CS-03 02 01 00 99

Contents

Chapter 9 Word Elements: Numbers and Measures *276*

Chapter 10 Word Elements: Thought and Belief *308*

Chapter 11   Word Elements: The Body and Health   *339*

Chapter 12   Word Elements: Speech and Writing   *370*

Preface

The World of Words, Fifth Edition, will help students master strategies for becoming independent learners of vocabulary, learn specific words that will be useful in their academic work, and develop a lifelong interest in words. Through a series of carefully paced lessons, students learn several hundred words directly. In addition, they master three vocabulary development strategies: using the dictionary, using context clues, and using ancient Greek and Latin word elements.

The Fifth Edition of **The World of Words** continues to link students' general knowledge to vocabulary, covering such topics as food, popular music, sports, and the origins of names. I find that students enjoy these features and begin to see that learning vocabulary *is* relevant to their lives. While reinforcing these links, the text also supplies information that will help students acquire a base for college academic work. Thus, as the book progresses, students read about science, the classics, and literature.

The word lists and the ancient Greek and Latin word elements have both been carefully selected on the basis of their appropriate level and usefulness in students' academic work. Word elements are presented so that students can easily recognize and use them in modern English words. Avoiding complex discussions of infinitive, participial, and stem forms, the text nevertheless provides the spellings of word elements most commonly found in English.

Feedback from students and instructors has enabled me to adapt this book to the needs of today's diverse student population. Instructors will find **The World of Words,** Fifth Edition, suitable for students of many cultural and linguistic backgrounds, including those for whom English is a nonnative language.

Organization

Part 1 concentrates on dictionary skills and context clues; Part 2 stresses word elements (ancient Greek and Latin prefixes, roots, and suffixes). A theme for each chapter (for instance, Words About People, Chapter 1) helps make vocabulary study more meaningful.

Each chapter of **The World of Words** contains these features:

- *Quiz Yourself* is a four-item true-false test by which students can determine their prior knowledge of four chapter words.

- *Did You Know?* presents interesting word facts to help spark students' interest in vocabulary.
- *Learning Strategy* provides instruction to help students independently learn new words.
- *Words to Learn* presents twenty-four vocabulary words with pronunciations, definitions, and example sentences. Related Words allow students to see how one base word can be adapted for use in several different ways, and usage notes help students use their new vocabulary words correctly. The Words to Learn are divided into two parts containing twelve words each. Word facts, etymologies, and trivia quizzes provide a context for the words and help students internalize the definitions.
- *Exercises* follow each set of Words to Learn; additional exercises are included at the end of each chapter. A wide variety of scaffolded exercises, including Matching Definitions, Words in Context, Related Words, Companion Words, Writing with Your Words, and Practicing Strategies, provide thorough practice in both the Words to Learn and the Learning Strategy.
- The *Passage* for each chapter uses many of the chapter words in context and gives students practice reading short essays. Each passage is followed by a brief exercise and three discussion questions.
- *Idioms* present the meanings of several widely used English expressions centered around a theme related to the chapter.
- *Quiz Again* presents again the quiz given at the beginning of the chapter, so that students may informally assess their progress.

New to This Edition

Having used this text for seventeen years at Northeastern Illinois University and having reviewed constructive comments on the Fourth Edition from users across the country, I have been able to refine those features students found most useful and add the following new features to the Fifth Edition:

- The *Quiz Yourself* and *Quiz Again* features at the beginning and end of each chapter that allow students to assess both their prior knowledge and their word learning
- Several interactive and entertaining quizzes that involve students while deepening their vocabulary and world knowledge by forming new links to words and strategies. (Answers to quizzes now appear at the end of the book on pages 405–407.)
- *Related Words* exercises based exclusively upon factual and cultural information designed to enhance background information. Some exercise sets form one continuous narrative

- Introductions to each *Passage* that engage students' interest and invite them to read extended text
- Exercises in review chapters based on the writing of other developmental students
- Revision and updating of contents to reflect contemporary developments, revisions in related words based upon word frequency, substantially revised example sentences and exercises, and three new passages

Support for Instructors

The *Instructor's Test Package* contains a complete testing program, as well as supplementary exercises. An *Instructor's Annotated Edition* provides answers to all exercises and teaching suggestions for each chapter. Additional exercises are also available through the Internet. Visit Developmental English at the Houghton Mifflin College Division website: http://www.hmco.com/college.

Acknowledgments

I wish to thank the many people who have contributed ideas, inspiration, and support for this book. The editorial staff of the Houghton Mifflin Company, especially Mary Jo Southern, Ellen Darion, and Jennifer Huber, who provided superb skills and a deep understanding of the purposes of this project. Editor Pam Bliss provided invaluable assistance in shaping the manuscript. Nancy Benjamin of Books By Design provided outstanding editorial and design aid. Thanks are also due to Perry Goldberg, Sandra Goldberg, Irene Nowicki, Stephen Richek, Jean Richek Markman, Milton Markman, Anne Feuerstein, Rodolfo Rodriguez Santiago, José Rodriguez Santiago, Jai Kim, Marina Ulanovskaya, Julia Ulanovskaya, Phyllis Glorioso, Eleanor Zeff, Daniel Zeff, Iris Cosnow, Kate Feinstein, David Lang, Neil Adelman, and Bill Zwecker. Special acknowledgment is reserved for Sophia Ruiz, Rocio Ruiz, Semir Mohammed, Ashanti Roberts, William Mojica, and Viem Nguyen, whose writing exercises appear in the review sections. The following reviewers helped to formulate the shape and direction of the manuscript: Edith Alderson, Joliet Junior College; Kenneth Bourn, Essex Community College; Joyce Crawford, Miami-Dade Community College; Patricia Gates, Community College of Allegheny County; and Darlene Pabis, Westmoreland Community College.

THE WORLD OF WORDS

1

Dictionary Skills
and Context Clues

Did you know that the size of your vocabulary predicts how well you will do in school? This book will improve your vocabulary so that you become a better reader, writer, listener, and speaker. As you master more words, you can improve your performance in all subjects—from astronomy to electronics to marketing to zoology. A larger vocabulary will also help you make a good impression in a job interview. People judge others by the way they communicate, and vocabulary is a key to communication.

This book will help you use words more precisely and vividly. Instead of describing a *friendly* gathering, you will be able to distinguish between a *convivial* party and an *amicable* meeting. Instead of saying that someone gave money to a charity, you may call that person a *philanthropist* or a *benefactor*. Learning these words will also help you understand the speech and writing of others.

As you work through this book, you will improve your vocabulary, first, by learning the words presented in each chapter and, second, by mastering learning strategies that will enable you to learn words on your own. Chapters 1 through 4 will teach you the strategies of using the dictionary and using context clues. In Chapters 5 through 12, you will learn how to use word elements such as prefixes, roots, and suffixes.

Each chapter contains several sections:

Quiz Yourself allows you to check your knowledge of chapter words before you study.
Did You Know? highlights interesting facts about English words.
Learning Strategy presents methods that will enable you to learn words independently.

Words to Learn defines, and gives examples of, twenty-four words that appear frequently in magazines, newspapers, and college texts. Each Words to Learn section is divided into two parts containing twelve words each.

The *Exercises* give you practice with the words and strategies. One set of exercises follows the first part of the Words to Learn section, another set follows the second part, and a final set appears at the end of the chapter.

The *Passage* presents a reading selection that includes several "Words to Learn" from the chapter. It is followed by an exercise that tests your understanding of words used in context and discussion questions that check your comprehension of the passage.

Quiz Again allows you to check your knowledge of some chapter words after you study.

Parts of Speech

Parts of speech are essential to the definition and use of words. In order to master the vocabulary words in this book, you will need to know the part of speech for each word. In addition, if you understand how words can be changed to form different parts of speech, you can multiply your vocabulary by using one word in many different ways.

Nouns, adjectives, verbs, and adverbs are presented in this book.

A **noun** is a person, place, thing, or idea.

> *Jocelyn* is a *nurse.*
> *San Diego* is a beautiful *city.*
> *Flowers* grew in the *garden.*
> *Liberty* and *justice* are precious.

An **adjective** describes, or modifies, a noun.

> The *happy* child played in the sun. (*Happy* modifies *child.*)
> The dog was *wet.* (*Wet* modifies *dog.*)

A **verb** expresses an action or a state of being.

> I *study* vocabulary.
> The class *is* interesting.

Verbs may be divided into two categories: transitive and intransitive. A **transitive verb** has an action that is directed toward someone or something. A transitive verb cannot stand alone in a sentence; it needs a direct object to make the sentence complete. In contrast, an **intransitive verb** does not need a direct object.

Transitive verb: Delphine *bought* a computer. (*Computer* is the
  direct object.)

Intransitive verb: The noise *stopped.* (No direct object is needed.)

Verbs may express past, future, or present action. Past-tense verbs
are usually formed by adding the ending *-ed.* In this case, the verb formed
with *-ed* is a **past participle.**

Scott *greeted* his friend.

The future tense is often expressed through the use of the helping
verb *will.*

I *will shop* in the mall tomorrow.

When we use the present tense, we add an *s* to third-person singular
verbs, that is, verbs that have any one person as the subject except *I* or
you. (Examples of subjects that require third-person singular verbs are
she, Joe, or *the door.*)

The doctor *sees* patients each morning.

Tucson *grows* rapidly each year.

We often express actions that started in the past and are still taking
place by using a form of the helping verb *to be* and adding *-ing* to the end
of the main verb. This is called the present progressive tense, and the *-ing*
form is called a **present participle.**

I *am waiting* for the mail delivery.

The sun *is shining.*

The *-ing* and *-ed* forms of verbs are also used to form other parts of
speech. The *-ing* forms of verbs are called **gerunds** when they are used
as nouns.

Smoking is forbidden in the theater.

Cuthbert and Ann went *dancing.*

The *-ing* and *-ed* forms of verbs are called **participles** when they are
used as adjectives.

The *insulting* man made others feel bad. (In this sentence, the
  man insults other people.)

The *insulted* man felt bad. (In this sentence, other people insult
  the man.)

An **adverb** modifies a verb, an adjective, or another adverb. Many
adverbs end in *-ly.*

The athlete ran *quickly.* (*Quickly* modifies *ran,* a verb.)

We admired the *brightly* colored mural. (*Brightly* modifies *colored*, an adjective.)

The disease spread *more rapidly* than we had expected. (*More*, an adverb, modifies *rapidly*, another adverb. *Rapidly*, in turn, modifies *spread*, a verb.)

In addition to nouns, adjectives, verbs, and adverbs, parts of speech also include pronouns, conjunctions, interjections, and prepositions.

A **pronoun** replaces a noun.

Brenda locked the door when *she* left.

We will meet *him* at the airport.

A **conjunction** connects words, phrases, or clauses.

Oswaldo bought a suit *and* a tie.

Will Marie go to the movies, *or* will she stay home?

An **interjection** is an exclamatory word that may appear by itself or in a sentence.

Great!

Oh, look at that!

A **preposition** joins a noun or pronoun with another word in a sentence. Prepositions are found at the beginning of prepositional phrases, which usually function as adjectives and adverbs.

I have a love *of* books.

In this sentence, the preposition *of* joins the noun *books* to another noun in the sentence, *love*. *Of* is the first word in the prepositional phrase *of books*. The entire prepositional phrase functions as an adjective because it modifies the noun *love*.

This sentence shows a prepositional phrase used as an adverb:

The child ran *over* the bridge.

Here, the preposition *over* connects the noun *bridge* to the verb *ran*. The prepositional phrase *over the bridge* functions as an adverb that modifies the verb *ran*.

Words and phrases commonly used as prepositions include *about, above, according to, across, after, against, before, below, beside, by, during, for, from, in, inside, into, like, of, off, on, out, over, through, to, toward, under, until, up,* and *with*.

Since it is often difficult to predict which preposition should be used in a sentence, mastery of these small words can come only with practice. Therefore, one exercise in this book, "Companion Words," provides practice in using the correct preposition with the words you will learn.

Word Endings and Parts of Speech

A single word can often be changed to form several different related words. These related words have similar meanings, but they usually function as different parts of speech. For example, as shown in the illustration, the word *nation* (a noun) can form *national* (an adjective), *nationally* (an adverb), *nationalize* (a verb), and *nationality* (another noun).

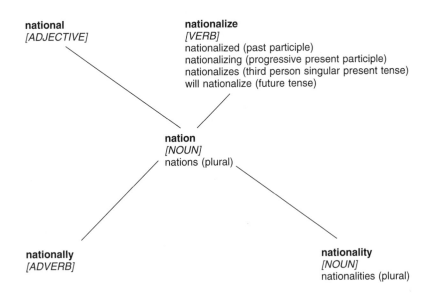

national
[ADJECTIVE]

nationalize
[VERB]
nationalized (past participle)
nationalizing (progressive present participle)
nationalizes (third person singular present tense)
will nationalize (future tense)

nation
[NOUN]
nations (plural)

nationally
[ADVERB]

nationality
[NOUN]
nationalities (plural)

Related words are formed by adding *suffixes*—groups of letters that are attached to the ends of words—to change the part of speech. The following table gives a list of such suffixes and examples of words formed with them.

Suffix	Base word	Suffixed word
Suffixes that form nouns		
-ance, -ancy	insure, truant	insurance, truancy
-ence	differ	difference
-er	teach	teacher
-ion, -tion	confuse, compete	confusion, competition
-ism	real	realism
-ity	reliable	reliability
-ment	require	requirement
-ness	happy	happiness
-ure	fail	failure

Suffixes that form adjectives

-able, -ible	wash, reverse	washable, reversible
-al	season	seasonal
-ful	watch	watchful
-ic	angel	angelic
-ous, -ious	fame, space	famous, spacious
-ive	react	reactive
-y	stick	sticky

Suffixes that form verbs

-ate	valid	validate
-ify	simple	simplify
-ize	idol	idolize

Suffix that forms adverbs

| -ly | rapid | rapidly |

When certain suffixes are added to words, they change the pronunciation of the new words that are formed. Some suffixes change the syllable of the word that we stress in speech. An accent mark (′) is used to indicate which syllable of a word receives the main stress. A light accent mark (′) shows that another syllable is also stressed, but not as strongly as the syllable with the darker accent mark. The following examples show the pronunciation changes in a word when these suffixes are added.

When *-ic* or *-tic* is added to a word, the stress moves to the syllable before the *-ic* or *-tic*.

cha′ os   cha′ ot′ ic
dip′ lo mat   dip′ lo mat′ ic

The stress remains on the syllable before the *-ic* or *-tic* even when another suffix is added.

cha′ os   cha′ ot′ ic   cha′ ot′ i cal ly
dip′ lo mat   dip′ lo mat′ ic   dip′ lo mat′ i cal ly

When *-ion* or *-tion* is added to a word, the main stress falls on the syllable before the suffix. Sometimes an *a* is added before the *-ion* or *-tion*. Note the light and heavy stresses in these words.

pro hib′ it   pro′ hi bi′ tion
con demn′   con′ dem na′ tion   (Note the added *a*.)

When *-ity* is added to a word, the main stress again falls on the syllable before the suffix.

gul′ li ble   gul′ li bil′ i ty
am′ i ca ble   am′ i ca bil′ i ty

As you can see, when you learn a new word, you will often be able to form a number of different, but related, words simply by adding suffixes. Related words formed in this way are listed with many of the words you will be studying. Since the changes in pronunciation caused by adding *-ic, -ion* (*-tion*), and *-ity* are explained in this section, these changes will not be repeated when related words are introduced in the text. As you work through this book, refer to the table of suffixes and the explanation of pronunciation changes when you meet words with these endings. To find out more about parts of speech and how related words can function in a sentence, you may want to consult a grammar book.

1

Words About People

The earth is home to over five billion people, and each of us is different in personality, lifestyle, and interests. It is no wonder that we have so many words to describe people! The words in this chapter will expand your ability to describe yourself and the people around you. You will be able to use these words in school, on the job, in your social life, and at home.

Chapter Strategy: Using the Dictionary

Chapter Words:

Part 1

adroit	capricious	gullible
aficionado	cosmopolitan	hypocritical
altruistic	disdain	intrepid
ascetic	fraternal	venerable

Part 2

affluent	candid	gauche
alien	dogmatic	novice
amicable	exuberant	renegade
astute	frugal	stoic

Quiz Yourself

To check your knowledge of some chapter words before you begin to study, identify these statements as true or false.

Gullible people usually believe what others tell them.	True	False
An **ascetic** lives a life of luxury.	True	False
A **frugal** person likes to save money.	True	False
A **stoic** often complains.	True	False

You will learn the answers as you study this chapter.

Did You Know?

What's in a Name?

Did you know that many first names have meanings? Some parents even research names before they select one for their baby. Here are the names most commonly chosen in the United States from 1990 to 1998. Each is listed with its meaning.

For Men

1. Michael—God-like
2. Christopher—carrier of Christ
3. Joshua—God saves us
4. Matthew—God's gift
5. David—well loved
6. Daniel—God is judge
7. Andrew—manly
8. Joseph—God's addition
9. Justin—fair-minded
10. James—person who takes the place of another

For Women

1. Jessica—person who sees truth
2. Ashley—ash tree grove
3. Brittany—from Britain or Brittany (in northern France)
4. Amanda—lovable
5. Stephanie—crown
6. Jennifer—pure, easy to influence
7. Samantha—God heard us
8. Sarah—princess
9. Megan—pearl
10. Lauren—the laurel plant

You may have noticed some differences between the men's and women's list. Frequently chosen men's names tend to have roots in religion; in contrast, women's names have broader origins.

Popular women's names seem to change yearly. In 1997, for example, the top ten names include four not found before: Taylor, Madison, Kayla (meaning "slim and fair"), and Alexis (meaning "protector"). Two of these new women's names, Taylor and Madison, are often given to men. In fact, the most popular man's name, Michael, is also the 799th most popular name for women. It seems that some people are comfortable giving newborn girls names that are usually given to boys. Some of these women later become famous, like the actress Michael Learned.

Throughout history, parents have also named children in honor of personal heroes. In the 1700s, although the Scots failed to bring Charles Stuart to the throne as their king, many Scottish people remained loyal to him. In tribute to "Bonnie" (handsome) Prince Charlie, one Scot named all fourteen of his sons *Charles*. Similarly, in the 1960s, many parents named their daughters *Jacqueline* after the popular Jacqueline Kennedy, wife of U.S. President John F. Kennedy. Similarly, the name *Kenyatta*, honoring Jomo Kenyatta, president of Kenya from 1964 to 1978, was given to boys. The continuing popularity of the name Michael may be partially due to the great basketball player Michael Jordan.

In some cultures, religious leaders, rather than parents, name babies. Traditional Buddhist families often ask monks to choose first names. After a name is given, the mother and father may not eat meat for one year.

Middle names may be used to show family ties. In Russia, a "patronymic" middle name contains the father's first name plus *-ovich* (son) or *-ovna* (daughter). Alexander Fekson's son, Gennady, is *Gennady Alexandrovich Fekson;* Alexander's daughter, Sophia, is *Sophia Alexandrovna Fekson.* The most respectful way to address a Russian is to use the first name and patronymic (Sophia Alexandrovna) without the last name.

Many Korean families express their unity by giving all boys of one generation the same middle name. Five names that mean *wood, fire, earth, metal,* and *water* are passed from father to son. If two brothers get the middle name *wood,* their sons are named *fire* and their grandsons are named *earth.* In the sixth generation, the cycle begins again.

Today many English-speaking parents give children hyphenated last (or family) names that contain the family names of both mother and father. This practice is similar to naming customs in Spanish-speaking countries. For instance, one Costa Rican teacher named *Beatrice* has a father whose family name is *Sandino* and a mother whose family name is *Rodriguez.* Beatrice's full name is *Beatrice Sandino-Rodriguez.*

In many Asian countries, family names are actually put first, giving special importance to family relationships. The family name of Chinese revolutionary leader Mao Zedong was *Mao,* not *Zedong,* and he was referred to as "Chairman Mao."

Learning Strategy

Using the Dictionary

The Learning Strategies presented in this book will teach you how to figure out the meanings of unknown words on your own. This book presents
about five hundred words that you will learn directly from the Words to
Learn sections. However, by using techniques from the Learning Strategy
sections, you will be able to multiply your vocabulary to include thousands of new words.

This chapter's Learning Strategy concentrates on the effective use
of the dictionary. The dictionary is an important tool for improving your
vocabulary, since it is the best source for finding the precise meaning of
a word.

There are many different types of dictionaries. The smallest is the
pocket or abridged dictionary, usually a paperback, which gives short
definitions. The most complete kind is the unabridged dictionary, which
includes many unusual words, extensive definitions, and full word histories. You may have seen an unabridged dictionary on a stand in the library or referred to an unabridged dictionary on the Internet or CD-ROM.
Between these two sizes is the college-level dictionary, which includes
enough detail for most college students.

Because a dictionary conveys much information in a small space,
learning to use this important tool takes practice. A skillful dictionary
user can find not only the meaning of a word but also its pronunciation,
its history, and other words related to it.

Here is an entry from a college-level dictionary, the *American Heritage Dictionary, Third College Edition*. Each part is labeled.

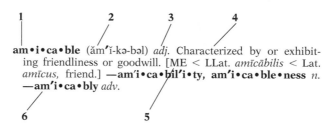

A standard dictionary entry contains the following parts:

1. **The word.** The entry word is printed in boldface type and divided into
   syllables.

2. **The pronunciation.** A key in the border of each fully opened page of
   a dictionary shows you how to interpret the pronunciation symbols.
   (You can also find a key to these symbols on the inside front cover of

this textbook.) This key gives a common word that contains the sound represented by that symbol. For example, the symbol ă (which represents the first sound in *amicable*) should be spoken like the sound of *a* in the word *păt*.

An accent mark (′) follows the syllable that should be stressed when you pronounce a word. In *amicable,* only the first syllable is stressed. If two syllables have accent marks, the syllable with the darker accent mark receives more stress.

At times, an entry will give two pronunciations for a word. The pronunciation that appears first is the preferred one.

3. **The part of speech.** The parts of speech you will most often encounter are commonly abbreviated as follows.

n.—noun   *tr. v.*—transitive verb
adj.—adjective   *intr. v.*—intransitive verb
adv.—adverb

These parts of speech and their functions are described in the Introduction to Part One.

4. **The definition.** Since some words have more than one definition, you must choose the one that best fits the sentence you are reading or writing. Choosing the best definition often requires some thought. Be sure to read all of the definitions before you select one.

Dictionaries have different methods of ordering definitions. In the *American Heritage Dictionary, Third College Edition,* published by Houghton Mifflin Company, the most general definition of a word is given first, and the least general is given last. In *Webster's Tenth New Collegiate Dictionary,* published by Merriam-Webster, the oldest definition of a word appears first, and the newest definition last. In the *Random House College Dictionary, Revised Edition,* published by Random House, definitions are ordered from the most commonly used to the least commonly used.

Dictionary definitions usually state only the precise, or *denotative,* meanings of words. But words also have implied, or *connotative,* meanings, which are suggested by the images, ideas, and emotions that we associate with them. For example, the words *skinny* and *slender* have the same denotative meaning, "thin," but they differ in connotative meaning. *Skinny* has negative associations, or connotations, and is an uncomplimentary word; *slender* has positive connotations and is a complimentary word. In the same way, *car* has a neutral connotation; *limousine* connotes an expensive, luxurious auto; and *wreck* connotes an auto that is worthless. Although dictionaries give some hints about connotative meanings, most information is learned simply by observing the ways people use words when they write and speak.

5. **The etymology.** In this section, the history of a word is traced to its origin. The word *amicable* comes to us in its present form from Middle

English. Before this, the word appeared in Late Latin as *amicabilis*, which can be followed back still further to the Latin word *amicus*, meaning "friend." The dictionary includes a complete list of the abbreviations for languages used in etymologies. A few of the most common abbreviations follow.

ME—Middle English, spoken in England from 1100 to 1500 C.E. (A.D. 1100 to 1500)

OE—Old English, spoken in England before 1100 C.E.

Fr.—French, spoken in France today

OFr.—Old French, spoken in France from 800 to 1200 C.E.

Lat.—Latin, spoken by the Romans in Italy about 2,000 years ago (LLat., Late Latin, was spoken at a later time.)

Gk.—Ancient Greek, spoken in Greece about 2,500 years ago

Etymologies are usually enclosed in square brackets ([ ]) in a dictionary entry.

6. **Related words.** Sometimes several forms of a word are listed under one dictionary entry. Related words usually differ from the entry word because they contain *suffixes*, or word endings. Often these suffixes make the related words into different parts of speech. For instance, under the main entry *amicable* (an adjective), two nouns (*amicability*, *amicableness*) and an adverb (*amicably*) are also listed. A discussion of suffixes and how they change the part of speech can be found in the Introduction to Part One.

While the dictionary entry for *amicable* is relatively simple, some entries are more complex. In the entry below, the word *key* has many definitions, which are separated according to different parts of speech.

(1) **key**[1] (kē) *n., pl.* **keys. 1.a.** A notched and grooved, usu. metal device that is turned to open or close a lock. **b.** A similar device for opening or winding: *the key of a clock.* **2.** A means of access, control, or possession. **3.a.** A vital, crucial element.
(5) **b.** A set of answers to a test. **c.** A table, gloss, or cipher for decoding or interpreting. **4.** A device, such as a wedge, inserted to lock together mechanical or structural parts. **5.** *Archit.* The keystone in an arch. **6.a.** A button or lever that is pressed to operate a machine. **b.** *Mus.* A button or lever
(10) that is pressed to produce or modulate the sound of an instrument, such as a clarinet. **7.** *Mus.* **a.** A tonal system consisting of seven tones in fixed relationship to a tonic; tonality. **b.** The principal tonality of a work: *an etude in the key of E.* **8.** The pitch of a voice or other sound. **9.** A characteristic
(15) tone or level of intensity, as of a speech. Often used in combination: *high-key; low-key.* **10.** *Bot.* The key fruit. **11.** An outline of the characteristics of a group of organisms, used in taxonomic identification. **12.** *Basketball.* An area at each end of the court between the base line and the foul line and in-
(20) cluding the jump-ball circle at the foul line. —*adj.* Of crucial importance; significant: *key decisions.* —*tr.v.* **keyed, key•ing, keys. 1.** To lock with or as if with a key. **2.** *Archit.* To furnish (an arch) with a keystone. **3.** *Mus.* To regulate the

(25) pitch of. **4.** To bring into harmony; adjust or adapt. **5.** To supply an explanatory key for. **6.a.** To operate (a device), as for typesetting with a keyboard. **b.** To enter (data) into a computer with a keyboard. **7.** To identify (a biological specimen). —*phrasal verb.* **key up.** To make intense, excited, or nervous. —*idioms.* **in key.** In consonance with other factors.

(30) **out of key.** Not in consonance with other factors. [ME *kai, kei* < OE *cǣg.*]

The entry shows that *key* can be used as three parts of speech: noun (line 1), adjective (line 20), and transitive verb (line 21). Sometimes a part of speech has several forms. In the entry above, *key* has different forms when it is used as a verb (see lines 21–22). These forms are (1) *keyed*—the past participle, (2) *keying*—the present participle, and (3) *keys*—the third-person singular verb form.

If the entry had been for a verb of more than one syllable, these forms might have been listed without the first syllable. For example, the forms for the verb *answer* are listed in the dictionary as -*swered,* -*swering,* and -*swers,* with the *an-* simply left out. Entries for nouns list the spelling of irregular plural forms, and entries for adjectives list spellings for comparative forms, such as *prettier* and *prettiest* for the word *pretty.*

As you look at the definitions within each part-of-speech category of *key,* you will notice several other features of the dictionary entry. First, two or more closely related definitions may be listed under one number. Definition 1 of *key* as a noun has two parts, 1a and 1b. This is also true of definitions 6 and 7 of *key* as a noun (lines 8–13) and definition 6 of *key* as a transitive verb (lines 25–27). Definition 3 of *key* as a noun (lines 4–6) actually has three parts, 3a, 3b, and 3c. The various parts of one definition are closely related to each other, as you can see by reading them. Next you will notice that a word or abbreviation in italics, such as *Archit.* (line 8), is included in some definitions. This is called a "label," and it indicates that this definition is used in a special field. For example, the fifth definition of *key* as a noun is used in architecture, the seventh is used in music, the tenth is used in botany, and the twelfth is used in basketball.

Other labels give information about the style or use of a definition. For example, the label *Informal* shows that a definition is acceptable in informal speech; *Slang* shows that a word is used only in slang, or very informal usage; and *Nonstandard* indicates that a usage is not commonly accepted. The labels *Obs.* (for "obsolete") and *Archaic* show that a meaning of a word is no longer commonly used. An explanation of labels is given in the front of each dictionary.

A dictionary entry may also include examples of the word being used in phrases or sentences. In line 3, note the phrase "the key of a clock." If sentences written by well-known authors are quoted, the author's name appears in parentheses after the quote. Finally, toward the end of the entry you may see *phrasal verb* and *idiom.* These show how the word is used with other words. A phrasal verb is a phrase that functions as a verb, such as *key up.* Idioms are common phrases, such as *in key* and *out of key.*

Notice, in the etymology, that the word *key* comes from Old English and is found later in Middle English. For some words, the etymology deals with the origins of the different word parts contained within the word. Finally, some etymologies refer the reader to other words.

To check your knowledge of the dictionary, read the following dictionary entry and then answer the questions below.

> **paw** (pô) *n.* **1.** The nailed or clawed foot of an animal, esp. of a quadruped. **2.** *Informal.* A human hand, esp. a large clumsy one. —*v.* **pawed, paw•ing, paws.** —*tr.* **1.** To strike with the paw or paws. **2.** To strike or scrape with a beating motion. **3.** To handle clumsily, rudely, or with too much familiarity. —*intr.* **1.** To scrape the ground with the forefeet. **2.** To paw someone or something as in rudeness. [ME *pawe* < OFr. *powe.*] —**paw′er** *n.*

1. What three part-of-speech functions does *paw* have? _____

   noun, transitive verb, intransitive verb

2. Which definition (including part of speech) is acceptable only in informal speech? **2, as a noun**

3. In which language was *paw* first recorded? **Old French**

Answers are on page 405.

Words to Learn

Part 1

1. **adroit** (adjective)   ə-droit′

   skillful; clever

   > The **adroit** politician avoided answering several embarrassing questions.

   > The boxer's **adroit** footwork allowed him to avoid his opponent's punches.

▶ *Related Word*

adroitness (noun)   Her *adroitness* at math enabled her to add fifty numbers in her head.

NOTE: The word *adroit* can refer to quickness of body or mind.

2. **aficionado** (noun)   ə-fĭsh′ē-ə-nä′dō

fan; admirer; follower

Aficionados of spicy food can subscribe to *Chili Pepper* magazine.

Sports **aficionados** can watch many different games on the split screens of one television.

3. **altruistic** (adjective)   ăl′trōō-ĭs′tĭk

dedicated to the good of others; unselfish

An **altruistic** one-hundred-year-old woman in Chicago distributes free food to poor people.

The **altruistic** man donated his kidney to save the life of a sick child.

▶ *Related Word*

altruism (noun)   (ăl′trōō-ĭz′əm)   The minister's *altruism* inspired him to run a shelter for abused children.

Famous sports figures Dikembe Mutombo and Sammy Sosa have displayed great *altruism*. Several-time winner of the Defensive Player of the Year award, basketball center Mutombo contributed two million dollars to build a hospital in his hometown of Kinshasa in the Congo. He also supports the Congo's women's Olympic basketball team. Mutombo honors the Luba tribe's tradition of the eldest taking responsibility for the family. Sosa, voted baseball's Most Valuable Player in 1998, was born to poverty in the Dominican Republic. As a child, he begged a peso to buy his mother a gift; now he has given her three homes. He has built a shopping center, sponsored baseball training, and given computers to his native town San Pedro de Macoris. After Hurricane Georges struck, Sosa led the effort to aid his native land.

---

4. **ascetic** (noun, adjective)   ə-sĕt′ĭk

a person who gives up pleasures and practices self-denial (noun)

St. Augustine, a leader of the early Christian Church, gave up wealth and family connections to live as an **ascetic.**

avoiding or giving up pleasures (adjective)

Sophia's **ascetic** diet included only vegetables, bread, and water.

NOTES: (1) *Ascetics* are often religious people who feel that self-denial and social isolation will bring them closer to God. (2) Be careful! Do not confuse *ascetic* with *aesthetic,* which means "beautiful" or "appealing to the senses." The two words sound almost the same.

An *ascetic* existence can be a source of great moral authority, as the life of the fourteenth Dalai Lama shows. Born into a humble family, Gyalwa Tenzin Gyatso was chosen when he was two years old to be the Dalai Lama, or reincarnation of the Buddha. He assumed leadership of the Tibetan people at sixteen. In 1959, during the brutal invasion of his country by China in which thousands were murdered, he was forced to flee to India. There, living in a small cottage, he rises at 4 A.M. to meditate and ends each day with prayer. In 1989, he was awarded the Nobel Peace Prize for his efforts to liberate Tibet without using violence. He often says, "I am a simple Buddhist monk, no more, no less."

---

5. **capricious** (adjective)   kə-prĭsh′əs

unpredictable; changeable; not based on reason or judgment; fickle

Because of **capricious** enforcement of the law, many speeding drivers did not receive tickets.

The teenager's **capricious** behavior was the first sign of her drug addiction.

▶ *Related Word*
capriciousness (noun)   The *capriciousness* of a hurricane's path prevents weather forecasters from predicting exactly where it will hit.

Newborns are known for seemingly *capricious* behavior, crying or refusing to eat for no apparent reason. Are teenagers ready to deal with such behavior? To find out, some high schools are giving students plastic "babies" known as Baby Think-It-Overs. Students must be on call 24 hours a day to care for the seven-pound "babies," who are programmed to cry. If the caretaker neglects the baby's needs, the Think-It-Over registers abuse. Being on 24-hour call to a baby's *capricious* behavior has convinced some students to delay parenthood.

6. **cosmopolitan** (adjective)   kŏz′mə-pŏl′ĭ-tn

from several parts of the world; international

> Los Angeles has a **cosmopolitan** population.

free from local bias; having a world view

> Travel throughout Europe and Asia gave the flight attendant a **cosmopolitan** view of the world.

▶ *Related Word*
  cosmos (noun)   (kŏz′məs)   The nature of the *cosmos* is still a mystery. (*Cosmos* means "universe.")

7. **disdain** (verb, noun)   dĭs-dān′

to scorn; to treat as unworthy (verb)

> The rich nobleman **disdained** the poor peasant.
>
> The politician **disdained** to respond to the insult.

scorn (noun)

> The opera critic treated rock music with **disdain.**
>
> The gang's drug dealing showed **disdain** for the law.

▶ *Common Phrase*
  disdain for

8. **fraternal** (adjective)   frə-tûr′nəl

referring to brothers

> Damon and Keenan Ivory Wayans are **fraternal** comedians who have starred in movies and on TV.

like a brother; very friendly

> Clarence had **fraternal** feelings for the men he had served with in the navy.

▶ *Related Word*
  fraternize (verb)   (frăt′ər-nīz′)   Our boss warned us not to *fraternize* on the job. (*Fraternize* means "to socialize.")

The word *fraternity* comes from *frater,* the Latin word for "brother." College *fraternities* are meant to foster brotherly relationships. Other *fraternal* organizations seek to foster friendships or associations in a community or a profession. Examples of these are the Knights of Columbus and the Fraternal Order of Police.

---

9. **gullible** (adjective)   gŭl′ə-bəl

easily deceived; easily cheated

> The **gullible** child believed the story that a man lived on the moon.
>
> The **gullible** man lost all the money he invested in the phony retirement plan.

▶ *Related Word*
gullibility (noun)   Marsha's *gullibility* allowed the crook to convince her that the brass ring was really gold.

10. **hypocritical** (adjective)   (hĭp′ə-krĭt′ĭ-kəl)

giving a false appearance of virtue; saying one thing while doing another

> The **hypocritical** governor spoke against public waste while using state employees to mow her lawn.

▶ *Related Words*
hypocrisy (noun)   (hĭ-pŏk′rĭ-sē)   We were shocked at the *hypocrisy* of the minister who robbed a bank.

hypocrite (noun)   That *hypocrite* told us to give our money to charity, but he gave none at all.

Many public officials have been accused of *hypocrisy*. Thomas Jefferson, U.S. President from 1801 to 1809, wrote the Declaration of Independence, stating that all men had a right to freedom. Yet he owned slaves, and in 1998, genetic testing showed that he probably fathered a son by one of his slaves, Sally Hemmings. Almost 200 years after Thomas Jefferson's presidency, his namesake, President William Jefferson Clinton, was impeached (but not convicted) on evidence concerning sex. Yet at least two of his accusers were found to have cheated on their wives.

NOTE: The word *hypocrite* comes from a Greek word meaning "actor."

11. **intrepid** (adjective)   ĭn-trĕp′-ĭd

    fearless; brave

    > The **intrepid** soldier led his men into battle.

12. **venerable** (adjective)   vĕn′ər-ə-bəl

    worthy of great respect because of dignity or age

    > The newly appointed university president sought advice from the **venerable** professor.
    >
    > The **venerable** Notre Dame Cathedral has stood in Paris since 1189.

    NOTE: 1. *Venerable* often refers to people or things of great age. 2. Do not confuse *venerable* with *vulnerable*. (*Vulnerable* means "easily injured or hurt.")

    ▶ *Related Words*
    > **venerate** (verb)   (vĕn′ə-rāt′)   We *venerate* the founders of our country.
    >
    > **veneration** (noun)   The beautiful Basilica of Our Lady of Guadalupe shows the *veneration* of Mexican people for this saint.

Exercises

Part 1

■ *Who's Who?*

The sentences below begin by naming a type of person. For each example, choose the letter of the word or phrase on the right that defines the type most accurately. Use each choice only once.

1. An adroit person ___i___ .

2. A hypocritical person ___c___ .

3. An altruistic person ___j___ .

4. Capricious people ___k___ .

5. A cosmopolitan person

   ___a___ .

a. has a world view

b. is brave

c. gives a false appearance of virtue

d. is a fan

e. are brothers or close friends

f. gives up pleasures

g. is easily fooled

6. An intrepid person __**b**__ .

7. An ascetic __**f**__ .

8. An aficionado __**d**__ .

9. A gullible person __**g**__ .

10. A person who shows disdain

   __**h**__ .

h. is scornful

i. is skillful

j. is unselfish

k. change their minds often

l. is worthy of respect

■ *Words in Context*

Complete each sentence with the word that fits best. Use each choice only once.

a. adroit   e. capricious   i. gullible
b. aficionado   f. cosmopolitan   j. hypocritical
c. altruistic   g. disdain   k. intrepid
d. ascetic   h. fraternal   l. venerable

1. My __**f, cosmopolitan**__ uncle was familiar with the customs of more than twenty different cultures.

2. The __**k, intrepid**__ explorer traveled without fear in the dangerous country.

3. The __**a, adroit**__ knitter moved her needles quickly.

4. The __**b, aficionado**__ of country and western music went to five or six concerts each month.

5. The __**j, hypocritical**__ boss took two-hour lunches, but complained if his workers took more than thirty minutes.

6. The rich person showed his __**g, disdain**__ for the poor person by refusing to talk to him.

7. Billionaire Li Ka-Shing showed his __**c, altruistic**__ nature by building roads in his native town of Shantou.

8. The __**i, gullible**__ man believed that money grew on trees in the United States.

9. The **d, ascetic** _____ lived alone in the mountains and prayed most of the day.

10. Family members consulted the **l, venerable** _____ grandfather on many problems.

■ *Using Related Words*

Complete each sentence by using a word from the pair of related words above it. You may need to capitalize a word when you write it in a sentence. Use each choice only once.

1. venerable, venerate, veneration

Although many of us think of chocolate as "junk food," it was considered precious by one of the world's most **venerable** _____

civilizations, the Aztecs. They showed their **veneration** _____ of chocolate by using it as money. In the 1700s, Europeans used it as a cure for asthma. Today, chemists are developing a low-calorie chocolate. If it tastes like the real thing, we may soon

venerate _____ it as much as the original.

2. capriciousness, capricious

What better symbol of love's **capriciousness** _____ is there than the Roman god Cupid? He aims arrows at the hearts of people who, when struck, fall instantly in love. Cupid is an infant, with-

out much sense, so he acts out of **capricious** _____ impulse rather than from reasoned thought. At times, he is even shown wearing a blindfold—a fitting symbol of romantic love.

3. adroit, adroitness

The **adroitness** _____ of the acrobats in the Great Moscow Circus amazes their audience. Pavel Lavrik balances on top of several steel barrels; the Doveiko Acrobats swing through the air from

a steel platform. The final act, an **adroit** _____ ballet done in the air, is dedicated to the Russians who died in World War II.

4. altruism, altruistic

Studies show that the more education people have, the more

altruistic
_____ they tend to be. In part, this may be because they have more money to give. However, people who are
more educated also are more likely to appreciate the value

of **altruism** _____ .

5. fraternize, fraternal

Soldiers from the U.S. 82nd Airborne Division developed

fraternal
_____ relationships when they served in the Per-
sian Gulf War. Although they later scattered throughout the coun-

try, they are able to **fraternize** _____ at yearly reunions.

■ *Which Should It Be?*

To complete the following sentences, choose the letter of the word that
makes better sense.

1. A good minister would be __**b**__ .
   a. gullible   b. altruistic

2. A person who could climb mountains would be __**a**__ .
   a. adroit   b. capricious

3. A brother would be a __**b**__ relative.
   a. venerable   b. fraternal

4. A person who travels around the world to watch car races would be

   an __**b**__ .
   a. ascetic   b. aficionado

5. A man who spoke out for gun control, yet carried a gun, would

   be __**b**__ .
   a. intrepid   b. hypocritical

Words to Learn

Part 2

13. **affluent** (adjective) ăf′lōō-ənt

wealthy; prosperous

> People with college degrees often become **affluent.**
>
> **Affluent** people can afford many vacations.
>
> Enormous oil reserves have made Kuwait an **affluent** country.

▶ *Related Word*
affluence (noun)   The hard-working immigrant rose from poverty to *affluence.*

14. **alien** (adjective, noun) ā′lē-ən

strange; foreign (adjective)

> Taking off one's shoes in a classroom is an **alien** custom to most Americans.
>
> Cruelty was **alien** to her kind nature.

a foreigner; a person who is not a citizen (noun)

> Many **aliens** come to Canada and the United States in search of peace and personal freedom.

a being from outer space (noun); coming from outer space (adjective)

> In the *Star Wars* movie series, Yoda, an **alien,** is a philosopher and leader of the Jedi. (noun)
>
> Scientists study **alien** rocks from the moon. (adjective)

NOTE: All three meanings have the connotation (or hint) of being unknown or strange.

▶ *Related Words*
alienate (verb)   The man's cruelty *alienated* his friends. (*Alienate* means "to make hostile or unfriendly.")

alienation (noun)   A fight about a friend led to Jamal's *alienation* from his father. (*Alienation* means "psychological isolation.")

Customs of public affection often differ. In Brazil, meetings with government ministers commonly end with hugs, and guests at parties kiss and hug everyone. These customs would be quite *alien* in Japan, where many gatherings begin with bows. Romantically involved couples have recently started to kiss in public, setting off a widespread debate. Many Japanese find public kissing to be disgusting.

---

15. **amicable** (adjective)   ăm′ĭ-kə-bəl

friendly; peaceful

> By settling the labor problem in an **amicable** manner, management and union leaders avoided a strike.

> The divorced couple maintained an **amicable** relationship for the sake of their children.

NOTE: Amicable indicates a friendly, but not very close, relationship.

▶ *Related Word*
   amicability (noun)   *Amicability* between the United States and Russia has existed only since the end of the Cold War.

16. **astute** (adjective)   ə-stoot′

shrewd; having good judgment

> **Astute** politicians know that a good economy is a key to public satisfaction.

> The **astute** worker knew that being well liked would help her get a promotion.

▶ *Related Word*
   astuteness (noun)   The lawyer's *astuteness* helped him get on powerful city committees.

NOTE: An *astute* person will know what is really important, rather than what people say is important.

In his classic *How to Win Friends and Influence People,* Dale Carnegie's *astute* advice is that people should make others feel important and give them honest compliments. Carnegie also feels that positive statements bring about more change in people than do criticisms. He emphasizes that people never see themselves as evil. Even the murderous gangster Al Capone saw himself as a basically good person.

17. **candid** (adjective)   kăn′dĭd

truthful; frank; honest in giving opinions

> The father was **candid** about his failure to support his family.
>
> Sinclair Lewis's book *The Jungle* was a **candid** description of the awful working conditions in meat factories.

not posed or rehearsed

> The **candid** photograph caught me with my mouth open and my eyes shut.

▶ *Related Word*
> **candor** (noun)   Joshua's *candor* about his girlfriend's outfit hurt her feelings.

18. **dogmatic** (adjective)   dôg-măt′ĭk

arrogant in belief; opinionated

> The **dogmatic** mother refused to listen to any suggestions about raising children.
>
> Workers found it hard to suggest new ideas to their **dogmatic** boss.

▶ *Related Word*
> **dogmatism** (noun)   (dôg′mə-tĭz′əm)   The *dogmatism* of the conservative candidate made many voters support his opponent.

19. **exuberant** (adjective)   ĭg-zoo′bər-ənt

very enthusiastic; joyfully energetic

> **Exuberant** at seeing his mother after ten years, Hean grabbed her and lifted her into the air.
>
> Fans applauded the **exuberant** cheerleaders.

▶ *Related Word*
> **exuberance** (noun)   In their *exuberance*, the audience ran onto the stage and began dancing.

20. **frugal** (adjective)   froo′gəl

thrifty; economical; attempting to save money; sparing

> The **frugal** student looked carefully for sales on food and clothing.
>
> Unfortunately, my husband is **frugal** with compliments.

▶ *Related Word*

frugality (noun)   The parents' *frugality* enabled them to save for their son's college education.

21. **gauche** (adjective)   gōsh

awkward; lacking in social graces

The **gauche** bride complained about her gifts at the wedding.

Our cousin was so **gauche** that he licked his fingers at a formal dinner.

In many languages, words that refer to the right side are positive and words that refer to the left side are negative. Two words in this chapter have their roots in the concepts of "right" or "left." In French, *à droit* means "to the right," and in both French and English *adroit* is a positive word meaning "skillful." *Gauche,* French for "left," means "socially awkward" or "clumsy" in English.

---

22. **novice** (noun)   nŏv′ĭs

beginner; person in a new situation

The expert chef patiently taught the **novice** how to make sauces.

Since the city council member was a political **novice,** he often said foolish things to the press.

23. **renegade** (noun)   rĕn′ĭ-gād′

traitor; deserter; outlaw

The **renegade** was captured and put on trial for desertion and treason.

The president of the country was a **renegade** who refused to follow international guidelines on nuclear weapons.

For centuries, Spain ruled over much of Mexico, Central America, South America, and what became the southwestern United States. As a result, most countries south of the United States are Spanish speaking. In addition, several million people within the United States speak Spanish. Not surprisingly, many Spanish words have entered American English. Two such words, *aficionado* and *renegade,* are introduced in this chapter. In Spanish, *aficionado* means "fan," in particular, a follower of the popular sport of bullfighting; and *renegado* means "deserter." Other examples of Spanish words found in American English are *corral, desperado, fiesta, patio,* and *rodeo.*

24. **stoic** (adjective, noun)   stô´ĭk

   not affected by pain or pleasure (adjective)

   > The **stoic** child remained still and silent during the painful medical treatment.

   ▶ *Related Word*
   stoicism (noun)   (stō´ĭ-sĭz´əm)   Uncomplaining Russian workers bore the late pay and harsh working conditions with *stoicism.*

   NOTE: In modern English usage, *stoic* is usually associated with pain, bad luck, or misfortune.

The word *stoic* refers to an ancient Greek school of philosophical thought founded in 308 B.C.E. The philosopher Zeno taught that, because gods had made the world, it was perfect. Therefore, human beings must accept their fates with expressing sorrow or joy. The word *stoic* is taken from the covered porch (*stoa* in Greek) where Zeno taught.

Exercises

Part 2

■ Who's Who

The following sentences begin by naming a type of person. For each example, choose the letter of the word or phrase on the right that defines the type most accurately.

1. An exuberant person is
   _**i**___ .

2. A stoic person is __**f**___ .

3. A frugal person is __**g**___ .

4. An alien is __**b**___ .

a. honest in giving opinions

b. a foreigner

c. a beginner

d. opinionated

e. friendly

f. not affected by pain

5. An amicable person is **e** _____ .

6. A renegade is **k** _____ .

7. A dogmatic person is **d** _____ .

8. A candid person is **a** _____ .

9. A novice is **c** _____ .

10. An astute person is **l** _____ .

g. thrifty, economical

h. awkward, lacking social graces

i. enthusiastic

j. wealthy

k. a rebel

l. shrewd

■ *Words in Context*

Complete each sentence with the word that fits best. Use each choice only once.

a. affluent   e. candid   i. gauche
b. alien   f. dogmatic   j. novice
c. amicable   g. exuberant   k. renegade
d. astute   h. frugal   l. stoic

1. As a freshman, I was a(n) **j, novice** _____ who knew nothing about college life.

2. The homes in that **a, affluent** _____ neighborhood are large and have swimming pools.

3. The **l, stoic** _____ farmer did not complain when cold weather killed his orange trees.

4. The **e, candid** _____ patient told her family the truth about her illness.

5. Because he was **d, astute** _____ at office politics, he rose from assistant to vice-president in just five years.

6. Spending money in a(n) **h, frugal** _____ manner helps people save for their retirement.

7. Her date was so **i, gauche** _____ that he poured Diet Pepsi into a wineglass.

8. Although I am now a(n) **b, alien** _____ living in Canada, I soon hope to be a Canadian citizen.

9. The army offered a reward for the capture of the **k, renegade** _____ .

10. My **f, dogmatic** _____ aunt insisted that there was only one right way of doing things.

■ Using Related Words

Complete each sentence by using a word from the pair of related words above it. You may need to capitalize a word when you write it in a sentence. Use each choice only once.

1. exuberance, exuberant

    In 1996, when the Chicago Bulls won the NBA championship, the **exuberant** _____ players raced onto the floor. Star player Michael Jordan held the ball tight to his chest with his eyes closed, while other team members showed their **exuberance** _____ by hugging him.

2. stoic, stoicism

    Queen Elizabeth of England has been **stoic** _____ in bearing the considerable bad publicity brought on by her children's behavior. She maintains this **stoicism** _____ by rarely talking to the press about her family's problems. In fact, the queen almost never displays her feelings to the public.

3. alien, alienated

    When an immigrant family comes to America, they must often adapt to **alien** _____ customs. Chroek Tao brought his family from Cambodia to the United States to escape danger and poverty. However, some of Tao's children find his traditional ways to be old-fashioned. Family differences have **alienated** _____ Tao from some of his children.

4. amicable, amicability

Morocco has a long history of **amicable** _____ relations with the United States. Only a year after the United States declared its independence in 1776, Morocco recognized the young country.

To further show his **amicability** _____, Sultan Moulay Suliman presented a lion house to the U.S. consulate in 1821. Located in Morocco, it is now a U.S. National Historic Landmark.

5. astute, astuteness

Before he became President of the United States, Abraham Lincoln was a successful lawyer. However, he was **astute** _____ enough not to reveal his full intelligence. Instead, he talked slowly and told long stories that charmed juries into thinking he was a simple man from the backwoods. His behavior in the courtroom led rivals to underestimate him. Research into the Lincoln law files is revealing the **astuteness** _____ and sophistication behind the innocent "country boy" mask.

■ *Which Should It Be?*

To complete the following sentences, choose the letter of the word that makes better sense.

1. Friends should be ___ **a** ___ .
   a. amicable   b. gauche

2. A difficult job should not be given to a ___ **a** ___ .
   a. novice   b. stoic

3. People who like to save money are ___ **b** ___ .
   a. exuberant   b. frugal

4. If you want an honest opinion, ask a person who is ___ **b** ___ .
   a. affluent   b. candid

5. A person who will never change his mind is ___ **a** ___ .
   a. dogmatic   b. alien

Chapter Exercises

■ *Practicing Strategies: Using the Dictionary*

Read the definitions, and answer the questions that follow.

> **fab•u•lous** (făb′yə-ləs) *adj.* **1.** Barely credible; astonishing. **2.** Extremely pleasing or successful: *a fabulous vacation.* **3.a.** Of the nature of a fable or myth; legendary. **b.** Told of or celebrated in fables or legends. [ME, mythical < OFr. *fabuleux* < Lat. *fābulōsus* < *fābula*, fable. See FABLE.] —**fab′-u•lous•ly** *adv.* —**fab′u•lous•ness** *n.*

1. What part of speech function does *fabulous* have? **adjective**

2. Which syllable of *fabulous* is stressed in pronunciation?

    first

3. What adverb is related to *fabulous*? **fabulously**

4. In which language did *fabulous* originate? **Latin**

> **piv•ot** (pĭv′ət) *n.* **1.** A short rod or shaft on which a related part rotates or swings. **2.** A person or thing on which something depends or turns; the central or crucial factor. **3.** The act of turning on or as if on a pivot. —*v.* **-ot•ed, -ot•ing, -ots.** —*tr.* **1.** To mount on, attach by, or provide with a pivot or pivots. **2.** To cause to rotate, revolve, or turn. —*intr.* To turn on or as if on a pivot. [Fr. < OFr.] —**piv′ot•a•ble** *adj.*

5. Which three part-of-speech functions does *pivot* have?

    noun, transitive verb, intransitive verb

6. What part-of-speech function does *pivotable* serve as? **adjective**

7. In total, how many definitions does *pivot* have? **six**

> **max•i•mum** (măk′sə-məm) *n., pl.* **-mums** or **-ma** (-mə). **1.a.** The greatest possible quantity or degree. **b.** The greatest quantity or degree reached or recorded; the upper limit of variation. **c.** The time or period during which the highest point or degree is attained. **2.** An upper limit permitted by law or other authority. **3.** *Astron.* **a.** The moment when a variable star is most brilliant. **b.** The magnitude of the star at such a moment. **4.** *Math.* **a.** The greatest value assumed by a function over a given interval. **b.** The largest number in a set. —*adj.* **1.** Having or being the maximum reached or attainable. **2.** Of, relating to, or making up a maximum. [Lat. < neut. of *maximus*, greatest. See **meg-***.]

8. Write the two full plural spellings of *maximum*.

   maximums, maxima

9. What two part-of-speech functions does *maximum* have?

   noun, adjective

10. Give the number and the part of speech of the definition of *maximum*

    most often used in astronomy. **3, as a noun**

■ Practicing Strategies: Using a Dictionary Pronunciation Key

It takes practice to use a pronunciation key efficiently. For each of the following words, use the key that is located on the inside of the front cover of this book to figure out the pronunciation. Try saying each word out loud several times.

1. accolade   ăk′ə-lād
2. pseudonym   so͞o′də-nĭm′
3. cuisine   kwĭ-zēn′
4. epitome   ĭ-pĭt′ə-mē
5. cliché   klē-shā′

■ Practicing Strategies: Using the Dictionary Independently

Use a college or unabridged dictionary to research the answers to the following questions. Be sure to consult a recently published dictionary.

1. In what language was the word *sheriff* first recorded? _____

   Old English

2. What is *myrrh*? _____

   an aromatic gum resin

3. Which syllable of the word *oxymoron* receives most stress? _____

   the third

4. If you do something *gingerly,* how do you do it? _____

   with great care _____

5. What is a *tupelo?* _____

   a tree _____

■ *Companion Words*

Complete each sentence with the word that fits best. Choose your answers from the words below. You may use words more than once.

Choices: for, of, with, about

1. The student was candid **about**_____ the fact that he didn't study.

2. My professor is an aficionado **of**_____ Toni Morrison's novels.

3. I have fraternal feelings **for**_____ my best friend.

4. Jose has amicable relationships **with**_____ his neighbors.

5. The renegade had disdain **for**_____ the government.

■ *Writing with Your Words*

This exercise will give you practice in using the vocabulary words in your own writing. Each sentence is started for you. Complete it with an interesting phrase that also indicates the meaning of the italicized word.

1. An *intrepid* traveler would _____

   _____ .

2. I am an *aficionado* of _____

   _____ .

3. In a *cosmopolitan* society, _____

   _____ .

4. I knew a person so *gauche* that _____

_____ .

5. A person might show *disdain* by _____

_____ .

6. A *novice* at driving might _____

_____ .

7. In my *candid* opinion, _____

_____ .

8. Only a *gullible* person would believe that _____

_____ .

9. One custom *alien* to me is _____

_____ .

10. I hope one day to be *affluent* enough to _____

_____ .

Passage

Two Real Guys: The Story of Ben & Jerry's Ice Cream

Their $8,000 investment grew to a business worth a hundred million dollars. Along the way, they became known for their sense of humor and their commitment to social concerns. This is the story of Ben Cohen and Jerry Greenfield, the two real guys behind Ben & Jerry's Ice Cream.

Ben Cohen and Jerry Greenfield met in junior high school and soon developed a relationship so close that it was almost **fraternal. (1)** Both **candidly** describe themselves as fat "nerds" who hated sports but loved to eat ice cream. **(2)** Ben, who left college without graduating, was a **renegade.** Once, when he was working in a kitchen, his boss ordered him to get rid of his beard. Instead, he simply shaved a thin line down the middle of his chin and declared that he now had sideburns. Not surprisingly, Ben was fired from a series of jobs, although he did do well at mopping floors. His partner, Jerry, managed to complete college, but was rejected by forty medical schools.

In 1978, Ben and Jerry decided to start an ice-cream shop in Burlington, Vermont, one of the coldest towns in the United States. **(3)** They completed a mail-order course in ice-cream making for **novices** and applied for a loan from the Merchant's Bank. Dressed in suits for the first time in years, their goal was to impress the **venerable** bankers. After the loan was granted, Ben and Jerry were able to start their business.

The next several months they worked day and night changing an abandoned gas station that lacked heating or adequate plumbing into an ice-cream shop. To save money, they lived in a trailer and existed on an **ascetic** diet of sardines and crackers. **(4)** In their desire to be **frugal,** Ben and Jerry paid construction workers with promises of free ice cream for life, instead of with money.

From the moment the shop opened, customers knew the ice cream was special. Ben, who lacked a strong sense of taste, had to approve each flavor. Because he could not taste mild things, **(5)** he **dogmatically** insisted that the flavors be strong and rich and have lots of crunchy additions. In 1981, *Time* magazine reported that Ben and Jerry's ice cream was among the best in the world.

Customers also loved the shop's **amicable** atmosphere, which featured personalized service, games, and live piano music. In keeping with the company motto, "If it's not fun, why do it?" Ben and Jerry threw a public festival that included an ice-cream eating contest and an award for the longest unbroken apple peel. An **exuberant** Jerry, who performed magic tricks, smashed a cinder block on Ben's stomach and demonstrated his fire-eating abilities.

Sales were great, but there was not much profit. **(6)** Since Ben and Jerry **disdained** standard business practices, they failed to keep track of their costs. They often supplied too much ice cream on their cones, and lack of **adroit** scooping meant that they did not serve people quickly enough to make money. **(7)** Their bookkeeping practices were so **capricious** that they often crumpled up checks, put them in their pockets, and forgot them. To help produce a profit, Ben and Jerry hired professional management staff and started to sell ice cream to grocery stores.

Despite Ben and Jerry's need to focus on the business, the fun continued as they created many imaginative and delicious flavors. **(8)** Two **aficionados** of the Grateful Dead rock group suggested the ice cream Cherry Garcia, a combination of chocolate and cherry named after the original leader of the group, Jerry Garcia. Ben and Jerry's rich-tasting

Ben and Jerry are the two real guys behind a large ice-cream company.

New York Super Fudge Chunk combined white and dark chocolate chunks with three kinds of nuts. Their best seller, Chocolate Chip Cookie Dough ice cream, contained raw cookie dough. Publicity also continued to be creative, as when Ben and Jerry crossed the United States in the summer of 1986 in a "Cowmobile" and gave away free ice-cream samples. In 1994, they hired Spike Jones to direct a humorous ad campaign for a new "Smooth" ice cream, without chunks.

Ben & Jerry's Homemade Inc. continued to grow in size and profits. Despite their new **affluence,** however, Ben and Jerry remained true to their original values. **(9)** Formality continued to be **alien** to the company style, for everyone from factory workers to bosses wore jeans, participated in Elvis Presley look-alike contests, and received three pints of ice cream per day. As another worker benefit, 5 percent of company profits were distributed to all employees. Since recycling was important to Ben and Jerry, the company bought 200 pigs—one of them named after Ben and another one after Jerry—to eat ice-cream waste. (Unfortunately, the pigs refused to eat mint ice cream.)

Ben and Jerry also became famous for their **altruism.** When they sold their first public stock nationally, they announced a policy of "linked prosperity," meaning that the company would use profits to support important causes. **(10)** The announcement turned out to be **astute,** for their **altruism** encouraged more people to buy their ice cream. Projects sponsored by Ben & Jerry's Homemade Inc. have included a New York "partnershop" that funds a drug counseling center and a homeless shelter, efforts to preserve the Brazilian rain forests, and a Mexican cooperative company that supports poor peasants. From 1991 to 1994, the company focused all of its charitable efforts on "Sav-a Child," a campaign to improve the lives of children. More recently, it has joined a campaign to eliminate land mines. Ben & Jerry's now employs over 600 people, and its stock is publicly traded. Ben and Jerry retain control and are committed to independence for the company, although others have offered to buy it. Despite the company's size and fame, its heart remains in the two real guys, Ben and Jerry, who, rich or poor, remain true to their values and to their community.

■ *Exercise*

Each numbered sentence below corresponds to a sentence in the Passage. Fill in the letter of the choice that makes the sentence mean the same thing as its corresponding sentence in the Passage.

1. Both ____**c**____ describe themselves as fat "nerds."
   a. politely b. secretly c. truthfully d. shyly

2. Ben, who left college without graduating, was a ____**b**____ .
   a. fan b. rebel c. tease d. failure

3. They completed a mail-order course in ice-cream making for ___**c**___ .
   a. foreigners b. poor people c. beginners d. skillful people

4. In their desire to be ___**c**___ , the partners paid with promises of free ice cream for life, instead of with money.
   a. friendly b. scornful c. thrifty d. excited

5. He ___**d**___ insisted that the flavors be strong and rich.
   a. sometimes b. happily c. truly d. stubbornly

6. Ben and Jerry __**d**__ standard business practices.
   a. kept   b. started   c. threw out   d. scorned

7. Their bookkeeping practices were __**b**__ .
   a. careless   b. unpredictable   c. bad   d. dishonest

8. Two __**a**__ of the Grateful Dead rock group suggested the ice cream Cherry Garcia.
   a. fans   b. friends   c. partners   d. singers

9. Formality continued to be __**a**__ to the company style.
   a. foreign   b. important   c. helpful   d. damaging

10. The announcement turned out to be __**b**__ .
    a. helpful   b. shrewd   c. charitable   d. friendly

■ Discussion Questions

1. Give two examples of the informality of Ben & Jerry's Homemade Inc.

2. Describe three factors that contributed to the success of Ben and Jerry's company. Defend your answers.

3. Name another company that is involved in charitable efforts, and describe these efforts.

ENGLISH IDIOMS

Color

Each chapter in this book gives the meaning of some English idioms. Idioms are groups of words that have special meanings, which are different from the usual meanings of the words. Since the passage in this chapter is about Ben and Jerry, two colorful (or lively and interesting) characters, the idioms for Chapter 1 are about colors.

Some color idioms have negative meanings. *Feeling blue* means feeling depressed or bad, and *yellow-bellied* means cowardly. The color words *green* and *rose* are used in idioms that have positive meanings. A person with a *green thumb* has a talent for gardening. People who look at the world *through rose-colored glasses* see things as much better than they really are.

Idioms containing the words *black* and *red* are used in business. A firm that is *in the red* is losing money, but one that is *in the black* is profitable.

During ancient Roman holidays, rival groups of young men would compete to see who could cover the most statues with red wine. Not surprisingly, the statue of Bacchus, god of wine, was particularly popular as a target. Today, when people go out for the evening to have a good time, they *paint the town red*.

Quiz Again

Now that you have finished studying this chapter, here is the brief true-false quiz you took when you began. Take it again.

Gullible people usually believe what others tell them.	True	False
An **ascetic** lives a life of luxury.	True	False
A **frugal** person likes to save money.	True	False
A **stoic** often complains.	True	False

Answers are on page 405. Did your score improve?

CHAPTER

Words in the News

Even on a remote mountaintop, we are never more than a few seconds away from the news. A touch of a radio button brings us the latest reports of international events, disasters, sports scores, and gossip about our favorite stars. Television transports images from thousands of miles away into our living rooms; we learn about the weather throughout the world, and in our own backyards. Daily newspapers give us in-depth political analysis, advice columns, and tips on daily living. We can get reports on traffic, weather, and the news instantly on the Internet. In a world so small that business events in Europe or Asia can affect U.S. markets within seconds, we need to broaden our understanding. This chapter presents words that deal with the news.

Chapter Strategy: Context Clues of Substitution

Chapter Words:

Part 1

accord	consumer	intervene
attrition	corroborate	media
bureaucracy	diplomacy	pacify
catastrophe	entrepreneur	Third World

Part 2

apprehend	ludicrous	radical
chaos	ominous	liberal
defer	supplant	conservative
epitome	thrive	reactionary

Quiz Yourself

To check your knowledge of some chapter words before you begin to study, identify these statements as true or false.

Things increase by a process of **attrition**.   True   False

An **ominous** warning is usually frightening.   True   False

A **radical** change is small.   True   False

Ludicrous things are funny.   True   False

You will learn the answers as you study this chapter.

Did You Know?

How Many Ways Can a Team Win or Lose?

If you read the sports pages of the newspapers, you know how cleverly they are written. Many sportswriters are masters of the English language, who express game results with drama and humor. Every day, football, basketball, baseball, or hockey games are reported in newspapers; yet day after day, sportswriters make their reports sound fresh and enthusiastic.

How do they do it? After all, most of the events are basically the same:

1. The game is played.
2. One team or player wins.
3. The other team or player loses.

Because sportswriters have had to report wins and losses over and over again, they have developed clever synonyms (words that mean the same thing) for the words *win* and *lose*.

Let's look at some of the many ways to say *win* with examples taken from newspaper sports pages.

A's *beat* Yankees.

Bears *top* Broncos.

And here are some examples of ways to say *lose*.

> Cubs *drop* heartbreaker.
>
> Ohio State *is canned* by Michigan.
>
> Hawks *are doormats* again.

Sportswriters vary their expressions depending on the amount of winning (or losing) points. For example, the connotations of these synonyms for *win* show that the victors won by a big score, really "killing" their opponents.

> Purdue *crushes* rival Indiana.
>
> Iowa State *rips* number 4 Kansas.
>
> Young, 49ers *clobber* Redskins.

On the other hand, the connotations of these words show that the winners barely got by.

> Nebraska *struggles past* Baylor.
>
> Chiefs *edge* Redskins.

This headline shows that the game changed in the middle.

> Bears *struggle,* then *cruise*.

Sometimes the name of a team is used in an imaginative way. The headlines that follow are *metaphors,* or figurative uses of names.

> Flyers *soar past* Islanders. (Something that flies can soar.)
>
> Flat Bulls *give* Rockets *a lift*. (Rockets are said to "lift off" when they begin to fly.)
>
> Pirates *slice up* Cubs. (The Pirates take their swords and "slice up" the Cubs.)
>
> 49ers *shear* Rams. (A ram is a sheep; sheep get sheared.)

At other times, rhyme is used.

> Bears *sack the Pack.*
>
> Hornets *shake, bake* Bulls. (The food product Shake 'n Bake has seasoned crumbs for coating chicken and pork.)
>
> Hoosiers *fake, shake, break* Illini.

Sometimes a short headline tells much about a game. What do you think happened in these games?

1. Bruins' rally on ice from 2 down stuns Rangers 4–3.

2. Iowa State surprises Minnesota in overtime.

3. Bulls surprise Bucks, end road slump.

Answers are on page 405.

Learning Strategy

Context Clues of Substitution

Using *context clues* is a powerful strategy that can help you to figure out the meaning of unknown words. *Context* refers to the group of words, sentences, or even paragraphs that surround a word. When you use context clues, you use the words that you do know in a sentence to make an intelligent guess about the meaning of an unknown word.

You may think that it is not a good strategy to guess at words. After all, it is better to know the answer on a test than just to guess. However, intelligent guessing is a very important strategy to use when you are reading. English has so many words that even the best readers cannot know them all. Good readers often use context clues, or intelligent guesses, when they meet unfamiliar words.

Context clues have two important advantages for you:

1. You do not have to interrupt your reading to go to the dictionary.

2. Using context clues allows you to rely on your own common sense. Common sense is your best learning tool.

In fact, you probably use context clues already, although you may not realize it. For example, context clues are the only way to choose the correct meaning for words that have more than one meaning, such as *cold*. You must use context clues to figure out what the word *cold* means in the following sentences.

a. She greeted him in a *cold* manner.

b. A cough and a stuffed-up nose are signs of a *cold*.

c. Alaskan winters are quite *cold*.

In which sentence does *cold* mean

1. having a low temperature?

2. a type of illness?

3. unfriendly?

Answers are on page 405.

Let's turn to a more difficult word. What are the meanings of the word *concession* in these sentences?

a. He bought some food at the hot-dog *concession*.

b. Because the country wanted peace, the leaders made a *concession* of land to the enemy.

In which sentence does *concession* mean

1. something that is surrendered or given up?

2. a business that sells things?

Answers are on page 405.

Context clues and the dictionary are natural partners in helping you to determine the meaning of unknown words. Context clues usually give you an approximate meaning for a word and allow you to continue your reading without interruption. After you have finished reading, you can look up the word in a dictionary. Why not use the dictionary first? People usually remember words they figured out for themselves far better than those they simply looked up in a dictionary.

You may be wondering exactly how to figure out unknown words that you find in your reading. Many people find the following steps helpful:

1. As you are reading, try to pinpoint words you do not know. This advice sounds almost silly, but it isn't. Many people lose the opportunity to learn words simply because they let unknown words slip by. Don't let this happen to you. Try to capture difficult words!

2. Use context clues to make an intelligent guess about an unknown word's meaning. The strategies you will learn here and in the following chapters will help you do this. Remember that context clues will often give you an approximate—not an exact—meaning.

3. Write down the word and later check it in a dictionary. This step will tell you whether you guessed correctly and will give you a more exact definition of the word.

How does a person learn to make these "intelligent guesses"? In this book, we will present three different methods: substitution in context (in this chapter), context clues of definition (in Chapter 3), and context clues of opposition (in Chapter 4).

Substitution in context is perhaps the most useful way to determine a word's meaning. To use this strategy, simply substitute a word or phrase that makes sense in place of an unknown word. The word you substitute will usually be an approximate definition for the unknown word. Here are some examples.

> Ron's two brothers were hitting each other, but Ron would not join the *fray*. (Since people often hit each other in a fight, the word *fight* is a good substitution and provides an approximate meaning.)

> The *indigent* student could not afford books or school supplies. (A person who cannot afford things necessary for school is poor, and the word *poor* may substitute for *indigent*.)

Of course, context clues of substitution cannot be used all the time. Some sentences simply do not provide enough context clues. For example, in the sentence "Jane saw the *conger*," it would be impossible to find a good substitution for *conger*. (A *conger* is a type of eel.) However, since many sentences do provide context clues, substitution in context will help you much of the time.

Two additional examples are given below. Try using context clues of substitution to make intelligent guesses about the meanings of the italicized words. To do this, take out the unknown word and substitute a word you know that seems to make sense in the sentence.

1. The famous star was *inundated* with letters from fans.

2. Carmen *entreated* her sick grandfather to sit down and rest.

Answers are on page 405.

Now try using the substitution strategy to make intelligent guesses about the meanings of some words to be studied in this chapter.

Each of the following sentences contains a word that will be presented in the Words to Learn section. Read the sentence and use a context clue of substitution to make an intelligent guess about the meaning of the italicized word.

1. A new computer *supplanted* the outdated one.

   Supplanted means **replaced** .

2. The rise in prices made us *defer* buying a home until next year.

   Defer means **delay** .

3. The two countries reached a final *accord* that enabled them to stop fighting.

   Accord means **agreement** .

Answers are on page 405.

Words to Learn

Part 1

1. **accord** (noun, verb)   ə-kôrd′

   agreement; harmony (noun)

   > The Lusaka Protocol, a 1994 **accord,** ended civil war in Angola.
   >
   > We are in **accord** with your proposal to increase money for education.

   to give or grant (verb)

   > Sherry Chayat, an American, was **accorded** the highest honor of Buddhism.

   ▶ *Common Phrases*
   in accord with

   reach an accord

2. **attrition** (noun)   ə-trĭsh′ən

   slowly wearing down; wearing away

   > Too much fishing and a polluted water supply have caused **attrition** in the salmon population.
   >
   > World War I (1914–18) was a war of **attrition,** in which the enemies gradually weakened each other.

Hawaii's land has been gradually worn away by the continuous *attrition* caused by the waves that pound against its shores. Thousands of years ago, Hawaii was one continuous piece of land, but water has slowly covered much of it, and today only eight islands remain. Known for its comfortable climate and breathtaking scenery, Hawaii is a favorite tourist spot. In 1959 it became the fiftieth of the United States, the only one not a part of North America.

3. **bureaucracy** (noun)   byŏŏ-rŏk′rə-sē

administration by employees who follow fixed rules and complex procedures

> The newly elected mayor promised to reform the inefficient city **bureaucracy.**

> My health insurance benefit was delayed because it had to be approved by several levels of **bureaucracy.**

NOTE: Bureaucracy is usually a negative word that refers to a government or organization involving too many officials and too much delay. In government, *bureaucrats* are appointed, not elected. Whether a *bureaucracy* is part of a government, business, or other organization, the officials often are more concerned with following rules than with getting things done.

▶ *Related Words*
  bureaucratic (adjective)   Because of *bureaucratic* problems in the registration office, my transcript was lost.

  bureaucrat (noun)   For twenty years, the *bureaucrat* made four copies of every letter he received.

Bureaucracy is often associated with the term *red tape* in sentences such as "There is too much bureaucratic red tape." In the 1700s, red tape was used to bind piles of English government documents. Since the government was bureaucratic and inefficient, *red tape* came to refer to excessive and silly official routines.

4. **catastrophe** (noun)   kə-tăs′trə-fē

a great disaster

> The bubonic plague of the 1400s was a **catastrophe** that killed one-third of all people in Europe.

> Nicaragua has survived two **catastrophes:** the earthquake of 1972 and the hurricane of 1998.

▶ *Related Word*

catastrophic (adjective)   kăt′ə-strŏf′-ĭk   Economic problems in Russia have had *catastrophic* effects on the lives of many people.

5. **consumer** (noun)   kən-soo′mər

a buyer

Consumers often buy goods through the Internet.

▶ *Related Words*

consume (verb)   People worldwide *consume* Coca-Cola. (*Consume* usually refers to eating and drinking.)

consumption (noun) (kən-səmp′shən)   The creation of drinks such as "mocha latte" and "venti cappuccino" has made the *consumption* of coffee more popular. (*Consumption* may refer to eating and drinking, as well as to buying.)

"Conspicuous *consumption*" means making unneeded purchases in order to impress other people.

6. **corroborate** (verb)   kə-rŏb′ə-rāt′

to confirm; to make more certain

Five eyewitnesses **corroborated** the police report.

Notes on doors **corroborated** the radio announcement that school had been canceled due to bad weather.

▶ *Related Word*

corroboration (noun)   The existence of the legendary Bigfoot has not received scientific *corroboration*.

7. **diplomacy** (noun)   dĭ-plō′mə-sē

the process of official international relations

United Nations Secretary General Kofi Annan used **diplomacy** to settle problems in Bosnia.

tact; politeness

It can be difficult to combine honesty and **diplomacy.**

▶ *Related Words*

diplomat (noun, person)   Prudence Bushnell, the *diplomat* serving as U.S. ambassador to Kenya, was injured during a 1998 embassy bombing.

diplomatic (adjective)   In 1993, Israel established *diplomatic* relations with Russia.

The United States has an enormous network of *diplomats* stationed in other countries. These diplomats represent U.S. interests, help U.S. citizens who travel abroad, and grant visas to foreigners who wish to visit the United States. *Diplomatic* work is sometimes dangerous. From 1979 to 1980, over 100 U.S. diplomatic employees were held captive in Iran for 444 days.

People in the U.S. diplomatic corps work in embassies, which are considered U.S. land. Foreigners who need protection from their own governments may "ask for asylum" by fleeing to a U.S. embassy, where other governments have no official control.

---

8. **entrepreneur** (noun)   ŏn′trə-prə-nûr′

a person who organizes and runs a business

> Bham Van Y, a Vietnamese **entrepreneur,** runs a profitable noodle soup business in the Philippine refugee camp where he lives.

▶ *Related Word*

entrepreneurial (adjective)   Berry Gordy's *entrepreneurial* skills helped make Motown Record Corporation a huge success.

Entrepreneurs have emerged from many backgrounds. African-American John H. Johnson founded the enormous Johnson Publishing Company. William and Ralph Cruz, both talented Hispanic musicians, codirect Miami-based Omega Research Company. Oprah Winfrey's *entrepreneurial* skills in the entertainment industry have made her one of the wealthiest women in the United States. Elizabeth Arden, Estee Lauder, Madam C.J. Walker, and Mary Kay Ash are legends in the cosmetics industry. Recent years have seen a change in the image of the *entrepreneur*. Wendy's founder Dave Thomas, who looks as if he would be uncomfortable in a suit, charms viewers with humorous TV commercials for his hamburgers.

---

9. **intervene** (verb)   ĭn′tər-vēn′

to act in a matter involving others; to interfere

> The teacher **intervened** to stop the fight between the two fifth graders.

> Concerned citizens **intervened** to prevent the historic building from being torn down.

▶ *Related Word*

intervention (noun)   In 1953, the United Nations' *intervention* ended North Korea's invasion of South Korea.

NOTE: To *intervene* can also mean to come between points of time, as in "Four years *intervene* between summer Olympics."

10. **media** (plural noun, adjective)   mē′dē-ə

means of communication, especially TV, radio, and newspapers (plural noun)

Х The impeachment of President Clinton was closely followed by the **media.**

referring to the media (adjective)

Х Reporters turned the terrible crime into a **media** event.

NOTES: (1) *Medium* is the singular form of the plural noun *media.* (2) These two words can also refer to the tools of artists, as in "The artist's main *medium* was oil, but she also used watercolor."

Is *media* coverage good or bad? A car chase by the press may have contributed to the death of Princess Diana of England in 1997. Several actors—George Clooney, Will Smith, and Woody Harrelson—have physically attacked photographers they claimed were hounding them. Carol Burnett and Tom Cruise won lawsuits against newspapers that published unproven stories. Yet media coverage is critical to a democracy. Courageous and vigilant journalists have reported such important stories as the Watergate break-in of 1972, government repression in Central America in the 1980s, and atrocities in Bosnia and Serbia in the 1990s. Every year, reporters are killed covering stories in the world's danger spots.

---

11. **pacify** (verb)   pas′ə-fī′

to calm; to establish peace

Х Mothers can often **pacify** crying infants.

Х Political reforms helped to **pacify** the country's angry farmers.

NOTE: Pacify can also mean to establish peace by conquering, as in "The army *pacified* the rebels."

In 1513, after crossing many miles of Central American jungle, the Spanish explorer Vasco Núñez de Balboa found himself faced by a large body of calm water. He chose the Spanish word for *peaceful* as a name for his discovery. In English it is now called the Pacific Ocean.

12. **Third World** (noun, adjective)   thûrd wûrld

economically underdeveloped countries of Asia, Africa, and Latin America (noun)

Only one in every four children born in the **Third World** attends school.

referring to countries of the Third World (adjective)

Many **Third World** countries are developing important industries.

Many *Third World* countries have precious knowledge of natural remedies. Living in Belize with the Nahuatl Indians, Rosita Arvigo learned the 5,000-year-old tradition of using plants to heal. She uses boiled roses to stop bleeding, wild lettuce to stop pain, and amaranth as a source of calcium and iron. Arvigo now directs the Ix Chel Tropical Research Foundation and has coauthored the book *Rainforest Remedies.*

NOTE: The term *Third World* originated when free enterprise countries, led by the United States, were called the First World; the Second World was Communist countries, led by the former Soviet Union (under Russia); and the Third World was nonaligned, often underdeveloped, countries. The first two terms are no longer common, but *Third World* still means underdeveloped countries.

Exercises

Part 1

■ *Matching Words and Definitions*

Check your understanding of words in the news by matching each word with the letter of its definition. Use each choice only once.

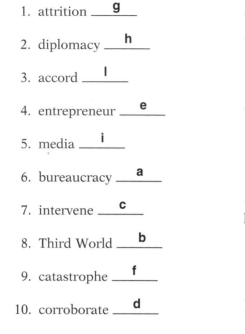

1. attrition __g__
2. diplomacy __h__
3. accord __l__
4. entrepreneur __e__
5. media __i__
6. bureaucracy __a__
7. intervene __c__
8. Third World __b__
9. catastrophe __f__
10. corroborate __d__

a. administration by employees who follow fixed rules
b. underdeveloped countries
c. to act in a matter involving others
d. to confirm; make more certain
e. person who runs a business
f. disaster
g. wearing away
h. the process of official international relations
i. means of communication
j. buyer
k. to calm
l. agreement

■ *Words in Context*

Complete each sentence with the word that fits best. Use each choice only once.

a. accord   e. consumer   i. intervene
b. attrition   f. corroborate   j. media
c. bureaucracy   g. diplomacy   k. pacify
d. catastrophe   h. entrepreneur   l. Third World

1. Many __l, Third World__ countries have important mineral resources that can be used to develop their economies.

2. Companies often use the __j, media__ to advertise their products.

3. Since we are in __a, accord__, we can easily reach a decision.

4. The government could not decide whether U.S. troops should __i, intervene__ to stop the fighting in the Sudan.

5. To __k, pacify__ his angry wife, the man washed the dishes.

6. Since I wasn't sure the Internet news report was correct, I tried to **f, corroborate**_____ it on the television and the radio.

7. Water changes stone to sand by a process of **b, attrition**_____ .

8. The **e, consumer**_____ called several stores to find the best price for a new printer.

9. Because of her great skill at **g, diplomacy**_____, Jantima was able to criticize others without hurting their feelings.

10. Workers in a(n) **c, bureaucracy**_____ often take days to process simple forms.

■ Using Related Words

Complete each sentence by using a word from the group of related words above it. You may need to capitalize a word when you write it in a sentence. Use each choice only once.

1. entrepreneur, entrepreneurial

Reverend Man Singh Das is an **entrepreneur**_____ who makes money while doing good. Owner of a service station and several apartment buildings, he has used his **entrepreneurial**_____ skills to provide jobs and housing to the needy. Instead of arresting a man who was trying to break into his gas station, Das offered him a job cleaning the station.

2. consume, consumption, consumers

Juice bars throughout the nation offer "smoothies," fruit drinks with herbal supplements, to **consumers**_____. Not only does the **consumption**_____ of such fruit juice provide a delicious treat, but smoothies that include ginseng, kava kava, or Saint Johns wort are also advertised as increasing health and energy. Walk into a juice bar, and you can choose to **consume**_____ a smoothie named Yang Yin, Stress Emerald Energy, Strawberry Blond, Energy Bee, or Da Blues.

3. catastrophe, catastrophic

Scientists are disturbed that a declining frog population may have

catastrophic consequences even for humans. Frogs dying throughout the world may signal that the earth is approaching

a **catastrophe** for all forms of life. Three of the suspected causes are infectious disease, a thinning of the ozone layer, and chemical pesticides.

4. bureaucratic, bureaucracy

Texan Calvin Graham won medals for bravery in World War II, but navy officials expelled him and took away his medals when they discovered he was only 12 years old! Graham spent the last

years of his life asking the military **bureaucracy** to re-

turn his medals. But **bureaucratic** agencies move slowly. The last medal, a Purple Heart, was returned only after his death.

5. diplomatic, diplomacy, diplomat

African American Ralph Bunche (1904–1971) had a distinguished

career as a writer and as a **diplomat** in the United

Nations. In 1949, his **diplomacy** and intelligence enabled him to bring about peace in the Middle East. In 1950, he was the first African American to be awarded the Nobel Prize for peace. By the time of his retirement, he held the highest

diplomatic rank of any U.S. citizen in the United Nations.

■ *Reading the Headlines*

This exercise presents five headlines that might appear in newspapers. Read each headline and then answer the questions that follow. (Remember that small words, such as *is, are, a,* and *the,* are often left out of newspaper headlines.)

THIRD WORLD COUNTRY PACIFIES REBEL FORCES

    1. Is the country economically developed? **no**

    2. Is there now peace? **yes**

TRANSPORTATION SYSTEM RUN BY BUREAUCRACY IS A CATASTROPHE

    3. Is transportation run by elected officials? **no**

    4. Is the transportation system working well? **no**

COUNTRIES REACH ACCORD NOT TO INTERVENE IN WAR OF ATTRITION

    5. Will the countries interfere? **no**

    6. Will the war be over quickly? **no**

DIPLOMATIC ENTREPRENEUR BUYS MEDIA COMPANY

    7. Is the entrepreneur polite? **yes**

    8. Is the company involved in communications? **yes**

CONSUMERS CORROBORATE THAT NEW CAR IS DANGEROUS

    9. Are consumers selling the car? **no**

    10. Were consumers the first to discover the danger? **no**

Words to Learn

Part 2

13. **apprehend** (verb)   ăp′rĭ-hĕnd′

to arrest or take a criminal into custody

> A call from a neighbor helped the police to **apprehend** the car thief.

to understand mentally; to grasp

> Scientists only vaguely **apprehend** the origin of the universe.

▶ *Related Words*
apprehension (noun)   The *apprehension* of the escaped convict calmed our fears. I had *apprehensions* about the test. (In the first sentence, *apprehension* means "arrest"; in the second sentence, it means "fear.")

apprehensive (adjective)   Tobacco farmers are *apprehensive* about the effect of new laws. (*Apprehensive* means "fearful.")

14. **chaos** (noun)   kā′ŏs′

a state of total disorder or confusion

> A power failure left the city in **chaos.**

> In a single day, the five active children reduced the orderly room to **chaos.**

▶ *Related Word*
chaotic (adjective)   The countryside became *chaotic* as people rushed to escape from the bombs.

15. **defer** (verb)   dĭ-fûr′

to delay

> Drivers can sometimes **defer** fixing problems with car mufflers for a few weeks, but brakes should be fixed immediately.

to show respect; to submit to the wishes of another

> When boarding a bus, you should **defer** to handicapped people by letting them on first.

> I **deferred** to my father's wishes and attended college.

▶ *Common Phrase*
defer to

▶ *Related Words*
deference (noun)   (dĕf′ər-əns)   He showed his *deference* by bowing to the king. (*Deference* means "respect.")

deferential (adjective)   The student used a *deferential* tone when talking to his professor.

16. **epitome** (noun)   ĭ-pĭt′ə-mē

a defining example; the best example; a symbol

Bill Gates, chairman of Microsoft Corporation, is considered the **epitome** of success in the field of computer technology.

Many consider Adolf Hitler to be the **epitome** of evil. (In this sentence, *epitome* is used in a negative sense.)

Jim Thorpe (1888–1953) *epitomizes* a great athlete. A Native American descended from the Sauk and Fox tribes, Thorpe first excelled in football at the Carlisle Indian School. After winning two Olympic events, Thorpe played baseball as an outfielder for six years. He then became one of the early stars of football and the first president of the American Professional Football League. Thorpe also excelled in swimming, hockey, lacrosse, basketball, and boxing. In 1950, U.S. sportswriters and broadcasters selected Thorpe as both the greatest American athlete and the greatest football player of the first half of the twentieth century.

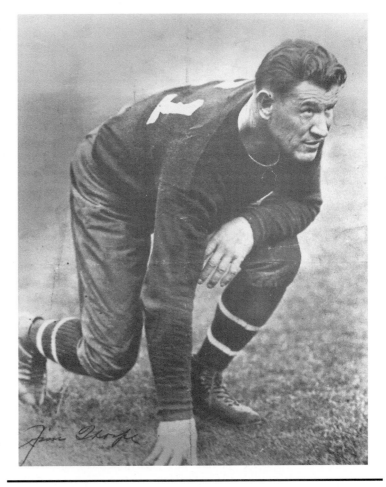

▶ *Related Word*

> **epitomize** (verb)   Rising 630 feet into the air, the graceful Gateway Arch has come to *epitomize* the city of St. Louis.

NOTE: The final *e* of *epitome* is pronounced.

17. **ludicrous** (adjective)   lōō′dĭ-krəs

very absurd, ridiculous, or outrageous

> It is **ludicrous** to think that an ant could carry an elephant.
>
> The fat, middle-aged singer looked **ludicrous** playing a young lover in the opera.

Advertising often uses *ludicrous* pictures to gain your attention. In an effort to boost milk sales, famous figures such as Mark McGwire, Leonardo DiCaprio, Kate Winslet, Amy Grant, Johnny Depp, and the Spice Girls have appeared in ads with "milk mustaches," as though they had just finished drinking milk without wiping their faces.

18. **ominous** (adjective)   ŏm′ə-nəs

warning of bad things; threatening evil

> The **ominous** black clouds warned us of a thunderstorm.
>
> The rising number of murders committed by teenagers is an **ominous** sign for society.

19. **supplant** (verb)   sə-plănt′

to replace

> No other pet could ever **supplant** the girl's first puppy in her affections.
>
> In the future, plastic "smart cards" may entirely **supplant** cash.
>
> In most of the world, electric lights have **supplanted** oil lamps and candlelight.

20. **thrive** (verb)   thrīv

to grow vigorously; to do well

> Protected by strong national laws, rain forests still **thrive** in Costa Rica.

Many athletes **thrive** on competition.

Scientists now think that bacteria may have been the first form of life on earth. Extremely hardy, some species of bacteria can *thrive* even without sunlight or oxygen. They survive in boiling water or steaming volcanic vents, within ice, and beneath the ground. So when scientists search for life in places like the frozen moons of Jupiter, they look for bacteria.

The next four words—*radical, liberal, conservative,* and *reactionary*—refer to political opinions that range from left to right.

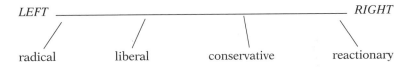

LEFT _____ *RIGHT*

radical · liberal · conservative · reactionary

Radical and liberal politicians are called *left-wing* because they sat on the left side (or wing) of the semicircular seating of the French National Assembly of 1789. Other European assemblies have continued this custom. Radical politicians want swift reforms that will benefit poor people, minorities, and others without political power. Liberal politicians favor the extension of rights and privileges through gradual reform. Between *liberals* and *conservatives,* in the middle, are *moderate* politicians.

Conservatives and reactionaries are spoken of as *right-wing* because they sat on the right wing of the French National Assembly. Conservative politicians favor tradition and oppose change. They want to protect business interests, religion, and the traditional family. Reactionary politicians oppose change so strongly that they often want to return to the way things used to be. *Radical, liberal,* and *conservative* also have nonpolitical meanings.

21. **radical** (adjective)   răd'ĭ-kəl

favoring great change; extreme

China experienced a **radical** social revolution during the 1950s and 1960s.

Radical politicians in some developing countries favor distributing all farmland to the peasants.

Leshan's new business suit was a **radical** departure from the jeans and T-shirt he usually wore.

▶ *Related Word*
> **radical** (noun)   In Iran, some *radicals* have been replaced with moderate leaders. (*Radical* means "a person who holds radical beliefs.")

NOTE: The definition of *radical* changes with the political situation. In many Muslim countries, for example, *radical* means favoring a return to strict obedience to religion. In Latin American countries, it means wanting a more equal distribution of land and wealth. Whatever the country, however, radicals favor great change.

22. **liberal** (adjective)   lĭb′ər-əl

favoring gradual progress and reform

> Many **liberal** politicians in this country favor providing health care for everyone.

favoring liberty; tolerant

> The college's **liberal** rules allowed all students to live in off-campus apartments.

plentiful; generous in amount

> If you want to please eight-year-olds, bring a **liberal** supply of chocolate bars.

▶ *Related Words*
> **liberal** (noun)   The *liberal* voted for increased legal aid for the poor. (*Liberal* means "a person who holds liberal beliefs.")
>
> **liberalize** (verb)   When the government *liberalized* rules on censorship, the number of newspapers increased.

23. **conservative** (adjective)   kən-sûr′və-tĭv

favoring traditional beliefs and actions; traditional

> The **conservative** senator favored prayer in schools.
>
> Coming from a **conservative** background, Fay was surprised to hear people swearing in public.
>
> George's nose ring was a strange contrast to his **conservative** business suit.

cautious or moderate

> We gave a **conservative** estimate that there were twenty thousand people at the rally; there may have been more.

▶ *Related Words*
> **conservative** (noun)   Senator Ruggles, a *conservative*, voted

against increasing taxes to fund welfare payments. (*Conservative* means a person who holds conservative beliefs.)

conserve (verb)   It is important to *conserve* trees by recycling newspapers. (*Conserve* means "to save.")

24. **reactionary** (adjective)   rē-ăk′shə-nĕr′ē

opposing progress in an extreme way

> The **reactionary** educator wanted to use century-old methods to teach reading.

▶ *Related Word*

reactionary (noun)   The *reactionary* wanted to take away the vote from eighteen-year-olds. (*Reactionary* means a person who holds reactionary beliefs.)

NOTE: Reactionary usually has a negative connotation.

Exercises

Part 2

■ *Matching Words and Definitions*

Check your understanding of words in the news by matching each word with the letter of its definition. Use each choice only once.

1. apprehend ____d____

2. ludicrous ____b____

3. radical ____l____

4. defer ____f____

5. liberal ____a____

6. conservative ____e____

7. reactionary ____g____

8. thrive ____j____

9. supplant ____c____

10. ominous ____h____

a. favoring gradual progress and reform

b. ridiculous

c. to replace

d. to arrest

e. favoring traditional beliefs

f. to delay

g. opposing progress in an extreme way

h. threatening evil

i. confusion

j. to grow vigorously

k. best example

l. favoring great change

■ *Words in Context*

Complete each sentence with the word that fits best. Use each choice only once.

a. apprehend   e. ludicrous   i. radical
b. chaos   f. ominous   j. liberal
c. defer   g. supplant   k. conservative
d. epitome   h. thrive   l. reactionary

1. In the future, computer-generated animation may **g, supplant** all other types of animation in feature films.

2. The storekeeper was able to **a, apprehend** the shoplifter and call the police.

3. After the hurricane, the house was in a state of **b, chaos**, with clothes and furniture scattered everywhere.

4. His wife's death resulted in a(n) **i, radical** change in the man's life, as he moved to another city and remarried.

5. The brilliant physicist Albert Einstein is often considered the **d, epitome** of genius.

6. The **j, liberal** wanted gradual reform in school funding.

7. Our guess that we would earn $100 was **k, conservative** because we actually made $200.

8. As I walked slowly up the sidewalk to the house, I heard the **f, ominous** growl of a vicious dog.

9. My father decided to **c, defer** quitting smoking until next year.

10. Children usually **h, thrive** in a warm, loving home.

■ *Using Related Words*

Complete each sentence by using a word from the group of related words above it. You may need to capitalize a word when you write it in a sentence. Use each choice only once.

1. apprehend, apprehended, apprehensive

   In most cities it is illegal to dine in a restaurant with your dog, and

   if you try, you could be **apprehended** by the police. But in New York, dogs can accompany owners to outdoor cafes. Al-

   though an occasional eater may become **apprehensive** when a huge dog looks longingly at his hamburger, most dogs be-have very well. In fact, at "Fido's," the first dog spa, dogs are served biscuits while humans eat. Fido's will soon start hosting dog birth-

   day parties for owners who cannot **apprehend** how a dog's birthday can pass without a celebration.

2. conserve, conservative, conservation

   In 1995, the U.S. Supreme Court decided to uphold a law to aid the spotted owl, an endangered species. The laws forbid logging on several thousand acres of forest that provide the bird's habitat.

   Although this helps the effort to **conserve** the bird, it harms business interests, including the jobs of loggers. The ban

   on logging has been opposed by **conservative** politi-cians. This case shows how difficult it can be to balance the need

   for **conservation** of wild animals with the needs of the economy.

3. deferred, deference

   In crowded cities, special lanes are reserved for cars that carry

   more than one passenger. In showing **deference** to group travelers, traffic controllers encourage people to ride to-gether and decrease traffic. However, people have long suspected that these uncrowded lanes are not used very much. The city of

   Los Angeles called for a study, but has recently **deferred** it.

4. chaotic, chaos

   The 1999 earthquake in Turkey left part of the country in **chaos** for several days, as water supplies, electric power, and road systems all failed to operate. Many charitable agencies helped to improve the __chaotic_____ situation.

■ *Reading the Headlines*

This exercise presents five headlines that might appear in newspapers. Read each headline and then answer the questions that follow. (Remember that small words, such as *is, are, the,* and *a,* are often left out of newspaper headlines.)

RADICAL CHANGE IN GOVERNMENT AN OMINOUS SIGN

1. Was the government changed slightly? __no____

2. Do people think that good things will come from the change? __no____

LUDICROUS SUMMER MOVIES THRIVE IN THEATERS

3. Are the movies serious? __no____

4. Are they doing well? __yes____

LIBERALS SUPPLANT CONSERVATIVES IN PARLIAMENT

5. Are there more conservatives than before? __no____

6. Is the number of liberals increasing? __yes____

EPITOME OF MORALITY APPREHENDED FOR DRUNK DRIVING

7. Is the person a symbol of morality? __yes____

8. Was the person arrested? __yes____

CHAOS ERUPTS AS STUDENTS REFUSE TO DEFER TO REACTIONARY PRINCIPAL

9. Is the principal old-fashioned? __yes____

10. Is the school orderly? __no____

Chapter Exercises

■ *Practicing Strategies: Context Clues of Substitution*

In each of the following sentences, one difficult word is italicized. Using context clues of substitution, make an intelligent guess about the meaning of the word as it is used in this sentence. Your instructor may ask you to look up these words in your dictionary after you've finished the exercise.

1. The rotten food gave off a *noisome* odor.

   Noisome means **disgusting** .

2. *Corpulent* people often become healthier after they lose weight.

   Corpulent means **fat; overweight** .

3. The child was so *contrite* about losing the money that we found it easy to forgive him.

   Contrite means **sorry; regretful; penitent** .

4. In the 1600s, true tales were told of *nefarious* pirates who kidnapped people and sold them as slaves.

   Nefarious means **famous for being wicked; wicked** .

5. The road was *truncated* when several miles were closed down.

   Truncated means **shortened** .

6. The *parsimonious* millionaire bought a cheap used car.

   Parsimonious means **stingy; cheap** .

7. On the exam, Antonio made a *grievous* error that lowered his grade from an A to a C.

   Grievous means **serious; bad** .

8. Eating fruits and vegetables, visiting the doctor regularly, and exercising have a *salubrious* effect.

   Salubrious means **healthy; health giving** .

9. Because we want to see justice done, we hope to *redress* the wrongs you have suffered.

   Redress means **set right; remedy; fix** .

10. Injuries to their two best players had a *deleterious* effect on the football team.

    Deleterious means **harmful; destructive; bad** .

■ *Practicing Strategies: New Uses of Familiar Words in Context*

Context clues can often help you determine the meaning of words used in unusual ways. Make an intelligent guess about the meaning of the italicized word or phrase in each of the following sentences.

1. Neslihan wanted to *air* her opinions in public.

   Air means **speak; express; say** .

2. He couldn't vote because he was a few months *shy of* eighteen.

   Shy of means **less than; younger than; short of** .

3. After spending the day at the library, they *repaired* to the restaurant.

   Repaired means **went** .

4. The President was alone *save for* a few friends.

   Save for means **except for** .

5. In her anger, she *stormed* out of the room.

   Stormed means **moved angrily** .

■ *Companion Words*

Complete each sentence with the word that fits best. Choose your answers from the words below. You may use each word more than once.

Choices: to, with, on, of, in, about

1. Babe Ruth was the epitome **of** a great baseball player.

2. Nobody dared to intervene **in**_____ the fight between the marines.

3. Children should defer **to**_____ the wishes of their parents.

4. The 1980–88 conflict between Iraq and Iran was a war **of**_____ attrition.

5. The radioactivity had catastrophic effects **on**_____ plants and animals in the area.

6. William showed deference **to**_____ his boss by addressing him as "sir."

7. Rocio was apprehensive **about**_____ flying in an airplane.

8. Monica thrived **on**_____ healthy food.

9–10. Sophia was **in**_____ accord **with**_____ her husband's decision to change jobs.

■ Writing with Your Words

This exercise will give you practice in writing effective sentences that use the vocabulary words. Each sentence is started for you. Complete it with an interesting phrase that also indicates the meaning of the italicized word.

1. In *Third World* countries _____

_____ .

2. My career will *thrive* when _____

_____ .

3. One thing I find *ludicrous* _____

_____ .

4. One *ominous* trend in society is that _____

_____ .

5. A *bureaucracy* _____

_____ .

6. I would like to *supplant* required courses with _____

_____ .

7. The *media* _____

_____ .

8. I would favor a *radical* change in _____

_____ .

9. I am in *accord* with the President on _____

_____ .

10. I cannot *apprehend* how _____

_____ .

Passage

The Dog—"Our Best Friend" and Coworker

Dogs are perhaps the best-loved of all animals. Throughout the ages, they have worked for us, protected us, and provided us with companionship and loyalty. Now they even sell products for us!

Dogs and humans have long been linked. Pictures of the animal on cave walls date back more than 12,000 years. **(1)** At times, humans' treatment of their favorite pets has bordered on the **ludicrous.** Ancient Egyptians provided dogs with servants and jewel-studded collars. Dogs were mummified to protect them in the afterlife.

How did dogs come to be so treasured by so many cultures? It seems likely that wild dogs first came near human campsites to eat the remains of meals. Humans were able to **pacify** dogs because of "pack behavior." In other words, dogs act in social groups and follow a leader. **(2)** Humans

supplanted other dogs as these leaders, and **(3)** an unspoken **accord** was reached. Dogs worked for humans by helping them to hunt and by providing protection. In return, dogs shared in the food that the humans gathered. If you own a dog, you are, in effect, the "leader of the pack."

Today, dogs have expanded their work roles and are regularly featured in the **media.** Television programs and movies cast dogs as companions and heroes. Newspapers and magazines carry stories about heroic dogs.

Dogs even star in advertisements. TBWA/Chiat/Day, an award-winning advertising agency, increased sales of the fast-food chain when the Taco Bell chihuahua, declared "Yo quiero Taco Bell." **(4)** Teenage **consumers** were particularly charmed when the chihuahua passed up romance in favor of a Taco Bell meal. Later, the dog starred in a commercial for Taco Bell Gorditas that was a takeoff on a political rally. Declaring "Viva Gorditas," a crowd led by the Taco Bell chihuahua stared at a shamefaced man who dared to eat a hamburger rather than a Gordita. In a "crossover" ad for the movie *Godzilla*, the tiny chihuahua tried to capture Godzilla in a box by calling, "Hey lizard, lizard, lizard." **(5)** But after seeing godzilla's huge, **ominous** shadow, the chihuahua decided he needed a bigger box! Chihuahuas were originally bred in Mexico as pet dogs small enough to sit in one's lap.

Although these ads have contributed to increased sales, some objections have been raised to them. Some feel that the Taco Bell chihuahua **epitomizes** a problem in advertising—the stereotyping of minorities, in this case, Hispanics. But many other critics enjoy the chihuahua's light-

hearted popularity. As one newspaper put it: "'Yo quiero Taco Bell' has been, in effect, added to English."

The ads are increasing the popularity of owning a chihuahua. According to one pet store **entrepreneur** in Oregon, many buyers want dogs that look just like the Taco Bell dog. Breeders warn that **(6)** chihuahuas need proper training to **thrive** as good pets. Otherwise, the small, sensitive dogs can become noisy and nervous. **(7)** Unprepared homes often have **catastrophic** results for dogs and their owners. **(8)** The sudden increase of chihuahuas in shelters for unwanted dogs **corroborates** the fact that an owner had better be prepared to handle the breed.

The tremendous success of the Taco Bell ads have led to more dogs working to sell products. **(9)** Some find humor in a **radical** departure from reality, as people follow the orders of their pets. For example, one Nissan ad shows a collie exercising mind control by waking up his owner and having him drive a car that picks up doggie friends. After the van is filled, the dogs want to make room for one more, rather attractive doggie passenger. The owner **defers** to the pets and, at the end, is left standing by the side of the road. We can only hope that the police will **apprehend** the car's new driver! In another ad, a terrier pushes an owner, who is sleeping in a reclining chair, through dangerous traffic to a Nissan dealer.

In one camera ad, an owner takes a picture of puppies, offering them for free to anyone who will take them. But when the picture is developed, the owner is actually offered "free to a good home."

(10) Owners of dogs who might be dreaming about living off a pet's **liberal** earnings should remember that training such a dog is expensive and time-consuming. At times, profits must be split among several owners. The movie *Air Bud*, about a basketball-playing dog, required six different golden retrievers. For most of us, dogs will simply be our "best friend" and companion, and who could ask for a better one?

■ *Exercise*

Each numbered sentence below corresponds to a sentence in the Passage. Fill in the letter of the choice that makes the sentence mean the same thing as its corresponding sentence in the Passage.

1. Humans' treatment of their favorite pets has bordered on the __d__.
   a. insane   b. unfair   c. disastrous   d. ridiculous

2. Humans __b__ other dogs as these leaders.
   a. used   b. replaced   c. trained   d. wanted

3. An unspoken __a__ was reached.
   a. agreement   b. finish   c. replacement   d. example

4. Teenage __d__ were particularly charmed.
   a. youngsters   b. delinquents   c. fans   d. buyers

5. After seeing the huge, __c__ shadow, the chihuahua decided he needed a bigger box.
   a. dark   b. dim   c. frightening   d. large

6. Chihuahuas need proper training to __b__ as good pets.
   a. serve   b. do well   c. guard   d. be considered

7. Unprepared homes often have __d__ results for dogs and their owners.
   a. unexpected   b. noisy   c. crowded   d. disastrous

8. The sudden increase of chihuahuas in shelters __b__ the fact that an owner had better be prepared.
   a. shows   b. confirms   c. conflicts with   d. predicts

9. Some find humor in a(n) __c__ departure from reality.
   a. funny   b. unreal   c. extreme   d. unexpected

10. Owners may dream about living off a pet's __a__ earnings.
    a. generous   b. helpful   c. typical   d. interesting

■ Discussion Questions

1. In what ways does the passage state that dogs have interacted with human beings?

2. How are the Nissan ads discussed a departure from reality?

3. How do you feel about the use of the chihuahua in the Taco Bell commercials? Discuss the reasons for your decision.

◀ ENGLISH IDIOMS

The Media and Communication

Although news sometimes comes to us *by word of mouth,* or through personal contact, we get most of our news from the media. On our way home, for example, we may *lend an ear to,* or listen to, the radio. If a reporter giving the news is not clear, we may not be able to *make heads or tails of,* or understand, what is being said. At other times, we may *see eye to eye with,* or agree with, a reporter's opinion.

On many television news broadcasts, people announcing the weather *ham it up,* or joke and overact. This may *rub us the wrong way,* or annoy us. Increasingly, talk shows have dealt with sex and violence. This practice has *raised eyebrows,* or shocked, some members of the public. Yet, talk shows have also *brought to light,* or made public, many important issues.

Yellow journalism refers to newspaper reporting that concentrates on shocking and sensational news, such as brutal murders and scandals. The term comes from the "Yellow Kid," the first comic strip in the United States, which was printed in yellow ink to attract attention. Because the newspaper containing the strip, the *New York World,* was known for its shocking news, *yellow paper* or *yellow journalism* came to mean shocking and sensational reporting.

Quiz Again

Now that you have finished studying this chapter, here is the brief true-false quiz you took when you began. Take it again.

Things increase by a process of **attrition**.	True	False
An **ominous** warning is usually frightening.	True	False
A **radical** change is small.	True	False
Ludicrous things are funny.	True	False

Answers are on page 405. Did your score improve?

Words for Feeling, Expression, and Action

Have you ever asked an instructor to *clarify* an assignment, yawned at a *bland* speech, heard the roar of a *boisterous* crowd, or been *elated* at winning a prize? This chapter presents words that you can use to describe the emotions, thoughts, and actions of yourself and others.

Chapter Strategy: Context Clues of Definition

Chapter Words:

Part 1

bland	confrontation	emulate
boisterous	dynamic	enigma
clarify	elated	skeptical
concise	emphatic	thwart

Part 2

appall	condemn	flaunt
articulate	contemplate	harass
belligerent	contend	prohibit
chagrin	elicit	undermine

Quiz Yourself

To check your knowledge of some of the chapter words before you begin to study, identify these statements as true or false.

When we **emulate** people, we do what they do.	True	False
Chagrin is a happy feeling.	True	False
An **enigma** is easy to understand.	True	False
When we **contemplate,** we take action.	True	False

You will learn the answers as you study this chapter.

Did You Know?

How Do Cars Get Their Names?

The process of naming cars shows how feeling, expression, and action can relate to one another. A car's name is an important part of its image. Before automakers bring out a new model, they research its name carefully. By using words that express speed, power, glamour, or even economy, manufacturers hope to give you positive feelings about their cars that translate into action when you decide to buy one.

Detroit auto pioneer Henry Leland named his early cars after personal heroes.

Cadillac is taken from Antoine de La Mothe Cadillac, the French adventurer who founded Detroit in 1701.
The *Lincoln* honored President Abraham Lincoln, the man Leland voted for in the 1860 election.

Names for sport utility vehicles, pick-up trucks, and minivans often suggest the power and openness of the American west.

Pontiac *Montana*—a western state
GMC *Sonoma*—county in California famous for wine
Yukon—a territory in Canada known for its mineral wealth; a lake in Canada and Alaska
Chevrolet's *Tahoe*—a lake bordering Nevada and California

The Chrysler Corporation seems to look upward for names.

Stratus and *Cirrus* refer to cloud types.

Sometimes carmakers simply create new names that suggest appealing images.

Cadillac *Escalade*—perhaps from *escalate,* meaning "go up," and *parade,*
    suggesting showy, upbeat travel
Nissan *Altima*—probably from *ultimate,* meaning "the last and best"
Mazda *Millenia*—suggesting the millennium
Toyota *Spyder*—a slight spelling change from the word *spider*
Oldsmobile *Bravada*—suggesting *bravado,* or showy courage (You will
    learn the word *bravado* later in this book.)

Animal names have proven to be popular. Five different car models have been named *Eagle.* But the 1912 *Dodo* was a disaster. It was named for a now extinct bird from the island of Mauritius that could not fly. Like the real dodo, the car "never got off the ground."

Eagle car sales soared.

Dodo car sales remained grounded.

Learning Strategy

Context Clues of Definition

The learning strategy in this chapter will focus on *context clues of definition.* Often, words that you don't know will actually be defined for you as they are used in sentences. Sometimes a sentence provides a *synonym* (a word that means the same thing or nearly the same thing) for the unknown word. For example, look at the word *effervescent* as it is used in a sentence.

> Coca-Cola® is an *effervescent,* or bubbly, beverage.

The word *effervescent* means? . . . bubbly. Thus, *bubbly* is a synonym for *effervescent.*

Such clues of definition are quite easy to use if you can recognize them. These clues include the following:

1. Words or phrases set off by commas, dashes, or parentheses:

   > The man's altruistic, *unselfish,* motives caused him to donate money to charity.
   >
   > The man's altruistic—*unselfish*—motives caused him to donate money to charity.
   >
   > The man's altruistic *(unselfish)* motives caused him to donate money to charity.

2. Direct definition:

   > She thought his motives were altruistic, *which means unselfish.*
   >
   > She thought his motives were altruistic, *that is to say, unselfish.*

3. Indirect definition:

   > He was an altruistic person *who often acted out of unselfish motives.*

4. The use of *or, and,* or *also:*

   > The man's altruistic, *or unselfish,* motives pleased his family.
   > (The use of commas with *or* is an extra hint signaling that a context clue of definition is being used.)
   >
   > The man's altruistic *and unselfish* motives pleased his family.
   > (Sometimes, however, words joined by *and* and *or* do not mean the same thing. Examples are "The man was lazy and dishonest" and "People shouldn't be lazy or dishonest.")

5. Words signaling agreement, such as *therefore, likewise, in the same way, as well as,* and *similarly:*

   > The man was altruistic; *therefore, he donated money to charity and did volunteer work with children.*

As you can see, the word *altruistic,* which you learned in Chapter 1, has been defined in each sentence. Many sentences use the synonym *unselfish.* Others provide a longer definition through examples, such as *donated money to charity* and *did volunteer work with children.*

Three more examples of context clues of definition are given below. Can you make an intelligent guess about the meaning of each italicized word?

1. The margin of the leaf was *sinuated,* and indented curves ran along the edge. (An *and* clue is used.)

2. The king took *draconian* measures against the rebels, and their supporters were also punished severely. (*And* and *also* clues are used.)

3. In 776 B.C.E. the first recorded Olympic games were held in *Olympia,* a city in Greece. (A following phrase is set off by a comma. This is an example of an "appositive" structure.)

Answers are on page 405.

Now try using context clues to figure out the meanings of some words you will be learning in this chapter.

1. The police thought the party was too *boisterous,* or noisy.

   Boisterous means __noisy_____.

2. The teenager tried to *emulate* Mariah Carey's personal style as well as to imitate her singing.

   Emulate means __copy; emulate_____.

3. The French philosopher Pascal was a *skeptical* thinker who doubted many accepted beliefs.

   Skeptical means __doubting_____.

Answers are on page 405.

Words to Learn

Part 1

1. **bland** (adjective)   blănd

   nonirritating

   > The mayor's **bland** responses calmed the angry crowd.

   > Rice is a **bland** food.

dull

> Patsy changed her hair color from **bland** brown to fiery red.
>
> A **bland** shopping mall, where all stores looked the same, replaced the colorful and varied shop fronts on the city street.

2. **boisterous** (adjective)   boi′stər-əs

noisy; rowdy; rough

> The **boisterous** crowd shouted and banged on their seats when a rival team stepped onto the field.

▶ *Related Word*
> **boisterousness** (noun)   After the *boisterousness* of the famous Mardi Gras celebration, New Orleans settles into the quiet time of Lent.

3. **clarify** (verb)   klăr′ə-fī′

to make clear or sensible

> We sent an e-mail asking the company to **clarify** the instructions in the manual.

▶ *Related Word*
> **clarification** (noun)   The senator asked for *clarification* of the special prosecutor's role.

4. **concise** (adjective)   kən-sīs′

short; clear but using few words

> Most students prefer a **concise** definition of a word to a more lengthy one.
>
> Computer manuals should give **concise** explanations.

5. **confrontation** (noun)   kŏn′frŭn-tā′shən

hostile meeting; direct fight

> **Confrontations** between students and Indonesian government forces have been deadly.
>
> To avoid a **confrontation** with her parents, Jane took the ring out of her lower lip when she went home.

▶ *Related Word*
> **confront** (verb)   (kən-frŭnt′)   A strong person is able to *confront* problems. (*Confront* means "to meet.")

6. **dynamic** (adjective)   dī-năm′ĭk

energetic; forceful

> The **dynamic** pastor doubled church membership and raised funds for a new building.

> Airports are a **dynamic** force in a city's economy because they bring employment, tourism, and new business.

fast moving; fast changing

> Prices change quickly in **dynamic** international currency markets.

▶ *Related Word*
  dynamics (noun)   Child psychologists often study family *dynamics*. Experts studied the *dynamics* of the hurricane. (*Dynamics* means "social or physical forces.")

The word *dynamite* is related to *dynamic,* since both are formed from the Greek root *dyne,* meaning "power." Dynamite, a powerful explosive, was invented by the Swedish scientist Alfred Nobel in the mid 1800s. After its invention, Nobel decided to find a positive use for the riches this destructive force had brought him, so he created prizes for peace, literature, medicine, physics, and chemistry. In 1969, a prize was added for economics. Today these Nobel Prizes are among the most prestigious in the world.

---

7. **elated** (adjective)   ĭ-lā′tĭd

thrilled; very happy

> Michael was **elated** when he won the hundred-million-dollar lottery.

8. **emphatic** (adjective)   ĕm-făt′ĭk

strong; definite; done with emphasis

> Piotr was **emphatic** in insisting that his car shouldn't have been towed.

> The Los Angeles Dodgers scored an **emphatic** victory over the Chicago Cubs.

▶ *Related Word*
  emphasis (noun)   The employer placed great *emphasis* on promptness.

9. **emulate** (verb)   ĕm′yə-lāt′

to try to equal or excel through imitating; to imitate

> Competitors try to **emulate** the success of Amazon.com at selling books over the Internet.

▶ *Related Word*
   emulation (noun)   Its model political and economic policies make the African country of Botswana worthy of *emulation*.

10. **enigma** (noun)   ĭ-nĭg′mə

something unexplainable or puzzling

> John was an **enigma** to his coach, who could not understand how the overweight, out-of-shape tennis player won every game.

> "Idiot savants," who may be mathematical geniuses but cannot manage everyday life, remain **enigmas** to scientists.

▶ *Related Word*
   enigmatic (adjective)   The humming sounds made by Mississippi's Pascagoula River remain *enigmatic*.

11. **skeptical** (adjective)   skĕp′tĭ-kəl

doubting; tending to disbelieve

> Because there were no other witnesses or photographs, people were **skeptical** that the man had seen a UFO.

> **Skeptical** people make good scientists because they demand proof of everything.

▶ *Common Phrase*
   skeptical of

▶ *Related Words*
   skeptic (noun)   *Skeptics* do not believe that universal insurance coverage will solve health care problems.

   skepticism (noun)   The doctor's *skepticism* about herbal remedies disappeared when one cured his patient's insomnia.

12. **thwart** (verb)   thwôrt

to prevent from happening

> A Spokane hotel clerk **thwarted** a theft by offering the robber food and a coat, rather than cash.

Mickey's efforts to score in the basketball game were **thwarted** by an alert guard.

Poverty can **thwart** a student's wish to finish college.

Exercises

Part 1

■ Definitions

The following sentences deal with feelings, expressions, and actions. Complete each statement by matching each word with the letter of its definition. Use each choice only once.

1. To clarify is to ____l____ .

2. An enigma is a(n) ____j____ .

3. To be dynamic is to

   be ____a____ .

4. To be elated is to be ____c____.

5. An emphatic statement

   is ____f____ .

6. A bland movie is ____g____ .

7. A concise statement

   is ____e____ .

8. To be boisterous is to

   be ____k____ .

9. To thwart is to ____d____ .

10. To emulate is to ____b____ .

a. energetic

b. imitate

c. thrilled; very happy

d. prevent from happening

e. short

f. definite; strong

g. dull

h. hostile meeting

i. doubtful

j. puzzle

k. noisy

l. make clear

■ Words in Context

Complete each sentence with the word that fits best. Use each choice only once.

a. bland   e. confrontation   i. emulate
b. boisterous   f. dynamic   j. enigma
c. clarify   g. elated   k. skeptical
d. concise   h. emphatic   l. thwart

1. The mysterious disappearance of Amelia Earhart remains a(n) **j, enigma** to this day.

2. I was **g, elated** when I was elected president of my class.

3. The **f, dynamic** woman swam three miles every day before going to work.

4. Many high school boys try to **i, emulate** famous basketball players.

5. After he made his paper more **d, concise**, it took less time to type.

6. We asked our accountant to **c, clarify** the instructions on our tax form.

7. People often speak loudly when they want to make a(n) **h, emphatic** statement.

8. The **e, confrontation** of the two armies on the battlefield resulted in great loss of life.

9. If you tell my brother about the party, you will **l, thwart** our plans to surprise him.

10. Ishmael had a(n) **a, bland** personality and never became excited.

■ *Using Related Words*

Complete each sentence by using a word from the group of related words above it. You may need to capitalize a word when you write it in a sentence. Use each choice only once.

1. skeptics, skeptical, skepticism

   From ancient times well into the 1800s, medicine made use of the blood-sucking leech. For the past two hundred years, however, modern medicine has viewed the leech's value with **skepticism** _____. But in recent years, many **skeptics** _____ have been surprised to find that leeches can help attach severed body parts. Furthermore, although there appears to be **skeptical** _____ reaction on the part of some doctors, the saliva of leeches may help treat certain tumors.

2. confront, confrontations

   Professional basketball has been marked by an increasing number of **confrontations** _____ between players. At times, these have even resulted in physical fights. Perhaps the National Basketball Association needs to **confront** _____ this problem directly and set up guidelines and penalties to reduce the number of hostile and violent contacts.

3. boisterous, boisterousness

   Are you tired of the **boisterous** _____ children who play on your street daily? Does the **boisterousness** _____ of your neighbor's parties offend you? Do you wish the elderly lady next door would stop bothering you about the noise *you* make? Cities in Colorado, California, New York, and Illinois have joined the Neighborhood Mediation Task Forces. In this program, volunteers are trained to help neighbors deal with their complaints by working together to solve them.

4. emulate, emulation

   Eating problems may arise when girls seek to **emulate** _____ the figures of extremely thin models. Since body types differ, a weight that is healthy for one girl may be underweight for another. **Emulation** _____ of a favorite star or model can actually result in death from starvation! A U.S. survey found that many eight-year-old girls felt they were overweight. In Argentina, it has been reported that 1 in 10 teenage girls suffers from an eating disorder.

5. enigma, enigmatic

In 1591, English explorers returning to the new colony of Roanoke, Virginia, found that everyone had vanished. The colonists' disappearance was an **enigma**_____. The initials *CR* carved into a doorpost were the only clue to this **enigmatic**_____ event. Were the people killed? Were they captured? Did they wander away? To this day, no one knows.

■ *True or False?*

Each of the following statements uses at least one word from this section. Read each statement and then indicate whether you think it is probably true or probably false.

T___   1. Emphatic views are stated in a strong way.

F___   2. We know the answer to an enigma.

F___   3. Confrontations are generally pleasant and quiet.

F___   4. When we thwart something, we accomplish it.

T___   5. We would be skeptical if told that a dish made with twenty-five chili peppers was bland.

F___   6. If we were seeking to emulate a concise report, we would write a long one.

T___   7. Before leaving, people should clarify directions to where they are going.

T___   8. A boisterous party is noisy.

F___   9. We would be elated if told that the world was coming to an end.

T___   10. Dynamic forces are fast moving.

Words to Learn

Part 2

13. **appall** (verb)   ə-pôl′

horrify; fill with horror, dismay, or shock

> The public was **appalled** when police found fourteen children living in a filthy, roach-infested apartment.

> Parents were **appalled** by the teacher's spelling mistakes.

▶ *Related Word*
appalling (adjective)   The violence in high schools is *appalling*.

NOTE: Appall can refer to very serious matters, such as murder or starvation, or simply annoying things, such as manners.

14. **articulate** (adjective)   är-tĭk′yə-lĭt;   (verb)   är-tĭk′-yə-lāt′

skilled in using language; clearly and well expressed (adjective)

> An **articulate** person often has a well-developed vocabulary.

> Jesse Jackson is an **articulate** spokesperson for civil rights.

to express clearly and distinctly (verb)

> Jose **articulated** his reasons for a raise so well that his boss gave him one immediately.

▶ *Related Word*
articulation (noun)   Frank Sinatra's *articulation* was clear enough that people understood every word he sang.

15. **belligerent** (adjective)   bə-lĭj′ər-ənt

hostile; engaged in warfare

> The two **belligerent** countries bombed each other's territory.

> The minor disagreement between drivers turned into a **belligerent** shouting match.

▶ *Related Word*
belligerence (noun)   Owners closed their shops for one day to protest the *belligerence* of local gangs.

Belligerent comes from the Latin words *bellum,* "war," and *gerere,* "to carry on." *Bellum* is also the root of the word *rebellion,* a war waged against a ruling power. The United States gained its independence in a rebellion against Great Britain that lasted from 1775 to 1783.

16. **chagrin** (noun)   shə-grĭn′

distress caused by failure, disappointment, or humiliation

> To my **chagrin,** I spilled spaghetti sauce all over my boyfriend's mother.

> To Anne's **chagrin,** she ruined the computer she had borrowed from her friend.

▶ *Common Phrase*
   to my (your/his/her/our/their) chagrin

17. **condemn** (verb)   kən-dĕm′

to express strong disapproval of

> Animal rights activists **condemn** the use of animals in experiments.

to give a punishment; to find guilty

> The judge **condemned** the criminal to life in prison.

> His lack of education **condemned** him to a low-level job.

> The city inspectors **condemned** the decayed old building. (In this case, *condemn* means "decide to destroy.")

▶ *Common Phrase*
   condemn to

▶ *Related Word*
   condemnation (noun)   (kŏn′dĕm-nā′shən)   The United Nations issued a *condemnation* of modern-day slavery.

18. **contemplate** (verb)   kŏn′təm-plāt′

to think about carefully

> Some Britons **contemplate** what their country would be like without the royal family.

> When Mario **contemplated** taking a vacation with his four children, he realized he would have to rent a minivan.

▶ *Related Word*

contemplation (noun)   Each day, the priest took time for religious *contemplation*.

19. **contend** (verb)   kən-těnd′

to compete; to struggle against something.

Greeks from Sparta, Athens, and many other cities **contended** in the ancient Olympic games.

Eighty high school students **contended** in the debating tournament.

Effie had to **contend** with a class of twenty boisterous children.

NOTE: The phrase *contend with* often means "to cope with."

Can you match these **contenders** with their sports?

1. Oscar de la Hoya	a. tennis
2. Goldberg	b. ice skating
3. Se Ri Pak	c. boxing
4. Venus Williams	d. golf
5. John Handegard	e. wrestling
6. Ilya Kulik	f. bowling

Answers are on page 405.

---

to put forth a point of view

Scientist Ron Clarke **contends** that he has found the oldest human remains, which date back three million years.

▶ *Related Words*

contender (noun, person)   Three *contenders* entered the Senate race.

contention (noun)   It was the museum curator's *contention* that the famous painting was a fake.

contentious (adjective)   A *contentious* person often starts fights. (*Contentious* means "tending to argue.")

20. **elicit** (verb)   ĭ-lĭs′ĭt

to draw forth (a response)

> The tender love story **elicited** sighs from the audience.
>
> Mouth-to-mouth resuscitation finally **elicited** a response from the child who had been pulled from the lake.

▶ *Related Word*
  elicitation (noun)   A comedian's *elicitation* of laughter from an audience requires skill.

21. **flaunt** (verb)   flônt

to display obviously or showily; show off

> The star **flaunted** her wealth by buying a huge mansion and a private jet.
>
> The military government **flaunted** its strength with parades of well-armed soldiers.

NOTE: Be careful not to confuse *flaunt* (to display) with *flout* (to disregard or ignore).

22. **harass** (verb)   hăr′əs or hə-răs′

to annoy or attack repeatedly

> The class bully **harassed** boys who wouldn't fight back.
>
> With a full-time job and three children, Milagros constantly felt **harassed**. (Here *harassed* means "bothered and under stress.")

▶ *Related Word*
  harassment (noun)   Sexual *harassment* can be a serious problem in the workplace.

Harass comes from the Old French *Hare!*—a command telling a dog to "Get it!" This cry was used in hunting, a traditional sport of nobles and rich landowners. Hunters set out on horseback with dogs that followed the scent (smell) of foxes. When the nobles finally saw the fox, they ordered "Hare!" and the dogs chased the fox.

---

23. **prohibit** (verb)   prō-hĭb′ĭt

    to forbid

    > Cars are **prohibited** on sidewalks.

    > Laws now **prohibit** tobacco companies from advertising on billboards.

    ▶ *Common Phrase*
    prohibit (someone) from

    ▶ *Related Word*
    prohibition (noun)   The city council issued a *prohibition* on new construction in the historic district.

    You may have read about the *Prohibition* Era in the United States. In 1919, a constitutional amendment *prohibited* people from making, selling, or drinking alcoholic beverages. Prohibition did not succeed in its aims. In fact, drinking became more fashionable than ever. Realizing that the law was a failure, Congress repealed Prohibition in 1933.

24. **undermine** (verb)   un′dər-mīn′

    to weaken or injure slowly

    > The spy **undermined** his country's security by selling secrets to the enemy.

    > Constant criticism can **undermine** a person's confidence.

Exercises

Part 2

■ *Definitions*

The following sentences deal with feelings, expressions, and actions. Complete each statement by matching each word with the letter of its definition. Use each choice only once.

1. To contend is to ___**c**___ .

2. To prohibit is to___**i**___ .

a. annoy repeatedly

b. display obviously

c. compete

3. To condemn is to ___h___ .

4. To appall is to ___f___ .

5. A belligerent person is ___k___ .

6. To feel chagrin is to feel ___e___ .

7. To undermine is to ___j___ .

8. When we elicit a response, we ___g___ .

9. To flaunt is to ___b___ .

10. Articulate people are ___l___ .

d. think about carefully

e. distress and humiliation

f. fill with shock

g. draw it out

h. express disapproval

i. forbid

j. weaken

k. hostile

l. skilled in using language

■ *Words in Context*

Complete each sentence with the word that fits best. Use each choice only once.

a. appall   e. condemn   i. flaunt
b. articulate   f. contemplate   j. harass
c. belligerent   g. contend   k. prohibit
d. chagrin   h. elicit   l. undermine

1. People can __l, undermine__ their health by eating poorly, not sleeping enough, and not exercising.

2. A boring lecture might __h, elicit__ yawns from students.

3. Do not __e, condemn__ people until you are sure that they have acted wrongly.

4. People should __f, contemplate__ what life with a husband or wife would be like before they decide to get married.

5. Dogs often __j, harass__ cats by chasing and barking at them.

6. If rich people **i, flaunt**_____ their clothes and jewels, others may become envious.

7. Alphonse was often asked to give speeches because he was **b, articulate**_____ .

8. To my **d, chagrin**_____ , my five-year-old child told some of our family secrets to her teacher.

9. The horrors of the brutal war will **a, appall**_____ the public.

10. The **c, belligerent**_____ nation invaded its neighbor's territory.

■ *Using Related Words*

Complete each sentence by using a word from the group of related words above it. You may need to capitalize a word when you write it in a sentence. Use each choice only once.

1. harass, harassment, harassed

Ducks and geese can annoy homeowners and damage their yards. Some owners complain they feel **harassed**_____ when dozens of birds choose their property as roosting grounds. Owners have tried several of their own methods of **harassment**_____ to make the birds leave. Laws may permit a homeowner to make loud noises and use chemicals that have short-term effects. However, people may not touch the birds or their eggs. If people **harass**_____ the birds illegally, they may be charged with a crime.

2. contemplated, contemplation

Contemplation_____ can sometimes lead to scientific breakthroughs. It is said that Sir Isaac Newton (1642–1727) discovered the principle of gravity as he **contemplated**_____ an apple falling from a tree.

3. contended, contender, contention, contentious

> The great African-American athlete Jesse Owens **contended** in the Olympic Games of 1936. These games, held in Germany, were presided over by Nazi leader Adolf Hitler. It was Hitler's racist **contention** that the white "Aryan" race was superior to all others and that no black **contender** could win. However, Owens earned four gold medals in running events. This outcome was so **contentious** that Hitler refused to attend the award ceremonies. Owens, who died in 1978, remains a symbol of black athletes' struggle for equality.

4. prohibition, prohibit

> The durian, an unusual fruit, is popular in Thailand. Although its taste is wonderful, its terrible smell reminds people of garbage. Because of the odor, some hotels and airlines **prohibit** the fruit. However, this **prohibition** has not affected the popularity of this delicious but strange-smelling food.

5. appalled, appalling

> The recent evidence that innocent people have been convicted of murder and sentenced to death has **appalled** the public. In one **appalling** case, Anthony Porter, who had come within two hours of being executed, was later found to be innocent. Based on such cases, there has been an outcry against the death penalty.

■ *True or False?*

Each of the following sentences uses at least one word from this section. Read each statement and then indicate whether you think it is probably true or probably false.

F   1. We take immediate action when we contemplate.

T   2. A contender competes in a contest.

_T_   3. You would be chagrined if the person you were with talked loudly during a quiet scene in a movie theater.

_T_   4. If you flaunt a diamond ring, people will notice it.

_T_   5. A disabled child often elicits sympathy from adults.

_F_   6. Belligerent people are peace-loving.

_T_   7. We would be appalled by a brutal murder.

_F_   8. When we articulate something, we keep it to ourselves.

_T_   9. Bosses should be prohibited from harassing employees.

_T_ 10. People would be likely to condemn you for undermining the interests of close family members.

Chapter Exercises

■ *Practicing Strategies: Context Clues of Definition*

In each of the following sentences, a difficult word is italicized. Using context clues of definition, make an intelligent guess about the meaning of the word as it is used in this sentence. Your instructor may ask you to look up these words in your dictionary after you have finished the exercise.

1. For years great chefs have been using the *chanterelle,* that is to say, a trumpet-shaped mushroom.

   Chanterelle means **a trumpet-shaped mushroom** .

2. The teenager *embellished* the story to the police, as well as exaggerating it to his friends.

   Embellished means **elaborated falsely; exaggerated** .

3. The *vestige,* or small remaining part, of the fossil revealed the impression of a bird's wing.

   Vestige means **small remaining part; remnant** .

4. Judge Learned Hand, *a paragon* of virtue, set an example of goodness every day that he lived.

Paragon means **model; model of perfection; excellent example** .

5. That *charlatan*—the awful faker—gave my aunt something for her illness that almost killed her.

Charlatan means **fraud; faker; imitator** .

6. The judge showed *clemency* to criminals by treating them with mercy.

Clemency means **mercy** .

7. The child's *dyslexia,* a serious reading disorder, was being investigated by a specialist.

Dyslexia means **serious reading disorder** .

8. The plans were *clandestine,* and almost no one knew about them.

Clandestine means **secret; hidden** .

9. President Calvin Coolidge was a *taciturn* person who seldom talked to others.

Taciturn means **quiet; not talkative** .

10. He *prevaricated,* which, put more plainly, means he lied.

Prevaricated means **lied** .

■ *Practicing Strategies: Using the Dictionary*

Read the following definition and then answer the questions below it.

> **pearl**[1] (pûrl) *n.* **1.** A smooth, lustrous, variously colored deposit, chiefly calcium carbonate, formed around a grain of sand or other foreign matter in the shells of certain mollusks and valued as a gem. **2.** Mother-of-pearl; nacre. **3.** One that is prized for beauty or value. **4.** *Print.* A type size measuring approximately five points. **5.** *Color.* A yellowish white. —*v.* **pearled, pearl•ing, pearls.** —*tr.* **1.** To decorate or cover with or as if with pearls. **2.** To make into the shape or color of pearls. —*intr.* **1.** To dive or fish for pearls or pearl-bearing mollusks. **2.** To form beads resembling pearls. [ME *perle* < OFr. < Lat. **pernula,* dim. of *perna,* ham, seashell.]

1. What three parts-of-speech functions does pearl have? **noun,**

   transitive verb, intransitive verb .

2. Which common word in the dictionary key contains a vowel pronounced like the *ear* in pearl? **urge** _____

3. In which language was pearl first recorded? **Latin** _____

4. Give the number and part of speech of the definition that best fits this sentence: "This famous stamp is the *pearl* of my collection."

   3, as a noun _____

5. Give the number and part of speech of the definition mostly used in the printing industry. **4, as a noun** _____

■ Companion Words

Complete each sentence with the word that fits best. Choose your answers from the words below. You may use each word more than once. You may have to capitalize a word.

Choices: to, of, by, from, for

1–2. The spies asked the head of intelligence **for** _____ clarification **of** _____ their mission.

3. Many great artists were condemned **to** _____ lives of poverty.

4. Our plans to ski were thwarted **by** _____ a lack of snow.

5. The writer was appalled **by** _____ his daughter's bad grammar.

6. The timing of earthquakes remains an enigma **to** _____ scientists.

7. **To** _____ my chagrin, my girlfriend kissed me in front of my boss.

8. People are prohibited **from** _____ eating in the theater.

9. My professor was skeptical **of**_____ my ability to get an A, but I did.

10. He undermined his happiness **by**_____ not marrying the woman he loved.

■ *Writing with Your Words*

This exercise will give you practice in writing effective sentences that use the vocabulary words. Each sentence is started for you. Complete it with an interesting phrase that also indicates the meaning of the italicized word.

1. My plans for getting a good job would be *thwarted* if _____

_____ .

2. If I wanted to *elicit* memories from my mother, _____

_____ .

3. I would like to *articulate* my grievances about _____

_____ .

4. You could *undermine* an enemy by _____

_____ .

5. A person who *contemplates* moving to another country _____

_____ .

6. Sam *flaunted* his expensive new watch by _____

_____ .

7. I am *skeptical* that _____

_____ .

8. I would feel *chagrin* if _____

_____ .

9. It is an *enigma* to me how _____

_____ .

10. It is *appalling* that _____

_____ .

Passage

Jackie Robinson, Baseball Hero

As incredible as it may seem today, at one time African Americans were prohibited from playing baseball in the major leagues. The ban was first broken by Jackie Robinson, a star athlete from the "Negro leagues," who went on to enrich major league baseball with his exciting and competitive style. This is Robinson's story, but as you read it, you should also think of "Smokey" Joe Williams, Rube and Willie Foster, Josh Gibson, Cool Papa Bell, "Bullet" Joe Rogan, and all the other earlier African-American greats who were denied the chance to play major league baseball.

Just over fifty years ago, a quiet man made baseball history. In 1947, Jackie Robinson became the first African American to play major league baseball in the twentieth century. **(1)** He bravely faced **appalling** persecution **(2)** and helped **undermine** racial prejudice in the United States. Jackie Robinson "broke the color line."

Before Robinson signed with the Brooklyn Dodgers, blacks had been **prohibited** from playing in major league baseball. Although many black players were as good as, or better than, white major league players, blacks were **condemned** to receive almost no national attention.

(3) When the Dodgers' management decided to sign Robinson, they issued a purposely **bland** announcement: "The Brooklyn Dodgers today purchased the contract of Jackie Roosevelt Robinson from the Montreal Royals." The baseball world reacted strongly. Some applauded the move to end discrimination. Others predicted disaster. How could a black succeed in white baseball? Some critics **contended** that Robinson would never be able to live peacefully with white teammates or tolerate the insults of fans. **(4)** Still others were **skeptical** of Robinson's ability as a baseball player.

All the doubters were wrong.

(5) The Dodgers' general manager, Branch Rickey, had **contemplated** the problem before making his choice. Rickey ensured Robinson's success in the major leagues by working with him on how to respond to **harassment.** "Hey," he would say, impersonating a hotel clerk. "You can't eat here." He imitated a prejudiced white ballplayer and charged into Robinson, saying, "Next time get out of my way, you bastard." Robinson was puzzled: "Are you looking for a Negro who is afraid to fight back?" Replied Rickey, "I'm looking for a ballplayer with guts enough not to fight back. Those **boisterous** crowds will insult you, **harass** you, do anything to make you start a fight. And if you fight back, they'll say, 'Blacks don't belong in baseball.'"

Of all the struggles Jackie was to have, the hardest one would be to keep calm in the face of insults. Nobody would be able to **elicit** an outburst of temper from Jackie Robinson. This fiercely competitive man, who had refused to sit in the back of an army bus, found the ultimate courage—the courage to be quiet.

In the 1947 season, Robinson was to face **harassment** that would have defeated a lesser man. **(6)** Roars of "Go home!" and "Kill him!" were heard from **belligerent** crowd members. Robinson was hit in the head by more "beanballing" pitchers than any other player in the major leagues. Sometimes it became too much for his friends. Robinson's teammate, Pee Wee Reese, once challenged some **harassers** by telling them to "take on somebody who could fight back." **(7)** But Robinson himself avoided **confrontations** and never **articulated** his grievances publicly.

Robinson gained revenge in another way. To the amazement of his critics, he succeeded brilliantly in the major leagues. **(8)** Although he never **flaunted** his skill, it was apparent that he was a marvelous ballplayer. For his first year in the majors, he had a batting average of .297, the team high, and was named Rookie of the Year. In his ten years in baseball, his superior playing helped his team win the pennant six times. He must have been **elated** when he was elected the first black member of the Baseball Hall of Fame.

Robinson is perhaps best remembered for his daring base stealing. Sleepy pitchers had to beware, for Robinson could steal a base at a moment's notice. As he ran from base to base, he confused infielders into making mistakes and losing control of the ball. **(9)** A fellow player gave a **concise** description of Robinson as "a hard out." He stole home base eleven times! Although many have tried to **emulate** him, this feat has never been equaled.

In his later years Robinson became ill with diabetes. Although he left baseball, he never stopped fighting for a just society. He championed civil rights and made investments to help build good housing in slum areas.

Jackie Robinson's name lives on in history. We all owe a debt to a brave man who bore the troubles of a prejudiced society. **(10)** No one could **thwart** the ambitions of this great baseball player and great man.

■ *Exercise*

Each numbered sentence below corresponds to a sentence in the Passage. Fill in the letter of the choice that makes the sentence mean the same thing as its corresponding sentence in the Passage.

1. He bravely faced __**b**__ persecution.
   a. frightening   b. shocking   c. violent   d. illegal

2. He helped __**a**__ racial prejudice in America.
   a. weaken   b. increase   c. delay   d. strengthen

3. The Dodgers' management issued a purposely __**d**__ announcement.
   a. short   b. exciting   c. long   d. dull

4. Still others were __**d**__ of Robinson's ability as a baseball player.
   a. confident   b. talking   c. hopeful   d. doubtful

5. The Dodgers' general manager, Branch Rickey, had __**b**__ the problem before making his choice.
   a. argued about   b. thought about   c. met with   d. planned for

6. Roars were heard from __**d**__ crowd members.
   a. excited   b. ridiculous   c. adoring   d. hostile

7. But Robinson himself avoided __**b**__ .
   a. hotels   b. fights   c. baseball   d. fans

8. He never __**c**__ his skill.
   a. talked about   b. thought about   c. showed off   d. tired of

9. A fellow player gave a(n) __**a**__ description of Robinson as "a hard out."
   a. short   b. silly   c. excellent   d. emotional

10. No one could __**c**__ the ambitions of this great man.
    a. accomplish   b. aid   c. prevent   d. know

■ *Discussion Questions*

1. What was Robinson's greatest skill as a baseball player?

2. Why was Robinson's refusal to lose his temper important?

3. In 1955, Rosa Parks refused to obey a law that required blacks to sit in the back of buses. How is Robinson's struggle similar to her act, and how is it different?

THE GREAT SATCHEL PAIGE 1906–1982

Playing for the Negro League Crawfords and Monarchs, and even in the Dominican Republic, Satchel Paige was so famous that his pitches were given names such as "bee-ball," "jump-ball," and "trouble-ball." With his great skill, sense of fun, and willingness to take risks, Paige was a legendary figure. After Jackie Robinson "broke the color line" in major league baseball, Paige became the oldest rookie ever to play in the majors. St. Louis Brown fans remember that he relaxed in his personal rocking chair when not on the field. Paige ended his career, several years later, at 59, the oldest man to pitch in a major league game.

◀ ENGLISH IDIOMS

Feelings and Actions

Many English idioms express feelings and actions. Some expressions deal with confusion. *To drive wild* and *to drive to the wall* mean to cause someone to become frantic or crazy. People who are *at loose ends* are unsettled and lack a clear direction for their lives. Such people may also have many *loose ends,* or undone things to finish.

Other idioms deal with preciseness. When we *hit the nail on the head,* we get something exactly right.

When teachers tell students *don't sweat* an exam, they mean don't worry about it. However, most students will improve their grades if they *hit the books,* or study. Computers, which are always improving, help us to study. If your old computer *can't hold a candle* to your new computer, your new computer is much better than your old one.

To *bury the hatchet* means to make peace. The early English settlers of the American colonies often fought and then made peace with Native American tribes. To symbolize that fighting had stopped, both sides buried a hatchet in the ground. In 1680, Samuel Sewall wrote that since the hatchet was a very important weapon for the Native Americans, this ceremony was more meaningful to them than any written agreement could be.

Quiz Again

Now that you have finished studying this chapter, here is the brief true-false quiz you took when you began. Take it again.

When we **emulate** people, we do what they do.   True   False

Chagrin is a happy feeling.   True   False

An **enigma** is easy to understand.   True   False

When we **contemplate,** we take action.   True   False

Answers are on page 405. Did your score improve?

Other Useful English Words

In this chapter you will find a variety of words that college students have identified as useful in their studies. The author's classes collected these words from textbooks, newspapers, magazines, and similar materials. Students reported seeing the words many times and felt they were important to learn. You, too, should find them valuable additions to your vocabulary.

Chapter Strategy: Context Clues of Opposition

Chapter Words:

Part 1

accolade	cryptic	meticulous
augment	indulge	obsolete
chivalrous	jeopardize	perpetual
complacent	mandatory	zealous

Part 2

accelerate	cultivate	pinnacle
adulation	euphemism	procrastinate
chronological	mammoth	successive
copious	mitigating	withstand

Quiz Yourself

To check your knowledge of some chapter words before you begin to study, identify these statements as true or false.

A **chivalrous** person is nasty.	True	False
A **zealous** person is enthusiastic.	True	False
Mitigating circumstances make hard things more difficult.	True	False
A **euphemism** is a harsh word for something.	True	False

You will learn the answers as you study this chapter.

Did You Know?

How Does English Get New Words?

What language is the second most widely spoken in the world? What language is used for international communication in business and science? What language has the most words? The answer to all three questions is English!

English is not the most widely spoken native language in the world. (Mandarin Chinese holds that position.) However, when we add people who speak English as a second language to native English speakers, it emerges as the world's most used language. About 775 million people spoke English in 1985, and the number is constantly growing. English is now the international language of science, technology, and business. Japanese and German companies, for instance, train many employees in English. People doing research often find that international scientific journals are published in English.

In keeping with the large number of people who speak English, many experts estimate that it has more words than any other spoken language. The complete *Oxford English Dictionary,* second edition (often called the OED), consists of twenty volumes, and it is available on compact disk for use on a computer. An abridged, or shorter, version, published in 1993, includes, for the first time, such words as *meltdown* (a nuclear disaster, now used also in business), *ankylosaur* (a dinosaur popularized by the movie *Jurassic Park*), and *gonzo* (a slang word for *bizarre* from *Rolling Stone* magazine).

The vocabulary of English grows continually as new inventions, discoveries, and customs emerge. Publications such as *Barnhart's Dictionary of New English Words* help us catalog additions to our language.

With our technology changing daily, computers—and the revolution they have sparked—are a major source of vocabulary growth. New words include *e-mail, netiquette, software, download,* and *user friendly.* Computer words are often slightly changed from old ones. *Retail* refers to buying at a store. The rhyming new word *e-tail* means buying on the Internet. Similarly, an *e-zine* is a *magazine* on the Internet.

Radio and television have inspired many new words. A large handheld radio is called a *boom box* because of its booming sound. Do you often like to just relax and watch television? If you do this several hours a day, you might be called a *couch potato.* Your exercise might be limited to *channel surfing* (rapidly changing channels by using a remote control) or watching *feevee* (channels available only to those who pay a fee).

Ancient Greek and Latin word parts are also used to create new words. A person who is interested in the latest forms of stereo equipment is an *audiophile.* This word is formed from the Latin verb *audire* (to hear) and the ancient Greek noun *philos* (love). People who are afraid of eating high-fat food may be said to suffer from *cholesterophobia,* a word formed from *cholesterol* and *phobia* (the ancient Greek noun for *fear*).

One new word can be formed from two old ones. Since traffic is often heavy in the Los Angeles area, people spend several hours per day in cars. Some treat their cars as miniature homes, furnishing them with expensive stereos, facilities for dressing, and telephones. The new word *carcoon* has been coined to describe this custom. *Carcoon* is composed of *car* and *cocoon.* Similarly, a newly built *tunnel* beneath the English *Channel* joins France and England. It is therefore called the *chunnel. Netiquette,* a new computer word noted above, is a combination of *net* and *etiquette;* it refers to how one behaves when using the Internet. The widely used term *e-mail,* also noted above, is a combination of *electronic* and *mail.*

The business world is a rich source of words. When Canada decided to replace dollar bills with coins, it put a picture of a loon, a water bird found in Canadian lakes, on one side of the coin. The dollar coin was nicknamed the *loonie.* Then, when Canada started issuing a two-dollar coin, it was promptly called the *toonie!* Both *loonie* and *toonie* have become popular slang usages.

English has also borrowed words from other languages. *Cotton* comes from Arabic; *pajamas* from Urdu, a language of India and Pakistan; *kiosk* from Turkish; and *tea* from Chinese. *Chocolate* and *tomato* came from languages spoken by the Aztecs, who lived in Mexico. The Algonquin Indians, of the northeastern United States, gave us *raccoon. Potato* came from the Taino, native inhabitants of the West Indies. *Banana* and *tote* came from Africa. *Piano* is from Italian, *boss* from Dutch, *ranch* from Spanish, and *hamburger* from German (named for the German city of Hamburg). A word for a trademarked video game entered English not too long ago. The relatively new game was given the name of a 100-year-old company in Kyoto, Japan: *Nintendo.*

Some words are "street language"—interesting and colorful words coined by people like you and me. Many are shortened forms of standard terms. One example is the new word *dis*, from *disrespect. Props,* perhaps from the word *property*, refers to the proper tributes and possessions that are due a person in a certain position, such as a well-known athlete. In the 1970s *bad* added a new meaning to its long list. It now can mean "great," "powerful," or, in a word, "good." We don't know who first used these words, but they certainly influenced English!

As you can see by the example of *bad*, English expands by using old words in new ways. The meanings of many words have changed over centuries of use. *Husband* once meant "master of the house." *Lady* meant "kneader of bread." The common word *nice*, which has been in English since 1100, has gone through several meanings, including "foolish or stupid," "sexy," "strange," "lazy," and "shy." None of these meanings is in common use today.

Can you match these new words with their definitions?

1. bloviate	a. what you see is what you get
2. WYSIWYG	b. calm down, relax
3. WIMP	c. to write or speak in an unnecessarily long and complex manner
4. bottom feeder	d. windows, icons, menus, pointers (for people who need all this support!)
5. chill out	e. a person who thrives on the bad luck of others

Answers are on page 405.

Learning Strategy

Context Clues of Opposition

Some sentences give the opposite definition or sense of a word you are trying to understand. A simple opposition clue is the word *not*. Take the following example:

The food was *not* hot, but cold.

Hot is, of course, the opposite of *cold*. Context clues of opposition can be used for more difficult words.

Since it was something not usual or normal in nature, it was considered an *anomaly*. (An anomaly is something not usual or normal, a "freak.")

Often a clue of opposition will provide an *antonym,* or a word opposite in meaning. In the first example, *hot* is an antonym of cold. Clues of opposition are easy to use if you become familiar with opposing structures in sentences. Some of the common structures are as follows.

1. The use of *not* and *no.*

    Peggy was *not happy,* but despondent.

2. Words signaling opposition. These include *but, nevertheless, despite, rather than, regardless of the fact, unless, if not,* and *although.*

    Peggy was despondent *despite* the fact that her sister was *happy.*

3. Words with negative senses. Certain words have a negative meaning, such as *merely, mere, barely, only, rarely, never, hardly, nowhere,* and *nothing.*

    Peggy was despondent and *rarely* felt happy.

4. Words containing negative prefixes, such as *anti-, un-, dis-, non-,* and *in-.* For example, when the prefix *un-* is added to *happy,* it forms *unhappy,* which means the opposite of *happy.*

    Peggy was despondent and felt *unhappy.*

From these examples, it is clear that *despondent* means "sad" or "depressed." In the examples, the antonym of *despondent (happy)* is given as a context clue.

Three examples of context clues of opposition are given below. Can you guess at the meaning of the italicized words? Remember that context clues of opposition, like all context clues, may give only the general sense of a word.

1. He was not shy and was, in fact, an *extrovert.* (A *not* clue is used.)

2. There was so much *enmity* between the two brothers that they almost never spoke to each other. (A word with a negative sense is used.)

3. Although Kristin thought the candidate was *despicable,* her friend thought he was wonderful. (A word signaling opposition is used.)

Answers are on page 405.

Some words that you will study in this chapter are used in the following sentences, which contain clues of opposition. Try to make an intelligent guess about the meaning of each italicized word.

1. The *meticulous* person rarely made a careless error. (A word with a negative sense is used.)

   Meticulous means **careful** _____ .

2. We were unable to understand the *cryptic* message. (A negative prefix is used.)

   Cryptic means **puzzling** _____ .

3. Because the course was not *mandatory,* we did not have to take it. (A *not* clue is used.)

   Mandatory means **required** _____ .

Answers are on page 405.

Words to Learn

Part 1

1. **accolade** (noun)   ăk′ə-lād′

   praise, honor, award

   > The hero received **accolades** from the press.

   > Garth Brooks has been awarded the **accolade** of Country Music Entertainer of the Year several times.

   NOTE: Accolade used in the singular means an award or honor; in contrast, *accolades,* the plural, usually signifies general praise or applause.

   At times, an **accolade** has been unjustly delayed. General Benjamin O. Davis, a West Point graduate, flew 1,500 fighter escort missions, often against great odds, with the Tuskegee Airmen during the Korean War. His powerful unit, made up entirely of African Americans, was nicknamed the "Black Birdmen." Yet not until 1998, three years after his retirement, was he given the **accolade** of promotion to four-star general. Benjamin was more fortunate than his father, who was turned away from West Point because of his race.

   ---

2. **augment** (verb)   ôg-měnt′

   to increase

   > The number of businesses selling on the Internet **augments** daily.

   > Congress is expected to **augment** assistance for poor families.

▶ *Related Word*
augmentation (noun)   Advertising often results in considerable *augmentation* of a store's sales.

3. **chivalrous** (adjective)   shĭv′-əl-rəs

having qualities of honor, including courtesy, loyalty, and generosity

A **chivalrous** man would never insult a woman.

The **chivalrous** knight used his body to shield his master from attack.

▶ *Related Word*
chivalry (noun)   Sir Lancelot followed the code of *chivalry.*

Chivalry was the code of conduct for European knights in the Middle Ages. A true knight was brave, loyal, and fair; he showed mercy to the defeated and loyalty to his overlord, or master. In the tradition of courtly love, a knight dedicated poems to his lady and fought tournaments in her name. However, this idealized passion involved only worship from afar. *Chivalrous* gestures, are considered somewhat old-fashioned in today's society, but in the Middle Ages they represented an improvement in women's lives.

The word *accolade* is also related to the code of *chivalry*. During the Middle Ages, when a warrior was made a knight, his lord gave him an *accolade* (embrace) and dubbed him (tapped him with a sword).

---

4. **complacent** (adjective)   kəm-plā**′**sənt

overly self-satisfied

> Once Rick achieved straight A's, he became **complacent** and hardly studied.
>
> After years of good health, Michael became **complacent** and stopped his yearly checkups.

NOTE: Complacent is a somewhat negative word.

▶ *Related Word*
> **complacency** (noun)   Lulled into *complacency* by the mild weather, Andrew neglected to winterize his car, and it stalled on the first freezing day.

5. **cryptic** (adjective)   krĭp**′**tĭk

puzzling; mysterious in meaning

> Nancy's **cryptic** smiles left us unsure of her feelings.
>
> Egyptian hieroglyphics remained **cryptic** until the discovery of the Rosetta Stone enabled them to be translated.

6. **indulge** (verb)   ĭn-dŭlj**′**

to pamper; to yield to desires

> People often **indulge** in daydreams while relaxing.
>
> After **indulging** in two pieces of chocolate cake, Julia went to the health club to work out.

▶ *Related Word*
> **indulgence** (noun)   A long, warm bubble bath is an *indulgence* after a stressful day.

▶ *Common Phrases*
> indulge in
>
> indulge oneself (*Indulge* often uses a reflexive pronoun, such as *myself, yourself,* or *herself.*)

7. **jeopardize** (verb)   jĕp**′**ər-dīz**′**

to risk loss or danger

Marcus **jeopardized** his savings by putting them in a risky investment.

A single computer virus can **jeopardize** an entire hard drive.

▶ *Related Word*
jeopardy (noun)   The soldier's loud whispering put the secret attack in *jeopardy*.

8. **mandatory** (adjective)   măn′də-tôr′ē

required; commanded

English 101 was **mandatory** for college graduation.

It is **mandatory** for employers to pay Social Security tax.

▶ *Related Words*
mandate (noun)   (măn′dāt′)   The government issued a *mandate* returning land to the Cherokee nation. (Here *mandate* means "command.")

The governor interpreted the wide margin of his election as a *mandate* to reduce taxes. (Here *mandate* refers to the unspoken wishes of the people who have elected an official.)

mandate (verb)   The government *mandates* taxes.

9. **meticulous** (adjective)   mĭ-tĭk′yə-ləs

extremely careful; concerned with details

Fine Turkish silk rugs are woven with **meticulous** care.

A computer programmer must be **meticulous,** for even a small mistake can ruin many hours of work.

▶ *Related Word*
meticulousness (noun)   Accountants value *meticulousness* in keeping business records.

10. **obsolete** (adjective)   ŏb′sə-lēt′

no longer in use; outmoded; old-fashioned

The horse and chariot have become **obsolete** in modern warfare.

The word *thou* is an **obsolete** way of saying "you."

Compact disks have made vinyl records **obsolete.**

▶ *Related Word*
obsolescent (adjective)   (ŏb′sə-lĕs′ənt)   No one wants to buy

an *obsolescent* computer. (*Obsolescent* means "becoming obsolete.")

11. **perpetual** (adjective)   pər-pĕch′oo-əl

lasting forever; eternal

Many religions teach that God is **perpetual.**

continuous and long lasting

The disorganized office was in a **perpetual** state of confusion.

▶ *Related Words*

perpetually (adverb)   The children's book *Tuck Everlasting* is about people whose lives continue *perpetually.*

perpetuate (verb) (pər-pĕch′oo-āt′)   The country name of Bolivia *perpetuates* the South American freedom fighter Simón Bolívar.

Chief Joseph's memory is being perpetuated.

In the shadow of the Bear Paw Mountains, south of Chinook, Montana, lies a field *perpetually* dedicated to the Nez Perce tribe and their chief, Joseph. Forced from their lands in 1877, 200 warriors, accompanied by women, children, and elderly people, fled from the enormous forces of the U.S. Army. The Nez Perce repeatedly outfought and outwitted the army. Only after a flight of some 2,000 miles did they finally surrender. The Montana field *perpetuates* the memory of their bravery and endurance.

12. **zealous** (adjective) zĕl′əs

extremely dedicated or enthusiastic

> The **zealous** prosecutor worked sixty hours a week on the murder case.

> The **zealous** minister dedicated his life to religion, preaching to anyone who would listen.

▶ *Related Word*
   zeal (noun) (zēl) In her *zeal* to be a perfect mother, Crystal sometimes forgot to take care of her own needs.

The first *zealots* were religious Jews who fought against Roman rule. After Romans destroyed the second Jewish temple in 70 C.E., the Zealots retreated to the ancient mountaintop fortress of Masada. There, 1,000 people held off a Roman force of 15,000 for more than two years. Preferring death to defeat, the Zealots committed suicide when they realized they could not win.

NOTE: Zealous can refer to enthusiasm that is excessive. Thus, the independent counsel who prosecuted President Clinton in the late 1990s was described by some, negatively, as *zealous*.

Exercises

Part 1

■ Matching Words and Definitions

Check your understanding of useful words by matching each word with the letter of its definition. Use each choice only once.

1. meticulous ___h___

2. jeopardize ___e___

3. mandatory ___l___

4. obsolete ___i___

5. perpetual ___k___

6. augment ___j___

7. zealous ___g___

8. accolade ___c___

9. cryptic ___f___

10. complacent ___a___

a. overly self-satisfied

b. having qualities of honor

c. award

d. yield to desires

e. to risk loss or danger

f. mysterious in meaning

g. dedicated or enthusiastic

h. very careful

i. no longer used

j. to increase

k. lasting forever

l. required

■ *Words in Context*

Complete each sentence with the word that fits best. Use each choice only once.

a. accolade   e. cryptic   i. meticulous
b. augment   f. indulge   j. obsolete
c. chivalrous   g. jeopardize   k. perpetual
d. complacent   h. mandatory   l. zealous

1. Since we didn't understand the many references to Greek myths, the

   professor's lecture was __e, cryptic__ to us.

2. Failure to wear a seat belt in a car can __g, jeopardize__ your
   safety.

3. The farm workers tried to be __i, meticulous__ about separating the good strawberries from the spoiled ones.

4. The gas lamp is a(n) __j, obsolete__ source of light; it has
   been replaced by electric power.

5. I would like to __f, indulge__ myself by taking a vacation.

6. When the champion boxer became **d, complacent** _____ and did not train, he was defeated.

7. U.S. General Colin Powell received the **a, accolade** _____ of the Purple Heart for wounds he received in combat.

8. In some states a breath test is **h, mandatory** _____ if you are stopped on suspicion of drunk driving.

9. In a(n) **c, chivalrous** _____ gesture, Walter Raleigh laid his cloak over a puddle so that Queen Elizabeth I could keep her feet dry.

10. Champion athletes are **l, zealous** _____ in their pursuit of victory.

■ *Using Related Words*

Complete each sentence by using a word from the group of related words above it. You may need to capitalize a word when you write it in a sentence. Use each choice only once.

THE GREAT ELEANOR OF AQUITAINE

1. chivalry, chivalrous

   The tradition of **chivalry** _____ owes much to Eleanor of Aquitaine, 1122–1204. As perhaps the most powerful woman of her century, she ran the court of Aquitaine (now part of France), which

   invited poets and performers to celebrate the **chivalrous** _____ deeds of legendary knights.

2. augment, augmentation

   The province of Aquitaine, which Eleanor inherited, was actually larger than France at the time. Thus, by marrying Eleanor, any

   king could considerably **augment** _____ the land under his control. In those days, when there was little commerce and hardly any currency, land was the only real source of power. Thus,

   an **augmentation** _____ of territory meant an increase in power. Eleanor was a sought-after bride, and her first marriage was to the French king Louis VII.

3. indulged, indulgences

But in her youth, beautiful Eleanor **indulged** in some wild behavior. In fact, King Louis VII divorced her for unfaithfulness. As the heir to enormous lands, she soon remarried. But her second marriage, to King Henry II of England, was also unhappy. This time, it was Henry's **indulgences** with other women that caused problems.

4. perpetual, perpetually, perpetuate

Nobles of this time traveled extensively, moving among their many properties. Even when pregnant, Eleanor was **perpetually** moving by horseback or small, often unsafe, boats. Unfortunately, her arguments with Henry were **perpetual**, and she even supported a revolt against him. In revenge he imprisoned her for sixteen years, until his death. She was freed when their son Richard the Lion-Hearted assumed the throne. In her last years, she became devoted to her family. When almost 80, she crossed the sea twice—a dangerous journey in those days—to fetch her granddaughter. One recorder described Eleanor as "beautiful and just, imposing and modest, humble and elegant." We **perpetuate** her memory every time we tell stories of knights in shining armor and courtly love.

■ *True or False?*

Each of the following statements contains at least one word from this section. Read each statement and then indicate whether you think it is probably true or probably false.

F   1. The newest cellular phones are obsolete.

T   2. Indulging in too much alcohol can jeopardize a person's health.

T   3. Complacent people tend to take things for granted.

F   4. We would be upset if our income augmented.

F   5. Cryptic messages are easily understood.

__F__   6. Perpetual care will end soon.

__T__   7. A chivalrous person is polite.

__T__   8. It is mandatory to obtain a license if you want to get married in the United States.

__T__   9. A meticulous housekeeper keeps an apartment well dusted.

__T__   10. A zealous worker would be likely to receive the accolade of being named employee of the month.

Words to Learn

Part 2

13. **accelerate** (verb)   ăk-sĕl′ə-rāt′

to speed up; to go faster

> The fax machine and e-mail have **accelerated** communication.
>
> The discovery and drilling of large oil deposits is **accelerating** Azerbaijan's economic development.

▶ *Related Words*
acceleration (noun)   Exposure to too much sun can cause *acceleration* of the aging process.

accelerator (noun)   The race car driver pressed the *accelerator* to the floor.

14. **adulation** (noun)   ăj′ə-lā′shən

extreme admiration or flattery

> The bride looked at the groom with **adulation** as she said, "I do."
>
> The Latin rock band Mana was greeted with **adulation** by adoring fans.

▶ *Related Words*
adulate (verb)   Teenagers of the past *adulated* Rudolph Valentino and Frank Sinatra.

adulatory (adjective) (ăj′ə-lə-tôr′ē)   Tony's *adulatory* comments flattered his boss.

15. **chronological** (adjective)   krŏn′ə-lŏj′ĭ-kəl

arranged in order of time

> John's job application listed his work experience in **chronological** order.

▶ *Related Word*
  chronology (noun)   (krə-nŏl′ə-jē)   A *chronology* of Egyptian pharaohs is listed in the front of the textbook.

16. **copious** (adjective)   kō′pē-əs

plentiful; abundant

> The student's **copious** lecture notes filled ten pages.

NOTE: Copious cannot be used to refer to a single large thing. We cannot say "a copious piece of cake." We can, however, refer to "copious notes," "a copious amount of sand," and "copious supplies."

17. **cultivate** (verb)   kŭl′tə-vāt′

to grow deliberately; to develop

> On the Basilan Islands of the Philippines, farmers **cultivate** seaweed.

> The basketball coach carefully **cultivated** the individual talents of her team.

> The lobbyist **cultivated** contacts with important senators.

> The poor student **cultivated** a relationship with his rich aunt, whom he hoped might help him pay his college tuition.

▶ *Related Words*
  cultivated (adjective)   John was a *cultivated* person who knew much about art and classical music. (*Cultivated* often describes people who are cultured and have interests in art, classical music, books, etc.)

  cultivation (noun)   John's musical *cultivation* impressed us.

Corn, or maize, is the most important product *cultivated* in the Americas. Food for humans and feed for animals, candy, and soap are all made from its products. When Christopher Columbus first saw corn in Cuba, he remarked on the meticulous efficiency of its cultivation. Early Americans developed modern corn over thousands of years, interbreeding it with grass to increase the size of the cobs. Modern scientists at the International Center for Improvement of Maize and Corn, in

Mexico, are making a new "lysine" corn that contains an important protein absent in traditional varieties.

---

18. **euphemism** (noun)   yoō′fə-mĭz′əm

a more positive word or phrase substituted for a negative one

> "Relaxed fit" is a **euphemism** referring to clothes designed for overweight people.

▶ *Related Word*
euphemistic (adjective)   "Peacekeeping forces" is a *euphemistic* expression for soldiers.

Euphemisms are used frequently. A bank recently announced that it was "rightsizing" itself by "lowering payroll costs through reducing head count." In other words, it was firing people.

Do you know what these common euphemisms stand for?

1. This will be a slightly *uncomfortable* procedure.
2. She *stretched the truth a bit.*
3. We watched an *encore telecast.*
4. He was *laid to rest.*
5. I bought a *pre-owned* car.

Answers are on page 405.

---

19. **mammoth** (adjective)   măm′əth

huge; very large

> Each day, one hundred thousand visitors shop, eat, play golf, ride roller coasters, and even get married in Minnesota's **mammoth** Mall of America.

> Effective handling of garbage has become a **mammoth** problem.

20. **mitigating** (adjective)   mĭt′ĭ-gāt′ĭng

making less severe or intense; moderating

> The ocean breeze has a **mitigating** effect on the tropical heat in southern Florida.

Tony admitted he was late, but offered the **mitigating** circumstance that his car had a flat tire on the way.

▶ *Related Word*
mitigate (verb)   Grandmother *mitigated* her harsh words with a wink.

21. **pinnacle** (noun)   pĭn′ə-kəl

top; highest point

The Keck telescope, the largest in the world, is located at the **pinnacle** of Mauna Kea in Hawaii.

At the **pinnacle** of his career, the TV news anchor earned more than a million dollars per year.

22. **procrastinate** (verb)   prō-krăs′tə-nāt′

to delay; to put off

I always manage to **procrastinate** when it is time to study.

Because Leshan **procrastinated** about seeing a dentist, he ended up losing his tooth.

▶ *Related Word*
procrastinator (noun)   The National *Procrastinators'* Club celebrates New Year's Day in October.

23. **successive** (adjective)   sək-sĕs′ĭv

following one after another without interruption

For six **successive** days in the fall of 1998, brutal rains caused by Hurricane Mitch pounded Central America.

My family has lived on the same farm for four **successive** generations.

▶ *Related Word*
succession (noun)   "Threepeat" was the word coined to describe the Chicago Bulls' *succession* of NBA championships in 1991, 1992, and 1993.

The prince's *succession* to the throne was greeted with joy. (*Succession* can mean the inheritance of a crown or title.)

24. **withstand** (verb)   wĭth-stănd′ (past tense: **withstood**)

not to surrender; to bear (the force of)

Russia has **withstood** many attacks, but has never been conquered.

People differ in their ability to **withstand** cold weather.

Unable to **withstand** the force of the hurricane, the tree broke in half.

Gitobu Imanyara, editor of *Nairobi Law Monthly,* has *withstood* much persecution as publisher of a magazine that speaks freely about Kenyan politics. At times, the magazine has been banned. Mr. Imanyara has been physically attacked and has served time in prison. For his bravery, Mr. Imanyara has received many awards from international organizations. We have failed to uncover any more recent news about this brave man since 1991, but we hope he is alive and well.

Exercises

Part 2

■ *Matching Words and Definitions*

Check your understanding of useful words by matching each word with the letter of its definition. Use each choice only once.

1. copious __h__

2. mitigating __j__

3. pinnacle __a__

4. euphemism __b__

5. successive __e__

6. adulation __i__

7. mammoth __f__

8. procrastinate __c__

9. accelerate __d__

10. chronological __k__

a. top

b. use of a more positive word in place of a negative one

c. to delay

d. to speed up

e. following without interruption

f. very large

g. not to surrender

h. plentiful

i. extreme admiration

j. making less severe

k. in order of time

l. to grow deliberately

■ Words in Context

Complete each sentence with the word that fits best. Use each choice only once.

a. accelerate
b. adulation
c. chronological
d. copious
e. cultivate
f. euphemism
g. mammoth
h. mitigating
i. pinnacle
j. procrastinate
k. successive
l. withstand

1. The boy's apology had a(n) **h, mitigating** effect on his mother's anger.

2. Edmund Hillary and Tenzing Norgay were the first people to reach the **i, pinnacle** of Mt. Everest.

3. The **g, mammoth** blue whale is one hundred feet long and weighs 400,000 pounds.

4. When my wife asks me to do the dishes, I simply **j, procrastinate** until she decides to wash them.

5. Unable to **l, withstand** the lack of rain, the crops died.

6. The man wished to **e, cultivate** the friendship of the famous artist.

7. The English teacher used the **f, euphemism** "not quite acceptable" to describe the failing paper.

8. Seattle has had light rain for four **k, successive** days, Monday through Thursday.

9. When I pressed the gas pedal to the floor, the car started to **a, accelerate**.

10. Because food was in **d, copious** supply at the picnic, we ate well.

■ Using Related Words

Complete each sentence by using a word from the group of related words above it. You may need to capitalize a word when you write it in a sentence. Use each choice only once.

THE LIFE OF ELVIS PRESLEY

1. adulated, adulation

   Elvis Presley, perhaps rock 'n' roll's most legendary performer, was

   adulated _____ by millions. So great was their **adulation** _____ that, thirty years after his death, his former home, Graceland, in Memphis, Tennessee, remains a popular tourist attraction.

2. chronology, chronological

   The **chronology** _____ of Elvis's life is simple. He was born in 1935 in Tupelo, Mississippi. He served in the army, was married, had a daughter, and got divorced. At the time of his sudden death at Graceland in 1977, his records had sold over 500 million copies,

   and he had made thirty-five movies. This **chronological** _____ retelling of his life, however, cannot capture his enormous influence.

3. cultivate, cultivating, cultivation, cultivated

   Growing up, Elvis was surrounded by the music of the American south. He listened to the Grand Ole Opry on the radio; he **cultivated** _____ a taste for gospel and sang in a church choir; he studied African-American artists performing the blues. Although largely unrecognized at the time, people of musi-

   cal **cultivation** _____ now give credit to the great heritage of the blues. Elvis's knowledge of it later guided him to

   cultivate _____ an intensely personal style. When per-

   forming, he was also known for **cultivating** _____ sex appeal, which gave him the nickname "Elvis the Pelvis."

4. withstand, withstood

   Elvis's performances **withstood** _____ attacks from many sources. In his early days, he was criticized by racists, who did not like the popularity of blues music. Later his reputation had

   to **withstand** _____ the attacks of those who felt he stole some of the fame due to such magnificent blues artists as Muddy Waters and B. B. King. Yet Elvis also gathered accolades. Twice he was awarded the Grammy for gospel music.

5. mitigated, mitigating

Tremendous success was **mitigated** by personal problems. His marriage failed, and, by the end, he was probably addicted to mood-controlling pills. Yet, Elvis's abiding love for his mother, even after her death, was a **mitigating** factor that counterbalanced his flaws. Today he is remembered for such classics as "Love Me Tender," "Hound Dog," "All Shook Up," and "Don't Be Cruel." Can you hum any of these?

■ *Reading the Headlines*

This exercise presents five headlines that might appear in newspapers. Read each headline and then answer the questions that follow. (Remember that small words, such as *is, are, a,* and *the,* are often left out of newspaper headlines.)

COPIOUS AMOUNTS OF GARBAGE ON STREETS AS STRIKE REACHES THIRD SUCCESSIVE WEEK

1. Was there much garbage? **yes**

2. Were the weeks continuous? **yes**

UNABLE TO WITHSTAND ACCELERATION IN TIMBER CUTTING, HILL EXPERIENCES MUDSLIDE

3. Before the mudslide, were trees being cut down at a faster rate? **yes**

4. Did the hill resist the force? **no**

EXCITING NEW PILL MITIGATES TENDENCY TO PROCRASTINATE

5. Do the people taking the pill always do things too quickly? **no**

6. Does the pill increase procrastination? **no**

SCIENTIST CULTIVATES MAMMOTH ROSE

7. Did the rose grow accidentally? **no**

8. Is the rose large? **yes**

AT PINNACLE OF CAREER, OPERA STAR RECEIVES ADULATION OF CROWD

9. Is the opera star at the beginning of her career? **no**

10. Does the crowd act positively toward the opera star? **yes**

Chapter Exercises

■ *Practicing Strategies: Context Clues of Opposition*

In each of the following sentences, a difficult word is italicized. Using context clues of opposition, make an intelligent guess about the meaning of the word as it is used in the sentence. Your instructor may ask you to look up each word in your dictionary after you have finished the exercise.

1. Although the editor's efforts were usually *disparaged,* she was occasionally praised.

   Disparaged means **criticized; spoken badly about** .

2. He *feigned* ignorance, although he knew about all of their plans.

   Feigned means **pretended; faked** .

3. He *dissipated* his money on parties and cars, and soon he was broke.

   Dissipated means **spent everything wastefully; wasted everything** .

4. Suddenly called upon to talk publicly, Jesse Jackson gave a brilliant *extemporaneous* speech.

   Extemporaneous means **unrehearsed; unprepared; spur of the moment** .

5. The *nebulous* clouds did not have a clear outline.

   Nebulous means **indistinct; lacking a clear outline** .

6. Although she was usually *garrulous,* Anne was quiet at the party.

   Garrulous means **talkative** _____ .

7. Barbara is *reticent* about revealing her background, despite the fact that she talks freely about other things.

   Reticent means **hesitant; shy; not revealing** _____ .

8. This *diminutive* type of hummingbird hardly ever grows over three inches long.

   Diminutive means **tiny; small** _____ .

9. She thought she would be *recompensed,* but she was never paid.

   Recompensed means **paid** _____ .

10. The *pusillanimous* soldier lacked courage.

    Pusillanimous means **cowardly** _____ .

■ *Companion Words*

Complete each sentence with the word that fits best. Choose your answers from the words below. You may use each word more than once.

myself, to, by, in, of

1–2. I would like **to** _____ indulge **myself** _____ by taking a long nap.

3. The effects of the cold rain were mitigated **by** _____ my warm jacket.

4. After a succession **of** _____ career failures, Harry Truman achieved great success as U.S. President.

5. American history is usually taught **in** _____ chronological order.

6. The rock star was greeted **by** _____ adulation.

7. The complacency **of** _____ the defending champion cost him the title.

8. Tom Hanks was awarded the accolade **of** _____ the Oscar.

9. The augmentation **of**_____ profits meant that employees got a raise.

10. The code **of**_____ chivalry protects the weak.

■ *Writing with Your Words*

This exercise will give you practice in writing effective sentences that use the vocabulary words. Each sentence is started for you. Complete it with an interesting phrase that also indicates the meaning of the italicized word.

1. The *mammoth* dog _____

_____ .

2. I might *mitigate* a friend's sadness by _____

_____ .

3. I would try to use a *euphemism* when _____

_____ .

4. The *chivalrous* knight _____

_____ .

5. A *cultivated* person _____

_____ .

6. I would like to *augment* _____

_____ .

7. I *procrastinate* when _____

_____ .

8. It is *mandatory* to _____

   _____ .

9. When I reach the *pinnacle* of success, I will _____

   _____ .

10. The crowd showed its *adulation* by _____

   _____ .

Passage

Australia: From Prison to Paradise

Today, when we think of Australia, we picture a sunny, prosperous country visited yearly by thousands of tourists. But for generations, the very name Australia brought fear to the heart. For Australia was founded to serve as a prison for England. This passage explores the clouded history of the continent, a history that was often rooted in social injustice.

In the late 1700s, England was a country of contrasts. The upper class lived on rich estates with beautiful gardens. Yet in the city of London, poor families crowded together into single rooms near the dark, evil-smelling factories where they worked. In the early days of industrialization, children as young as six held jobs. **(1)** Young girls ruined their eyesight by doing **meticulous** sewing in dim light. Boys grew up with backs bent from years of carrying coal.

Yet those who worked were relatively fortunate, for thousands had no jobs. Without government help, the unemployed were simply left to starve. **(2)** The crime rate **augmented,** as more poor families were forced to steal or starve.

The rich of England knew little about the fate of the poor. **(3) Complacent** in their own situations and unaware of the depth of this poverty, many simply believed that there was a "criminal class." To try to control it, the government passed laws of extreme harshness. Hanging was made **mandatory** for stealing property worth 40 shillings, burning a pile of straw, or cutting down an ornamental bush. Public executions were considered "educational." Despite the fact that **(4)** the smallest offense could **jeopardize** one's life, desperate poverty caused the crime rate to **accelerate.**

Finally, sickening of the sight of death for small offenses, **(5)** the government began to **mitigate** the harsh punishments. It was decided that if "royal mercy" were granted, the death sentence could be replaced by sending prisoners out of the country to do forced labor. However, no one could decide where to send criminals, so within a few years, prisons became stuffed with convicts awaiting transportation. **(6)** Government officials could **procrastinate** no longer; they had to send the prisoners somewhere.

The **(7) mammoth** island of Australia seemed a wise choice. The British had claimed rights to it and needed to support this claim with settlement. Prisoners could do the hard labor needed to establish farms, and those who wished to escape would simply drown. Best of all, the "criminal element" would be 8,000 miles from England.

Who were the "criminals" transported to Australia in 1787? They included Thomas Chaddick, who ate twelve cucumber plants, and William Francis, who stole a book. Eleven-year-old James Grace took ribbons and a pair of stockings; Elizabeth Beckford, seventy years old, stole some cheese.

For these crimes, each was sentenced to years of hard labor in an unknown land. Many prisoners believed that exile would be **perpetual,** and they would never see England again. Parting from their families was difficult to **withstand.** One man wrote to his wife, "I don't mind where I go nor what I suffer, if I have your company to cheer my almost broken heart." Yet he sailed off alone, in chains.

In the first years of Australia's English settlement, many prisoners died. **(8)** The land proved difficult to **cultivate.** For three **successive** years, supply ships from England failed to come, forcing the population into near starvation. One Australian remembered living on a diet of boiled seaweed and whale blubber.

Nature, too, was unfamiliar and unwelcoming. People tried to build ships from Australia's **copious** supply of pines, but the trees had brittle, useless wood. Winter and summer were reversed in the Southern Hemisphere. Unfamiliar kangaroos and parakeets replaced cows and horses. The ground had aloe plants, but grew no grass.

Convicts were forced to work for bosses who might refuse them food or sentence them to whippings. **(9)** Humane governors received criticism, rather than **accolades,** from the English government. Doctors who treated the poor might earn the **adulation** of convicts, but they received little pay.

Yet, convicts built the country. One freed convict, Samuel Terry, became the largest landowner in Australia. Simeon Lord became an important manufacturer; James Underwood's firm constructed ships. Mary Haydock, transported at age thirteen, built a chain of warehouses and boats. As the "criminal class" became a powerful force in Australia's success, it became more respectable. **(10)** Soon the **euphemism** "government man" was substituted for "convict." Later the term became "empire

Australia is now a prosperous country with a low crime rate.

builder." Amazingly, the children of the so-called "criminal class"—the transported convicts—committed almost no crimes.

Today, Australia, a prosperous country with a cosmopolitan population, continues to have one of the world's lowest crime rates. For these blessings, Australia must thank the 160,000 "criminals" who were sentenced to years of hard labor in a strange land for crimes as small as shoplifting.

■ *Exercise*

Each numbered sentence below corresponds to a sentence in the Passage. Fill in the letter of the choice that makes the sentence mean the same thing as its corresponding sentence in the Passage.

1. Young girls ruined their eyesight doing ___**d**___ sewing.
   a. dark   b. difficult   c. horrible   d. careful

2. The crime rate ___**d**___ .
   a. hurt   b. paid   c. stopped   d. grew

3. ___**c**___ in their own situations, many simply believed there was a "criminal class."
   a. Trusting   b. Wealthy   c. Satisfied   d. Blinded

4. The smallest offense could ___**a**___ one's life.
   a. risk   b. improve   c. save   d. weaken

5. The government began to ___**d**___ the harsh punishments.
   a. consider   b. change   c. increase   d. soften

6. Government officials could ___**d**___ no longer.
   a. help   b. stay   c. finish   d. delay

7. The ___**d**___ island of Australia seemed a wise choice.
   a. difficult   b. warm   c. rich   d. large

8. The land proved difficult to ___**b**___ .
   a. hold   b. farm   c. build   d. buy

9. Humane governors received criticism, rather than ___**b**___ .
   a. time off   b. praise   c. help   d. employment

10. Soon the ___**b**___ "government man" was substituted.
    a. longer phrase   b. nicer phrase   c. harsher phrase   d. more accurate phrase

■ Discussion Questions

1. How did "royal mercy" change a punishment?

2. From the evidence in this passage, does crime appear to stem from evil people or from economic conditions? Defend your answer.

3. Do you find parallels between the treatment of criminals as described in the passage and in today's world? Why or why not?

◀ **ENGLISH IDIOMS**

Rhyme and Repetition

Speakers of English create many forceful and appealing idioms by putting together two words that sound almost alike. Most of these idioms are informal and more appropriate in everyday speech than in formal conversation and writing.

To *dilly-dally* means to delay, or to take too much time. A person who cannot hold a firm opinion, or whose mind is easily changed, is called *wishy-washy*.

To *hobnob* means to associate closely with, as in "He hobnobs with the rich people in town." If you *hobnob* with the rich, you may be considered *hoity-toity,* which means that people think you're a snob. (A snob is also referred to as *stuck up.*)

Something that contains many things that don't fit together is said to be a *hodgepodge*. For example, an essay might be a *hodgepodge* of unrelated ideas. However, if the essay contained many false or silly ideas, it could be called *claptrap*.

In 1919, cartoonist Billy DeBeck created the comic strip "Barney Google," about the adventures of a man and his racehorse. On October 26, 1923, DeBeck coined the phrase *heebie-jeebies* to refer to nervousness. Since then "to have the *heebie-jeebies*" is to be nervous or upset. So popular was the term that trumpeter Louis Armstrong even made a record called "Heebie Jeebies."

Quiz Again

Now that you have finished studying this chapter, here is the brief true-false quiz you took when you began. Take it again.

A **chivalrous** person is nasty.	True	False
A **zealous** person is enthusiastic.	True	False
Mitigating circumstances make hard things more difficult.	True	False
A **euphemism** is a harsh word for something.	True	False

Answers are on page 405. Did your score improve?

REVIEW

Chapters 1–4

■ Reviewing Words in Context

Read the passage below. Then complete each sentence with a word from the group of words below.

THE "TROUBLE TWINS"

a. adroit	e. chronological	i. epitome	m. intrepid
b. articulate	f. conservative	j. exuberant	n. ludicrous
c. belligerent	g. contemplate	k. fraternal	o. meticulous
d. chagrined	h. enigma	l. frugal	p. thwarted

Background: Sophia and Rocio, students in the author's class, are identical twins who have been together since they shared a cradle. They sometimes find that they are independently humming the same song or thinking the same thoughts. Here is more about them.

1. Rocio and Sophia are identical twins, not **k, fraternal** _____ twins.

2. Both have **j, exuberant** _____ personalities; they are bubbly and get excited over things.

3. In addition, they both are **b, articulate** _____ people who express themselves forcefully and well.

4. In **e, chronological** _____ order, Sophia, who was born five minutes before Rocio, came first.

5. Their wonderful relationship is the **i, epitome** _____ of how sisters should get along.

6. Being twins made them feel secure, so they grew up to be **m, intrepid** _____ and afraid of nothing.

7. In fact, it is difficult for them to **g, contemplate** _____ what life would be like if they didn't have each other.

8. However, there are some differences between them; Rocio is **l, frugal** _____ and shops carefully, but Sophia spends money freely.

9. Rocio, who is more **f, conservative** _____, values marriage and family more highly than Sophia, who values independence.

10. They are both **a, adroit** _____ musicians who move their fingers skillfully when playing the violin and piano.

11. When they were young, their mother **p, thwarted** _____ their desire to look like individuals by dressing them the same; people teased them by calling them "the Trouble Twins."

12. To most people, it is a(n) **h, enigma** _____ which twin is Rocio and which is Sophia.

13. However, if you examine their faces with **o, meticulous** _____ care, you can see that Rocio, who is called "la gorda" ("fat one") has slightly rounder cheeks than Sophia, who is called "la flaca" ("thin one").

14. Once a **c, belligerent** _____ playmate, who was angry with Rocio, started to fight with Sophia!

15. More recently, Sophia's boyfriend was __d, chagrined__ when he realized he was trying to kiss Rocio!

■ *Passage for Word Review*

Complete each blank in the Passage with the word that makes the best sense. The choices include words from the vocabulary lists along with related words. Use each choice only once.

MY JOB IN TELEMARKETING

a. amicable	e. concise	i. elicit	m. mandatory
b. appalled	f. consumers	j. harassment	n. perpetual
c. candid	g. contemplated	k. intervene	o. skeptical
d. clarify	h. disdain	l. jeopardize	p. withstand

Background: In this passage Ashanti, another student in the author's class, gives insight into an interesting, but difficult, job.

To support my family while I attend college, I work as a market researcher. This job has many positive features. I bring home a decent paycheck. I work sitting down, unlike most jobs, which require you to be on your feet all day. The job has very flexible hours; I make my own schedule and work overtime whenever I want to. The process of finding how

(1) __f, consumers__ react to a product they have bought can also be interesting. However, the job also has some negative features. To be

(2) __c, candid__, the process of interviewing people over the phone can be extremely stressful.

It can be difficult to **(3)** __i, elicit__ a response from a respondent. When I introduce myself, I am careful to speak in a(n)

(4) __a, amicable__ manner so that the respondent will want to cooperate. But, no matter how friendly I try to be, people do not always

respond politely. In fact, I am **(5)** __b, appalled__ at how rude they can be. People have cursed and screamed at me, and one man even

barked! There seem to be endless ways to show **(6)** __h, disdain__ for me and my job. I become especially frustrated because, no matter

what they do, I must be polite. I **(7)** __l, jeopardize__ my job if I am the least bit rude. The company monitors all of my calls to make sure I am always agreeable. I certainly understand if a respondent is busy or simply does not want to participate in the survey. I appreciate those who say they are not interested and hang up. Sometimes, however, they do not hang up. Then I must try to persuade them to do the survey by giving them three reasons to do it. At times, this persuasion is so strong that it almost amounts to **(8)** **j, harassment**. Yet I must do it, for my company says this is **(9)** **m, mandatory**. To help persuade them, I tell them I am not selling anything, but, in fact, I am giving items away.

Still, many remain **(10)** **o, skeptical** and think I am trying to make them buy something.

At other times, people agree to participate, but, since they are obviously lonely, they talk on and on. Doing an interview with such people can seem like a(n) **(11)** **n, perpetual** task. They often give long speeches to questions that simply require **(12)** **e, concise** responses. At times, these responses make little sense, and I must take extra time to **(13)** **d, clarify** their answers so that I can understand them.

Worst of all, I am sometimes appalled at what I have to do. People have told me of their illnesses or how their spouse has recently died. As a human being, I feel I should listen sympathetically to them, but my job is to take a survey.

For all these reasons, at times, I have seriously **(14)** **g, contemplated** quitting this job. But I have a family that needs money. So I must try to **(15)** **p, withstand** the pressure until I can graduate and find a more satisfying job. The next time you answer the phone, I may be the one calling to ask you, "Would you like to take a survey?"

■ *Reviewing Learning Strategies*

Dictionary Skills Complete each sentence with the answer that fits best.

1. An etymology gives the **c, history** of a word.
   a. pronunciation   b. meaning   c. history

2. The most complete dictionary is called a(n) __**a, unabridged**__ dictionary.

   a. unabridged   b. college   c. pocket

Context Clues   Using context clues, make an intelligent guess about the meaning of the italicized word in each sentence.

3. The *refractory* mule refused to move from the spot, despite our urging.

   Refractory means __**stubborn**__ .

4. You are *niggling* again, and I'd be grateful if you would not argue about small points and discuss the issues instead.

   Niggling means __**arguing about small points**__ .

5. He had a *propensity* to be lazy; in other words, he tended to avoid work.

   Propensity means __**tendency**__ .

6. As a child, Beverly Sills *evinced* so much musical talent that she gave her first performance at the age of three.

   Evinced means __**showed**__ .

7. There was *bedlam,* or total confusion, after the riot.

   Bedlam means __**total confusion**__ .

8. Since the dodo bird died out centuries ago, it is no longer *extant.*

   Extant means __**living**__ .

9. The *fervor* of his plea was emphasized by his wild gestures.

   Fervor means __**passion; wildness**__ .

10. The *noxious* gas caused sickness and death.

    Noxious means __**harmful**__ .

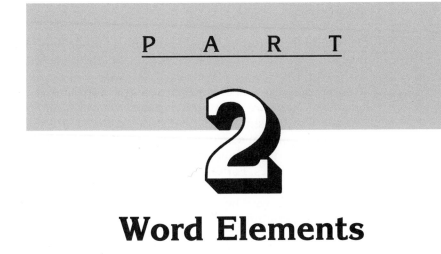

P A R T 2

Word Elements

In Part 1 of this book, you learned about context clues. Part 2 focuses on word elements, the parts of words that have their own meanings. Unlike context clues, which provide hints from the sentence surrounding a word, word elements give hints within the word itself. For example, the parts *re-* (meaning "back") and *tract* (meaning "pull") are the two elements in the word *retract* (meaning "to pull back"). If you break up an unknown word into separate elements, you can often figure out its meaning. If you combine context clues with the word element clues you will learn in Part 2, you will have a powerful approach to understanding new words.

Prefixes, Roots, and Suffixes

There are three kinds of word elements: prefixes, roots, and suffixes. A **prefix** is a group of letters that is attached to the beginning of a word root. A **root** is the central, or main, portion of a word. A **suffix** is a group of letters that is attached to the end of a root. An example of a word that contains all three elements is *impolitely: im-* is the prefix, *polite* is the root, and *-ly* is the suffix. Now let us look at each element separately.

Prefixes. A prefix, such as *im-* (the hyphen at the end indicates a prefix) attached to the beginning of a root, results in a new word with a different meaning. In the word *impolite*, for example, the prefix *im-* means "not." When *im-* is joined to the root *polite*, the new word formed by the prefix and root means "not polite." Next, we can see what happens when the prefix *co-*, which means "together," is joined to two familiar word roots.

co- (together) + *exist* = *coexist* (to exist together)
co- (together) + *operate* = *cooperate* (to work or operate together)

139

In both of these examples, the prefix *co-* changes the meaning of the root word.

Roots.   A root is the central portion of a word, and it carries the basic meaning. There are two types of roots: base words and combining roots. A **base word** is simply an English word that can stand alone, such as *polite* or *operate,* and may be joined to a prefix or a suffix. **Combining roots** cannot stand alone as English words; they are derived from words in other languages. For example, the combining root *ject* is derived from the Latin word *jacēre,* which means "to throw." Although the root *ject* is not an English word by itself, it can combine with many prefixes to form words. Two examples are *reject* and *eject.*

e- (a prefix meaning "out") + *ject* (a root meaning "throw") = *eject*
re- (a prefix meaning "back") + *ject* (a root meaning "throw") = *reject*

How do a prefix and a root create a word with a new meaning? Sometimes the new word's meaning is simply the sum of its root and prefix. Thus, *eject* means "to throw out." At other times the meaning of a word may be somewhat different from the combined prefix and root. *Reject* does not mean "to throw back," but rather "not to accept." These two meanings are related, since we could imagine that someone who did not accept something might throw it back. In fact, "to throw back" gives an imaginative mental picture of *reject.* Prefixes and roots often give an image of a word rather than a precise definition. This image can help you to remember the meaning of a word. The formation of several words from *ject* is illustrated below.

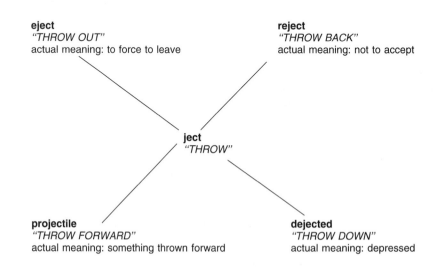

eject
"THROW OUT"
actual meaning: to force to leave

reject
"THROW BACK"
actual meaning: not to accept

ject
"THROW"

projectile
"THROW FORWARD"
actual meaning: something thrown forward

dejected
"THROW DOWN"
actual meaning: depressed

Suffixes.   A suffix, such as *-ly* (the hyphen at the beginning indicates a suffix) is added to the end of a root. Most suffixes change a base word from one part of speech to another (see the table on pages 5 and 6). For example, *-able* changes a verb *(reach)* to an adjective *(reachable)*. Suffixes may also indicate a plural or a past tense, as in boy*s* and reach*ed*. A few suffixes extend the basic meaning of a word root. The root *psych* (mind), and the suffix *-logy* (study of) are joined to form *psychology* (the study of the mind).

Many common words contain word elements. Each of the following words consists of a prefix, a root, and a suffix: *reaction, unlikely, exchanges, reviewing,* and *invisibly.* Can you identify each element?

Answers are on page 405.

Using Word Elements

Word elements provide valuable clues to the meanings of unknown words, but they must be used carefully.

Some word elements have more than one spelling. For example, the root *ject* is occasionally spelled *jac*. The prefix *anti-* is also spelled *ant-* (as in *antacid* and *antagonist*). Some spelling differences make words easier to pronounce. Others reflect the history of a word element. Fortunately, spellings usually vary by only one or two letters. Once you learn to look for the common letters, you should easily be able to identify word elements.

Some word elements have more than one meaning. For example, the combining root *gen* can mean both "birth" and "type." This book gives all the common meanings of many combining roots, prefixes, and suffixes, and some hints about when to use them. When you encounter word elements that have more than one meaning, remember to use the context clues you learned in Part 1 of this book. If you combine your knowledge of word elements with context clues, you can usually determine the most appropriate meaning.

Finally, when you see a certain combination of letters in a word, those letters may not always form a word element. For instance, the appearance of the letters *a-n-t-i* in a word does not mean that they always form the prefix *anti-*. To find out whether or not they do, you must combine context clues with your knowledge of word elements. To illustrate this, *a-n-t-i* is used in two sentences below. Which sentence contains the prefix *anti-* (meaning "opposite" or "against")?

1. The *antihero* was a villain.

2. We *anticipate* you will come.

The answer is the first sentence; *antihero* ("villain") is the opposite of *hero*. (The *anti-* in *anticipate* is actually a varied spelling of the prefix *ante-*, meaning "before.")

Despite these cautions, the use of word elements is an excellent way to increase your vocabulary. Prefixes, roots, and suffixes can help you unlock the meanings of thousands of difficult words. The chapters in Part 2 of this book present many different word elements. Each one is illustrated by several new words that will be valuable to you in college. If you relate these words to the word elements they contain, you will remember both more effectively.

As you work through the word elements in Part 2, keep in mind the context clues that you learned in Part 1. Together, word elements and context clues will give you very powerful strategies for learning new words on your own.

CHAPTER

5

Word Elements: Prefixes

The rich cultural heritage that the ancient Greeks and Romans left to us includes many word elements that are still used in English. This chapter introduces some prefixes from ancient Greek and from Latin, the language of the ancient Romans. Learning these prefixes will help you figure out the meanings of many unfamiliar words.

Chapter Strategy: Word Elements: Prefixes

Chapter Words:

Part 1

anti-	antidote	re-	reconcile
	antipathy		revelation
	antithesis		revert
equi-	equilibrium	sub-	subconscious
	equitable		subdue
	equivocal		subordinate

Part 2

auto-	autobiography	im-, in-	impartial
	autocratic		incongruous
	autonomous		ingenious
ex-	eccentric		interminable
	exorbitant		invariably
	exploit		
	extricate		

Quiz Yourself

To check your knowledge of some chapter words before you begin to study, identify these statements as true or false.

Two things that are **incongruous** are similar.	True	False
Eccentric behavior is odd.	True	False
When we **equivocate,** we state our position clearly.	True	False
Antipathy is hatred.	True	False

You will learn the answers as you study this chapter.

Did You Know?

Where Does English Come From?

The origins of language are lost in the mists of time. Archaeologists discover examples of ancient jewelry, weapons, and art, but no one knows how or why people first spoke. We do know that most of the languages of Europe, the Middle East, and India are descended from a common source. Linguists trace these languages back to a possible parent language called *Indo-European,* which would have been spoken at least five thousand years ago. The Indo-European root *mater* (mother), for example, shows up in many different languages.

Languages No Longer Spoken		*Modern Languages*	
Ancient Greek	mētēr	English	mother
Latin	mater	German	mutter
Old English	modor	Italian	madre
		Spanish	madre
		French	mère
		Polish	matka

English vocabulary descends from Indo-European through several other languages that are no longer spoken. Much of the higher-level vocabulary of modern English comes from ancient Greek and Latin. (These are often called the *classical languages.*) A knowledge of the Greek and Latin word elements used in English will help you master thousands of modern English words.

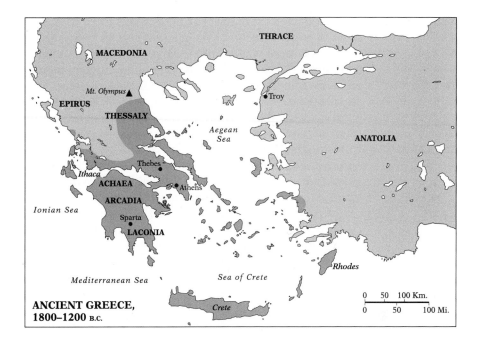

The dark area of the map shows Ancient Greece.

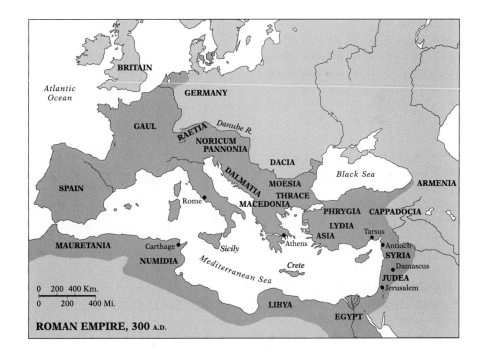

The dark area of the map shows the Roman Empire.

Who were these Greeks and Romans from whom so much language flows? The civilization of the ancient Greeks flourished between 750 and 250 B.C.E. Greece was a land of small, separate city-states that created the first democracies and the first concept of citizenship. Sparta and Athens were two important city-states. The citizens of Sparta were accomplished athletes who excelled in warfare, whereas Athens was a center of art and learning. Athenians produced the first lifelike sculpture, wrote the first tragedies and comedies, and learned philosophy from Socrates and Plato. Unfortunately, ancient Greek civilization also had its dark side. The economic system was based on slavery, and only a small percentage of the population—free men—were full citizens. Women had few political rights. Greek history was also marred by tragic wars between city-states.

In contrast to the divided Greek city-states, the city of Rome steadily took over first the whole of Italy, and then more territory, until it finally ruled over a vast empire. From about 200 B.C.E. to 450 C.E. Rome brought its way of life to much of the Mediterranean world and beyond. Roman officials introduced a highway system, a postal service, water supplies, public baths, and border patrols to many less advanced areas. They also spread their language, Latin. But, like ancient Greece, Rome had its problems. After the first emperor, Augustus, died, plots and murders became common in the Roman court. Several Roman emperors were poisoned, stabbed, or smothered. Meanwhile, officials and the army continued to rule the empire efficiently.

If you have studied the ancient Greeks and Romans, you may be able to answer these questions.

1. An epic poem, the *Iliad,* tells of a Greek war that started when Helen, the daughter of Zeus, was stolen from her husband. Helen is often

   called "Helen of <u>**c**_____</u> ."
   a. Athens   b. Sparta   c. Troy   d. Crete

2. <u>**d**_____</u> was a famous Roman leader who said, "I came, I saw, I conquered."
   a. Augustus   b. Brutus   c. Cato   d. Julius Caesar

3. Cleopatra, queen of Egypt, did *not* have a romance with <u>**a**_____</u> .
   a. Augustus   b. Julius Caesar   c. Mark Antony

Answers are on page 406.

Learning Strategy

Word Elements: Prefixes

Our heritage from the Greeks and Romans includes many word elements that are still used in English. The Learning Strategy in this chapter concentrates on *prefixes,* word elements "added to" the beginning of word roots. The seven prefixes presented in this chapter (see the following table) are very common, and learning them will help you build a large vocabulary. One dictionary lists over four hundred words that use *ex-* and more than six hundred formed from *in-* or *im-*.

Element	Meaning	Origin	Chapter Words
			Part 1
anti-, ant-	against; opposite	Greek	antidote, antipathy, antithesis
equi-, equa-	equal	Latin	equilibrium, equitable, equivocal
re-	back; again	Latin	reconcile, revelation, revert
sub-	below; under; part of	Latin	subconscious, subdue, subordinate
			Part 2
auto-	self	Greek	autobiography, autocratic, autonomous
ex-, e-, ec-	out of; former	Latin	eccentric, exorbitant, exploit, extricate
im-, in-	not; in	Latin	impartial, incongruous, ingenious, interminable, invariably

Prefixes give clues to word meaning when they join with word roots. Let us look first at how prefixes can combine with roots that are base words.

anti- (against) + *poverty* makes *antipoverty,* meaning "against poverty."
   Food stamps were part of the *antipoverty* program.
sub- (below) + *normal* makes *subnormal,* meaning "below normal."
   Subnormal temperatures are colder than usual.
auto- (self) + *suggestion* makes *autosuggestion,* meaning "a suggestion made to yourself."
   Some people use *autosuggestion* when they try to stop smoking.

See if you can use prefixes to determine the meaning of the following words. Write in the word and its meaning.

equi- (equal) + *distant* makes **equidistant** , meaning
equal in distance .

in- (not) + *direct* makes **indirect** , meaning
not direct .

re- (again) + *appear* makes **reappear** , meaning
appear again .

Answers are on page 406.

Now let's look at how prefixes join with combining roots (roots that cannot stand alone as English words). The Latin root *scrib* or *script* (meaning "write") combines with some prefixes in our list to make English words whose meanings are the combined meanings of the prefix and root.

in- (in) + *scrib* makes *inscribe*, "to write in."
People often *inscribe* their names in books.
sub- (under) + *script* makes *subscript*, "written under."
A *subscript* is a tiny number or letter written beneath a line, such as the 2 in H_2O, the chemical symbol for water. Subscripts are often used with symbols in math and science.

At other times, the meaning of a word is not precisely the combined meanings of a prefix and combining root. Still, these word elements will give you valuable clues to the meaning of the word. The Latin root *vert* (to turn) combines with three prefixes that you will study in this chapter to make three different English words, but the idea of "turn" appears in all of them.

re- (back) + *vert* (turn) makes *revert*, or "turn back."
When people *revert* to an old habit, they start to do it again. Perhaps you know a child who *reverted* to sucking his thumb after having outgrown the behavior.
in- (in) + *vert* (turn) makes *invert*, or "turn in."
Invert means to turn inside out or upside down, or to change in order.
If you *invert* a pocket, you turn it inside out.
sub- (under) + *vert* (turn) makes *subvert*, or "turn under."
Subvert means to make something worse by corrupting it or trying to overthrow it. Traitors seek to *subvert* their countries' governments.

As you can see, using prefixes sometimes requires a little imagination. Prefixes and roots may not give the *entire* meaning of an unknown word, but they do provide excellent hints. If you combine the use of context clues with the use of word elements, you can often figure out the precise meaning of an unfamiliar word.

Two words formed from a prefix and a root are presented below. The meanings of the roots and prefixes are given, followed by a sentence using the word. Write in the meaning of each word.

revive, from *re-* (again) and *vivere* (to live).
The plant *revived* after we gave it water.

Revive means __to live again__ .

incredulous, from *in-* (not) and *cred* (to believe)
She was *incredulous* when she heard the fantastic story.

Incredulous means __not believing__ .

Answers are on page 406.

Prefixes

Part 1

Four prefixes are presented in Part 1 of this chapter. Each prefix is described below.

anti-, ant- (against; opposite)

The two meanings of *anti-* are related and therefore easy to remember. *Antifreeze* protects a car radiator from freezing, *antiaircraft* missiles shoot down aircraft, and *antigambling* laws outlaw gambling. New English words continue to be formed with *anti-*, especially since people always seem to find new things to protest.

equi- equa- (equal)

Equi- is used in many English words. Two homes that are *equidistant* from a school are the same, or **equal,** distance from the school. *Equivalent* sums of money have the same, or **equal,** value. For example, one dollar is *equivalent* to four quarters. Two equally powerful forces may be called *equipotent.*

re- (back; again)

Re- has two distinct meanings. It usually means "again" when it is attached to other English words (or base words). For example, when *re-* is added to the base words *wind* and *do* it forms *rewind* (wind **again**) and *redo* (do **again**). However, when *re-* is added to combining roots, which cannot stand alone, it often means "back." *Recede,* for instance, means "to go **back**" and comes from *re-* (back) and *cēdere* (to go).

sub- (below; under; part of)

In the word *substandard, sub-* means "below": *below* the standard." *Sub-* can also refer to a classification that is "part of" something else, as a *subdivision,* which is *part of* a division. In biology, animals from one species may be further classified into several *subspecies.*

Words to Learn

Part 1

anti-, ant-

1. **antidote** (noun)   ăn′tĭ-dōt′

    From Greek *anti-* (against) + *didonai* (to give) (to give a remedy against something harmful)

    a substance that acts against a poison

Dimercaprol is used as an **antidote** to arsenic poisoning.

something that acts against a harmful effect

Research has shown that artificial sunlight can be an **antidote** to depression for short winter days.

Treatment programs are the most effective **antidote** to drug addiction.

The prefix *anti-* is widely used in medicine. Health care professionals prescribe *antibiotics* such as penicillin and neomycin to kill organisms that can cause disease. The word *antibiotic* comes from *anti-* and *bio,* meaning "life." We take an *antihistamine* to stop the sneezing and runny nose of a cold or an allergy. *Antihistamine* comes from *anti-* plus *histi,* the ancient Greek word element meaning "tissue," or body substance. Immunizations against smallpox, measles, polio, and tuberculosis allow us to form *antibodies* that prevent these diseases. Currently, medical researchers are trying to locate substances that will form antibodies against the deadly AIDS virus.

---

2. **antipathy** (noun)   ăn-tĭp′ə-thē

From Greek: *anti-* (against) + *patho* (feeling)

great hatred, opposition, or disgust

Mara's **antipathy** toward her abusive father made her move to another city.

People in the neighborhood felt **antipathy** toward the violent gang members who had made the streets dangerous.

3. **antithesis** (noun)   ăn-tĭth′ĭ-sĭs (plural: **antitheses**)

From Greek: *anti-* (against) + *tithenai* (to put)

contrast; opposite

John's rude behavior was the very **antithesis** of his brother's polished good manners.

Although service in the Peace Corps might seem the **antithesis** of preparing for a career, many employers feel it helps people develop job-related skills.

Censorship is the **antithesis** of freedom of expression.

▶ *Related Word*
  antithetical (adjective) (ăn′tĭ-thĕt′ĭ-kəl) Demolishing old buildings is *antithetical* to keeping the traditions of a neighborhood.

equi-, equa-

4. **equilibrium** (noun)   ē′kwə-lĭb′rē-əm

   From Latin: *equi-* (equal) + *libra* (balance)

   balance between forces; stability

   > Traditional Chinese philosophy discusses the importance of keeping the forces of yin, or passivity, and yang, or activity, in **equilibrium.**

   > The tightrope walker almost lost his **equilibrium.**

   > The reporter's nasty question disturbed the mayor's **equilibrium** and he began to yell.

   ▶ *Common Phrase*
   in equilibrium

   NOTE: The concept of balance can be used in several ways, including evenness of temperament.

5. **equitable** (adjective)   ĕk′wĭ-tə-bəl

   From Latin: *equi* (equal)

   fair; just

   > To help poor children, we need more **equitable** ways to fund education.

   > Laws should provide for **equitable** payment to victims of crimes.

   NOTE: In *equitable*, the *equi* word element is used as a root.

Many early rock stars were not given *equitable* treatment. In the early 1950s, New York's Morrisania High School echoed with the sound of "doo-wop," vocal music with complex harmonies and nonsense syllables (such as "sh-boom"). Famous songs included "Pretty Little Angel Eyes," "Who Put the Bomp," and "Nag." Unfortunately, the young singers often were unaware of copyright laws and were easily cheated. In the 1990s, doo-wop singers released a compact disk titled *Voices: A Legendary Morrisania Review*. This time they hoped for *equitable* artistic and financial rewards.

---

6. **equivocal** (adjective)   ĭ-kwĭv′ə-kəl

   From Latin: *equi-* (equal) + *vox* (voice) (When something is equivocal, it seems as if two equally strong voices are sending different messages.)

   open to different interpretations, often misleading or avoiding the truth

The President's **equivocal** reply, "I will serve our national interest," did not answer the question of whether he would support
a war. (In this sentence, there is an intention to mislead or
avoid the truth.)

Studies of the effects of welfare payments on family stability
have shown **equivocal** results. (There is no intention to mislead in this sentence.)

doubtful

Although people pay high prices for her paintings, her position
as a great artist is **equivocal.**

NOTE: Equivocal statements are often meant to mislead and even
deceive people.

▶ *Related Words*

    equivocate (verb) (ĭ-kwĭv′ə-kāt′) Don't *equivocate;* answer
directly.

    equivocation (noun) The defendant's *equivocation* on the
question of where he was the night of the robbery made him
look guilty.

re-

7. **reconcile** (verb)   rĕk′ən-sīl′

From Latin: *re-* (back) and *concilare* to bring together (to bring back
together)

To bring to peace, agreement, or understanding

Democrats and Republicans worked to **reconcile** their differences on environmental policy.

Computer programs help me to **reconcile** my bank statement
with my checking account records.

After she married, Aretha had to **reconcile** herself to living with
two troublesome teenage stepdaughters.

▶ *Related Word*

    reconciliation (noun) After a period of separation, the mar-
ried couple decided to try a *reconciliation.*

According to Lakota Sioux tribal legend, the birth of a white buffalo
brings *reconciliation* among nations. A story is told that a beautiful
woman once appeared to rescue Indians from starvation. As she left,
promising to return, she turned into a white buffalo. In the 1990s, a
rare white buffalo was born in Wisconsin. Named "Miracle," it has captured the imagination of many who hope for world peace.

8. **revelation** (noun)   rĕv′ə-lā′shən

From Latin: *re-* (back) + *vēlāre* (to veil) This makes *revēlāre*, "to draw back the veil." (When a veil is drawn back, something surprising or even shocking may be discovered.)

dramatic disclosure; surprising news

> The Islamic holiday of Ramadan marks God's **revelation** of the Koran to the prophet Mohammed. (Here, *revelation* has a positive, religious meaning.)

▶ *Related Word*
reveal (verb)   (rĭ-vēl′)   The newspaper reporter *revealed* that the public official had cheated on his wife.

9. **revert** (verb)   rĭ-vûrt′

From Latin: *re-* (back) + *vert* (turn)

to return to a former practice or condition

> The land on the abandoned farm **reverted** to its natural prairie state.

> Whenever his brother was around, my boyfriend **reverted** to childish behavior.

> After ninety-nine years of British rule, the city of Hong Kong **reverted** to Chinese control in 1997.

▶ *Common Phrase*
revert to

▶ *Related Word*
reversion (noun)   (rĭ-vûr′zhən)   The mayor promised there would be no *reversion* to the former terrible conditions in public housing.

sub-

10. **subconscious** (adjective, noun)   sŭb-kŏn′shəs

From Latin: *sub-* (under) + *conscius* (aware of)

not aware (or conscious) in the mind (adjective)

> Colors can have **subconscious** meanings; red often suggests excitement, and blue suggests peace.

> Advertisers try to appeal to our **subconscious** desires.

the part of the mind that is beneath awareness (noun)

> When the psychiatrist Sigmund Freud explored the **subconscious,** he found that some dreams were disguised wishes.

NOTE: The *unconscious* (not conscious) is that part of the mind that can *never* become conscious. The word *unconscious* also describes a sleeping person or someone in a coma. The *subconscious* can be made conscious, but only with great effort.

11. **subdue** (verb)   səb-d$\overline{oo}$′

From Latin: *sub-* (under) + *dūcere* (to lead) (Someone who is subdued is led by, or placed under, the control of another.)

to conquer or bring under control

>   Alexander the Great (356–323 B.C.E.) **subdued** lands now occupied by Greece, Iran, Turkey, Afghanistan, and Egypt.

>   It is difficult to **subdue** a desire to overeat when faced with a plentiful buffet table.

to make less intense or noticeable

>   We **subdued** our voices to avoid waking the infant.

▶ *Related Word*
>   **subdued** (adjective)   My mother wears *subdued* colors, such as black and gray.

12. **subordinate** (adjective, noun)   sə-bôr′də-nĭt;   (verb)   sə-bôr′də-nāt

From Latin: *sub-* (under) + *ōrdīnāre* (to arrange in order)

less important; of lower rank (adjective)

>   District courts and courts of appeals hold **subordinate** positions to the Supreme Court.

>   Regina holds a **subordinate** position to the president of the company.

a person of lower rank or importance (noun)

>   A **subordinate** delivered the U.S. President's message to the press.

to place in a lower or less important position (verb)

>   I try to **subordinate** my personal wishes to the needs of the rest of my family.

▶ *Common Phrases*
>   subordinate to (adjective)

>   a subordinate of (noun)

NOTE: The pronunciation of the verb *subordinate* differs from the adjective and noun forms.

▶ *Related Word*
subordination (noun)   The southern portion of the **Sudan** has not freed itself from economic *subordination* to the north.

Exercises

Part 1

■ *Definitions*

Match each word in the left-hand column with a definition from the right-hand column. Use each choice only once.

1. revelation _____ **k**

2. equitable _____ **h**

3. subdue _____ **a**

4. antithesis _____ **d**

5. subordinate _____ **j**

6. subconscious _____ **l**

7. equilibrium _____ **b**

8. antipathy _____ **f**

9. revert _____ **g**

10. antidote _____ **e**

a. conquer

b. balance

c. bring to peace

d. opposite

e. something that acts against a poison

f. hatred

g. return to a former practice

h. fair

i. doubtful

j. less important in rank

k. surprising news

l. beneath awareness

■ *Meanings*

Match each prefix to its meaning. Use each choice only once.

1. re- _____ **d**

2. equi-, equa- _____ **a**

3. anti- ant- _____ **b**

4. sub- _____ **c**

a. equal

b. against

c. under, below, part of

d. again, back

■ *Words in Context*

Complete each sentence with the word that fits best. Use each choice only once.

a. antidote   e. equitable   i. revert
b. antipathy   f. equivocal   j. subconscious
c. antithesis   g. reconcile   k. subdue
d. equilibrium   h. revelation   l. subordinate

1. Her answer was so **f, equivocal** _____ that he couldn't tell whether she accepted his proposal or not.

2. After losing her savings, Natasha had to **g, reconcile** _____ herself to a lower standard of living.

3. The **e, equitable** _____ decision enabled everyone to feel that justice had been done.

4. Because the housewife kept her **d, equilibrium** _____, she was able to deal calmly with three crying children and a broken window.

5. We feel **b, antipathy** _____ for our bitter enemy.

6. The university provost, Dr. Esmeralda Lopez, was so busy that her **l, subordinate** _____ had to handle many details for her.

7. After a dangerous snakebite, a(n) **a, antidote** _____ to the poison must be administered quickly.

8. The loud rock music was the **c, antithesis** _____ of the quiet classical piece.

9. Many people are tempted to **i, revert** _____ to smoking in tense situations, even after they have quit for a few years.

10. Using a stun gun, the forest rangers were able to **k, subdue** _____ the bear that invaded our campsite.

■ *Using Related Words*

Complete each sentence by using a word from the group of related words above it. You may need to capitalize a word when you write it in a sentence. Use each choice only once.

A Brief History of Ancient Rome

1. reconcile, reconciliation

   For almost 500 years, until about 40 B.C.E., the Roman republic was governed by a Senate. However, continual fighting among Senators, with few attempts at **reconciliation**_____, led to greater concentration of power. Eventually, the Romans had to **reconcile**_____ themselves to living under an emperor. The story starts with Julius Caesar.

2. subordinate, subordination

   After achieving much political success, the great Julius Caesar set out to **subordinate**_____ Gaul (now France and Belgium) to the Romans. He achieved this **subordination**_____ and returned home a hero.

3. equivocated, equivocation

   After some **equivocation**_____, Julius Caesar, Crassus, and Pompey formed a triumvirate, or group of three, to rule Rome. Pompey was Caesar's son-in-law, yet their position as allies was short-lived. Pompey was jealous of Caesar's popularity; Caesar was power hungry. Eventually they fought, and Caesar won. As Caesar **equivocated**_____ about whether he wanted to be emperor, Senate members murdered him.

4. revelation, revealed

   While Augustus, nephew of Caesar, was in Illyria, a letter from his mother brought the shocking **revelation**_____ that Caesar had been murdered. His mother warned Augustus to flee. Instead, his decision **revealed**_____ his character: he immediately went to Rome. This courage later helped him become Rome's first emperor. For the next 500 years, Rome remained an empire.

5. antithesis, antithetical

   Many years after Augustus took power, the city of Rome was weakened by a series of barbarian invasions. With their lack of technology and art, the invaders' culture was **antithetical**_____ to the highly civilized Romans. The destructive violence of the attacks was the **antithesis** _____ of the principles on which the Roman Empire stood. After many invasions, the last Roman emperor was forced to resign in 467 C.E.

■ *True or False?*

Each of the following statements contains one or more words from this section. Read each sentence carefully and then indicate whether you think it is probably true or probably false.

F ___   1. A subordinate is in a superior position to a boss.

F ___   2. A revelation is the antithesis of a surprise.

F ___   3. We know all about our subconscious wishes.

T ___   4. Equitable treatment is just.

T ___   5. We should try to subdue our urge to revert to childish temper tantrums.

F ___   6. An antidote makes us sicker.

T ___   7. Antipathy is hatred.

T ___   8. A person who loses his equilibrium may fall down.

T ___   9. An equivocal statement is clear and easy to interpret.

T ___   10. When we reconcile ourselves to something, we accept it.

Prefixes

Part 2

The following three prefixes are introduced in Part 2.

auto- (self)
This prefix comes from the Greek word for "self." The word *automobile* comes from *auto-* and *mobile,* meaning "moving." When the automobile was invented, it was named for the amazing sight of something moving all by *itself.*

ex-, e-, ec- (out of; former)

When *ex-* is combined with the base words, it usually means "former." The words *ex-wife* (*former* wife) and *ex-president* (*former* president) show *ex-* used in this sense. The hyphens in these words give a hint that the "former" meaning is being used. When *ex-* is used with combining roots, it usually means "out of," as in *exhale* (to breathe *out*). The words introduced in this lesson join *ex-* to combining roots, so *ex-* means "out of" in all these words. However, you should remember that *ex-* can also mean "former."

im, in- (not; in)

This prefix is spelled in two different ways, and either spelling may have two different meanings. The most common meaning of *im-* and *in-* is "not," as in the words *impure* (*not* pure) and *indecent* (*not* decent). *Im-* and *in-* can also mean "in," as in *inhale* (to breathe *in*) and *import* (to carry *into* a country). The prefix is spelled *ir-* or *il-* before roots that begin with *r* or *l*, such as in *irregular* and *illogical*. The *il-* and *ir-* spellings always mean "not."

Words to Learn

Part 2

auto-

13. **autobiography** (noun)   ô'tō-bī-ŏg'rə-fē

From Greek: *auto-* (self) + *bio* (life) + *graph* (to write)

account of a person's life written by that person

> Although blind and deaf, Helen Keller composed a moving **autobiography** titled *The Story of My Life*.

Can you match these famous people with the names of their autobiographies?

1. Glen Campbell	a. *Little Girl Lost*
2. Howard Stern	b. *What Falls Away: A Memoir*
3. Christopher Reeve	c. *Private Parts*
4. Michael Jordan	d. *Still Me*
5. Drew Barrymore	e. *Rhinestone Cowboy*
6. Mia Farrow	f. *For the Love of the Game*

Answers are on page 406.

▶ *Related Word*

autobiographical (adjective) The *autobiographical* song "*Qax*," meaning "refugee," relates singer Maryam Mursal's escape from Somalia.

14. **autocratic** (adjective) ô'tə-krăt′ək

From Greek: *auto-* (self) + *krates* (ruling)

having absolute power; domineering

Spain established a constitutional democratic government after the death of the **autocratic** ruler Francisco Franco.

The **autocratic** CEO ran the company without any input from other executives.

▶ *Related Words*

autocrat (noun; person) (ô′tə-krăt′) The *autocrat* Peter the Great ruled Russia from 1682 to 1725.

autocracy (noun) (ô-tŏk′rə-sē) Mexico is changing from what was, in effect, a one-party *autocracy* to a multiparty democracy.

15. **autonomous** (adjective) ô-tŏn′ə-məs

From Greek: *auto-* (self) + *nomos* (law)

self-governing; independent

The Vatican is an **autonomous** area within the country of Italy.

People usually need to be self-supporting before they can truly be **autonomous.**

▶ *Related Word*

autonomy (noun) Slaves have no *autonomy*.

ex-, e-, ec-

16. **eccentric** (adjective) ĕk-sĕn′trĭk

From Greek: *ek-* (out) + *kentron* (center)

odd; different from normal or usual

The **eccentric** man attached strings to large bugs and walked them like dogs.

▶ *Related Word*

eccentricity (noun) (ĕk′sĕn-trĭs′ə-tē) One of Albert Einstein's *eccentricities* was going without socks in cold weather.

17. **exorbitant** (adjective)   ĭg-zôr′bĭ-tənt

From Latin: *ex-* (out) + *orbita* (path)

expensive; unreasonable; exceeding proper limits

> Because frost killed much of the crop, oranges were selling for an **exorbitant** fifteen dollars per pound.

> Management refused to meet the baseball player's **exorbitant** contract demands.

18. **exploit** (verb)   ĭk-sploit′; (noun)   ĕks′ploit′

From Latin: *ex-* (out) + *plicāre* (to fold), making *explicāre* (to unfold) (When we *exploit* something, we "fold it out" and make it work for us.)

to take advantage of; to use (verb)

> Because his low wages made Samir feel **exploited,** he decided to open his own business.

> Several child athletes have claimed that their parents have **exploited** them by living on their earnings.

> Alaska **exploited** its rich oil and natural gas reserves while trying not to harm the environment.

great adventure; great deed (noun)

> Homer's *Odyssey* relates the **exploits** of the Greek hero Odysseus as he returns home from the Trojan War.

NOTE: (1) *Exploit,* when used as a verb, often suggests taking unfair advantage (as in the exploitation of women or minorities). However, it can mean simply "to take advantage of" or "to use wisely." (2) Notice the difference in pronunciation stress between *ex-ploit′* (verb) and *ex′ploit* (noun).

▶ *Related Word*

> **exploitation** (noun)   (ĕk′sploi-tā′shən)   Many consumers have begun to protest the *exploitation* of child labor in clothing factories.

19. **extricate** (verb)   ĕk′strĭ-kāt′

From Latin: *ex-* (out) + *tricae* (difficulties), making *extricāre* (to disentangle, to free)

to free from difficulty; to disentangle

> Rescue workers **extricated** the boy who had fallen down an old well.

Roy **extricated** himself from an embarrassing situation by leaving the room.

▶ *Common Phrase*
to extricate (oneself) from

Harry Houdini (1874–1926) was a world-famous escape artist. Houdini *extricated* himself from many seemingly escape-proof devices, including ten pairs of handcuffs, jail cells, nailed crates, and an airtight tank filled with water. Once, tied into a straitjacket and hung upside-down from the top of a tall building, he extricated himself within minutes.

---

im-, in-

20. **impartial** (adjective) ĭm-pär′shəl

From Latin: *im-* (not) + *pars* (part)

fair; just; not biased

It is important for a basketball referee to be **impartial.**

My dad remained **impartial** in the fight between my brother and me.

The peacekeepers were **impartial** toward both countries involved in the war.

▶ *Common Phrase*
impartial toward

▶ *Related Word*
impartiality (noun) (ĭm′pär-shē-al′ə-tē) It is difficult to judge a good friend with *impartiality.*

21. **incongruous** (adjective) ĭn-kŏng′groo-əs

From Latin: *in-* (not) + *congruere* (to agree)

out of place; not consistent or in harmony

The modern furniture looked **incongruous** in the ancient castle.

The violent attack seemed **incongruous** with the peaceful village atmosphere.

The stingy tip seemed **incongruous** with the patron's expensive limousine.

▶ *Related Word*
incongruity (noun) People noted the *incongruity* of the housekeeper's mild manner and the terrible crime she was charged with committing.

22. **ingenious** (adjective) ĭn-jēn′yəs

From Latin: *in-* (in) + *gen* (born), making *ingenium* (inborn talent)

clever; inventive

> Scientists are perfecting an **ingenious** plastic wrap that will produce electric power from sunlight.

> The **ingenious** slogan "snap, crackle, pop" has sold many boxes of Rice Krispies.

▶ *Related Word*
> **ingenuity** (noun) (ĭn′jə-nōō′ĭ-tē) Technological *ingenuity* has led to the design of tiny laptop computers.

Benjamin Franklin, a Philadelphian who lived in the 1700s, produced many *ingenious* inventions, including the lightning rod, bifocals (glasses with two visual corrections), and the Franklin stove (which stood in the middle of a room, heating all parts evenly). Franklin also developed some valuable public services, such as the public library and the volunteer fire department.

---

23. **interminable** (adjective) ĭn-tûr′mə-nə-bəl

From Latin: *in-* (not) + *terminus* (end, boundary)

endless; too long

> The lecture seemed **interminable,** but we were afraid to get up and leave.

> In the subzero weather, the wait in the ticket line seemed **interminable.**

NOTE: 1. *Interminable* has a negative connotation. 2. This word often describes something that seems endless rather than actually is endless.

24. **invariably** (adverb) ĭn-vâr′ē-ə-blē

From Latin: *in-* (not) + *variabilis* (changeable)

consistently; always

> Superman and Batman **invariably** win their fights against evil.

Exercises

Part 2

■ Definitions

Match each word in the left-hand column with a definition from the right-hand column. Use each choice only once.

1. autocratic __a__   a. holding all power

2. invariably __k__   b. endless; too long

3. ingenious __e__   c. the story of one's own life

4. autobiography __c__   d. odd

5. eccentric __d__   e. clever

6. exploit __f__   f. to take advantage of

7. exorbitant __j__   g. to free from difficulty

8. incongruous __l__   h. not biased

9. extricate __g__   i. self-ruling

10. interminable __b__   j. very expensive

                             k. always; consistently

                             l. out of place; not in harmony

■ Meanings

Match each prefix to its meaning. Use each choice only once.

1. im-, in- __b__   a. self

2. ex-, e-, ec- __c__   b. in; not

3. auto- __a__   c. out; former

■ Words in Context

Complete each sentence with the word that fits best. Use each choice only once.

a. autobiography   e. exorbitant   i. incongruous
b. autocratic   f. exploit   j. ingenious
c. autonomous   g. extricate   k. interminable
d. eccentric   h. impartial   l. invariably

1. The **d, eccentric** lady kept ninety-nine cats in her home.

2. To help ensure that the scholarship board would be **h, impartial**, the members were not told the names of the applicants.

3. Eighty dollars seems like a(n) **e, exorbitant** price to pay for a sweatshirt.

4. As a(n) **c, autonomous** person, I make all my own decisions.

5. In a(n) **j, ingenious** plan to prevent water shortages, Alaska's plentiful water may be shipped in huge bags to dry areas.

6. The college professor and waitress seemed like a(n) **i, incongruous** couple, but they were very much in love.

7. The **b, autocratic** ruler suddenly announced that everyone had to pay a new tax.

8. People **l, invariably** close their eyes when they sneeze, since it is not possible to keep them open.

9. When my dog got its paw caught in a mousetrap, we tried to **g, extricate** it carefully.

10. The time I spent waiting to find out if I got the job seemed **k, interminable**.

■ *Using Related Words*

Complete each sentence by using a word from the group of related words above it. You may need to capitalize a word when you write it in a sentence. Use each choice only once.

FACT AND FICTION FROM ANCIENT GREECE

1. ingenious, ingenuity

   Euclid, who lived in Alexandria at about 500 B.C.E., was a mathematician of great **ingenuity**_____. His **ingenious**_____
   system of teaching geometry through proofs is still used in class-
   rooms today.

2. autonomy, autonomous

   In 490 B.C.E., Darius, king of the vast Persian empire, decided to
   conquer the city-state of Athens and end its **autonomy**_____.
   Against all odds, Athens defeated the Persian army on the

   Plain of Marathon and remained **autonomous**_____.
   Pheidippides ran twenty-six miles to deliver news of the victory to
   Athens. Since then, a race of twenty-six miles, or any long, difficult
   contest, has been called a "marathon."

3. impartial, impartiality

   The philosopher Socrates was among the most famous citizens of
   ancient Athens. Unfortunately, he criticized the city leaders, and
   in 399 B.C.E. he was brought to trial for corrupting youth. Emotions

   were so strong that it was difficult to be **impartial**_____
   in the debate. Socrates was condemned to die by drinking poison hemlock. Although the city elders stated they had acted

   with **impartiality**_____, others disagreed.

4. exploitation, exploited

   Is there anyone who has never heard of Aesop's fables? Aesop
   himself lived about 500 B.C.E. In one of his fables, a couple had
   a goose that laid one golden egg each day. When the couple

   exploited_____ their good fortune wisely, they grew
   wealthier. However, one day they decided to get all the gold immediately. They killed the goose, only to find that there was no gold

   inside it. Thus, their attempt at greedy **exploitation**_____ cost them dearly. From this fable comes the phrase "to kill the goose that lays the golden egg."

5. extricated, extricate

Homer's *Iliad* tells the story of the Trojan War. After several years of fighting, the Greeks had not conquered the Trojans. Finally, the Greeks used a trick to **extricate** _____ themselves from the conflict. Greek soldiers hid inside a large wooden horse just outside the gates of Troy. Assuming the horse was a gift, the Trojans brought it inside. When night fell, the Greeks **extricated** _____ themselves from the horse, attacked, and conquered Troy.

■ *True or False?*

Each of the following statements contains at least one word from this section. Read each sentence carefully and then indicate whether you think it is probably true or probably false.

F ___   1. Someone else writes your autobiography.

T ___   2. If you exploit ingenious ideas, you are likely to become wealthy.

T ___   3. An exorbitant price on an old car seems incongruous.

T ___   4. It is difficult to extricate the last bit of ketchup from a narrow jar.

F ___   5. An eccentric person behaves like everyone else.

T ___   6. Rain is invariably wet.

F ___   7. An interesting movie seems interminable.

T ___   8. An impartial judge is fair.

F ___   9. An autocratic ruler listens to everyone.

F ___   10. An autonomous person is controlled by others.

Chapter Exercises

■ *Practicing Strategies: New Words from Word Elements*

See how your knowledge of prefixes can help you understand new words. Complete each sentence with the word that seems to fit best. Use each choice only once. You may need to capitalize a word.

a. antibacterial   e. equipotential   i. reattach
b. antislavery   f. impression   j. refill
c. autoinoculation   g. invalid   k. subliminal
d. equator   h. irresponsible   l. subculture

1. If a finger has been cut off, a surgeon may be able to **i, reattach** it.

2. You cannot drive with a(n) **g, invalid** license.

3. The **b, antislavery** movement fought for the right of African Americans to be free.

4. In a process called **c, autoinoculation** , chemicals from your own body are injected back into you to fight disease.

5. The sociologist studied the gang **l, subculture** within the larger culture of American society.

6. The **d, equator** divides the earth equally into the Northern and Southern hemispheres.

7. **e, Equipotential** means having equal potential.

8. After I drank all of my coffee, the waiter offered to **j, refill** my cup.

9. Something **k, subliminal** is beneath the limits of your hearing or vision.

10. A(n) **f, impression** is made when something is pressed into soft cement.

■ *Practicing Strategies: Combining Context Clues and Word Elements*

Combining the strategies of context clues and word elements is a good way to figure out unknown words. In the following sentences, each italicized word contains a word element that you have studied in this chapter. Using the meaning of the prefix and the context of the sentence, make an intelligent guess about the meaning of the italicized word. Your instructor may ask you to check the meaning in your dictionary after you have finished.

1. Using the *auto-focus* feature of the camera, even an amateur can take a clear picture.

   Auto-focus means **self-focusing** .

2. The criminal was *extradited* from England and sent to the United States.

   Extradited means **removed/taken out of** .

3. At the time of an *equinox,* there are twelve hours of daylight and twelve hours of darkness.

   Equinox means **the time of year when day and night are of equal length** .

4. Since our computer is *infallible,* the mistake must be due to human error.

   Infallible means **perfect; never wrong** .

5. The *subcellar* was the first room to flood during the storm.

   Subcellar means **room (or space) beneath the cellar** .

■ *Practicing Strategies: Using the Dictionary*

Read the following definition and then answer the questions that follow.

bloom[1] (bloom) *n.* **1.** The flower of a plant. **2a.** The condition of being in flower. **b.** A condition or time of vigor and beauty; prime: *"the radiant bloom of Greek genius"* (Edith Hamilton). **3.** A fresh, rosy complexion: *"She was short, plump, and fair, with a fine bloom"* (Jane Austen). **4.a.** A waxy or powdery coating sometimes occurring on the surface of plant parts, such as the fruits of certain plums. **b.** A similar coating, as on newly minted coins. **c.** *Chem.* See **efflorescence** 3a. **5.** Glare that is caused by a shiny object reflecting too much light into a television camera. **6.** A colored area on the surface of water caused by planktonic growth. —*v.* **bloomed, bloom•ing, blooms.** —*intr.* **1a.** To bear a flower or flowers. **b.** To support plant life in abundance. **2.** To shine; glow. **3.** To grow or flourish with youth and vigor. **4.** To appear or expand suddenly. —*tr.* **1.** To cause to flourish. **2.** *Obsolete.* To cause to flower. [ME *blom* < ON *blōm.* See **bhel-³*.] —**bloom′y** *adj.*

1. Which common word in the dictionary key contains a vowel pronounced like the *oo* in *bloom*? **boot**

2. Give the number and part of speech of the definition in which a quote is used from author Jane Austen to define *bloom*. **3, as a noun**

3. Give the definition of *bloom* that is no longer in use. **2, as a transitive verb: "to cause to flower"**

4. Give the number and part of speech of the definition that best fits this sentence: "To avoid the *bloom*, the assistant on the TV show took the metal pans off the wall." **5, as a noun**

5. In which language did *bloom* appear just before it entered modern English? **Middle English**

■ *Companion Words*

Complete each sentence with the word that fits best. Choose your answers from the words below. You may use each word more than once.

Choices: to, toward, of, from

1. The graduate assistant is a subordinate **of** the professor.

2. The graduate assistant is in a subordinate position **to** the professor.

3. The party was an antidote **to** her depression.

4. We felt antipathy **toward** our enemy.

5. After his divorce, Ken had to reconcile himself **to** living alone.

6. Hearing of her engagement made his thoughts revert **to** the last time he had seen her.

7. The revelations **of** cheating on tests shocked the administration.

8. We extricated ourselves **from** the stuck elevator by climbing up to the next floor.

9. It is difficult to maintain an impartial attitude **toward** our own children.

10. We enjoyed hearing about the exploits **of** Dr. Livingstone.

■ *Writing with Your Words*

This exercise will give you practice in writing effective sentences that use the vocabulary words. Each sentence is started for you. Complete it with an interesting phrase that also indicates the meaning of the italicized word.

1. I would like to *subdue* _____

_____ .

2. In her *autobiography,* the famous star _____

_____ .

3. I hope I never have to *reconcile* myself to _____

_____ .

4. A person would be considered *eccentric* if _____

_____ .

5. I *invariably* have difficulty _____

_____ .

6. An *antidote* to envy is _____

_____ .

7. A truly *autonomous* person _____

_____ .

8. The world needs an *ingenious* solution to the problem of _____

_____ .

9. Winter seems *interminable* when _____

_____ .

10. The *exorbitant* price of the car _____

_____ .

Passage

Food of the People

It has fed our nation for more than sixty years, inspiring poetry and song. It has even been counted among the one hundred greatest inventions of the twentieth century. Yet it has come under attack for its nutritional value as well as its strange appearance. What is it? SPAM® luncheon meat, of course!

SPAM® luncheon meat, known originally as "Hormel Spiced Ham," was first produced in 1935. A few years later, **(1)** the Hormel company invented an **ingenious** process that allowed the food product to be preserved in a can, without refrigeration. But sales didn't really take off until the company changed the name. It ran a contest, choosing "Spam," a blend of the words "spiced" and "ham." The person who coined the name received $100. While perhaps this would be considered **exploitation** by today's standards, it was quite a bit of money at the time.

(2) The economic depression of the 1930s made the price of many fresh meats **exorbitant.** So with its new, appealing name, SPAM found its way into many U.S. homes. People might have preferred fresh food, but with many out of a job, **(3)** they had to **reconcile** themselves to eating protein that could be stored cheaply in cans. A can of SPAM was easy to get, store, and prepare.

World War II (1939–45) made SPAM luncheon meat a truly common food. With its new, square-cornered cans, designed to military needs, SPAM could easily be shipped to provide protein to soldiers. **(4)** Its high calorie count quickly **subdued** hunger. SPAM fed the armies of many nations. In his **autobiography,** *Khrushchev Remembers,* the former head of the Soviet Union credited SPAM with saving the Russian army from starvation. And, back in the United States, when other meats were rationed, SPAM was not.

SPAM luncheon meat continued to feed troops in other wars. **(5)** Jess Loya, a Vietnam veteran, remembers that SPAM was an **antidote**

SPAM® luncheon meat is a registered trademark of Hormel Foods Corporation.

to his homesickness. **(6)** Opening a can would **invariably** remind him of his childhood when, living with a single father, he ate it many times.

With its gelatin-like condition and odd, boxlike shape, SPAM has long been a source of conversational fun. Its pink color, similar to ham but more intense, seems to spark strong reactions. **(7)** SPAM has inspired **antipathy** as well as devotion. Advertisements have also added to SPAM's popularity. Radio featured "Spammy the Pig" and the musical "Hormel Girls," who toured the United States. In 1940, SPAM was quite possibly the subject of the world's first singing commercial. Sung to the tune of "My Bonny Lies Over the Ocean," it went "SPAM, SPAM, SPAM, SPAM, Hormel's new miracle meat in a can. Tastes fine, saves time. If you want something grand, ask for SPAM."

Although Hormel called it "the miracle meat in a can," others have referred to it as "the mystery meat." This is unfair, for, **(8)** as **impartial** observers have pointed out, the ingredients are listed on the can. (They are chopped pork shoulder with ham meat added, salt, water, sugar, and sodium nitrite.) In these more health-conscious times, SPAM's calorie count and high percentage of calories from fat have become a concern. In fact, Hormel now makes SPAM Lite, as well as several other varieties, including smoked SPAM.

SPAM is now manufactured in several countries. In fact, in Korea, SPAM is sold in stylish gift boxes. **(9)** It seems **incongruous** to see SPAM alongside expensive watches and perfume, but Koreans consider it a great treat. Within the United States, Hawaiians eat the most SPAM per capita, averaging four cans per person each year. SPAM can be prepared in many ways, including sliced, fried, wrapped in a tortilla, spread on a sandwich, wrapped in sushi, or mixed with wild rice. SPAM cooking contests are popular throughout the United States.

(10) It may come as a **revelation** that SPAM has some uses that have nothing to do with food. Joey Green has become famous for using it to polish furniture and bathroom fixtures. Reporter James Barron, however, noted that it left a greasy film. Although its merits as polish may be **equivocal,** others have found that SPAM can be used to spackle a wall, fill holes in a canoe, and soothe a black-and-blue eye. These seem like **eccentric,** but amusing, uses for a food. Would you want your furniture, wall, or canoe—not to mention your eye—to smell like meat?

SPAM has also been the subject of verse, including haiku, a form of seventeen-syllable poetry originally from Japan. One author writes:

Pretty pink Spam ham
Shining on the white platter.
Where did my fork go?

Sonnets and limericks have also been written to SPAM.

With all the fun and nutrition that SPAM has given us, it is good to know that the product is doing well. Hormel continues to be an **autonomous,** family-run company. SPAM's continuing popularity is shown by the fact that if all the cans ever sold were laid end to end, they would circle the earth at least twelve times!

■ *Exercise*

Each numbered sentence below corresponds to a sentence in the Passage. Fill in the letter of the choice that makes the sentence mean the same thing as its corresponding sentence in the Passage.

1. The Hormel company invented a(n) **c**_____ process.
   a. speedy   b. interesting   c. clever   d. independent

2. The economic depression of the 1930s made the price of many fresh meats **b**_____.
   a. unfair   b. high   c. low   d. different

3. They had to **a**_____ eating protein out of a can.
   a. accept   b. enjoy   c. mind   d. go back to

4. Its high calorie count **b**_____ hunger.
   a. increased   b. controlled   c. caused   d. killed

5. Jess Loya remembers that SPAM was a __d____ his homesickness.
   a. cause of   b. reaction to   c. reminder of   d. cure for

6. Opening a can would __d____ remind him of his childhood.
   a. never   b. sometimes   c. often   d. always

7. SPAM has inspired __b____ as well as devotion.
   a. love   b. hatred   c. anger   d. unhappiness

8. __d____ observers have pointed out that the ingredients are listed on each can.
   a. Intelligent   b. Strange   c. Bossy   d. Fair

9. It may seem __b____ to see SPAM alongside expensive watches and perfume.
   a. not acceptable   b. out of place   c. inventive   d. natural

10. It may come as a __c____ that SPAM has some uses that have nothing to do with food.
    a. joke   b. rumor   c. surprise   d. fact

■ Discussion Questions

1. Give two nonfood uses for SPAM.

2. Describe two things that appeal to you about SPAM and two things you find unappealing or bad.

3. Why do you think SPAM has become famous beyond its use as a food?

Spam has a new meaning related to computers. Sending out large numbers of advertisements, that were not asked for, by e-mail is called *spamming*. Laws are being considered to limit this annoying practice.

◀ **ENGLISH IDIOMS**

Beginnings, Ends, and Time

Since this chapter deals with prefixes, elements that start words, our idioms will deal with beginnings, ends, and time. To *start from scratch* means to start from the beginning. However, to *start up with someone* means to argue with that person.

To *wind up* something means to end it, as in "winding up my assignment." People *at the end of their rope* or *at the end of their tether* are desperate and do not know what to do.

If a woman *takes her time*, she does things slowly, at her own rate. If she *has time on her hands*, she has time to spare, or extra time. If she has *the time of her life*, she has a *good time*, or is enjoying herself very much.

When something is done that is long overdue, we say, "It's *high time*" for it to be done. When something is no longer in fashion or up-to-date, we call it *behind the times*.

Until the invention of quartz controls, most clocks and watches were driven by small wheels with notches, or *nicks*, in them. You may actually have some clocks with these ticking gears. The nicks catch on a wheel and move as frequently as every second. Therefore, to be *in the nick of time* means to be on time to the second, or nearly late. A person who catches a train *in the nick of time* almost misses it.

Quiz Again

Now that you have finished studying this chapter, here is the brief true-false quiz you took when you began. Take it again.

Two things that are **incongruous** are similar.	True	False
Eccentric behavior is odd.	True	False
When we **equivocate,** we state our opinion clearly.	True	False
Antipathy is hatred.	True	False

Answers are on page 406. Did your score improve?

CHAPTER 6

Word Elements: People and Names

Many English words come from people's names. Characters from classical myths, as well as actual people, have been a rich source of vocabulary. The first part of this chapter introduces four word roots that relate to people. The second part adds two prefixes taken from names of characters in Greek mythology and then introduces words that perpetuate the names of specific people.

Chapter Strategy: Word Elements About People

Chapter Words:

Part 1

anthrop	anthropological	nom	nominal
	misanthrope		pseudonym
	philanthropist		renowned
gen	congenital	viv	viable
	genesis		vital
	genocide		vivacious

Part 2

pan-	pandemonium	Name Words	boycott
	panorama		chauvinism
psych-	psyche		gargantuan
	psychosomatic		martial
			maverick
			odyssey
			quixotic
			spartan

Quiz Yourself

To check your present knowledge of some of the chapter words, identify these statements as true or false.

Vivacious means lacking energy.   True   False

You are born with a **congenital** condition.   True   False

A **maverick** follows rules.   True   False

A **psychosomatic** illness has a physical basis.   True   False

You will learn the answers as you study this chapter.

Did You Know?

Which Words Come from Names?

Many English words are taken from names in classical myths. The Greeks and Romans had well-developed and colorful mythologies, whose legends reflected the violence and passion of life in a time when humans were almost totally at the mercy of natural forces and disease.

According to mythology, Jupiter, king of the gods, ruled thunder—a fearful force to ancient people. His many exploits included dethroning his father and turning himself into a swan in order to seduce a young girl. He loved to play nasty jokes on others. The word *jovial*, meaning "merry," was taken from Jove, another name for Jupiter.

Mercury, often shown in paintings with wings on his feet, was the speedy messenger of the gods. The metal *mercury*, used in thermometers, is a quickly moving liquid at room temperature. A quick-tempered person is often called *mercurial*.

Venus, or Aphrodite, was the goddess of love. An *aphrodisiac* is a drug or food that is said to increase sexual desire.

Two English words derive from the Titans, giants who ruled the earth before Jupiter's thunderbolts conquered them. Something of enormous size and power is called *titanic*. Since one Titan, Atlas, was condemned to support the world on his shoulder, a book containing maps is now called an *atlas*.

Modern characters have also been the source of English words. In the 1920s, to amuse himself during lonely hours, struggling artist Walt

Disney drew a comic-strip mouse called Mortimer. The mouse, renamed Mickey, later became the hero of many cartoons. Something that is silly or easy might now be called *Mickey Mouse,* as in a "Mickey Mouse job."

Words are also based on the names of real people. The Earl of Sandwich (1718–1792) loved to gamble so much that he refused to leave the game, even to eat. Instead he had meat brought to him between two pieces of bread, thus creating the *sandwich. Braille,* the system of raised dots that allows blind people to read, was first published in 1829 by Louis Braille, who had lost his vision in childhood. U.S. Union Civil War general Ambrose Burnside, a fashion leader, allowed his hair to grow down the side of his face, inventing a style we still call—reversing Burnside's name—*sideburns.*

Many flower names honor botanists. *Zinnia* was named for Johann Zinn, *magnolia* for Pierre Magnol, and *dahlia* for Anders Dahl.

Some words come from the names of organizations. The coffee drink *cappuccino* comes from the Italian Capuchin order, a group of Roman Catholic monks. The idea for the *frisbee* came from the easy-to-catch pie tins manufactured by the Frisbie company in Bridgeport, Connecticut.

Places also have donated their names. The word *dollar* comes from *taler,* short for *Joachimstal,* the city in Bohemia where it was first used. The *tuxedo,* a type of men's formal wear, comes from Tuxedo Park in New York State. *Scotch* liquor comes from Scotland. *Peach* comes from the Latin word for Persia (now Iran), where this fruit originated.

Even imaginary places have lent their names to English. In about 1500, a Spanish novelist described a beautiful, imaginary island inhabited by strong women. When exploring the Americas, one Spaniard used the novelist's word to name a real place of great natural beauty, at first thought to be an island. The name, *California,* is still used today.

In this chapter, you will be learning several words derived from names and places. Perhaps one day a word will be coined from your name!

Can you match the given name to the person or place behind it?

1. McIntosh apple
2. Melba toast
3. Pulitzer Prize
4. cologne
5. Listerine
6. ritzy

a. the founder of the *St. Louis Post-Dispatch*
b. a farmer in Ontario, Canada
c. the physician who originated antiseptic surgery
d. the wife of a Roman emperor
e. a hotel founder who was the thirteenth child of a peasant couple
f. an Australian opera star on a diet

Answers are on page 406.

Learning Strategy

Word Elements About People

This first part of Chapter 6 discusses word roots and how they function in words. Four specific roots dealing with people are used as examples. The second part of the chapter continues with prefixes, presenting two prefixes taken from names.

Element	Meaning	Origin	Function	Chapter Words
				Part 1
anthrop	human	Greek	root	anthropological, misanthrope, philanthropist
gen	birth; type	Latin; Greek	root	congenital, genesis, genocide
nom, nym	name	Latin; Greek	root	nominal, pseudonym, renowned
vit, viv	life	Latin	root	viable, vital, vivacious
				Part 2
pan-	all	Greek	prefix	panorama, pandemonium
psych-	mind; soul	Greek	prefix	psyche, psychosomatic

A root is the word element that carries the central meaning. Although prefixes and suffixes may alter the meaning of a root, they never carry as much meaning as the root itself.

Remember that there are two kinds of roots—base words and combining roots. Base words can stand alone as English words. They may or may not have prefixes and suffixes attached to them. *Work* is an example of a base word.

Combining roots cannot stand alone as English words. They require a prefix, a suffix, or at least a change in spelling in order to form a word. Most of the roots you will study in this book are combining roots that come from ancient Greek and Latin. Although they were words in these ancient languages, they appear in modern English only as root word elements.

The root *anthrop* (human) is an example of a combining root. It can form a word when it is attached to a prefix (*misanthrope*) or a suffix (*anthropological*).

Nom or *nym*, meaning "name," is another example of a combining root. This root has more than one spelling because it comes from both Latin and Greek. It forms over thirty English words. Slight changes in spelling give us the words *name* and *noun;* adding a suffix gives us *nominate;* adding different prefixes gives us *antonym* and *synonym*.

Each of the words formed from the root *nom* or *nym* carries a meaning related to "name." Sometimes the meaning is directly related to "name"; at other times the word root gives a hint about a word's meaning rather than supplying a direct meaning. The word *name* has the same meaning as the root *nom* or *nym;* thus, the word and the root are directly related. Other words have an indirect relationship to *nom* and *nym:*

A *noun* is a word that **names** a person, place, idea, or thing.

To *nominate* is to **name** somebody to a position, or to **name** somebody as a candidate in an election.

A *synonym* is a word that means the same thing as another word; two synonyms **name** the same thing. (*Syn* means "same.")

An *antonym* is a word opposite in meaning to another word; two antonyms **name** opposite things. (As you learned in Chapter 5, *ant-* means "opposite.")

Word Roots

Part 1

The four roots presented in Part 1 of this chapter all deal with people and their lives.

anthrop (human)

The root *anthrop* comes from the Greek word for "human," *anthropos.* Perhaps you have taken a course in *anthropology,* the study of **human** life.

gen (birth; type)

Because it forms over fifty English words, *gen* is an extremely useful root to learn. *Gen* has two meanings: "birth" and "type." The ancients felt that these meanings were related because when someone was born, he or she was a certain "type" of person. *Gen* means "birth" in the word *gene,* which refers to the hereditary information in each cell of a living plant or animal. We are all **born** with our genes. Currently, an enormous *genome* research project is attempting to define the function of all human genes. Another word, *generation,* refers to people **born** during the same time period.

Gen means "type" in the word *gender,* which tells what **type** of person you are, male or female. Perhaps you buy *generic* foods at the grocery. These have no brand names and are of a general **type.** The use of context clues will help you to determine whether *gen* means "birth" or "type" when you see it in a word.

nom, nym (name)

As you read above, this root word comes from both Latin and Greek. *Nomen* is Latin for "name," and the word originally appeared in Greek as *onoma*.

vit, viv (life)

In Latin, *vita* means "life." *Vit* forms such words as *vitamin*, a chemical necessary for human **life.** Manufacturers have used this root to make brand names, such as the hair product Vitalis, which is supposed to add **life** to your hair. Victuals (pronounced and sometimes spelled informally as *vittles*) means "food." It comes from *vivere*, "to live," for food enables us to live.

Words to Learn

Part 1

anthrop-

1. **anthropological** (adjective) ăn'thrə-pə-lŏj'ĭ-kəl

   referring to the study of human beings

   > In landmark **anthropological** research, Margaret Mead studied the social structure of tribes on the island of Samoa.

   ▶ *Related Words*
   anthropologist (noun) Colin Turnbull, an *anthropologist*, has described the gentle Pygmy tribes of Africa and their great respect for the balance of nature.
   anthropology (noun) Judy MacDonald's specialty in *anthropology* is Vietnamese culture.

   The field of *anthropology* studies the physical and social characteristics of human beings. Physical *anthropology* gives insight into human origins. Through cultural studies, we see how fundamental human needs for food, reproduction, and companionship are met. *Anthropologists* sometimes research exotic cultures by living with the people and learning their languages. They can also study more familiar environments, such as shopping malls, hospitals, and factories.

   ---

2. **misanthrope** (noun) mĭs'ən-thrōp'

   From Greek: *misein* (to hate) + *anthrop* (human)

   a person who hates or distrusts other people

   > A failure in business and personal life, the **misanthrope** resented the happiness of others.

▶ *Related Words*

misanthropic (adjective) (mĭs′ən-thrŏp′ĭk) *Misanthropic* people can make cruel remarks to salespeople and waiters.

misanthropy (noun) (mĭs-ăn′thrə-pē) The boss showed his *misanthropy* by refusing to allow his workers any vacations or holidays.

Two famous literary characters exemplify *misanthropy.* Ebenezer Scrooge, created by Charles Dickens in the classic novel *A Christmas Carol*, mistreats his employee and wishes ill to everybody, especially at Christmastime. Scrooge has become famous for his classic expression "Bah, Humbug!" A more modern *misanthrope*, the Grinch, actually steals Christmas. The Grinch was created by the famous children's author Theodor Geisel, better known as Dr. Seuss.

---

3. **philanthropist** (noun)   fĭ-lăn′thrə-pĭst

From Greek: *philos* (loving) + *anthrop* (human)

one who wishes to help humanity; a person who makes large gifts to charity

Steelmaker Andrew Carnegie was a **philanthropist** who donated money to establish public libraries throughout the United States.

▶ *Related Words*

philanthropic (adjective) (fĭl′ən-thrŏp′ĭk) The *philanthropic* efforts of the American Jewish community helped to build the state of Israel.

philanthropy (noun) Mexican workers who make money in the United States often demonstrate *philanthropy* by donating money to improve their home towns.

gen

4. **congenital** (adjective)   kən-jĕn′ĭ-təl

From Latin: *com-* (together; with) + *gen* (birth) (If something is *congenital*, you are born with it.)

existing at birth

Spina bifida, a **congenital** condition, is failure of the spinal column to close correctly.

According to recent studies, fingerprint patterns can often reveal **congenital** health problems.

naturally being a certain way; habitual

The criminal was a **congenital** liar who could not tell the truth, no matter how much pressure was put on him.

Duncan Kennedy, three-time contestant in the Olympics and the American who won the most sledding awards in history, was then diagnosed with a *congenital* condition affecting the formation of his brain. He also fought shoulder and back problems. However, Kennedy's response was not to give up, but to switch sports! He turned to competing in the sport of snowboarding.

5. **genesis** (noun)   jĕn′ĭ-sĭs

From Greek: *gen* (birth) (*Genesis* meant "birth" or "origin" in ancient Greek.)

origin; beginning

The **genesis** of agriculture dates back more than ten thousand years.

Many scientists think that the **genesis** of the universe was an enormous explosion called the "big bang."

Genesis, the first book of the Bible, tells the story of a great flood that only Noah, his family, and two of each type of animal survived. Many other religions and cultures have tales of a large flood. In southern Mesopotamia (now largely Iraq), references to a flood are recorded on a stone tablet (dated 2100 B.C.E.) and in the Babylonian Epic of Gilgamesh (about 700 B.C.E.). Other references are found in India, Burma, Australia, and among Native American tribes. Was there ever a great flood? In 1929, Sir Leonard Woolley, after exploring lower Mesopotamia, concluded that a widespread area had been badly flooded in about 3000 B.C.E.

NOTE: Sega Genesis® is a computer system that starts, or originates, many popular video games.

6. **genocide** (noun)   jĕn′ə-sīd′

From Greek: *gen* (type) + Latin: *-cidium* (killing) (*Genos* meant "race" in ancient Greek, so *genocide* means "the killing of an entire race.")

the planned murder of an entire group

The **genocide** of Armenians during World War I resulted in over a million deaths.

▶ *Related Word*

genocidal (adjective)   In the early 1900s, Belgium's *genocidal* control of the Congo resulted in thousands of deaths.

The most horrible recent example of *genocide* occurred from 1939 to 1945, when the leader of Nazi Germany, Adolf Hitler, planned the destruction of all of Europe's Jews. This dreadful plan, often called the Holocaust, resulted in the deaths of over six million people. Another six million civilians were murdered in countries occupied by the Nazis because of their ethnic origins, beliefs, or resistance to Nazi oppression.

---

nom; nym

7. **nominal** (adjective)   nŏm′ə-nəl

From Latin: *nom* (name)

in name only

> Although Queen Elizabeth is the **nominal** ruler of England, the prime minister and Parliament actually hold most of the power.

a very small amount

> The accountant did the charity's financial work for the **nominal** sum of $20 per year.

8. **pseudonym** (noun)   sood′n-ĭm′

From Greek: *pseudes* (false) + *nym* (name)

assumed name; pen name

> James G. Janos, who competed in professional wrestling under the **pseudonym** Jesse "the Body" Ventura, won the governorship of Minnesota in 1998.

> Norma Jean Mortenson performed under the **pseudonym** of Marilyn Monroe.

> Stephen King has published successful novels using the **pseudonym** Richard Bachman.

NOTE: The word *pseudonym* often refers to authors or artists. In contrast, *alias,* which usually refers to names assumed by criminals, has a negative connotation.

James G. Janos competed under the pseudonym of Jesse "the Body" Ventura.

▶ *Common Phrase*
under the pseudonym of

Many celebrities have adopted *pseudonyms*. Can you match the following pseudonyms to the real names?

1. Martin Sheen   a. Terry Bollea

2. Hulk Hogan   b. Pal

3. Alice Cooper   c. Reginald Kenneth Dwight

4. Elton John   d. Ramon Girard Estevez

5. Ice T   e. Vince Furnier

6. Lassie   f. Tracy Marrow

Answers are on page 406.

9. **renowned** (adjective) rǐ-nound′

famous; well regarded

From Latin: *re-* (again) + *nom* (to name) (A person who is "named repeatedly" becomes famous.)

Renowned Spanish opera star Placido Domingo has raised money for many worthy causes.

Jamaica is **renowned** for its beautiful beaches and pleasant climate.

▶ *Related Word*
  renown (noun)   Jonas Salk won *renown* for developing a vaccine to prevent polio.

vit; viv

10. **viable** (adjective)   vī′ə-bəl

From Latin: *vit* (life), becoming French *vie* (life)

capable of living; capable of success; workable

  Mosquito eggs remain **viable** for four years, awaiting enough rain to hatch.

  Because of scandals in his past, the governor was not a **viable** candidate for president.

11. **vital** (adjective)   vīt′l

From Latin: *vit* (life)

referring to life

  The doctor measured her pulse, blood pressure, and other **vital** signs.

necessary; essential

  Food is **vital** to life.

  Computers are **vital** to today's libraries.

lively; full of life; busy

  Seattle's **vital** downtown area attracts many tourists.

▶ *Common Phrase*
  vital to

▶ *Related Word*
  vitality (noun)   (vī-tăl′ĭ-tē)   The teacher's *vitality* enabled him to work long hours in after-school programs. (*Vitality* means "life energy.")

12. **vivacious** (adjective)   vĭ-vā′shəs

From Latin: *viv* (to live) (*Vivax* meant "lively.")

lively; full of spirit

No picture could capture the **vivacious** spirit of the high school cheerleader.

The girl's **vivacious** temperament and sense of fun made her popular at school.

▶ *Related Word*
vivacity (noun) (vĭ-văs′ə-tē) Lisa Kudrow's *vivacity* adds to the appeal of her role as Phoebe in the hit TV series *Friends*.

Exercises

Part 1

■ *Definitions*

Complete each sentence in the left-hand column with a definition from the right-hand column. Use each choice only once.

1. A vivacious person is
   __h__ .

2. Genocide is __a__ .

3. Genesis is __e__ .

4. A congenital condition
   is __j__ .

5. A viable idea is __g__ .

6. A philanthropist is __b__ .

7. Something vital to a person
   is __k__ .

8. Anthropology is __l__ .

9. A pseudonym is __c__ .

10. A person in nominal control
    is __i__ .

a. the murder of an entire group

b. charitable

c. a false name

d. famous

e. a beginning

f. a person who distrusts others

g. workable

h. lively

i. not really in power

j. present at birth

k. necessary

l. the study of human beings

■ Meanings

Match each word element to its meaning. Use each choice only once.

1. vit, viv ___**a**___

2. nom, nym ___**b**___

3. gen ___**c**___

4. anthrop ___**d**___

a. life
b. name
c. birth; type
d. human

■ Words in Context

Complete each sentence with the word that fits best. Use each choice only once.

a. anthropological
b. misanthrope
c. philanthropist
d. congenital

e. genesis
f. genocide
g. nominal
h. pseudonym

i. renowned
j. viable
k. vital
l. vivacious

1. Endurance is ___**k, vital**___ to a champion swimmer.

2. The small chick was not ___**j, viable**___ , so it soon died.

3. The ___**e, genesis**___ of our current writing system dates back more than 3,500 years to the Sumerians.

4. Some people are born with hemophilia, a(n) ___**d, congenital**___ condition that slows the ability of their blood to clot.

5. The ___**i, renowned**___ scientist Marie Curie gained fame for experiments with uranium.

6. The founder of the manufacturing company had become only its ___**g, nominal**___ head, since his daughter, the vice-president, now made all the decisions.

7. Singer and actor Cherlyn Sarkisian La Pierre performs under the ___**h, pseudonym**___ of Cher.

8. The ___**c, philanthropist**___ donated money to build a new student center.

9. In the horror movie *Plan Nine from Outer Space,* evil creatures from another planet plotted the __**f, genocide**__ of the entire human race.

10. Only a(n) __**b, misanthrope**__ would turn away from this scene of human happiness.

■ *Using Related Words*

Complete each sentence by using a word from the group of related words above it. You may need to capitalize a word when you write it in a sentence. Use each choice only once.

THE ANCIENT GREEKS

1. vivacious, vivacity

   In one of Aesop's fables, as a __**vivacious**__ girl walked to town carrying a jug of milk on her head, she thought of how the milk would make cream to buy eggs. The eggs would make chickens, and she could sell the chickens for a gown, which would attract a rich husband. As she fantasized, her __**vivacity**__ overcame her. She tossed her head and spilled the milk. From this story comes the proverb "Don't count your chickens before they're hatched."

2. misanthrope, misanthropic

   In the ancient Greek classic the *Odyssey,* hero Odysseus has to choose between two __**misanthropic**__ monsters, Scylla, a six-headed horror that eats people for lunch, and Charybdis, a whirlpool that sucks in ships. Deciding that the less dangerous __**misanthrope**__ is Scylla, he loses only six men, rather than his entire crew. Today, to have two bad choices is referred to as being "between Scylla and Charybdis."

3. vital, vitality

   In Greek mythology, the hero Achilles was __**vital**__ to the success of the Greeks over Troy. At his birth, Achilles' goddess mother wanted to make her son immortal, so she dipped him in the River Styx to preserve his **vitality**_____ . However, the heel she held him by was not touched by the protective water. As battle raged in Troy, an arrow struck Achilles in that heel, killing him. A point of weakness is now called an "Achilles heel."

4. renown, renowned

   Odysseus, a hero of great **renown**_____ , went to fight in the Trojan War. He entrusted the education of his son to the

   renowned_____ tutor Mentor. In today's sports and business, a coach or adviser is often called a "mentor."

5. anthropological, anthropologist

   Originally staged by the ancient Greeks, the Olympic Games took place from 776 B.C.E. to 394 B.C.E. In the 1800s, Frenchman Pierre de Coubertin spent his life reviving them. The modern Olympics, begun in 1896, are now a tradition. John MacAloon, an

   anthropologist_____ at the University of Chicago, studies the meaning of the games. He concludes that, from an

   anthropological_____ point of view, they bring a sense of national identity and allow people throughout the world to share a common event.

■ *True or False?*

Each of the following statements uses at least one word from this section. Read each statement and then indicate whether you think it is probably true or probably false.

__F__   1. A plan would be viable without the thing that is vital to its success.

__F__   2. A nominal sum is large.

__T__   3. A congenital problem is present at the genesis of life.

__F__   4. Anthropologists mainly study animals.

__T__   5. A vivacious person is usually energetic.

__T__   6. When Amandine-Aurore-Lucile Dudevant published as George Sand, she was using a pseudonym.

F

    7. When other people pay someone money, that person becomes a philanthropist.

T

    8. Genocide is evil.

T

    9. A misanthrope hates humanity.

F

    10. A renowned person is not well known.

Prefixes and Name Words

Part 2

Part 2 of this chapter deals with words taken from names. The two prefixes presented also occur as names in Greek mythology. Four words using these prefixes and eight words taken directly from names are introduced.

pan- (all)

The prefix *pan-* is the Greek word for "all." It appears in two names in Greek mythology. Pan was the god of woods, fields, and shepherds. He had the lower body of a goat and the upper body of a man. He got his name "because he delighted **all**," wrote Homer. Pandora (*pan-*, all, + *dora*, gifts) was the first woman. The gods sent her to Earth and gave her a box that she was told not to open. When curiosity got the better of her, she disobeyed, and out flew **all** the world's troubles. Only Hope remained shut up in the box. (Like Eve in the Bible, Pandora was a woman blamed for causing all the world's problems.) The prefix *pan-* is used in such words as *pan-American,* which refers to **all** of America: North, South, and Central.

psych-; psycho- (mind; soul)

The Greek word *psyche* originally meant "breath" and refers to the soul or the spirit of a person. This is personified in Greek mythology as Psyche, a beautiful mortal, who was loved by Eros (or Cupid), the god of love. He visited her every night but told her never to look at him. One night, overcome by curiosity, Psyche held a lamp up to Eros as he slept. A drop of oil dripped on his shoulder, waking him, and he fled. Psyche searched frantically for Eros and performed many difficult tasks to win the favor of the gods. As a reward, they made her immortal and allowed her to marry Eros. In this story, Psyche, with her beauty and dedication, symbolizes the soul. When she is made immortal, Psyche shows how the human soul finally goes to heaven. In modern words, *psych-* usually means "mind" rather than "soul." *Psychobiology* is the study of the biology of the **mind.** In some words, *psych* functions as a root. Perhaps you have taken a class in *psychology,* the study of the **mind.**

Words to Learn

Part 2

pan-

13. **pandemonium** (noun)   păn′də-mō′nē-əm

From Greek: *pan-* (all) + *daimōn* (demon)

chaos, wild disorder, and noise

> **Pandemonium** broke out when people realized they were trapped inside the burning building.

> In John Milton's poem *Paradise Lost,* published in 1667, *Pandaemonium* was the principal city of Hell, where "all the demons" lived.

---

14. **panorama** (noun)   păn′ə-răm′-ə

From Greek: *pan-* (all) + *horan* (to see)

a clear view over a wide area

> The view from a hilltop in Carmel, California, was a breathtaking **panorama** of the Pacific Ocean.

a wide-ranging survey

> The book *Europe in the Middle Ages* offered a **panorama** of its subject.

▶ *Related Word*
  panoramic (adjective)   From the top of the ski slope, we had a *panoramic* view of the beautiful Colorado mountains.

NOTE: Panorama can refer either to a physical view of something or a "view" in one's mind, as in a wide-ranging presentation of a subject.

psych-

15. **psyche** (noun)   sī′kē

    From Greek: *psych-* (soul)

    mental state; soul

    > Mozart's beautiful music gives no clue to his troubled **psyche.**

    > Psychologists believe that the human **psyche** is governed by basic needs for food and love.

    NOTE: Psyche usually refers to the part of the mind that is not rational and deals with feelings such as self-esteem and happiness.

16. **psychosomatic** (adjective)   sī′kō-sō-măt′ĭk

    From Greek: *psych-* (mind; soul) + *soma* (body)

    referring to physical disorders that are caused by the mind

    > Pet ownership can reduce **psychosomatic** symptoms caused by stress, such as high blood pressure.

Name Words

17. **boycott** (verb, noun)   boi′kŏt′

    to refuse to use or buy something as an act of protest (verb)

    > The professional golf tournament decided to **boycott** country clubs that did not admit minorities.

    the act of boycotting (noun)

    > A **boycott** of grapes helped migrant workers to unionize.

    The Irish potato famine of the mid 1800s had made farmers so poor that a law was passed in 1881 to reduce rents. Captain Charles C. Boycott, a cruel English land agent, angered the Irish people by insisting on the old payments, thus forcing many farmers out of business. In response, the Irish Land League *boycotted* him by refusing to deal with him in any way.

    ---

18. **chauvinism** (noun)   shō′və-nĭz′əm

    prejudiced devotion to a group or country

    > Jim's **chauvinism** was evident from the dozens of "Buy American" bumper stickers on his Chevy pickup.

Men of the primitive Yanomamo tribe are so **chauvinistic** that they feel women are too clumsy to make pottery.

▶ *Related Words*
chauvinist (noun, person)   Slam poets frequently attack male *chauvinists*.

chauvinistic (adjective)   Many European settlers were so *chauvinistic* toward Native Americans that they saw nothing wrong with forcing the Indians onto reservations.

NOTE: The commonly used term *male chauvinism* refers to the view that men are superior to women, and a *male chauvinist* shows by his words and behavior that he shares this view.

Nicholas Chauvin was a legendary lieutenant in the French army who was extremely devoted to his general, Napoleon Bonaparte. Even after Napoleon's defeat, Chauvin continued in his blind loyalty. Such excessive devotion is now called *chauvinism*.

---

19. **gargantuan** (adjective)   gär-găn′choo-ən

huge; immense

Steve's **gargantuan** breakfast consisted of a three-pound steak and a dozen eggs.

The fossil skeleton of "Sue," a *Tyrannosaurus rex,* is a **gargantuan** forty feet long.

Poverty is a **gargantuan** problem in Third World countries.

Gargantua appears in *Gargantua and Pantagruel,* a series of stories by the French author François Rabelais, published between 1532 and 1562. Gargantua was an enormous giant with an appetite to match. At one point, he ate five people in a salad! He arranged his hair with a comb nine hundred feet long. Right after his birth, he cried out, "Drink, drink!" The book may be a satire—a work that makes fun—of Francis I, the French king. Rabelais led a colorful life, which is reflected in the vitality of his book's hero.

---

20. **martial** (adjective)   mär′shəl

referring to war or soldiers

Dressed in armor and carrying a sword, the knight had a splendid **martial** appearance.

▶ *Common Phrase*

martial law In 1981, when Poland declared *martial law,* U.S. President Ronald Reagan halted trading with the country. (Martial law is rule by military authorities imposed on a civilian population.)

martial arts *Martial arts* will be featured as Olympic sports for the first time in 2004. (Martial arts are such sports as karate and tae kwon do, which teach one how to defend oneself.)

Mars was the Roman god of war, after whom the month of March is named. His name is also honored as the name of a planet, Mars, which appears to be faintly red, suggesting the color of blood. Except for Earth, each of the planets in our solar system is named for a Greek or Roman god. Closest to the sun is *Mercury,* the quickly rotating planet named for the messenger god. *Venus,* named for the god of love, is followed by *Earth* and *Mars. Jupiter* is named for the king of the gods. *Saturn* is Jupiter's father, and *Uranus* is his grandfather. *Neptune* is ruler of the sea. Finally, *Pluto,* the planet farthest from the sun, honors the gloomy god of the underworld, the region of the dead.

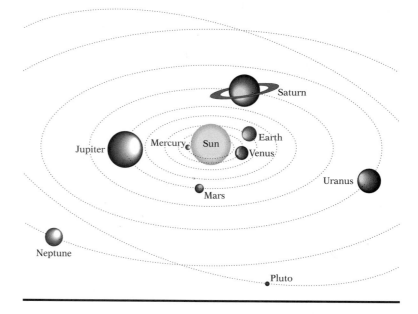

---

21. **maverick** (noun)   măv′ər-ĭk

an independent-minded person who does not conform or adhere to rules

Ross Perot is a **maverick** who opposed both Democrats and Republicans in the 1992 U.S. presidential election.

In the 1800s, cattlemen began branding their calves to indicate ownership. Samuel Maverick, a Texan rancher of independent spirit, refused to follow this custom. This annoyed the other ranchers, who called all unbranded cattle *mavericks.* Maverick led a colorful life, fighting duels, spending time in prison, and serving in the Texas legislature.

---

22. **odyssey** (noun)   ŏd′ĭ-sē

a long and adventurous journey

> People have made **odysseys** to the United States in overcrowded, dangerous boats.

> During his spiritual **odyssey** to acceptance of the Nation of Islam, Malcolm Little changed his name to Malcolm X.

The *Odyssey,* a classic ancient Greek poem, details the journey of Odysseus (also known as Ulysses) home from the Trojan wars. His adventures include a shipwreck, a visit to the underworld, the irresistible songs of the dangerous Sirens, and a choice between meeting one of two monsters, Scylla and Charybdis (mentioned earlier in this chapter). Since then, an intense physical or spiritual journey has been called an *odyssey* in honor of this epic poem by Homer.

---

23. **quixotic** (adjective)   kwĭk-sŏt′ĭk

noble, but not practical; having unreachable ideals; idealistic

> Scott spent three years in a **quixotic** effort to block the construction of a high-rise in a historic neighborhood.

Miguel de Cervantes published his classic novel *Don Quixote* in 1605. In the book, an old man, Don Quixote, decides to become a wandering knight and does noble but strange deeds that no one quite understands. For example, he duels with a windmill that he thinks is a giant. He mistakes an inn for a castle and a peasant girl for a noble lady. His squire (helper), Sancho Panza, sees how ridiculous all of this is, but remains loyal to his master.

Although *Don Quixote* was originally written in Spanish, many of its famous phrases are used in modern-day English. These include "in a pickle," "too much of a good thing," "a wink of sleep," "a stone's throw," "smell a rat," "honesty is the best policy," "turn over a new leaf," and "faint heart never won fair lady."

Don Quixote traveled with his squire, Sancho Panza.

24. **spartan** (adjective)   spär′tn

lacking in comfort; requiring self-discipline

His **spartan** routine included walking ten miles each day.

The professional football players were annoyed when they had to stay at a **spartan** college dorm rather than at a luxurious hotel.

The ancient Greek city of Sparta was known for its devotion to athletics and fighting, just as Athens was known for its intellectual life. Spartans valued physical stamina, rough living, and bravery. Sparta was known for its warriors. So *spartan* was their training process that they were taken away from their mothers when they were seven and put in training camps.

Exercises

Part 2

■ Definitions

Complete each sentence in the left-hand column by choosing a word or phrase from the right-hand column. Use each choice only once.

1. To boycott is ___a___ .

2. A quixotic person is ___h___ .

3. A maverick is ___f___ .

4. An odyssey is ___j___ .

5. Psychosomatic illness has ___b___ .

6. The psyche is ___l___ .

7. Pandemonium is ___d___ .

8. Chauvinism is ___c___ .

9. A gargantuan man is ___k___ .

10. A spartan life is ___e___ .

a. not to buy or use

b. a mental cause

c. prejudiced devotion

d. confusion

e. without comforts

f. an independently minded person

g. warlike

h. idealistic

i. a wide view

j. a journey

k. huge

l. the mind or soul

■ Meanings

Match each word element to its meaning. Use each choice only once.

1. pan- ___b___

2. psych- ___a___

a. mind; soul

b. all

■ Words in Context

Complete each sentence with the word that fits best. Use each choice only once. You may need to capitalize words.

a. panorama   e. boycott   i. maverick
b. pandemonium   f. chauvinism   j. odyssey
c. psyche   g. gargantuan   k. quixotic
d. psychosomatic   h. martial   l. spartan

1. For over a year, **k, quixotic** _____ Julia Hill has lived in a six-hundred-year-old redwood tree to prevent it from being cut down.

2. From the window of the fortieth floor, we could see a beautiful **a, panorama** _____ of the New York skyline.

3. Lan's **d, psychosomatic** _____ headaches disappeared when she got a good job.

4. **b, Pandemonium** _____ broke out as the crowd realized someone was firing a gun.

5. The **g, gargantuan** _____ tree was over three hundred feet tall.

6. The parade of **h, martial** _____ strength featured soldiers and military equipment.

7. In Bev's **j, odyssey** _____ across Russia, she traveled through eleven time zones.

8. People decided to **e, boycott** _____ the store until it lowered its high and unfair prices.

9. The political **i, maverick** _____ refused to follow the policies of his party.

10. Mike had trouble adjusting to the **l, spartan** _____ living conditions in army boot camp.

■ Using Related Words

Complete each sentence by using a word or phrase from the group of related words or phrases above it. You may need to capitalize a word when you write it in a sentence. Use each choice only once.

1. panorama, panoramic

Pictures of Mars taken from the *Pathfinder* in 1998 are available in *Mars: Uncovering the Secrets of the Red Planet*. The marvelous photos offer a color **panorama** of the planet. The book comes with glasses that, when worn, show a 180-degree **panoramic** view in three dimensions.

2. psyche, psychosomatic, psychosomatically

How much does the **psyche** govern the body? A study done at Ohio State University found that healing may be aff-ected by **psychosomatic** factors. Wounds inside the mouth healed more slowly during exam time, indicating that the body is **psychosomatically** affected by stress.

3. chauvinism, chauvinists, chauvinistic

During World War II, when British men went to fight, women called "land girls" were asked to work on farms. Some **chauvinists** doubted that the women would be able to save the crops. But despite outdated equipment and poor conditions, the women succeeded, proving that male **chauvinism** was uncalled for. Season after season, they proved their **chauvinistic** peers to be wrong.

4. martial, martial law

Ferdinand Marcos declared **martial law** in the Philippines in 1962. In 1972, he used **martial** force to arrest people he suspected of trying to overthrow his government. After a fraudulent presidential election in 1986, he was forced to leave the country.

■ *Reading the Headlines*

This exercise presents five headlines that might appear in newspapers. Read each headline and then answer the questions that follow. (Remember that small words, such as *is*, *are*, *a*, and *the*, are often left out of newspaper headlines.)

MARTIAL FORCE USED BY GOVERNMENT AGAINST THOSE IN BITTER BUS BOYCOTT

1. Is the government using peaceful methods? __no__

2. Did people ride the buses? __no__

SPARTAN LIVING CONDITIONS FOUND TO CURE PSYCHOSOMATIC ILLNESSES

3. Are the living conditions luxurious? __no__

4. Are the illnesses based in the mind? __yes__

STUDY FINDS CHAUVINISM CAN DAMAGE PSYCHE

5. Can prejudiced devotion cause the damage? __yes__

6. Is the body damaged? __no__

ANNOUNCEMENT OF GARGANTUAN LOSS IN SALES CAUSES PANDEMONIUM AT COMPANY MEETING

7. Was the loss large? __yes__

8. Did the meeting stay calm? __no__

QUIXOTIC MAVERICK MAKES ODYSSEY TO DISCOVER MEANING OF LIFE

9. Is the person both idealistic and willing to follow orders?

   __no__

10. Did the person go on a short journey? __no__

Chapter Exercises

■ *Practicing Strategies: New Words
   from Word Elements*

See how your knowledge of roots and prefixes can help you understand new words. Complete each sentence with the word that seems to fit best. Use each choice only once. You may need to capitalize some words.

a. anthropoids
b. genealogy
c. generation
d. homogenize

e. nomenclature
f. pan-African
g. pandemic
h. psychopath

i. psychotherapy
j. rename
k. revive
l. vivarium

1. __**i, Psychotherapy**__ is a treatment for problems of the mind.

2. Apes that resemble human beings are called __**a, anthropoids**__ .

3. The word __**f, pan-African**__ refers to all of Africa.

4. When referring to plants and animals, scholars often use scientific __**e, nomenclature**__ .

5. A worldwide epidemic of a disease is __**g, pandemic**__ .

6. Since *-logy* means "study of," __**b, genealogy**__ is the study of your heredity, or the family into which you were born.

7. The root *path* can mean "sick," so a person with a sick mind is a(n) __**h, psychopath**__ .

8. The prefix *homo-* means "same," so to __**d, homogenize**__ milk is to make it the same type, or mixture, throughout.

9. In a(n) __**l, vivarium**__ , plants and animals can live in natural conditions.

10. When someone faints and then awakens, he or she is said to __**k, revive**__ , or "live again."

■ Practicing Strategies: Combining Context Clues and Word Elements

Combining the strategies of context clues and word elements is a good way to figure out unknown words. In the following sentences, each italicized word contains a word element that you have studied in this chapter. Using the meaning of the word element and the context of the sentence, make an intelligent guess about the meaning of the italicized word. Your instructor may ask you to check the meaning in your dictionary after you have finished.

1. Defenders of animal rights oppose the *vivisection* of animals to study their organs.

   Vivisection means **taking animals apart while they are still living** .

2. The television program *generated* much discussion.

   Generated means **started** .

3. It is a *misnomer* to call only citizens of the United States "Americans," for America consists of North, Central, and South America.

   Misnomer means **wrong term** .

4. It is impossible to find a *panacea* for all the problems of humanity.

   Panacea means **cure; complete cure** .

5. Conditions of poverty can *engender* criminal behavior.

   Engender means **start; give birth to** .

■ *Companion Words*

Complete each sentence with the word that fits best. Choose your answers from the words below. You may use each word more than once.

Choices: of, for, to, under

1. After Indonesia was placed **under** martial law, its president, Suharto, resigned.

2. From the mountaintop, we saw a breathtaking panorama **of** the Hong Kong skyline.

3. Vitamins are vital **to or for** health.

4. Mother Teresa was renowned **for** her work with the poor.

5. The boycott **of** tuna greatly reduced sales and led fishing boats to use dolphin-safe nets.

6. The book *Money Management* was written **under** the pseudonym of Adam Smith.

7. The genesis **of** the steam engine dates back to the Greeks.

■ *Writing with Your Words*

This exercise will give you practice in writing effective sentences that use the vocabulary words. Each sentence is started for you. Complete it with an interesting phrase that also indicates the meaning of the italicized word.

1. The *maverick* _____

   _____ .

2. A *gargantuan* workload might include _____

   _____ .

3. It is *vital* that _____

   _____ .

4. A *vivacious* teenager _____

   _____ .

5. Your plan is not *viable* because _____

   _____ .

6. When Betty saw the *spartan* living conditions, _____

   _____ .

7. *Pandemonium* broke out when _____

   _____ .

8. The *nominal* ruler _____

   _____ .

9. A *pseudonym* I would like to use _____

   _____ .

10. We *boycotted* the store because _____

   _____ .

Passage

The Greek Myth of Winter

In modern times, science has explained the causes of storms, floods, earth-quakes, and disease, but ancient people were puzzled and awed by these mysterious events. Perhaps to gain a sense of control, they created tales about the world around them.

(1) Since humans are **chauvinistic,** it was natural for the ancients to assume that the forces driving nature were just like themselves. Stories were told of gods who ate, loved, and hated just as we do, but on a larger scale. Because these gods had **gargantuan** powers, their smallest wish could mean disaster or good fortune for all the world. **(2)** A **misanthropic** god might send deadly storms; a **philanthropic** one might share the secrets of fire and food.

(3) One ancient Greek tale of humanlike gods deals with the **genesis** of winter. According to the ancient Greeks, the world was once a warm, green paradise where the goddess Demeter provided summer throughout the year. But one day, **(4)** Persephone, Demeter's beautiful and **vivacious** daughter, wandered away from her friends to explore a flowered field. Unfortunately, Hades, the god of the underworld, was visiting the world and **(5)** enjoying a **panoramic** view of the very same place. With one look at Persephone, Hades fell in love. Unable to control himself, he carried her off to the underworld and made her his bride.

(6) Pandemonium broke out when word of Hades' crime reached the other gods. Demeter frantically tried to get her daughter back, begging Zeus, king of the gods, to order her return. **(7)** But although Zeus was **renowned** for his power, **(8)** Hades, a **maverick** among the gods, refused to return Persephone.

In her desperation, Demeter forgot to provide the world with the warmth and sunshine **vital** to growing crops, and the earth plunged into winter. Plants began to die one by one, and when no crops were left, humans faced starvation. Through her grief, Demeter was causing the death of the human race. Zeus appealed to Hades, who finally agreed to let Persephone return home, as long as she had not eaten anything.

What had Persephone been doing while Demeter was trying to release her? Sitting unhappily in the underworld, she had led a **spartan** existence, refusing all the luxuries that Hades offered. She had eaten no food—except for seven pomegranate seeds. Alas! **(9)** Persephone had eaten only a **nominal** amount, but she had eaten. Hades did not have to let her go.

(10) Zeus and Demeter quickly thought of a **viable** arrangement. For nine months of the year, Persephone would live with her mother, and for three months she would live with Hades. Just as Persephone's life was divided, Demeter decreed that for nine months the earth would have warm weather, and for three months it would have winter.

And that is how, according to the ancient Greeks, winter began.

■ *Exercise*

Each numbered sentence below corresponds to a sentence in the Passage. Fill in the letter of the choice that makes the sentence mean the same thing as its corresponding sentence in the Passage.

1. Because humans are ___**a**___, they assumed the forces controlling nature were like themselves.
   a. prejudiced toward themselves   b. naturally violent
   c. not able to control themselves   d. searching for familiar answers

2. A ___**d**___ god might send deadly storms.
   a. human-loving   b. human-fearing   c. lonely   d. human-hating

3. One ancient Greek tale deals with the ___**c**___ of winter.
   a. hunger   b. coldness   c. beginning   d. problems

4. Persephone was Demeter's beautiful and ___**d**___ daughter.
   a. shy   b. quiet   c. rebellious   d. lively

5. Hades was enjoying a ___**b**___ view of the same place.
   a. beautiful   b. wide, clear   c. breathtaking   d. lonely

6. ___**c**___ broke out when word of Hades' crime reached the other gods.
   a. Punishment   b. Revenge   c. Disorder   d. Sadness

7. Zeus was ___**c**___ for his power.
   a. feared   b. envied   c. famous   d. rewarded

8. Hades was a(n) ___**a**___ god who resisted all control.
   a. independent   b. strong   c. clever   d. romantic

9. Persephone had eaten a ___**b**___ amount.
   a. large   b. small   c. sufficient   d. healthy

10. Zeus and Demeter thought of a ___**b**___ arrangement.
    a. silly   b. workable   c. tricky   d. brilliant

■ *Discussion Questions*

1. What reasons explain why the Greeks thought of their gods as being like humans, but on a larger scale?

2. Was Zeus's power limited? Explain your answer.

3. Describe a human situation that would bring forth the same types of emotions that Demeter felt.

> ◀ **ENGLISH IDIOMS**
>
> ### Body Words
>
> Since this chapter concerns people and their names, the idioms presented here all deal with the human body. Many such idioms use the concept of cold. For example, to *give people the cold shoulder* means to ignore them. When people get *cold feet*, they become nervous, and just before they plan to do something, they may refuse to do it, or *back out*. When a man becomes nervous, something *freezes his blood, makes his blood run cold*, or *makes his hair stand on end*. When people are made to wait, they *cool their heels*.
>
> People who put forth an opinion that is completely wrong, or not supported by evidence, *don't have a leg to stand on*. If you listen to another person, you *lend an ear*. If, on the other hand, you do not listen carefully, information goes *in one ear and out the other*.
>
> To *raise eyebrows* is to shock people. When a person is embarrassed or shamed by a failure, that person *loses face*.
>
> Long ago in China, the emperor was considered a god. To mention his body or health in any way was forbidden, since it implied that he was human. People who made this mistake had their feet pulled upward and forced into their mouths, remaining in this position for several hours. Today, to *put your foot in your mouth* means to say something that should not be said.

Quiz Again

Now that you have finished studying this chapter, here is the brief true-false quiz you took when you began. Take it again.

Vivacious means lacking energy.	True	False
You are born with a **congenital** condition.	True	False
A **maverick** follows rules.	True	False
A **psychosomatic** illness has a physical basis.	True	False

Answers are on page 406. Did your score improve?

CHAPTER

7

Word Elements: Movement

Many word elements from the classical languages of Greek and Latin originally referred to physical movement. Each of the six roots and two prefixes in this chapter describes an action, such as pulling or turning. These word elements help to form many widely used English words.

Chapter Strategy: Word Elements: Movement

Chapter Words:

Part 1

duc, duct	abduction	*stans, stat*	stature
	conducive		status quo
	deduction		staunch
ject	dejected	*tain, ten*	abstain
	eject		tenable
	jettison		tenacious

Part 2

tract	distraught	*circum-*	circumscribe
	extract		circumspect
	retract		circumvent
vers, vert	adversary	*trans-*	transcend
	inadvertently		transformation
	perverse		transitory

Copyright © Houghton Mifflin Company. All rights reserved.

Quiz Yourself

To check your knowledge of some chapter words before you begin to study, identify these statements as true or false.

To **jettison** is to throw out.	True	False
A **staunch** supporter would probably betray you.	True	False
Things change quickly in the **status quo.**	True	False
A **perverse** person is cooperative.	True	False

You will learn the answers as you study this chapter.

Did You Know?

How Did Inventions Get Their Names?

What would life be like if we could not switch on a light bulb, refrigerate our leftovers, and turn a faucet handle for water? The last three hundred years have seen tremendous numbers of inventions and discoveries. If we were put back on earth in 1700, we would have to live without electricity, refrigeration, and running water. In fact, we would hardly recognize the way of life. Travel, food, and medicine would be vastly different from what we experience today.

Three hundred years ago, people traveled on foot or used horses, on unpaved roads with deep ruts. A twenty-mile trip from an English country village to London took all day. Today the same trip takes less than half an hour by automobile or subway.

Because there were no stoves or refrigerators, people cooked over open fires and just hoped that the temperature would be suitable. Meat was either eaten immediately, salted, or preserved as sausage. Pepper and other spices were very valuable, for they helped keep meat from spoiling quickly.

Medical science was primitive. In fact, fewer than half of all children survived to adulthood. Because germs had not yet been discovered, operations were done under unclean conditions. The most common medical treatment was to apply leeches that sucked the "bad blood" from the sick. Medical historians now think that such "bleeding" caused George Washington's death.

In today's world, automobiles, trains, and airplanes provide rapid transportation. We use freezers and refrigerators to preserve our food and temperature-regulated stoves to cook it with precision. Many diseases have been controlled, and the average life expectancy has almost doubled.

The past one hundred years have been especially productive times for inventors. Such widely used devices as the computer, television (as well as the TV dinner and TV remote), vacuum cleaner, automatic washer, cell phone, zipper, paper clip, and Post-it® note were all invented after 1900.

Each invention brought a new word into English. Often, scientists and inventors took names from ancient Greek and Latin word elements. This tradition started in 1611 when a Greek poet suggested a name for Galileo's new invention, using two Greek word elements, *tele-* (far) and *-scope* (look). The invention is called the *telescope*.

Modern inventors continue to create names from ancient Greek and Latin word elements. This makes a knowledge of classical word elements more useful than ever.

The following inventions and discoveries have made your life easier. Each contains at least one classical prefix, root, or suffix. You will be studying some of these elements in this book.

Invention	*Classical Word Elements*	*Approximate Date of Invention*
microscope	*micro-* (small) + *-scope* (look)	1665
antiseptic	*anti-* (against) + *sepsis* (rotten)	1745
photography	*photo-* (light) + *-graph* (written)	1780
anesthetic	*an-* (without) + *aisthēsis* (feeling)	1850
bicycle	*bi-* (two) + *kuklos* (wheel)	1862
phonograph	*phono-* (sound) + *-graph* (written)	1875
telephone	*tele-* (far) + *-phone* (sound)	1880
automobile	*auto-* (self) + *movēre* (to move)	1885
refrigerator	*re-* (again) + *frigus* (cold)	1890
television	*tele-* (far) + *visus* (sight)	1925
computer	*com-* (together) + *-putāre* (to reckon)	1940
microwave	*micro-* (small) + *wave*	1963

Learning Strategy

Word Elements: Movement

Each of the word elements in this chapter describes a type of movement, such as leading *(duct)*, pulling *(tract)*, or turning *(vert)*. Many words use classical word elements that refer to movement. Every one of these elements forms at least fifty English words, so learning them will help you multiply your vocabulary knowledge.

Element	Meaning	Origin	Function	Chapter Words
				Part 1
duc, duct	lead	Latin	root	abduction, conducive, deduction
ject	throw	Latin	root	dejected, eject, jettison
stans, stat	standing; placed	Latin; Greek	root	stature, status quo, staunch
tain, ten	hold	Latin	root	abstain, tenable, tenacious
				Part 2
tract	pull	Latin	root	distraught, extract, retract
vers, vert	turn	Latin	root	adversary, inadvertently, perverse
circum-	around	Latin	prefix	circumscribe, circumspect, circumvent
trans-	across	Latin	prefix	transcend, transformation, transitory

Words formed from word elements describing movement often have interesting histories. Many started out describing physical movement but over the years gained abstract, nonphysical meanings. Although these words may no longer describe the movement itself, the elements in them will still give you hints about their meanings.

The word element *ject* (throw) illustrates how word elements and meanings relate. Two *ject* words in this chapter consist of a prefix and a root. If you think about the meanings of the word elements below, you will be able to picture each word's meaning in your mind.

The word elements *de-* (down) and *ject* (throw) make *deject,* or "throw down." The word *dejected* actually means depressed, or how we feel when our mood is "thrown down."

The word elements *e-* (out of) and *ject* (throw) make *eject,* or "throw out of." When a candy bar is *ejected* from a vending machine, it is "thrown out."

Circumstance is another word in which the elements give us a mental picture. It combines two word elements presented in this chapter, the prefix *circum-* and the root *stans. Circumstances* are things that are "standing" *(stans)* "around" *(circum-)* an event; in other words, they surround it. Circumstances that might "stand around" and keep you from studying are noise in the library or a friend who wants to talk!

Word Roots

Part 1

The four word roots of movement presented in Part 1 are discussed below.

duc, duct (lead)
> This root appears in many different words. The *ducts* in a building **lead** air and water to different rooms. A *conductor* **leads** an orchestra so that all the players stay together. (*Con-* means "together.") European noblemen are called *dukes* because long ago their ancestors **led** troops into battle.

ject (throw)
> This root appears as *jet,* a stream of water or air **thrown** into space. *Ject* can also represent the idea of **throwing** rather than the physical action itself. Although the word elements of *reject* actually mean "to **throw** back," the word itself has the related but nonphysical meaning of "not to accept."

stans, stat (standing; placed)
> This root indicates a lack of movement, as in *statue. Stans* and *stat* can also refer to standing in an abstract, nonphysical way. For example, one's *status* is one's **standing** or placement in society.

tain, ten (hold)
> This root can mean "hold" in a physical sense; a pan *contains,* or **holds,** baked beans. This root can also mean "hold" in a nonphysical sense. For example, a *tenet* is a belief that somebody **holds.**

Words to Learn

Part 1

duc, duct

1. **abduction** (noun) ăb-dŭk'shən

    From Latin: *ab-* (away) + *duct* (lead)

    kidnapping

    > The **abduction** of children is a serious problem in the United States.

▶ *Related Word*
abduct (verb)   The extremist group *abducted* people and held them for ransom.

2. **conducive** (adjective)   kən-d$\overline{oo}$′sĭv

From Latin: *con-* (together) + *duc* (lead)

contributing to; leading to

> A quiet library is **conducive** to studying.
>
> Candlelight and soft music are **conducive** to romance.

▶ *Common Phrase*
conducive to

3. **deduction** (noun)   dĭ-dŭk′shən

From Latin: *de-* (away) + *duct* (lead)

something subtracted from a total

> The monthly **deduction** in Wallace's paycheck covered his health insurance.
>
> As a salesperson, Pat got a **deduction** on clothing from the Gap.

a conclusion drawn from evidence

> After I got sick each time I ate chocolate, I made the **deduction** that it was causing my illness.
>
> Because the hotel restricted smoking to the fourth floor, we made the **deduction** that our third-floor room would be smoke-free.

▶ *Related Words*
deductive (adjective)   The mathematician's well-developed *deductive* skills enabled her to solve difficult logic problems.

deduce (verb)   (dĭ-d$\overline{oo}$s′)   We *deduced* that a child lived in the house from the toys on the floor.

Sherlock Holmes, a fictional English detective created by Sir Arthur Conan Doyle, is a master of *deductive* reasoning. Holmes amazes his companions by drawing brilliant conclusions from the smallest bits of evidence. The famous, but fictional, Holmes was based on a real-life Scottish doctor, Joe Bell, who was an expert in diagnosing disease from a minimum of evidence.

ject

4. **dejected** (adjective)   dĭ-jĕk′tĭd

   From Latin: *de-* (down) + *ject* (throw)

   depressed; downcast

   > Albert was **dejected** after he failed the exam for his driver's license.

   ▶ *Related Word*
   dejection (noun)   Marisol was in a state of *dejection* after she lost her job.

5. **eject** (verb)   ĭ-jĕkt′

   From Latin: *ex-* (out) + *ject* (throw)

   to force to leave; to expel

   > The manager **ejected** the noisy teenagers from the fast-food restaurant.

   > We put in fifty-five cents, pushed the button, and watched the machine **eject** a bag of potato chips.

   ▶ *Related Word*
   ejection (noun)   Seconds before the plane crashed, an automatic *ejection* device saved the pilot.

6. **jettison** (verb)   jĕt′-ĭ-sĕn

   From Latin: *ject* (throw)

   To throw out forcefully; to throw overboard

   > The lifeboat was able to hold two more sailors after we **jettisoned** the extra supplies.

   > The television network **jettisoned** the unpopular talk show.

   NOTE: Jettison can also apply to nonphysical things, as in to "jettison an unworkable plan."

stans, stat

7. **stature**   stăch′ər

   level of achievement and honor

   > Nobel Prize winner Robert Lucas has great **stature** in the field of economics.

   physical height

   > Achondroplasia is a condition that prevents people from developing to average **stature.**

8. **status quo** (noun)   stā′təs kwō′

From Latin: *stat* (standing, placed) + *quo* (in which), making "the condition in which"

the existing conditions; present state of things

> The young idealist challenged old-fashioned politicians to change the **status quo.**

The American Revolution (1775–83) established the first democracy in the modern world. In some ways, however, the French Revolution that followed (1789–99) changed the *status quo* in more fundamental ways by bankrupting many of the rich, deposing a king, and temporarily changing days of the week and holidays. The Russian Revolution of 1917 changed the economic and social system of the country to communism. In the 1980s, however, the status quo was upset once again by a move toward capitalism.

The pending unification of Europe will, once again, change the *status quo*. In 1999, the euro, Europe's unified currency, was the first substantial move toward this change.

---

9. **staunch** (adjective)   stônch

From Latin: *stans* (standing), through the French word *étanche* (watertight, firm) (Something *staunch* stands firm and strong.)

faithful; firmly supporting

> My **staunch** friend stood by me through my difficult divorce.
>
> Athlete Jackie Joyner-Kersee is a **staunch** supporter of her home town, East St. Louis, Illinois.

healthy; strong

> My **staunch** constitution can withstand cold easily.
>
> A **staunch** defense saved the town from attack.

▶ *Related Word*
> **staunchness** (noun)   The *staunchness* of a friend's support helped me during my difficult divorce.

tain, ten

10. **abstain** (verb)   ăb-stān′

From Latin: *abs-* (away) + *tain* (hold) ("To hold away from" is not to do something.)

not to do something by choice

> Members of Alcoholics Anonymous **abstain** from drinking liquor.

My mother **abstains** from smoking whenever she visits my grandmother.

not to vote

Seven people voted yes, seven voted no, and seven **abstained.**

▶ *Common Phrase*
abstain from

▶ *Related Words*
abstinence (noun)   (ăb'stə-nəns)   The month-long Muslim holiday of Ramadan requires *abstinence* from eating during daylight hours. (*Abstinence* usually refers to self-denial.)

abstention (noun)   (ăb-stən'shən)   China's *abstention* allowed the resolution to pass in the United Nations. (*Abstention* usually refers to voting.)

11. **tenable** (adjective)   tən'ə-bəl

From Latin: *ten* (hold)

capable of being defended; logical

The theory that a comet may have caused the extinction of dinosaurs is now considered **tenable.**

The commander decided that the high hill was a **tenable** position for his troops to defend.

▶ *Related Words*
tenability (noun)   Trung convinced others that his argument had *tenability*.

untenable (adjective)   The theory that the world is flat is now considered *untenable*. (*Untenable* is the opposite of *tenable*.)

When the great Polish scientist Copernicus (1473–1543) proposed that the Earth revolved around the sun, many thought that his theory was *untenable*. It seemed ridiculous that the Earth, with its heavy mass, could move around the sun, which appeared so small in the sky. Most people believed the Earth was the center of the universe. However, as more evidence accumulated, it became clear that Copernicus' theory had great *tenability*. Today, it is accepted as scientific fact.

12. **tenacious** (adjective)   tə-nā'shəs

From Latin: *ten* (hold)

firmly holding; gripping; retaining

The ship's captain kept a **tenacious** grasp on the wheel throughout the storm.

My **tenacious** uncle never gives up on a crossword puzzle until he has filled in every word.

▶ *Related Words*

tenaciousness (noun)   Winston Churchill's *tenaciousness* in believing that Nazi Germany was a threat helped prepare England for World War II.

tenacity (noun)   (tə-năs′ə-tē)   In 1998 U.S. gymnastics champions Blaine Wilson and Kristen Maloney showed their *tenacity* by competing despite injuries.

The *tenacious* Aung San family has fought for political freedom in Myanmar (formerly Burma) for many years. The father, General Aung San, was a famous independence leader. Daughter Aung San Suu Kui, who spent some years under house arrest, has been repeatedly attacked by the country's news media. Although the military leaders would like her to leave the country, she *tenaciously* refuses, preferring to serve as a symbol of freedom. Her efforts have earned her calls for her deportation, detention for thirteen days inside her car, and death threats, as well as the 1991 Nobel Peace Prize.

Exercises

Part 1

■ Definitions

Match each word in the left-hand column with a definition from the right-hand column. Use each choice only once.

1. jettison __h__

2. dejected __e__

3. staunch __j__

4. abstain __k__

5. conducive __d__

6. status quo __i__

a. something thrown forward

b. kidnapping

c. gripping

d. contributing to

e. depressed

f. logical

g. something subtracted

h. to throw overboard

7. deduction ___g___   i. the present state of things

8. abduction ___b___   j. faithful

9. stature ___l___   k. not to do

10. tenacious ___c___   l. level of achievement

■ Meanings

Match each word root to its meaning. Use each choice only once.

1. ject ___c___   a. hold

2. tain, ten ___a___   b. lead

3. duc, duct ___b___   c. throw

4. stans, stat ___d___   d. standing; placed

■ Words in Context

Complete each sentence with the word that fits best. Use each choice only once.

a. abduction   e. ejection   i. staunch
b. conducive   f. jettison   j. abstain
c. deduction   g. stature   k. tenable
d. dejected   h. status quo l. tenacious

1. Since he couldn't decide whether to vote yes or no, the senator decided to __j, abstain__ .

2. The wise minister had great __g, stature__ in her community.

3. To avoid a fire, the crew of the airplane had to __f, jettison__ its fuel into the sea.

4. The __i, staunch__ Democrat always votes for every candidate the party nominates.

5. The __l, tenacious__ mathematician worked on the problem for twenty years before he solved it.

6. Defense of the city was no longer **k, tenable** _____, so the army surrendered.

7. Moderate amounts of rain are **b, conducive** _____ to plant growth.

8. If all money were divided equally among people, there would be quite a change in the **h, status quo** _____ .

9. After her mother died, the woman became **d, dejected** _____ .

10. The man took a(n) **c, deduction** _____ for business expenses on his income taxes.

■ *Related Words*

Complete each sentence by using a word from the group of related words above it. You may need to capitalize a word when you write it in a sentence. Use each choice only once.

1. tenacious, tenacity

Inventor Jerome Lemelson, who holds the most patents in the United States after Thomas Edison, displayed tremendous **tenacity** _____ in court battles he fought against companies who took his ideas without getting his permission. The **tenacious** _____ Lemelson was forced to fight for years to protect the rights to inventions such as the technology for automatic warehouses, video camcorders, bar code scanners, and the Hot Wheels toy system. After a long struggle, when he finally became affluent, he funded a yearly $500,000 award to help inventors who had been exploited.

2. tenable, untenable

During the Middle Ages, people believed that attitudes and general health were controlled by four types of "humors": choleric (angry), melancholic (sad), sanguine (happy), and phlegmatic (easygoing).

Scientific evidence has shown that this theory is **untenable** _____ . However, the theory that mental states can affect physical health is considered **tenable** _____ by today's physicians.

3. abducted, abduction

Joggers, walkers, and drivers whose cars break down may be in danger of **abduction** _____ . Two modern inventions have helped to protect them. Mace, a substance that works like tear gas, may be sprayed at an assailant. Or, the cellular phone can be used to call for help. People who fear being **abducted** _____ , or even robbed, can carry one or both.

4. abstain, abstinence

Because of the concern over AIDS and teenage pregnancies, some schools have opened clinics that give advice about sexual activity. While the clinics teach **abstinence** _____ as the surest way to avoid problems, they also talk about contraception. Studies show that the clinics both reduce pregnancy rates and help teens to **abstain** _____ from premarital sex.

5. deductive, deduce, deduction

Identifying a person by DNA, the genetic material in cells, is coming into wider use. DNA testing enables law officials to **deduce** _____ who is the father of a child or who has committed a crime. As of 1999, this type of testing had freed fifty-seven prisoners who were wrongly convicted. DNA analysis allowed detectives to make the **deduction** _____ that these people were innocent. This **deductive** _____ method will not take the place of normal police detective work, but will certainly add to its accuracy.

■ *Reading the Headlines*

This exercise presents four headlines that might appear in newspapers. Read each headline and then answer the questions that follow. (Remember that small words, such as *is, are, a,* and *the,* are often left out of newspaper headlines.)

DETECTIVE OF GREAT STATURE SOLVES ABDUCTION THROUGH TENACIOUS INVESTIGATION

1. Is the detective well thought of? **yes** _____

2. Was the crime a robbery? **no** _____

3. Was the solution to the crime investigated thoroughly? **no** _____

FAMOUS HOST DEJECTED THAT HE WILL BE JETTISONED FROM TALK SHOW

4. Is the host happy? **no** _____

5. Will he stay on the talk show? **no** _____

ECONOMIC STATUS QUO FOUND CONDUCIVE TO INVESTMENT

6. Is the economy described as changing? **no** _____

7. Is the situation good for investment? **yes** _____

THEORY THAT STAUNCH FRIENDS HELP US TO ABSTAIN FROM BAD HABITS IS NOW THOUGHT TO BE TENABLE

8. Are these friends helpful? **yes** _____

9. Are we more likely to have bad habits if we have staunch friends? **no** _____

10. Is the theory believable? **yes** _____

Prefixes of Movement

Part 2

Part 2 continues with more word elements that show movement: first, two additional roots, *tract* (pull) and *vert* (turn); and then two prefixes, *circum-* (around) and *trans-* (across).

tract (pull)

> *Tractor,* a machine that **pulls** plows and other equipment through the earth, is an example of a common word formed from this root. Like many movement roots, *tract* is used in words that no longer carry the physical meaning of "pull." For example, when we distract someone's attention, we "**pull** it away" in a mental rather than in a physical sense.

vers, vert (turn)

> *Vert* can mean "turn" in a direct sense. When we *invert* a cup, we **turn** it upside down. The root can also hint at a nonphysical meaning of "turn." When we *advertise,* we "**turn** attention toward" a product.

circum- (around)

> *Circum-* is a prefix with the movement meaning of "around." The distance **around** a circle is called its *circumference.* Like other movement word elements, *circum-* can indicate the idea, rather than the action, of "around." For example, a library book that *circulates* "goes **around**" and is used by many different people.

> *Circus* is the Latin word for "circle." A circus was originally a circular area surrounded by seats used for viewing shows. Emperors were said to stay in power by giving the people "bread and circuses"—that is, food and entertainment. In modern English, a "three-ring circus" is a commonly used expression. This originally was a very large circus, but it has come to mean any event that causes a great deal of excitement.

---

trans- (across)

> *Transcontinental* jets **cross** a continent—as from New York to Los Angeles. The prefix *trans-* can also suggest the idea of "across" rather than physical movement. When we *translate* something, it goes "across" languages, or from one language to another.

Words to Learn

Part 2

tract

13. **distraught** (adjective)   dĭs-trôt´

> From Latin: *dis-* (apart) + *tract* (pull) (*Tract* changed to *traught* in Middle English.)

> crazy with worry

> **Distraught** over his troubled marriage, Wayne broke into tears.

Jasmine became **distraught** when she lost the diamond bracelet her friend had lent her.

NOTE: Distracted, which comes from the same word elements as *distraught,* has a less extreme meaning. It can be used simply for "confused" or "not attentive."

14. **extract** (verb)   ĭk-străkt´;   (noun) ĕk´străkt

From Latin: *ex-* (out) + *tract* (pull)

to pull out; to draw out (verb)

My mother **extracted** the last bit of juice from the orange.

Scientists **extracted** a large amount of information from the pictures of Mars.

something that is drawn out (noun)

An **extract** of the aloe plant is used for treating burns and cuts.

▶ *Related Word*

extraction (noun)   The *extraction* of oil from shale is an expensive process.

I am of Polish *extraction.* (Here, *extraction* means "ancestry.")

Vanilla *extract,* a popular flavoring for baked goods, is drawn from the pods of orchids. The ancient Aztecs of Mexico used it to flavor their *xocolatl* (chocolate) drinks. The Spanish explorer Hernando Cortés drank it at the court of the Aztec ruler Montezuma and brought it to Europe, where it soon became popular. Vanilla *extract* is widely used as an ingredient in perfume. In an effort to make gasoline more pleasant, the French have even added the odor of vanilla *extract* to it.

---

15. **retract** (verb)   rĭ-trăkt´

From Latin: *re-* (back) + *tract* (pull)

to withdraw a promise or statement; to pull something back

The newspaper **retracted** its false statements about the political candidate.

The frightened turtle **retracted** into its shell.

▶ *Related Word*

retraction (noun)   The company issued a *retraction* of its error-filled profits statement.

vers, vert

16. **adversary** (noun)   ăd′vər-sĕr′ē; plural: adversaries

    From Latin: *ad-* (toward) + *vert* (turn) (When we "turn toward" an enemy or adversary, we prepare to fight.)

    opponent; foe

    > After a hard-fought tennis match, the two **adversaries** shook hands.

    > In the Civil War, former slaves proved to be brave **adversaries** of the Confederate Army.

    ▶ *Related Word*
    adversarial (adjective)   Prosecutors and defense lawyers have *adversarial* relationships.

    NOTE: Adversary connotes a stubborn and determined foe.

    _____

    Can you match these adversarial pairs?

1. Napoleon	a. Max Schmeling
2. Octavian	b. Luke Skywalker
3. Utah Jazz	c. The Duke of Wellington
4. Darth Vader	d. Jake, Cassie, Rachel, Tobias, Marco, and Homer
5. Tweety Bird	e. Bugs Bunny
6. Joe Louis	f. Chicago Bulls
7. Elmer Fudd	g. Sylvester
8. Yeerks	h. Mark Antony

    Answers are on page 406.

17. **inadvertently** (adverb)   in′əd-vûr′tnt-lē

    From Latin: *in-* (not) + *ad-* (toward) + *vert* (turn) (When you are "not turned toward" something, events often happen inadvertently, or accidentally.)

    unintentionally; by accident

    > Tom **inadvertently** locked his keys in the car.

    > Fishing nets meant for tuna may **inadvertently** capture dolphins.

▶ *Related Word*
  inadvertent (adjective)   We forgave Rodney's *inadvertent* insult.

18. **perverse** (adjective)   pər-vûrs′

From Latin: *per-* (completely) + *vert* (turn) (A perverse person is "completely turned away" from what is natural.)

contrary; determined not to do what is expected or right

> The **perverse** child refused to wear a coat in the freezing weather.

> In a **perverse** trend, cheap used clothing became fashionable among wealthy people.

▶ *Related Word*
  perversity (noun)   Out of sheer *perversity,* my mother-in-law ordered us to cook corned beef and then refused to eat it.

circum-

19. **circumscribe** (verb)   sûr′kəm-skrīb′

From Latin: *circum-* (around) + *scrib* (to write)

to limit; to restrict; to enclose

> The new constitution of the country sought to **circumscribe** the president's power.

> Paris was originally **circumscribed** by a protecting wall.

20. **circumspect** (adjective)   sûr′kəm-spĕkt′

From Latin: *circum-* (around) + *spec* (to look) (To be circumspect is "to look around" or be careful.)

cautious; careful; considering results of actions

> Since scandal has ruined many careers, public figures should be **circumspect** in their personal lives.

▶ *Related Word*
  circumspection (noun)   The senator's *circumspection* kept her from accepting any gifts.

21. **circumvent** (verb)   sûr′kəm-vĕnt′

From Latin: *circum-* (around) + *venīre* (to come)

to avoid; to outwit

> We **circumvent** problems with mail delivery by sending e-mail messages.

Le Shan **circumvented** the traffic jam by taking a side street.

After years of **circumventing** taxes, the man was caught by the Internal Revenue Service.

▶ *Related Word*
circumvention (noun)   *Circumvention* of child support payments has become more difficult in recent years.

trans-

22. **transcend** (verb)   trăn-sĕnd′

From Latin: *trans-* (across) + *scandere* (to climb) (When we transcend something, we "climb across" limits and overcome them.)

to overcome; to go above limits

Marcy **transcended** a background of poverty to graduate from college and get a good job.

Grief **transcended** hatred as people from the two fighting nations mourned together for their dead.

Many mysteries of the universe **transcend** our understanding.

Can a person *transcend* a physical disability to become a professional athlete? Jim Abbott, born without a right hand, went on to become a major league baseball pitcher who played for the California Angels, Chicago White Sox, and Milwaukee Brewers. He uses his left hand both to catch and to throw the ball. Abbott's career shows the power of the human will to *transcend* obstacles.

---

23. **transformation** (noun)   trăns′fər-mā′shən

From Latin: *trans-* (across) + *forma* (shape), making *transformāre* (to change shape)

a complete change

Trang Le **transformed** the bankrupt company into a profit-making venture.

The second-graders were amazed when they saw the **transformation** of the caterpillar into a butterfly.

▶ *Related Word*
transform (verb)   (trăns-fôrm′)   The start of the semester *transformed* the video-game addict into a hard-working student.

24. **transitory** (adjective)   trăn′sĭ-tôr′ē

From Latin: *trans-* (across) + *īre* (to go), making *transīre* ("to go across" or to pass through quickly)

short-lived; existing briefly; passing

> People hope their sorrows will be **transitory.**

> The child's wish for a dog was just **transitory;** the next week she wanted a pony.

Exercises

Part 2

■ Definitions

Match each word in the left-hand column with a definition from the right-hand column. Use each choice only once.

1. adversary __d__
2. circumvent __e__
3. retract __c__
4. transitory __j__
5. transcend __b__
6. perverse __l__
7. extract __a__
8. circumspect __g__
9. circumscribe __k__
10. distraught __h__

a. something taken out
b. to overcome
c. to withdraw
d. opponent
e. to avoid
f. complete change
g. cautious
h. crazy with worry
i. accidentally
j. short-lived
k. to limit
l. determined not to do what is right or expected

■ Meanings

Match each word element to its meaning. Use each choice only once.

1. tract- __b__
2. vers, vert __c__
3. circum- __a__
4. trans- __d__

a. around
b. pull
c. turn
d. across

■ *Words in Context*

Complete each sentence with the word that fits best. Use each choice only once.

a. distraught   e. inadvertently   i. circumvent
b. extract   f. perverse   j. transcend
c. retract   g. circumscribe   k. transformation
d. adversary   h. circumspect   l. transitory

1. Marian Anderson was able to **j, transcend** _____ racial prejudice to become the first African-American soloist at the New York Metropolitan Opera.

2. The snail can **c, retract** _____ into its shell when danger threatens.

3. Some students **i, circumvent** _____ the long lines at school by using the telephone to register for classes.

4. The mother on the beach became **a, distraught** _____ when she realized that her child was missing.

5. We were amazed by the **k, transformation** _____ of the awkward teenager into a beautiful woman.

6. The child's sadness was **l, transitory** _____, and he soon was smiling again.

7. My **f, perverse** _____ uncle complained constantly about his illnesses yet refused to call a doctor.

8. The government agency was **h, circumspect** _____ in dealing with foreign firms and checked them carefully.

9. To **g, circumscribe** _____ the professor's power, the college president took some responsibilities away from her.

10. I **e, inadvertently** _____ tripped when I got out of the car.

■ *Using Related Words*

Complete each sentence by using a word from the group of related words above it. You may need to capitalize a word when you write it in a sentence. Use each choice only once.

INVENTIONS AND DISCOVERIES

1. adversaries, adversarial

    The refrigerator is used in more than 99 percent of U.S. households. Invented in the early 1900s, it has revolutionized food storage. However, Freon 12, used as a cooling liquid, has negative effects on the world's protective ozone layer. People concerned about the environment have become **adversaries** _____ of using this chemical. Because of their **adversarial** _____ position, legislation was enacted to substitute other compounds.

2. inadvertent, inadvertently

    In 1928, while Sir Alexander Fleming was researching bacteria, he went on vacation. During his absence, a test-tube lid **inadvertently** _____ slipped off, and his sample was killed by an unknown mold. Fleming returned and was just about to throw the sample out when he realized that the mold might be able to kill harmful bacteria. In this **inadvertent** _____ manner, he discovered the great antibiotic, penicillin.

3. transformed, transformation

    Invented in 1901, the paper clip has been hailed as one of the world's most useful items. Yet this elegant invention can be **transformed** _____ into something even more useful. A **transformation** _____ of the traditional paper clip, the new Super Clip, invented by the Froehlich family, is three inches long and holds over one hundred papers. The Super Clip can be used to hold men's ties, to attach hair curlers, to seal bags, and to decorate Christmas trees.

4. extracted, extract, extraction

    Before the invention of the washing machine, people pounded clothes on rocks and used water in lakes and streams to wash away dirt. William Blackstone, from Bluffton, Indiana, built the first washing machine as a present for his wife. Soon, and not surprisingly, he was selling them. Early washing machines swished

clothes around in soapy water to __**extract**__ dirt.
Then, to remove the soap, the clothes were rinsed in clean water.

Finally, a separate "wringer" was used for the __**extraction**__
of excess water, before the clothes were dried. In the 1930s, John
Chamberlain invented a single machine that washed, rinsed, and

__**extracted**__ water, like the washing machines of today.

5. circumspect, circumspection

Carrying an umbrella is a mark of a __**circumspect**__ person, one who is prepared for rain. In London, businesspeople show

their __**circumspection**__ by carrying umbrellas at all times, for
rain is always possible in Britain's damp climate. For centuries,
umbrellas were used as sunshades by people in Egypt, Mesopotamia, China, and India. Introduced in 1720 to Europe, they soon
made their way to the American colonies. However, the first person
to carry an umbrella in a Connecticut rain was followed by a laughing crowd.

■ *Reading the Headlines*

This exercise presents five headlines that might appear in newspapers.
Read each headline and then answer the questions that follow. (Remember that small words, such as *is, are, a,* and *the,* are often left out of newspaper headlines.)

MAYOR FORCES HIS ADVERSARY TO RETRACT FALSE STATEMENTS

1. Have the statements been taken back? __**yes**__

2. Was the person making the statements a friend of the

mayor? __**no**__

INADVERTENTLY DISCOVERED SUBSTANCE TRANSFORMS MAN

3. Was the substance discovered purposely? __**no**__

4. Did the man remain the same? __**no**__

LAWS TO CIRCUMVENT TAX PROBLEMS ARE ONLY TRANSITORY

5. Do the laws remain? <u>**no**</u>

6. Do the laws cause tax problems? <u>**no**</u>

DISTRAUGHT GIRL TRIES TO TRANSCEND DIFFICULTIES AND WIN RACE

7. Is the girl happy? <u>**no**</u>

8. Is she trying to overcome her problems? <u>**yes**</u>

NO CONFESSIONS OF WRONGDOING CAN BE EXTRACTED FROM CIRCUMSPECT MAN

9. Is the man careful? <u>**yes**</u>

10. Are people trying to get something out of him? <u>**yes**</u>

Chapter Exercises

■ *Practicing Strategies: New Words from Word Elements*

See how your knowledge of prefixes and roots can help you understand new words. Complete each sentence with the word that seems to fit best. Use each choice only once.

a. aqueducts   e. induct   i. tenor
b. attract   f. injection   j. traction
c. circuitous   g. statement   k. transatlantic
d. conduct   h. stationary   l. vertigo

1. The woman stood <u>**h, stationary**</u> in the doorway, not moving a muscle.

2. When we get a(n) <u>**f, injection**</u>, medicine is "thrown into" our bodies.

3. Making a <u>**k, transatlantic**</u> crossing from Southampton, England, to New York, the *Titanic* hit an iceberg and sank.

4. A __c, circuitous__ path goes in a roundabout way.

5. *Ad-* or *at-* can mean "toward," so to __b, attract__ is to pull someone toward you.

6. The __i, tenor__ voice was so named because these singers held the melody in a song with many different parts.

7. When we __e, induct__ people into a club, we "lead" them "in" as new members.

8. When your leg is broken, __j, traction__ , or a pulling motion, may help the bones mend properly.

9. You suffer from __l, vertigo__ when you get dizzy and things around you seem to turn and spin.

10. *Aqua* means "water"; the ancient Romans built __a, aqueducts__ to lead water to their cities.

■ *Practicing Strategies: Combining Context Clues and Word Elements*

Combining the strategies of context clues and word elements is a good way to figure out unknown words. In the following sentences, each italicized word contains a word element that you have studied in this chapter. Using the meaning of the word element and the context of the sentence, make an intelligent guess about the meaning of the italicized word. Your instructor may ask you to check the meaning in your dictionary when you have finished.

1. The company offered many *inducements* to attract qualified computer specialists.

    Inducements means __attractions, offers that lead to something__ .

2. In a terrible *subversion* of justice, the man's innocent words were twisted to seem evil.

    Subversion means __undermining; overturning__ .

3. Because of the blockage, the blood in the artery was in a state of *stasis*.

    Stasis means __standing still__ .

4. For hundreds of years, alchemists sought methods to *transmute* iron and copper into gold.

Transmute means **change; change across forms**   .

5. In 1522, the ships of Magellan became the first to *circumnavigate* the world.

Circumnavigate means **circle completely; travel completely around**   .

■ *Practicing Strategies: Using the Dictionary*

Read the following definition and then answer the questions below it.

> **de•mand** (dĭ-mănd′) *v.* **-mand•ed, -mand•ing, -mands.**
> —*tr.* **1.** To ask for urgently or peremptorily. **2.** To claim as just or due: *demand payment.* **3.** To ask to be informed of. **4.** To require as useful, just, proper, or necessary; call for. **5.** *Law.* To claim formally; lay legal claim to. —*intr.* To make a demand. —*n.* **1.** The act of demanding. **2.** Something demanded. **3.** An urgent requirement or need. **4.** The state of being sought after: *in demand as a speaker.* **5.** *Econ.* **a.** The desire to possess a commodity or make use of a service, combined with the ability to purchase it. **b.** The amount of a commodity or service that people are ready to buy for a given price: *supply and demand.* **6.** *Comp. Sci.* A coding technique in which a command to read or write is initiated as the need for a new block of data occurs, thus eliminating the need to store data. **7.** *Law.* A formal claim. **8.** *Archaic.* An emphatic question or inquiry. —*idiom.* **on demand. 1.** When presented for payment. **2.** When needed or asked for. [ME, *demanden* < OFr. *demander*, to charge with doing, and < Med.Lat. *dē-mandāre*, to demand, both < Lat., to entrust : *dē*, de- + *mandāre*, to entrust; see **man-²*.**] —**de•mand′a•ble** *adj.*

1. In which language was *demand* first recorded? **Latin**

2. Give the number and part of speech of the definition that is no longer used. **8, as a noun**

3. Give the idiom that uses *demand.* **on demand**

4. List the three part-of-speech functions that *demand* has. _____

   transitive verb, intransitive verb, noun

5. Give the number and part of speech of the definition that best fits this sentence: "At fifty cents a pound, the *demand* for cotton appears to be about five million pounds." **5b, as a noun**

■ *Companion Words*

Complete each sentence with the word that fits best. Choose your answers from the words below. You may use each word more than once.

Choices: about, from, of, to, that, over

1. The Queen of England is circumspect __about__ her personal life, but her children often are not.

2. We have witnessed a transformation __of__ communication from paper mail to e-mail.

3. The NAACP is a staunch defender __of__ the rights of African Americans.

4. The extraction of information __from__ the large database involved many months of work.

5. Freedom is conducive __to__ creativity.

6. Miss Marple made a deduction __that__ a murder had taken place.

7. She was distraught __over, about__ her husband's death.

8. Circumvention __of__ difficulties would be desirable.

9. The professor issued a retraction __of__ his statement after realizing it was based on faulty evidence.

10. I must abstain __from__ eating for twelve hours before the medical test.

■ *Writing with Your Words*

This exercise will give you practice in writing effective sentences that use the vocabulary words. Each sentence is started for you. Complete it with an interesting phrase that also indicates the meaning of the italicized word.

1. One theory that is no longer *tenable* is _____

_____ .

2. One difficulty I would like to *transcend* is _____

_____ .

3. You must be *tenacious* in order to _____

_____ .

4. If I underwent a *transformation,* I would _____

_____ .

5. People should *abstain* from _____

_____ .

6. I *inadvertently* _____

_____ .

7. The most *perverse* thing someone could do is _____

_____ .

8. People often try to *circumvent* lines for ticket sales by _____

_____ .

9. A change I would like to see in the *status quo* is _____

_____ .

10. The college student felt *dejected* because _____

_____ .

Passage

What Body Language Tells Us

The posture of your body, where you place your arms, and how you walk may reveal more to others than the words you are speaking. In fact, social psychologists tell us that body language is one of the most effective forms of communication.

A first-grade teacher stands by the door, smiling and greeting the children with friendly words. **(1)** But if her arms are crossed, she is **inadvertently**

Body language sends out powerful messages.

communicating another message. Crossed arms indicate negative feelings, and the children will probably see her as a threat rather than as a friend.

In a nearby high school, a student sits in math class, his body straight, his hands folded, **(2)** fixing a **tenacious** stare on the teacher. Is he paying attention? Probably not! His lack of movement indicates that his thoughts are far away (perhaps on his girlfriend). If the student were interested in the lesson, he would move and react. **(3)** Only an inexperienced teacher would make the **deduction** that a student who remains perfectly still is thinking about math.

In contrast to the math student's rigid posture, tilting one's head indicates friendliness and interest. A student who tilts her head and sits on the edge of her chair is paying attention to a lecture. People often bend their heads or bodies forward slightly to show interest in members of the opposite sex. Enlarged pupils in one's eyes also indicate this interest.

Smiling is a body language that may not always mean what you think. Most people believe that smiling indicates happiness. But scientists observing animals have found that **(4)** another conclusion is sometimes more **tenable:** a smile indicates apology, or the wish to avoid an attack. A gorilla often smiles when showing stronger animals that it doesn't want to fight. Similarly, a person who has accidentally poked a stranger with an elbow **(5)** will give a **transitory** smile that silently requests the injured person not to become angry.

Hands communicate much body language. **(6)** An open-handed gesture is **conducive** to friendliness. Perhaps this is the origin of the handshake, in which people open their hands and then join them.

In contrast, arms folded on the chest indicate defensiveness. Baseball fans have seen this behavior many times when **(7)** an umpire makes a call that a team manager wants him to **retract.** As the manager approaches, the formerly neutral umpire undergoes a **transformation** into an **adversary** simply by folding his arms. **Abstaining** from movement, he listens to the manager's arguments. Finally, the umpire shows his rejection just by turning his back. The **dejected** manager walks back to the dugout, shrugging his shoulders.

Walking styles can also communicate messages. We all have seen the controlled and measured walk of a person trying to appear dignified and **circumspect.** People who are **distraught** often walk with their heads down and their hands clasped behind their backs. The person with energy and will power moves rapidly, hands swinging freely from side to side. **(8)** Those who walk with their hands in their pockets may be **perverse** and critical of others. **(9)** People who look toward the ground may be trying to **circumvent** the glances of others.

Body language sends out powerful messages both to others and ourselves. Research has shown that it helps us to think. Gesturing with hands helps people to retrieve words from memory and express abstract concepts. But, of course, we also communicate messages to each other with these gestures. The next time you shake hands, tilt your head, or fold your arms, **(10)** think about the messages that others may **extract** from your movements.

■ *Exercise*

Each numbered sentence below corresponds to a sentence in the Passage. Fill in the letter of the choice that makes the sentence mean the same thing as its corresponding sentence in the Passage.

1. But if her arms are crossed, she is ____**a**____ communicating another message.
   a. accidentally   b. hopefully   c. strongly   d. probably

2. The student is fixing a(n) ____**a**____ stare on the teacher.
   a. stubborn   b. friendly   c. hateful   d. interested

3. Only an inexperienced teacher would ____**a**____ that a student who remains perfectly still is thinking about math.
   a. conclude   b. question   c. hope   d. picture

4. Another conclusion is sometimes more __**d**__ .
   a. ridiculous b. negative c. desirable d. logical

5. A person will give a __**d**__ smile that silently requests the injured person not to become angry.
   a. happy b. false c. friendly d. brief

6. An open-handed gesture is __**b**__ to friendliness.
   a. opposed b. leading c. hopeless d. given

7. An umpire makes a call that a team manager wants him to __**a**__ .
   a. take back b. be firm about c. discuss intelligently
   d. delay slightly

8. Those who walk with their hands in their pockets may be __**d**__ and critical of others.
   a. lonely b. unhappy c. observant d. contrary

9. People who look toward the ground may be trying to __**b**__ the glances of others.
   a. capture b. avoid c. greet d. notice

10. Think about the messages that others may __**b**__ from your movements.
    a. ignore b. draw out c. try to miss d. misunderstand

■ Discussion Questions

1. According to the passage, what may be the "hidden message" of smiling?

2. Identify two situations in which the position of a person's arms or hands indicates an attitude.

3. Suggest three ways in which dogs communicate by using body language.

◀ **E**NGLISH **I**DIOMS

Movement

Since this chapter concerns word elements of movement, the idioms introduced here all deal with action. Some idioms relate to negative actions. When people are *axed,* they are fired or lose their jobs. If a worker does something wrong, her boss may *call her on the carpet,* scold her, or *bawl her out.* If her boss makes her feel bad, she would be *cut down to size.*

To *draw the line* means to set a limit. For example, you might help a friend to study, but *draw the line* at writing his paper for him. A professor who *covers a lot of ground* in a lecture gives much information. (Similarly, a traveler might *cover a lot of ground* by going a long distance.)

If people go to a theater to see a mystery and they are kept in suspense until the last minute, the mystery is called a *cliffhanger.* If audience members enjoy the performance, clapping and cheering loudly, they would be said to *bring the house down.*

In the hill tribes of northern India, it was the custom to bend over backwards while doing a yoga exercise that symbolized submission to God. *To bend over backwards* now means to do everything possible to please or accommodate another person. A professor might *bend over backwards* to help a student who is having difficulty in a course.

Quiz Again

Now that you have finished studying this chapter, here is the brief true-false quiz you took when you began. Take it again.

To **jettison** is to throw out.	True	False
A **staunch** supporter would probably betray you.	True	False
Things change quickly in the **status quo.**	True	False
A **perverse** person is cooperative.	True	False

Answers are on page 406. Did your score improve?

8

Word Elements:
Together and Apart

People come together in classes, clubs, concerts, parties, and sports events. Yet disagreements and disputes can push them apart. This chapter concentrates on word elements meaning "together" and "apart." Three prefixes and two roots are presented. The chapter also introduces several words that came into English as English speakers came in contact with people who spoke other languages and "borrowed" non-English words.

Chapter Strategy: Word Elements: Together and Apart

Chapter Words:

Part 1

co-, com-, con-		dis-	
coherent		discord	
collaborate		disparity	
communal		disreputable	
compatible	*sym-, syn-*	syndrome	
concur		synopsis	
contemporary		synthesis	

Part 2

greg		*Borrowed Words*	
congregate		bravado	
gregarious		charisma	
segregate		cliché	
sperse	disperse		cuisine
	intersperse		nadir
	sparse		zenith

Quiz Yourself

To check your knowledge of some chapter words before you begin to study, identify these statements as true or false.

A **disparity** is a difference.   True   False

Charisma attracts people.   True   False

Gregarious people hate parties.   True   False

Disreputable people enjoy good reputations.   True   False

You will learn the answers as you study this chapter.

Did You Know?

What Are Two Sources of English?

Modern English has roots in two languages, Old French and Old English. Old French was a Romance language; that is, it descended from Latin, which was spoken by the Romans. Old French was an ancestor of the French spoken today. Old English, spoken in England from about the beginning of the eighth century to the middle of the twelfth century, was a Germanic language, similar in many ways to the German used today. The two languages first came into contact in 1066.

In 1066, William the Conqueror crossed the English Channel from northwestern France, conquered England, and made himself king. He replaced the English nobility with his fellow Norman countrymen, who spoke a version of Old French. For many years, then, the ruling class of England spoke Old French, and the rest of the people continued to speak Old English.

Gradually the two languages merged into Middle English, which was spoken until about the fifteenth century, when it became what we know as Modern English. But to this day, many rare, fancy English words (like the ones you find in vocabulary books) tend to be of Old French origin. The common words of English are usually from Old English.

What does this mean to you? Perhaps you speak or have studied Spanish, Italian, French, or Portuguese. If so, you may realize that these languages are related to the Old French that William the Conqueror brought to England. They are all Romance languages. If you speak a Romance language, you can easily learn many difficult English words. All you need to do is to think of a *cognate,* a word that sounds the same and has the same meaning, from a Romance language. As an example, *furious* is an English word descended from Old French. The Spanish cognate is *furioso.*

Modern English is full of pairs of words that have the same or similar meanings. In these cases, one word is often derived from Old French and the other from Old English. Several of these word pairs are listed below. Notice that the words descended from Old French are often longer and less common.

Old English (Germanic Origin)	*Old French (Romance Origin)*
eat	devour
talk	converse
give	donate
earth	terrain
top	pinnacle
late	tardy

During the Renaissance (in the 1400s and the 1500s), interest in the ancient Greeks and Romans resulted in another great expansion in English vocabulary. Writers sometimes coined new words from ancient Greek and Latin ones. In this way, words such as *compatible, congenital,* and *conspicuous* (all found in this book) entered the English language. The great English playwright, Shakespeare, was the first to use the words *misanthrope* and *frugal.*

Finally, English has borrowed words from many other languages, including Arabic, Hindi, Urdu, Italian, German, and Spanish. If you know another language, you'll probably recognize many words that are similar in English. In this chapter you will study several words that English has taken from other languages. These words are a spoken and written record of the explorations that brought English speakers together with people of other cultures and languages.

Learning Strategy

Word Elements: Together and Apart

Part 1 of this chapter presents three common prefixes that refer to being together or apart: *com-* and *syn-* mean "together"; *dis-* means "apart." These prefixes are very useful to know, since each one is used to form more than one hundred English words.

Part 2 presents two roots that are related to the idea of together and apart, *greg* (flock, herd) and *sperse* (scatter).

Element	Meaning	Origin	Function	Chapter Words
				Part 1
co-, col-, com-, con-, cor-	together	Latin	prefix	coherent, collaborate, communal, compatible, concur, contemporary
dis-	apart; not	Latin; Greek	prefix	discord, disparity, disreputable
sym-, sy-	together; same	Greek	prefix	syndrome, synopsis, synthesis
				Part 2
greg	flock	Latin	root	congregate, gregarious, segregate
sperse	scatter	Latin	root	disperse, intersperse, sparse

Prefixes

Part 1

The three prefixes presented in Part 1 are discussed in more detail below.

co-, col-, com-, con-, cor- (together)
This prefix is used in several hundred English words. Its five spelling variations help us pronounce it more easily when it is attached to various roots, as in these examples: *coworker, collect, communicate, contact,* and *correspond.* Each of these words carries some sense of "together." For example, a *coworker* is someone who works **together** with another worker. To *collect* means "to bring things **together.**" When people *communicate* or *correspond,* they come **together** through speech or writing. When two electrical wires establish *contact,* they come **together** by touching.

dis- (apart; not)
Dis- means "apart" in some words. For example, students often *dissect* (cut **apart**) frogs in biology classes. A noisy student may *disrupt* (break **apart** into confusion) a class. *Dis-* can also mean "not." The word *distrust,* formed from the prefix *dis-* and the base word *trust,* means "**not** to trust." A person in *disgrace* is **not** in the "grace," or favor, of others. In a new slang usage, "dis" appears as a verb meaning *to show disrespect for* as in "She dissed me."

sym-, syn- (together; same)

The two meanings of *syn-* and *sym-* are related, making them easy to remember. For example, *sympathy* is composed from *sym-* (same) and the root *path* (feeling). *Synagogue,* a place where Jewish people meet to worship, is composed from *syn-* (together) and *agein* (to lead).

Words to Learn

Part 1

co-, col-, com-, con-, cor-

1. **coherent** (adjective)   kō-hîr′ənt

   From *co-* (together) + *haērere* (to cling or stick)

   logical; consistent; clearly reasoned

   > The Canadian government worked out a **coherent** policy for admitting refugees.

   > There is no **coherent** regulation of the information available on the Internet.

   ▶ *Related Words*
   coherence (noun)   Lacking any *coherence,* the student's paper was simply a disorganized collection of sentences.

   cohere (verb)   In the cold weather, ice *cohered* to the surface of the road. (*Cohere* means "to stick.")

   incoherent (adjective)   The English directions were *incoherent* to the Korean tourist. The frightened child spoke so rapidly that her speech was *incoherent.* (*Incoherent* is the opposite of *coherent.*)

There are so many laws that often people have trouble finding out what the law in a given situation actually is. The ancients had this problem too, and they dealt with it through law codes. These *coherent* collections of laws classified each one by subject and made certain all were consistent. The oldest code, in Ebla (northern Syria), dates to 2400 B.C.E. and is carved in stone. The Code of Hammurabi, assembled in Mesopotamia in approximately 1750 B.C.E., was publicly displayed. The Napoleonic Code applied to territory under that French emperor. In fact, the state of Louisiana, once controlled by the French, still operates partially under the Napoleonic Code. The rest of the United States is under English Civil Law.

---

2. **collaborate** (verb)   kə-lăb′ə-rāt′

From Latin: *col-* (together) + *labōrāre* (to work)

to work together

> Metal-rock band Metallica was scheduled to **collaborate** with the San Francisco Symphony on a project.

> J. D. Watson and F. H. C. Crick **collaborated** to find the structure of DNA, which carries the genetic information of all living organisms.

▶ *Related Words*
collaboration (noun)   Working in *collaboration*, José, Phillip, and Suzuki produced an award-winning science project.

collaborator (noun, person)   The two *collaborators* sold defense secrets to a foreign country.

NOTE: The word *collaborator* can have the negative meaning of "one who aids an enemy occupying one's country."

3. **communal** (adjective)   kə-myoo′nəl

From Latin: *com-* (together) (*Communis* meant "shared," "public.")

referring to a community or to joint ownership

> Some formerly homeless Los Angeles residents now live in Dome Village, where they have individual fiberglass domes, but **communal** baths and kitchens.

> The swimming pool was **communal** property, so everybody in the condo association paid dues to keep it clean.

▶ *Related Word*
commune (noun)   (kŏm′yoon′)   A *commune* is a place where people live as a group, sharing their incomes.

4. **compatible** (adjective)   kəm-păt′ə-bəl

From Latin: *com-* (together) + *path* (feeling)

harmonious; living in harmony

> Zoning laws in the suburb required that the outside of new homes be **compatible** with those of existing homes.

▶ *Common Phrase*
compatible with

▶ *Related Words*

compatibility (noun)   *Compatibility* is an important factor in a happy marriage.

incompatible (adjective)   My new printer was *incompatible* with my software. (*Incompatible* means *not* compatible.)

5. **concur** (verb)   kən-kûr′

From Latin: *con-* (together) + *currere* (to run)

to agree

The findings of several studies **concur** that women find it more difficult to quit smoking than men.

In a 1998 pact, forty-four nations **concurred** on principles for restoring stolen art to victims of the Holocaust.

The court of appeals **concurred** with the decision of the district court.

▶ *Common Phrase*
concur with

▶ *Related Words*

concurrence (noun)   The mayor needed the *concurrence* of the city board to appoint a chief of police.

concurrent (adjective)   The man was serving two *concurrent* prison sentences for robbery. (*Concurrent* means "at the same time." If people were given two *concurrent* ten-year sentences, they would serve ten years. If they were given two *consecutive* ten-year sentences, they would serve twenty years.)

6. **contemporary** (noun, adjective)   kən-tĕm′pə-rĕr′ē (plural: *contemporaries*)

From Latin: *com-* (together) + *tempus* (time)

a person living during the same time period as another person

Thomas Jefferson was a **contemporary** of Alexander Hamilton.

Great artists are often not appreciated by their **contemporaries.**

NOTE: Typically *contemporary* refers to people who are about the same age. You, for example, would not be a contemporary of your grandfather, even if both of you are alive at the same time.

existing at the same time (adjective)

The expansion of railroads and the migration to the West were **contemporary** developments in U.S. history.

current; modern (adjective)

> At the exhibit, a **contemporary** photo of each man was placed beside a photo of him taken during the Vietnam War.

> According to **contemporary** medical beliefs, it is healthy for mothers to breast-feed their babies.

▶ *Related Word*

contemporaneous (adjective) During World War II, the United States fought *contemporaneous* battles in Europe and the Pacific.

dis-

7. **discord** (noun)   dĭs′kôrd′

From Latin: *dis-* (apart) + *cor* (heart, mind)

strife; lack of agreement

> According to experts, money is the most common cause of **discord** in marriage.

▶ *Related Word*

discordant (adjective) (dĭ-skôr′dnt) The horns of the cars stuck in traffic made *discordant* sounds.

A Greek legend tells the story of the apple of *discord*. The goddess of discord, Eris, had not been invited to a wedding at which all the other gods were to be present. Enraged, she arrived at the party and threw onto the table a golden apple intended "for the most beautiful." Three goddesses, Hera, Athena, and Aphrodite, all claimed it. Paris, prince of Troy, was asked to settle the dispute. He chose Aphrodite. As a reward, Aphrodite promised him the world's most beautiful woman, Helen, who was, unfortunately, married to the Greek king Menelaus. When Paris abducted her, a Greek army went to Troy to get her back. This military expedition resulted in the Trojan War, the subject of Homer's *Iliad*.

---

8. **disparity** (noun)   dĭ-spăr′ĭ-tē

From Latin: *dis-* (not) + *par* (equal)

inequality; difference

> Despite the **disparity** in their ages, the boy and his grandfather enjoyed playing Nintendo and fishing together.

> According to economists, income **disparity** in the United States has increased in the last twenty years.

Research indicates that a college degree increases income. The 1990 census found considerable *disparity* in the earning power of college graduates and nongraduates. On average, the difference amounted to $600,000 over a working life, or about $15,000 each year. An advanced degree (such as an M.A. or Ph.D.) can increase earning power by as much as two million dollars over a lifetime.

▶ *Related Word*

disparate (adjective)   (dĭs′pər-ĭt)   Airlines sometimes find it difficult to please the *disparate* demands of promptness and safety.

9. **disreputable** (adjective)   dĭs-rĕp′yə-tə-bəl

From Latin: *dis-* (not) + *re-* (again) + *putāre* (to think) (Literally, *disreputable* means "not worth a second thought.")

not respectable; having a bad reputation

> The student's appearance was so **disreputable** that we thought he was a beggar.

> The **disreputable** bar owner was rumored to be dealing in illegal drugs.

▶ *Related Word*

disrepute (noun)   (dĭs′rĭ-pyo͞ot′)   Some in the military forces have fallen into *disrepute* because of accusations of sexual harassment.

The chemist who had reported false results was held in *disrepute*.

sym-, syn-

10. **syndrome** (noun)   sĭn′drōm′

From Greek: *syn-* (together) + *dramein* (to run)

a group of symptoms that indicates a disease or disorder

> Carpal tunnel **syndrome** can include pain, tingling, weakness, and numbness in the hands and fingers.

> After head injuries, football players can develop post-concussion **syndrome,** with speech and balance problems.

> In the late 1800s, the U.S. economy suffered from a **syndrome** of alternating growth and sudden declines.

Medical and educational specialists have defined several *syndromes* that affect childhood learning, including conduct disorders and attention deficit disorders. For reasons not fully understood, boys are more likely to suffer from these. Some researchers believe that because boys are more active, they are seen as having more behavior problems. However, scientists have also shown that, even before birth, the brains of boys are more likely to be injured than those of girls.

11. **synopsis** (noun)   sĭ-nŏp′sĭs   plural: synopses

From Greek: *syn-* (together) + *opsis* (view) (In a synopsis, something is viewed "all together.")

a short summary

The **synopsis** of the book told the plot in a few short paragraphs.

12. **synthesis** (noun)   sĭn′thĭ-sĭs   plural: syntheses

From Greek: *syn-* (together) + *tithenai* (to put)

something made from combined parts; the making of something by combining parts

The music of Brazilian composer Heitor Villa-Lobos is a **synthesis** of folk melodies and classical forms.

Steroids can help treat multiple sclerosis because they help the body in the **synthesis** of myelin, the white substance composed of fat and protein that protects nerves.

▶ *Related Words*
   synthesize (verb)   Soy protein is healthy for many people because it reduces the body's ability to *synthesize* cholesterol.
   synthetic (adjective)   (sĭn-thĕt′ĭk)   Nylon and polyester are examples of *synthetic* materials made from petroleum.
   synthetically (adverb)   *Synthetically* produced vitamins are not always as good as natural products.

NOTE: Synthetic and *synthetically* refer to products produced chemically, or by other artificial means, rather than those of natural origin.

Exercises

Part 1

■ *Definitions*

Match each word in the left-hand column with a definition from the right-hand column. Use each choice only once.

1. coherent ___d___
2. syndrome ___c___
3. concur ___k___
4. discord ___a___
5. synthesis ___b___
6. contemporary ___e___
7. synopsis ___i___
8. disreputable ___l___
9. disparity ___f___
10. communal ___g___

a. strife; lack of agreement
b. something made from combined parts
c. symptoms that make up a disease
d. logical; consistent
e. current; modern
f. inequality
g. jointly owned
h. harmonious
i. summary
j. to work together
k. to agree
l. not respectable

■ Meanings

Match each prefix to its meaning. Use each choice only once.

1. con- ___c___
2. dis- ___a___
3. syn- ___b___

a. apart; not
b. together; same
c. together

■ Words in Context

Complete each sentence with the word that fits best. Use each choice only once.

a. coherent   e. concur   i. disreputable
b. collaborate   f. contemporary   j. syndrome
c. communal   g. discordant   k. synopsis
d. compatible   h. disparity   l. synthesis

1. During summer camp, eight children slept in a ___c, communal___ cabin.

2. Jewish and Catholic groups will ___b, collaborate___ in providing a free meal for people in shelters.

3. People felt that the **i, disreputable** _____ shopkeeper cheated his customers.

4. Since we are the same age, Alice is my **f, contemporary** _____ .

5. I was annoyed by the **g, discordant** _____ noise from five radios playing different music on the bus.

6. The **d, compatible** _____ children often played together.

7. Students who read a **k, synopsis** _____ of a book, rather than the book itself, will miss the richness of the original language.

8. Critics and fans **e, concur** _____ in judging Miles Davis as a great jazz trumpeter.

9. People often suffer from a withdrawal **j, syndrome** _____ when they stop taking drugs.

10. There is a great **h, disparity** _____ of power between a master and a slave.

■ *Using Related Words*

Complete each sentence by using a word from the group of related words above it. You may need to capitalize a word when you write it in a sentence. Use each choice only once.

1. compatibility, compatible

When blood is donated, both giver and receiver must have

compatible _____ blood types. There are four blood types: A, B, AB, and O. People with type O can donate to people with any other blood type. People with AB blood may receive blood from people with any other blood type. Otherwise, blood types must be

matched for **compatibility** _____ .

2. synthetic, synthesize, synthesized, synthetically

Although the human body can produce many substances, vitamin

C cannot be **synthesized** _____ . Now, however, Nicholas

Smirnoff has found how plants **synthesize** _____ this

chemical, and may be able to produce plants that contain more of the vitamin. Currently, people must eat many foods such as oranges and grapefruits or rely on __synthetic__ vitamin C. In the future, there may well be less reliance on __synthetically__ produced vitamin C, as smaller amounts of food will supply more of the vitamin.

3. collaboration, collaborated

   Several Peruvian women have __collaborated__ to form a radio station that presents programs on women's health and welfare. A __collaboration__ has also been formed between women's groups in Mexico and in Boston. Latinas (Latin American women) are leading the world in this type of networking.

4. contemporaries, contemporaneous, contemporary

   Wolfgang Amadeus Mozart, who lived from 1756 to 1791, was musically __contemporaneous__ with composer Franz Joseph Haydn. Mozart was a child prodigy who performed throughout Europe at the age of six. However, as an adult, he had many problems. His __contemporaries__, other than Haydn, often ignored his best music. __Contemporary__ reports tell us that he lost the sponsorship of royalty. He died in poverty when he was thirty-six years old, but his great music lives on today.

■ *True or False?*

Each of the following statements contains one or more words from this section. Read each sentence carefully and then indicate whether you think it is probably true or probably false.

__F__   1. Discord is pleasant.

__T__   2. People who are not compatible should not live in a communal setting with each other.

__F__   3. People should only collaborate with others who they consider disreputable.

__F__   4. Disparity means equality.

T
___   5. A synopsis is shorter than the original work.

F
___   6. Contemporary refers to things that happened long ago.

T
___   7. Something coherent makes sense.

F
___   8. A synthesis is made up of one thing.

T
___   9. A syndrome is a group of symptoms.

T
___   10. To concur is to agree.

Word Roots

Part 2

Part 2 presents two word roots that are concerned with coming together and moving apart, but do not carry these meanings directly. These roots are *greg* and *sperse*.

This part also presents some words that were taken from other languages when English speakers came into contact with them.

greg (flock; herd)
   Greg once referred to a flock of sheep or a herd of cattle. By extension, *greg* has come to be used as a word element meaning the action of coming, or "flocking," together. For example, one word you will learn, *gregarious,* describes people who like to **come together** with other people.
sperse (scatter)
   When we scatter things, we move them apart. Thus, the root *sperse* is concerned with being apart. *Disperse,* one of the words in this lesson, means "to **scatter** widely."

Words to Learn

Part 2

greg

13. **congregate** (verb)   kŏng′grĭ-gāt′

    From Latin: *con-* (together) + *greg* (flock, herd)

    to meet; to assemble

Both houses of Congress **congregated** to hear the President's State of the Union address.

Crowds **congregated** around the Pope during his visit to Cuba.

The cold children **congregated** around the door, waiting to be let into school.

▶ *Related Word*

congregation (noun)   The *congregation* listened intently to the minister's sermon.

Congregation is a religious word, meaning the members of a religious organization, such as a church or synagogue. Many other religious words have interesting origins.

Catholic, from the meaning "universal"   When spelled with a small *c*, *catholic* still means "universal," rather than the religion.

Protestant, from *protest*   In the early 1500s, Martin Luther and his followers protested against certain Catholic practices. They formed a new set of "protesting" religions.

Jewish, from the Hebrew word *Judah*, the ancient Jewish Kingdom

Muslim, from the Arabic word *aslama*, meaning "he surrendered," referring to people who are obedient to Allah's will

Hindu, from the Persian word for India, *Hind*

---

14. **gregarious** (adjective)   grĭ-gâr′ē-əs

From Latin: *greg* (flock; herd)

sociable; fond of company

Since Thelma was **gregarious,** she loved to talk to clients while she styled their hair.

Politicians are usually **gregarious** people who love crowds, meetings, and public appearances.

▶ *Related Word*

gregariousness (noun)   Because of his *gregariousness*, George hated to work at home alone.

15. **segregate** (verb)   sĕg′rĭ-gāt′

From Latin: *sē-* (apart) + *greg* (flock; herd) (*Sēgregāre* meant "to separate from the flock.")

to separate

In some religious traditions, men are **segregated** from women during prayer services.

Although laws do not **segregate** them, there has been increasing separation of the living quarters of Turkish immigrants from others in Cologne, Germany.

▶ *Related Word*
segregation (noun)   The laws of apartheid, requiring the *segregation* of blacks and whites in South Africa, were repealed only in the early 1990s.

sperse

16. **disperse** (verb)   dĭ-spûrs′

From Latin: *dis-* (apart) + *sperse* (scatter)

to scatter; to distribute widely

Refinishing furniture outdoors allows harmful chemical fumes to **disperse** into the open air.

Antifreeze allows moisture that has accumulated in a gas tank to **disperse.**

The crowd **dispersed** after the parade ended.

▶ *Related Word*
dispersion (noun) (dĭ-spûr′zhən)   The students observed the *dispersion* of light through a prism.

17. **intersperse** (verb)   ĭn′tər-spûrs′

From Latin: *inter-* (between) + *sperse* (scatter)

to scatter here and there; to distribute among other things

The Sublime band, a rock-ska fusion, **interspersed** music with clips of phone messages and police broadcasts.

Most people **intersperse** their speech with expressions like "hmmm" and "uh."

The paved highway was **interspersed** with stretches of dirt road.

▶ *Common Phrase*
intersperse with

18. **sparse** (adjective)   spärs

From Latin: *sperse* (scatter)

thinly scattered or distributed; meager

Rain is so **sparse** in western Nebraska that ruts of wagon wheels made over a hundred years ago can still be seen.

Several medical conditions cause **sparse** hair growth.

▶ *Related Word*
  sparsity (noun)   Due to a *sparsity* of minority teachers through-
    out the school district, the school board sent representatives
    to a hiring fair.

Borrowed Words

19. **bravado** (noun)   brə-vä′dō

From Spanish

false bravery; showy display of courage

  In a show of **bravado,** the teenager challenged the famous gun-
    slinger to a shootout.

20. **charisma** (noun)   kə-rĭz′mə

From Greek

quality of leadership that attracts other people

  Oprah Winfrey's **charisma** has transformed her from a TV per-
    sonality into an important spokesperson of popular culture,
    concerns, and causes.

▶ *Related Word*
  charismatic (adjective)   (kăr′ĭz-măt′ĭk)   Church attendance
    increased dramatically under the *charismatic* leadership of the
    new minister.

Although the special quality of *charisma* is hard to define, history records many charismatic leaders. Pancho Villa's *charismatic* leadership
popularized the cause of the Mexican Revolution of 1910.

  Napoleon Bonaparte became emperor of France in 1804, eleven
years after the French had beheaded King Louis XVI and declared
the country a republic. It is said that Napoleon's *charisma* was so
strong that anybody who met him would be captured by his personality. Napoleon united the French behind him and managed to conquer half of Europe before he was defeated by England and Austria in
1815.

  In his powerful speeches, the modern African-American leader
Martin Luther King, Jr., inspired all who heard him with the justice of
his great cause. King employed nonviolent peace marches to win rights
for African Americans.

21. **cliché** (noun)   klē-shā′

From French

an overused, trite expression

An example of a **cliché** often used in sports is "no pain, no gain."

The official's speech was full of **clichés** and promises, but it gave no plan of action.

Popular **clichés,** ones you have undoubtedly heard, include "Every cloud has a silver lining," "Don't cry over spilt milk," "That's how the cookie crumbles," "A stitch in time saves nine," and "Home is where the heart is."

22. **cuisine** (noun)   kwĭ-zēn′

From French

a style of food or cooking

Puerto Rican **cuisine** features delicious pasteles, which are made of cornmeal and stuffed with meat, raisins, olives, capers, and almonds.

The elegant restaurant featured Northern Chinese **cuisine.**

NOTE: Generally, a *cuisine* refers to food prepared by skilled cooks or chefs.

Cuisines of different regions feature various specialties. Can you match each food item with its country or group of origin?

1. curry
2. sushi
3. crepes
4. phò tai
5. fajitas
6. hummus

a. Arab
b. Japanese
c. Mexican
d. French
e. Vietnamese
f. Indian

Answers are on page 406.

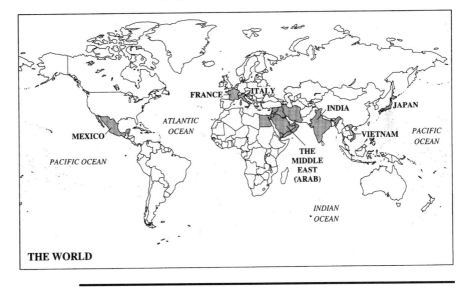

THE WORLD

23. **nadir** (noun)   nā′dər

From Arabic: *nazīr as-samt* (the lowest point; opposite the zenith)

the lowest point

> Homeless and alone, the man had reached the **nadir** of his life.
> Human behavior reaches its **nadir** in the act of genocide.

24. **zenith** (noun)   zē′nĭth

From Arabic: *samt ar-ra's* (the path overhead; the highest point in the heavens)

the highest point

> Centered in present-day Iraq, the Assyrian empire was at the **zenith** of its power from 900 to 650 B.C.E.

Arabic and early Middle Eastern cultures made many important contributions to astronomy. As early as 800 B.C.E., Babylonians and Assyrians had calculated new moons and composed a seasonal calendar. The Chaldeans (about 500 B.C.E.) had a table of lunar eclipses and knew the cycles of five planets around the sun. The work of Abū Ma'shar (born in 787 C.E.), who calculated the length of the year and catalogued the stars, was translated from Arabic into Latin. This work was one of the first books printed in Germany.

NOTE: *Zenith* is not used to refer to a physical high point, such as the top of a mountain. In that case, we refer to the *pinnacle* of a mountain.

Exercises

Part 2

■ Definitions

Match each word in the left-hand column with a definition from the right-hand column. Use each choice only once.

1. sparse __b__

2. zenith __i__

3. cuisine __a__

4. cliché __d__

5. gregarious __g__

6. charisma __f__

7. intersperse __k__

8. bravado __j__

9. segregate __c__

10. congregate __l__

a. style of cooking

b. thinly scattered

c. to separate

d. overused expression

e. to distribute among other things

f. a quality that attracts others

g. sociable

h. lowest point

i. highest point

j. showy display of bravery

k. to scatter; to distribute widely

l. to gather together

■ *Meanings*

Match each word root to its meaning. Use each choice only once.

1. sperse ___**b**___   a. flock; herd

2. greg ___**a**___   b. scatter

■ *Words in Context*

Complete each sentence with the word that fits best. Use each choice only once.

a. congregate   e. intersperse   i. cliché
b. gregarious   f. sparse   j. cuisines
c. segregate   g. bravado   k. nadir
d. disperse   h. charisma   l. zenith

1. The __**b, gregarious**__ couple went to many parties.

2. Because of his __**h, charisma**__, the rock star attracted fans and imitators.

3. At the political rally, they are planning to __**e, intersperse**__ speeches with videotaped presentations about the candidate's life.

4. The expression "Here today, gone tomorrow" is a __**i, cliché**__ that most of us have heard many times.

5. The young boxer displayed true __**g, bravado**__ when he publicly dared the champion to a fight.

6. Health officials wanted to __**c, segregate**__ the sick cows from the healthy ones.

7. Child abuse shows human nature at its __**k, nadir**__.

8. Elephants are now found only in __**f, sparse**__ locations in Africa; however, at one time they lived over a much wider territory.

9. At the __**l, zenith**__ of his power, Genghis Khan ruled a vast Asian empire.

10. In recent decades, Americans have extended their tastes beyond meat and potatoes and tried many different types of __**j, cuisines**__.

■ *Using Related Words*

Complete each sentence by using a word from the group of related words above it. You may need to capitalize a word when you write it in a sentence. Use each choice only once.

1. segregated, segregation

   During criminal trials, a jury is often "sequestered," or
   segregated——————— from other people. This helps to ensure that jury members will be influenced only by the evidence pre-
   sented in the trial. Without this **segregation**———————, they might make decisions based upon media reporting, the opinions of their friends or families, or other factors that should not be allowed to enter into decisions.

2. dispersion, disperse

   Small, fast-moving hummingbirds **disperse**——————— the pollen that fertilizes flowers. The birds' long bills gather nectar, and as hummingbirds move, they carry it from flower to flower. In this
   way, **dispersion**——————— allows flowers to be fertilized. Hummingbirds are especially attracted to red and orange flowers. If you wear these colors, they will be attracted to you too!

3. charisma, charismatic

   With his riveting blue eyes and mysterious manner, the Russian spiritual adviser Rasputin (1872–1916) was extremely
   charismatic———————. His **charisma**——————— attracted many followers, including Czarina Alexandra. Her devotion to Rasputin, deeply resented by the Russian people, may have been a factor leading to the revolution of 1917.

4. interspersed, interspersion

   The great playwright Shakespeare often **interspersed**——————— a
   few comic scenes into his tragic plays. This **interspersion**——————— allowed the audience some comic relief from the dramatic tension.

5. sparse, sparsity

In many portions of Canada, settlement is **sparse** _____ .
One can go for hundreds of miles without ever seeing other people.

This **sparsity** _____ of settlement is due to the cold climate and difficult living conditions.

■ *Reading the Headlines*

This exercise presents four headlines that might appear in newspapers. Read each one carefully and then answer the questions that follow. (Remember that little words, such as *is, are, a,* and *the,* are often left out of headlines.)

CHARISMATIC OUTLAW DISPLAYS BRAVADO AT NADIR OF FORTUNES

1. Does the outlaw have a following of people? **yes** _____

2. Does the outlaw appear to be a coward? **no** _____

3. Is the outlaw currently enjoying good luck? **no** _____

PEOPLE CONGREGATE TO HEAR POLITICIAN AT ZENITH OF POWER SPOUT CLICHÉS

4. Are there many people listening? **yes** _____

5. Is the politician currently powerful? **yes** _____

6. Is the politician saying something new and interesting?
   no _____

MILK SPARSE IN ASIAN CUISINES

7. Is there a lot of milk? **no** _____

8. Are Asian stores being described? **no** _____

LOW-COST HOUSING DISPERSED THROUGHOUT CITY USED TO COUNTER EFFECTS OF ETHNIC SEGREGATION

9. Is the housing in just a few locations? **no** _____

10. Have people been living in separate groups? **yes** _____

Chapter Exercises

■ *Practicing Strategies: New Words from Word Elements*

See how your knowledge of word elements can help you understand new words. Complete each sentence with the word that seems to fit best. Use each choice only once.

a. aggregate	e. compress	i. distrust
b. coexist	f. conform	j. disqualified
c. collide	g. disassociate	k. sympathize
d. community	h. discourteous	l. synchronized

1. Groups of people or animals that live together are said to

    b, coexist .

2. A person who is not qualified to compete in a race should be

    j, disqualified .

3. If we do not trust someone, we feel **i, distrust** for that person.

4. *Chronos* means "time," so two things that happen at the same time

    are **l, synchronized** .

5. When all of something is herded or gathered together, the total is

    called the **a, aggregate** .

6. To press together is to **e, compress** .

7. *Path-* means "feeling," so when we feel the same as another

    person, we **k, sympathize** .

8. Someone who is not courteous is **h, discourteous** .

9. A(n) **d, community** consists of many people together.

10. When we come apart from people we have been associated with, we

    g, disassociate ourselves from them.

■ *Practicing Strategies: Combining Context Clues and Word Elements*

Combining the strategies of context clues and word elements is a good way to figure out unknown words. In the following sentences, each italicized word contains a word element that you have studied in this chapter. Using the meaning of the word element and the context of the sentence, make an intelligent guess about the meaning of the italicized word. Your instructor may ask you to check the meaning in your dictionary when you have finished.

1. Because of the total *concordance* of the aims of the delegates, the meeting was a complete success.

   Concordance means ___agreement; togetherness___ .

2. After seven active children played in the house all day, it was in a state of *disarray*.

   Disarray means ___disorder; messiness___ .

3. In many movie musicals, stars *lip-synch* lyrics that are actually sung by other people.

   Lip-synch means ___mouthing the words at the same time that some-___

   ___one else is singing them___ .

4. The man was so *disheartened* by his failure to find a job that he stopped his search.

   Disheartened means ___upset; discouraged___ .

5. At the *confluence* of the Green River with the Colorado River, the color of the water is a mix of both sources.

   Confluence means ___flowing together; joining together___ .

■ *Companion Words*

Complete each sentence with the word that fits best. Choose your answers from the words below. You may use each word more than once.

Choices: with, on, of, in

1. There was a disparity ___in___ the money spent for education of rich and poor children.

2. The student read a five-page synopsis **of**_____ *Romeo and Juliet.*

3. There is a sparsity **of**_____ rain in a desert.

4. The high school class collaborated **on**_____ plans for a graduation party.

5. This style is a synthesis **of**_____ many different fashion trends.

6. In the evening, people congregate **in**_____ the town square.

7. Good speakers often intersperse their presentations **with**_____ jokes.

8. The taste of ketchup is not compatible **with**_____ that of ice cream.

9. My adviser concurred **with**_____ my choice of classes.

10. The Beatles were contemporaries **of**_____ my professor.

■ *Writing with Your Words*

This exercise will give you practice in writing effective sentences that use the vocabulary words. Each sentence is started for you. Complete it with an interesting phrase that also indicates the meaning of the italicized word.

1. An example of a *cliché* is _____

   _____ .

2. A *communal* dormitory _____

   _____ .

3. Because of her *charismatic* personality, _____

   _____ .

4. A *syndrome* _____

   _____ .

5. My favorite *cuisine* is _____

   _____ .

6. After I *dispersed* the money, _____

_____ .

7. At the *nadir* of his career, the athlete _____

_____ .

8. Because the plot of the movie was not *coherent,* _____

_____ .

9. You would call a person *gregarious* if _____

_____ .

10. Because of their continuing *discord* _____

_____ .

Passage

Intelligence Under Fire: The Story of the Navajo Code Talkers

When Marines raised the U.S. flag on the island of Iwo Jima in 1945, the picture of Ira Hayes, a Navajo Indian, became world famous. A statue modeled from this picture stands in Arlington National Cemetery as a tribute to one of the hardest-fought battles of World War II. But unlike Hayes's picture, the heroic role of the Navajo code talkers in the battle has only recently become known. This is their story.

In many ways, the **nadir** of United States justice is the country's treatment of Native Americans. In 1863, for example, the U.S. Army destroyed crops and animals, exiled the Navajos from their lands, and ordered them onto reservations. There Navajo children attended Bureau of Indian Affairs schools, where they were forbidden to use their own language. One man remembers being chained in a basement for daring to speak Navajo! Navajos faced other forms of discrimination too, including being **(1) segregated** in restaurants and movie theaters.

But the language that the schoolmasters disdained would prove to be a powerful weapon in World War II. When the United States entered the war in 1941, over one hundred Navajos, some as young as 15, volun-

Ira Hayes, a Navajo, helps to plant a flag celebrating victory at Iwo Jima.

teered to fight. In a show of **bravado,** some even brought their own rifles, which would have been useless against the powerful weaponry of Japan and Germany. But, as it turned out, Navajos provided one of the most precious resources of the war.

(2) Experts **concur** that communication is an extremely difficult problem during warfare. Fighting units can be miles apart, **(3)** yet they must **collaborate** in making decisions, so that fighting is coordinated. Messages may be put into code, but the enemy will have "code breakers" specially designed to decode the messages. In World War II, what could the U.S. Army do?

Philip Johnston, an army engineer, had lived on a Navajo reservation as a child. He understood some Navajo and recognized what a complex, sophisticated, and precise language it was. Because it had no written symbols, it was almost impossible for the Japanese enemy to study. He asked the armed forces to gather Navajo enlistments and have them create a code for their native language.

In response, twenty-nine Navajos who could speak both English and Navajo gathered in San Diego and **(4)** began a **communal** effort to write the code. Messages could not simply be given in Navajo, for a captured Navajo might be forced to decode them for an enemy. **(5)** So, the coders **synthesized** symbols and spelling. Some words got symbols, such as *bird* for *airplane* and *fish* for *ship*. In addition, each letter of the alphabet was given a Navajo word, so that other words could be spelled. *A*, for example, was given the Navajo word for *ant*, which is *wol-la-chee*. Since symbols for words were **interspersed** with symbols for letters, the code could not be understood, even by those who spoke Navajo. **(6)** One had to speak Navajo, speak English, and know the code for a message to be **coherent.**

After composing the code, **(7)** the twenty-nine Navajos were **dispersed** into Marine battalions fighting the Japanese in the Pacific. Within a few weeks, they had proved their worth. In one battle, one American force accidentally attacked another. When the force under attack radioed their fellow Americans, the attackers refused to stop unless they heard the message in Navajo code. A code talker was located, and within minutes, the firing had ceased.

But code talking reached its **zenith** during the attack on Iwo Jima, one of the most dangerous missions of the war. U.S. Marines had to land on the Japanese island and then cross loose volcanic ash. With their movements slowed and **(8)** only **sparse** tree growth to hide them, the Americans were easy targets. In contrast, the Japanese were hidden in deep trenches. Under terrible fire, the Marines painfully made their way to Mount Suribachi. During the assault, the code talkers sent more than eight hundred messages, all without error. Six worked continuously, without sleep, for forty-eight hours. When the Marines got to the peak of Suribachi, Ira Hayes planted the U.S. flag. Another Navajo sent the message of victory: "Sheep-Uncle-Ram-Ice-Bear-Ant-Cat-Horse-Itch." The first letters spell "Suribachi." **(9)** The language that was too **disreputable** to use in school had enabled the United States to take Iwo Jima. One official referred to the Navajos as "walking, talking weapons."

When World War II ended, the code talkers were released with no special honors or awards. In fact, the armed forces cautioned them not to talk about their experiences, for the code might be used again. **(10)** There was a shameful **disparity** between the priceless service the men had given during the war and the way Navajos continued to be treated. In fact, the men who had served their country so well were not even permitted to vote in their own states.

Today, the Navajo code talkers, as well as most of their **contemporaries,** are gone, but their story is becoming widely known. Their intelligence under fire serves as a reminder of a nation's shameful past, war's most heroic moments, and the enduring value of different cultures to the United States.

■ *Exercise*

Each sentence below corresponds to a sentence in the Passage. Fill in the letter of the choice that makes the sentence mean the same thing as its corresponding sentence in the Passage.

1. Navajos were ___**c**___ in restaurants and movie theaters.
   a. helped   b. picked on   c. separated   d. crowded

2. Experts ___**b**___ that communication is a difficult problem during warfare.
   a. discover   b. agree   c. feel   d. know

3. Yet they must ___**d**___ in making decisions.
   a. help each other   b. be agreed   c. not harm each other
   d. work together

4. Navajos began a(n) ___**d**___ effort to write the code.
   a. extended   b. essential   c. hopeless   d. community

5. The coders ___**b**___ symbols and spelling.
   a. commonly used   b. put together   c. found out about   d. left alone

6. One had to speak Navajo, speak English, and know the code for a message to be ___**b**___ .
   a. easy   b. logical   c. translated   d. useful

7. The twenty-nine Navajos were ___**d**___ into Marine battalions.
   a. shipped   b. forced   c. trapped   d. scattered

8. They had only ___**a**___ tree growth to hide them.
   a. scattered   b. short   c. one type of   d. green

9. The language too ___**b**___ to use in school had enabled the United States to take Iwo Jima.
   a. lacking in easiness   b. lacking in respect
   c. lacking in translation   d. lacking in speakers

10. There was a shameful ___**b**___ .
   a. discrimination   b. difference   c. response   d. hopelessness

■ *Discussion Questions*

1. Name two ways in which Navajos have been deprived of their rights.

2. In what way was the Navajo code a synthesis?

3. Would you have been a code talker if given the opportunity? Why or why not?

◀ **E**NGLISH **I**DIOMS

Agreement and Anger

English has many idioms that express agreement, which brings us together with others, and anger, which sets us apart. People who become angry are said to *lose their heads, blow their tops,* or *lose their cool.* Such individuals *let off steam* through harsh words or actions.

Other idioms concern negative feelings that are not quite as strong as anger. *To speak one's piece* is to speak frankly, and usually with some anger, but without losing one's temper. Somebody who annoys you *rubs you the wrong way.*

People calm their anger and make peace, or *make up* with others. When people realize they have been wrong and want to regain friendship or influence, they *mend fences,* perhaps by apologizing. Similarly, when people find that they are in agreement or have interests in common, they are said to have *common ground.*

If you are angry with people, you might *read them the riot act,* or give a strong warning or scolding. The original riot act was passed in 1774 to stop protests against King George III of England. When more than a dozen people gathered, a riot act was read, ordering them to disperse. If they did not obey, they were imprisoned or shot.

Quiz Again

Now that you have finished studying this chapter, here is the brief true-false quiz you took when you began. Take it again.

A **disparity** is a difference.	True	False
Charisma attracts people.	True	False
Gregarious people hate parties.	True	False
Disreputable people enjoy good reputations.	True	False

Answers are on page 406. Did your score improve?

REVIEW

Chapters 5-8

■ Reviewing Words in Context

Complete each sentence with the word or term that fits best. You may have to capitalize some words.

A JOURNEY FROM VIETNAM TO THE UNITED STATES

a. abducted	e. congregated	i. reconcile	m. tenacity
b. antipathy	f. interminable	j. status quo	n. transcend
c. circumvent	g. jettison	k. staunch	o. transformations
d. communal	h. odyssey	l. transitory	p. vital

Background: Viem, a student in the author's class, was born in Vietnam. This is the story of his life there and his escape to the United States.

1. I was born in Saigon, Vietnam. My father had fought for the U.S. allies against the communists. The communists felt much _**b, antipathy**_ for people like him. He was even put in jail for six months.

2. I too felt some discrimination, and had to _**n, transcend**_ many difficulties. To get into college, I needed a higher exam score than children of people who had fought for the communists.

3. I knew that unless the _**j, status quo**_ changed, I would have a hard time in Vietnam.

4. Since I could not _**i, reconcile**_ myself to such a life, I decided to escape.

5. _**m, Tenacity**_ was very important, because ten of my efforts failed. In 1982, I finally succeeded.

6. I made my way to the seacoast, carefully trying to _**c, circumvent**_ the police, who would have arrested me.

7. Forty-three people _**e, congregated**_ on a beach to board the small, open fishing boat that would take us from Vietnam to Malaysia.

8. The sea was so rough that at times we had to bail water out of the boat and even _**g, jettison**_ some of our belongings.

9. We ran short of food, water, and other **p, vital** _____ supplies.

10. Although the trip seemed **f, interminable** _____ , it was actually only four days.

11. In fact, we were very lucky. The boat before us was lost at sea for fifty-two days and many died. The boat after us was captured by the Vietnamese police. Other boats were stopped by pirates who **a, abducted** _____ passengers and held them for ransom. Some pirates even killed the passengers.

12. Once I arrived in Malaysia, I was put in a refugee camp with **d, communal** _____ living quarters that I shared with several men.

13. My **h, odyssey** _____ to the United States included transfers to two other refugee camps.

14. When I came to the United States, my **k, staunch** _____ health enabled me to quickly adapt to the cold weather and the snow in Chicago, the city I live in.

15. In the ten years that I have been here I have made many **o, transformations** _____ in my lifestyle, my language, and my career. Currently I am looking forward to graduating college and working in the field of computers.

■ *Passage for Word Review*

Complete each blank in the passage with the word that makes the best sense. The choices include words from the vocabulary lists along with related words. Use each choice only once. You may have to capitalize some words.

RUNNING TRACK

a. abstained	e. dejected	i. renowned	m. synopsis
b. compatible	f. gregarious	j. spartan	n. tenaciously
c. conducive	g. psyche	k. stature	o. viable
d. congregated	h. reconcile	l. subdue	p. vital

Background: William, a student in the author's class, describes what competitive running did for him—and to him.

When I started high school, I was only about 5 feet 2 inches in

(1) **k, stature** _____ and weighed about 95 pounds. As you can imagine, I was very small in size. I wanted to play a sport, and I didn't have much of a choice of which one. I didn't have the size for football, the height for basketball, or an interest in baseball. But I could run fast, so joining the track team seemed to be my only

(2) **o, viable** _____ option. I was afraid of the coach, but I decided to go ahead. After a week of tryouts, I finally made it.

Being in good shape is (3) **p, vital** _____ to an athlete. I worked out every day, including weekends. After a boring job, I remember going home to do yet another workout. I also trained

(4) **n, tenaciously** _____ , practicing my running whenever I could. I was so tired that I would sometimes fall asleep while eating my dinner.

I (5) **a, abstained** _____ from doing anything unhealthy, like smoking. I lived a(n) (6) **j, spartan** _____ existence, concentrating on school, work, and running.

My teammates were (7) **f, gregarious** _____ people, who liked to socialize. I found that their interests were (8) **b, compatible** _____ with my own and enjoyed spending time with them. This atmosphere was

(9) **c, conducive** _____ to a winning team spirit.

By my senior year, I was captain of a(n) (10) **i, renowned** _____ track team that had set records throughout the state. People

(11) **d, congregated** _____ to see our races. I even had a personal fan or two!

Then, during the indoor track season of my senior year, a terrible thing happened. I pulled both my hamstrings. I went through two months of physical therapy before I could walk normally. You can imagine that

I was extremely (12) **e, dejected** _____ when I was told I would never compete again.

But I could not (13) **l, subdue** _____ my desire to run. After therapy, I began working out again and told my coach I wanted to run in the city meets. He let me run, although I now had to

(14) **h, reconcile** _____ myself to the fact that it would hurt. Despite this, I qualified for the city meet. But the following week I had to quit running in the middle of my race—the race I was favored to win. As I

walked across the finish line, I heard the crowd cheer! You can imagine

that this helped my **(15)** **g, psyche** _____ .

I have not given up on my dream of competing. At the moment, I am training to run track later in my college years.

■ *Reviewing Learning Strategies*

New Words from Word Elements   Below are words you have not studied that are formed from classical word elements. Using your knowledge of these elements, write in the word that best completes each sentence. You may have to capitalize some words. Use each choice only once.

a. anthropogenesis   e. immortal   i. regenerates
b. co-counsel   f. inequity   j. sympathy
c. distaste   g. intractable k. synonym
d. ex-member   h. invisible   l. vivid

1. A person who used to belong to a club is a(n) **d, ex-member** _____ .

2. A word with the "same name," or same meaning, as another is a(n) **k, synonym** _____ .

3. If you do not like a particular food, you may have a(n) **c, distaste** _____ for it.

4. The legal counsel shared all the responsibilities with a(n) **b, co-counsel** _____ .

5. **a, Anthropogenesis** _____ refers to the origins of human beings.

6. When two things are not fair, or equal, there is a(n) **f, inequity** _____ .

7. A person who lives forever would be **e, immortal** _____ .

8. When a plant grows new leaves or is "born again," after appearing to be dead, it **i, regenerates** _____ .

9. A(n) **g, intractable** _____ person is stubborn or "cannot be pulled."

10. Something that cannot be seen is **h, invisible** _____ .

Word Elements: Numbers and Measures

In ancient times the lives of most human beings were organized around farming. People needed words that dealt with numbers and measurement to tell them *when* planting should take place, *how many* units of grain the soil yielded, and *how much* in trade or in money they would get for their crops. From these words were developed modern words for quantities. This chapter presents Latin and ancient Greek word elements that will help you with the meanings of thousands of words.

Chapter Strategy: Word Elements: Numbers and Measures

Chapter Words:

Part 1

uni-	unanimity	*di-, du-*	dilemma
	unilateral		duplicity
mono-	monarchy	*tri-*	trilogy
	monopoly		trivial
bi-	bilingual	*dec-*	decade
	bipartisan		decimate

Part 2

cent-	centennial	*integer*	disintegrate
	centigrade		integrity
ambi-, amphi-	ambiguous	*magn-, mega-*	magnanimous
	ambivalence		magnitude
ann, enn	annals	*meter, -meter*	metric
	perennial		symmetrical

Quiz Yourself

To check your knowledge of some chapter words before you begin to study, identify these statements as true or false.

Unanimity involves agreement.	True	False
To **decimate** something is to improve it.	True	False
Friends generally demonstrate **duplicity** toward each other.	True	False
Something that is **perennial** disappears quickly.	True	False

You will learn the answers as you study this chapter.

Did You Know?

How Were the Months of the Year Named?

Did you ever wonder how the months got their names? Some of the names are based on number word elements; other months are named after gods. It took civilization thousands of years to develop an accurate calendar. Ancient ones were so inaccurate that people often found themselves planting crops when the calendar claimed that winter was approaching. The Roman leader Julius Caesar ordered the calendar reformed about two thousand years ago, and hence, the months bear Latin names. There have been other changes since then, but even now the calendar is not perfect. We must adjust the length of our years by adding an extra day (February 29) in every fourth, or leap, year.

January gets its name from the god Janus, the doorkeeper of the gate of heaven and the god of doors. Since doors are used to enter, Janus represented beginnings, and the first month of the year is dedicated to him. Janus is pictured with two faces; one looks back to the past year, and one looks forward to the new year.

February comes from Februa, the Roman festival of purification. *March* is named for Mars, the Roman god of war. *April* has an uncertain origin. It may be from *apero*, which means "second," for at one time it was the second month of the year, or from *aperīre* (to open) since it is the month when flowers and trees open out in bloom.

May comes from the goddess of fertility, Maia. It was natural to name a spring month for the goddess who was thought to control the crops. *June* was named either for the Junius family of Roman nobles or for the goddess Juno, wife of Jupiter. *July* honors Julius Caesar, the Roman leader we have mentioned. You will read about him in the Passage for this chapter.

August is named for Augustus Caesar, the nephew of Julius Caesar and the first emperor of Rome. His actual name was Octavian, but he took the title of *Augustus* because it meant "distinguished." The word *august* still means "distinguished" when the second syllable of the word is stressed.

The last four months all contain number prefixes: *September, sept* (seven); *October, oct* (eight); *November, nov* (nine); *December, dec* (ten). As you can see, the number roots are wrong! How did the ninth, tenth, eleventh, and twelfth months get the elements of seven, eight, nine, and ten?

Until 153 B.C.E. the new year was celebrated in March, so the months corresponded to the correct numbers. Then a change in the calendar left these months with the wrong meanings.

Learning Strategy

Word Elements: Numbers and Measures

Every word element in this chapter has a meaning of number or measurement. A list of the prefixes for the first ten numbers is given below. Although you won't be studying all of them in this chapter, you will find this list a handy reference for textbooks and everyday reading. English uses these number prefixes frequently; in fact, we are still making new words from them.

Prefix	Meaning	Example Word
uni-	one	unidirectional (in one direction)
mono-	one	monologue (speech by one person)
bi-	two	bidirectional (in two directions)
di-, du-	two	diatomic (made up of two atoms)
tri-	three	trio (a musical group of three)
quad-, quar-	four	quartet (a musical group of four)
quint-, quin-	five	quintet (a musical group of five)
sex-	six	sextet (a musical group of six)
sept-	seven	septet (a musical group of seven)
oct-	eight	octet (a musical group of eight)
nov-	nine	novena (a prayer offered for nine days)
dec-	ten	decade (ten years)

*You will study these word elements intensively in this chapter.

To test your understanding of these number word prefixes, fill in the blanks in the following sentences.

a. A duplex is an apartment with __**two**__ floors.

b. A trilingual person speaks __**three**__ languages.

c. A quadruped is an animal that walks on __**four**__ feet.

d. When a mother has quintuplets, __**five**__ children are born.

e. Sextuple means to multiply by __**six**__ .

f. If something is produced in septuplicate, there are __**seven**__ copies of it altogether.

Answers are on page 406.

All the word elements you will study in this chapter are either number prefixes *(uni-, mono-, bi-, di-, tri-, dec-, cent-)* or measurement roots and prefixes *(ambi-, ann, integer, magn-, meter)*.

Element	Meaning	Origin	Function	Chapter Words
				Part 1
uni-	one	Latin	prefix	unanimity, unilateral
mono-	one; single	Greek	prefix	monarchy, monopoly
bi-	two	Latin	prefix	bilingual, bipartisan
di-, du-	two	Greek; Latin	prefix	dilemma, duplicity
tri-	three	Greek; Latin	prefix	trilogy, trivial
dec-	ten	Greek; Latin	prefix	decade, decimate
				Part 2
cent-	hundred	Latin	prefix	centennial, centigrade
ambi-, amphi-	both; around	Latin; Greek	prefix	ambiguous, ambivalence
ann, enn	year	Latin	root	annals, perennial
integer	whole; complete	Latin	root	disintegrate, integrity
magn-, mega-	large	Latin; Greek	prefix	magnanimous, magnitude
meter, -meter	measure	Greek; Latin	root suffix	metric, symmetrical

This chapter presents a large number of word elements for study, twelve in all. However, the number prefixes follow a clear pattern. They are arranged in order of the numbers they represent, rather than in alphabetical order. The first six are discussed below.

Prefixes

Part 1

uni- (one)

The Latin prefix for one, *uni-*, is used in many English words. To *unite,* for example, is to make several things into **one.** *Unisex* clothing uses **one** design that is suitable for both men and women.

The *unicorn* was a mythical animal of great grace and beauty. Named for its one horn, it was supposed to have the legs of a deer, the tail of a lion, and the body of a horse. It is often represented as white with a red head and a horn of white, red, and black. Certainly, this animal would have had an interesting appearance!

---

mono- (one, single)

The Greek prefix for one, *mono-*, is usually joined to Greek combining roots. For example, *monogamy* is marriage to **one** person. A *monologue* is a speech given by **one** person. *Mono-* is also used to form many technical words used in scientific fields.

bi- (two)

The Latin prefix for two, *bi-*, forms words such as *bifocals,* glasses that contain **two** visual corrections. When the *bicycle* was invented in the 1860s, it was named for its **two** wheels.

di-, du- (two)

This Greek prefix for two is often used in scientific and technical words, so you will find it useful in your college courses. For example, the word *dichromatic* refers to animals that change their colors in different seasons and, therefore, have **two** colors.

tri- (three)

A *triangle* is a **three**-sided figure. A *tricornered* hat has a brim turned up on **three** sides. A *tricycle* has **three** wheels.

dec- (ten)

The *decimal* system uses the base **ten.** The common word *dime,* a **tenth** part of a dollar, is also taken from the prefix *dec-*.

Words to Learn

Part 1

uni-

1. **unanimity** (noun)   yo͞o′nə-nĭm′ĭ-tē

   From Latin: *uni-* (one) + *animus* (soul) (When people agree, they seem to have one soul.)

   complete agreement

   > If jurors cannot reach **unanimity** in a verdict, a hung jury is reported.
   >
   > The people of the nation demonstrated **unanimity** in opposing the aggressor's threat.
   >
   > In a surprising display of **unanimity,** every city council member voted to ban parking on Main Street.

   ▶ *Related Word*
   > **unanimous** (adjective) Scholars are *unanimous* in their praise for Shakespeare's plays and sonnets.

2. **unilateral** (adjective)   yo͞o′nə-lăt′ər-əl

   From Latin: *uni-* (one) + *latus* (side)

   arbitrary; one sided; relating to only one side or part

   > Without waiting for approval by Congress, the U.S. President made a **unilateral** decision to send troops into the small country.
   >
   > Students and faculty were angered when the dean of student services made a **unilateral** decision to ban all smoking from campus.

mono-

3. **monarchy** (noun)   mŏn′ər-kē   (plural: monarchies)

   From Greek: *mono-* (one) + *arkein* (rule)

   a state ruled by a king, queen, or emperor

   > Saudi Arabia is a **monarchy.**

   NOTE: Rule in a monarchy is hereditary and passes from parent to child, usually in the male line. However, in the modern world, women can reign. In Sweden, a change to the constitution in 1980 dictated that the eldest child of the royal couple—whether male or female—would be heir to the throne. In 1998, Queen Elizabeth of England changed centuries of tradition when she put the same rule of succession in place for Great Britain.

▶ *Related Word*

monarch (noun)   One *monarch,* Henry VIII of England (1491–1547), was married six times.

Although *monarchs* once held absolute power, there are now many constitutional *monarchies,* or governments that limit the power of kings. Bhumibol Adulyadej, constitutional monarch of Thailand (formerly Siam), has provided stable leadership by supporting democratic institutions. He is the world's longest-reigning *monarch.* His ancestors led the way for strong leadership. Chulalongkorn (or Rama V, 1869–1910) abolished slavery and maintained independence against English and French colonialism. His father, Mongkut (1804–1868), had prepared for modernization by welcoming foreigners. The famous play and movie *The King and I* tells the story of an English governess who worked in Mongkut's court.

---

4. **monopoly** (noun)   mə-nŏp′ə-lē

From Greek: *mono-* (single) + *pōlein* (to sell) (When only one company or person can sell something, a monopoly exists.)

exclusive possession or control

England once maintained a **monopoly** over the sale of salt in India.

Some states have a **monopoly** on the sale of liquor.

▶ *Related Words*

monopolistic (adjective)   *Monopolistic* control of an industry by one company generally leads to high prices for the consumer.

monopolize (verb)   The teenager *monopolized* the family telephone.

bi-

5. **bilingual** (adjective)   bī-lĭng′gwəl

From Latin: *bi-* (two) + *lingua* (tongue, language)

having or speaking two languages

Children can easily become **bilingual,** but adults have more difficulty learning a second language.

The **bilingual** prayer book was printed in Hebrew and English.

▶ *Related Word*

bilingualism (noun) *Bilingualism* is essential for students who run WRTE, a Chicago radio station featuring music, news, and documentaries in Spanish and English.

A large number of people in both Canada and the United States are *bilingual.* Many Canadians speak French and English. In the United States, the most widely spoken languages, after English, are Spanish, Vietnamese, Hmong, Cantonese, Cambodian, Korean, Laotian, Navajo, Tagalog, and Russian.

---

6. **bipartisan** (adjective) bī-pär′tĭ-zən

From Latin: *bi-* (two) + *pars* (part)

supported by members of two parties

Both Republicans and Democrats on the **bipartisan** committee worked on tax reform.

di-, du-

7. **dilemma** (noun) dĭ-lĕm′ə

From Greek: *di-* (two) + *lēmma* (proposition) (A choice between two propositions or alternatives puts us in a *dilemma.*)

problem; difficult choice between equally bad things

Dorothy was faced with the **dilemma** of having either to drop the course or to flunk it.

As scientists map the human genetic code, moral *dilemmas* arise. Prediction of illnesses can lead people to seek earlier treatment. On the other hand, if insurance companies can demand genetic information from individuals, they may use it to limit benefits. The issue of financial rewards from the information gained by mapping genes is also a *dilemma.* Recently, the Icelandic government granted a *monopoly* on genetic mapping to Decode, a private company. There is lively discussion about whether one company should be alone in profiting from this important scientific process.

---

8. **duplicity** (noun) dōō-plĭs′ĭ-tē

From Latin: *du-* (two) + *plicāre* (to fold or complicate) (A person who is involved in duplicity is not straightforward but is "folded in two ways.")

deceitfulness; double-dealing

The spy's **duplicity** was revealed to a shocked nation.

In an act of **duplicity,** Mona's friend taped their private conversations and passed them on to her boyfriend.

▶ *Related Word*
duplicitous (adjective)   The *duplicitous* leader betrayed his allies.

tri-

9. **trilogy** (noun)   trĭl′ə-jē

From Greek: *tri-* (three) + *log* (word; to speak)

a group of three books, plays, or stories

The *Cairo **Trilogy*** by Naghib Mafouz tells the story of a traditional Egyptian family in a rapidly changing country.

10. **trivial** (adjective)   trĭv′ē-əl

From Latin: *tri-* (three) + *via* (road) (In Latin, *trivium* meant "where three roads meet," the public square where people would gossip.)

unimportant; silly

Fashion is a **trivial** topic when compared to world peace.

The teenager's fight with her friend upset her, but seemed **trivial** to her parents.

Such **trivial** issues as folding towels or squeezing toothpaste tubes from the bottom can cause problems in a marriage.

ordinary; commonplace

It was a **trivial** task for the experienced electrician to install a new plug on the toaster.

▶ *Related Words*
trivia (noun)   Marisa was an expert on movie *trivia*. (*Trivia* is unimportant information.)
triviality (noun)   This *triviality* is not worth our attention.
trivialize (verb)   A focus on gifts and parties can *trivialize* the religious meaning of Christmas.

dec-

11. **decade** (noun)   dĕk′ād′

From Greek: *dec-* (ten) (*Dekas* meant "group of ten.")

a ten-year period

During the **decade** of the 1950s, images of women concentrated on the roles of wife and mother.

Because of the demands of supporting a family, it took Mr. Markman almost a **decade** to complete his college degree.

12. **decimate** (verb)   dĕs′ə-māt′

From Latin: *dec-* (ten) (*Decimāre* meant "to take the tenth." This was the severe practice of killing every tenth soldier, chosen by lot, in order to punish a mutiny.)

to destroy or kill a large part of

Introduced accidentally in cartons for imports, the Asian long-horn beetle has **decimated** trees in some U.S. urban areas.

Starvation **decimated** the ship's crew.

Hailstones **decimated** the farmer's crop.

▶ *Related Word*
decimation (noun)   After its *decimation* by bombing during World War II, the Dutch city of Rotterdam was completely rebuilt.

Exercises

Part 1

■ Definitions

Match each word in the left-hand column with a definition from the right-hand column. Use each choice only once.

1. monarchy __l__

2. trilogy __h__

3. decade __f__

4. unanimity __g__

5. decimate __i__

6. duplicity __b__

7. trivial __c__

8. monopoly __j__

9. bipartisan __e__

10. dilemma __k__

a. arbitrary

b. deceitfulness

c. unimportant

d. speaking two languages

e. supported by both sides

f. ten-year period

g. complete agreement

h. three books or plays

i. to destroy most of something

j. control by one person or company

k. problem

l. a state ruled by a king or queen

■ *Meanings*

Match each word element to its meaning. Two of the choices in the right-hand column should be used twice.

1. tri- __**b**__

2. uni- __**c**__

3. dec- __**a**__

4. mono- __**c**__

5. bi- __**d**__

6. di- __**d**__

a. ten

b. three

c. one

d. two

■ *Words in Context*

Complete each sentence with the word that fits best. Use each choice only once. You may have to capitalize some words.

a. unanimity   e. bilingual   i. trilogy
b. unilateral   f. bipartisan   j. trivial
c. monarchy   g. dilemma   k. decade
d. monopoly   h. duplicity   l. decimate

1. One famous film __**i, trilogy**__ consists of *Star Wars, The Empire Strikes Back,* and *Return of the Jedi.*

2. Since people are different, things that seem __**j, trivial**__ to some may be important to others.

3. Until 1893, Hawaii was a(n) __**c, monarchy**__ ruled by a queen.

4. For many years, the government of Japan had a complete __**d, monopoly**__ on tobacco and, thus, full control of cigarette sales.

5. The __**k, decade**__ between 1960 and 1970 was marked by growing freedom in lifestyles and politics.

6. __**e, Bilingual**__ teachers can instruct children in two languages.

7. By their 9–0 vote, the Supreme Court members showed their

   a, unanimity in declaring school segregation unconstitutional in the 1954 case *Brown* v. *Board of Education*.

8. Lubna was faced with the **g, dilemma** of living in poverty or going to an unfamiliar country.

9. Without asking for advice, the general made a(n) **b, unilateral** decision to attack.

10. Both Canadian Liberals and Conservatives alike supported the

    f, bipartisan measure.

■ *Using Related Words*

Complete each sentence by using a word from the group of related words above it. You may need to capitalize a word when you write it in a sentence. Use each choice only once.

1. decimation, decimated

   In recent times, there has been an alarming **decimation** of the world's forests; over 13 percent disappeared in the 1980s alone. However, new, more responsible methods of logging trees are coming into use. In northern Michigan, foresters are harvesting mature trees, not young ones. In Paraguay, a timber company is cutting trees a few at a time, using oxen, rather than tractors, in order to protect soil. These companies help

   to prevent our forests from being **decimated** .

2. trivial, triviality, trivialize

   Compared to educational achievement, a boy's right to wear

   an earring to school may seem like a **triviality** , yet it is being hotly debated. In 1996, an Indiana court decision denied a fourth-grader the privilege; yet more recently school

   boards have allowed it. We should not **trivialize** this issue. It involves freedom of expression, which is not a

   trivial matter.

3. bilingual, bilingualism

Many people living in India are **bilingual**_____ . They speak both English and another language, such as Hindi, Telugu, or Bengali. This **bilingualism**_____ enables people to communicate in distant areas of the country as well as near their home.

4. duplicity, duplicitous

There is no more shocking **duplicity**_____ than that of a general who betrays his own country. Entrusted with defending a fort during the American Revolution, Benedict Arnold planned to surrender it to the British. When his plot was discovered, he fled to England. To this day the name of the **duplicitous**_____ Arnold symbolizes a traitor.

5. monopolize, monopoly

Can one have a **monopoly**_____ on the name Monopoly? Ralph Anspach decided that the popular game glorified monopolies and he created Anti-Monopoly, a game in which free trade wins. After several years, the courts decided that Parker Brothers could no longer **monopolize**_____ the name. Currently, Anti-Monopoly II, which features entrepreneurs, is also available.

■ *True or False?*

Each of the following statements contains one or more words from this section. Read each sentence carefully and then indicate whether you think it is probably true or probably false.

F___   1. An illness with a trivial effect on health would decimate a population.

T___   2. A monopoly involves unilateral control by one company.

F___   3. A person who speaks only English is bilingual.

T___   4. A bill that Democrats and Republicans vote for has bipartisan support.

T___   5. In one decade, a child's age would increase from five to fifteen.

F   6. Most dilemmas have an easy solution.

F   7. Duplicity is a valuable trait in a best friend.

T   8. A trilogy contains three books, plays, or stories.

F   9. A monarch is elected to rule a country.

F   10. A vote of five "for" and ten "against" shows unanimity.

Word Elements

Part 2

Part 2 presents the last number prefix, *cent-*, as well as five roots and prefixes that refer to quantities.

cent- (one hundred)
    The prefix *cent-* is used in many common words. A *century* is a period of **one hundred** years. A *cent* is a coin worth **one-hundredth** of a dollar.

Thanks to medical advances, over 60,000 people in the United States are *centenarians,* or people *one hundred* years old or older. By 2060, the number will increase to two and a half million.

---

ambi-, amphi- (both; around)
    These prefixes have two meanings. The meaning of "both" occurs in the word *ambidextrous,* meaning "able to use **both** hands." The meaning of "around" is found in *amphitheater,* a theater with seats on all sides of, or **around,** the stage. This prefix comes from ancient Greek and Latin: *amphi-* is the Greek form; *ambi-* is the Latin form.

The common word *ambitious* is derived from the Latin verb *ambīre* (to go around). In ancient Rome, an ambitious person was a candidate who "went around" asking people to vote for him. Now, of course, an ambitious person is one who desires achievement.

---

ann, enn (year)
    An *annual* event occurs every **year.** At times, *ann* is spelled *enn,* as in the word *perennial.*

integer (whole; complete)

This root can refer to numbers, as in the English word *integer*, which means a **whole** number without a fraction value. Thus, 3 is an integer, but 3.5 is not. In Latin, *integer* also describes a "**whole**" person, who does not have serious character flaws. Such a person is said to have *integrity*.

magn-, mega- (large)

To *magnify* something is to make it **larger.** Recent books have appeared about *megatrends*, meaning **large** trends in society. A *megalopolis* is a region including several **large** cities. *Magn-* is the Latin spelling; *mega-* is the Greek spelling.

meter, -meter (measure)

This element often appears as a root but can also be used as a suffix. One word using *meter* as a root is *metronome*, an instrument for **measuring** musical time. The element *-meter* is used as a suffix in the words *thermometer*, an instrument for **measuring** heat, and *speedometer*, an instrument for **measuring** speed.

Words to Learn

Part 2

cent-

13. **centennial** (noun)   sĕn-tĕn′ē-əl

    From Latin: *cent-* (one hundred) + *ann* (year)

    one-hundred-year anniversary; a period of one hundred years

    > One hundred years after its founding, the city celebrated its **centennial** with special events that lasted throughout the year.

    The Roman numeral C meant 100. Abbreviations we use today are related to this numeral. For example, the cent sign—¢—and the abbreviation for century—C.—remind us that the root *cent* means 100. The root for 1,000 is *mil,* and in fact, a "mil" is a thousandth part of a dollar. You have heard this root used in the word *millennium.*

    ---

14. **centigrade** (adjective)   sĕn′tĭ-grād′

    From Latin: *centi-* (one hundred) + *gradus* (step)

    referring to a temperature scale based on one hundred degrees

    > A temperature of 35 degrees **centigrade** indicates summer heat.

Many signs now display outdoor temperatures in both the **centigrade** and Fahrenheit scales.

NOTE: 1. The *centigrade scale* is also referred to as *Celsius.* In fact, *Celsius* is the name formally used in science. 2. In the *centigrade* scale, 0° marks the freezing point of water and 100° marks its boiling point. In the Fahrenheit scale, named for its inventor, Daniel Fahrenheit, water freezes at 32° and boils at 212°.

ambi-, amphi-

15. **ambiguous** (adjective) ăm-bĭg′yo͞o-əs

From Latin: *ambi-* (around) + *agere* (to lead) (When something is ambiguous, two meanings are equally possible, and a person is led around rather than "straight toward" the meaning.)

not clear; having two or more meanings

> The **ambiguous** test item was difficult to answer.

▶ *Related Word*
> **ambiguity** (noun) (ăm′bĭ-gyo͞o′ĭ-tē) Federal copyright laws contain many *ambiguities* that make them difficult to follow precisely. The *ambiguity* of my mother's answer left me confused.

The great linguist Noam Chomsky has pointed out the *ambiguity* of the sentence "They are flying planes." This sentence can mean either "The planes are meant for flying" or "Those people are flying the planes."

---

16. **ambivalence** (noun) ăm-bĭv′ə-ləns

From Latin: *ambi-* (both) + *valēre* (to be strong) (A person who is ambivalent about something has two equally strong feelings about it.)

existence of mixed or conflicting feelings

> The child felt **ambivalence** toward the roller-coaster ride, which inspired both excitement and fear.

▶ *Related Word*
> **ambivalent** (adjective) Ajay was *ambivalent* about registering for the difficult, but worthwhile, math course.

ann, enn

17. **annals** (noun) ăn′əlz

From Latin: *ann* (year) (*Annālis* meant "yearly." Written *annals* are often divided by the year.)

a written record of events

> Inspiring speeches are recorded in the **annals** of the U.S. Congress.

general records

> Italian explorers famous in the **annals** of American history include Christopher Columbus, Giovanni Caboto (John Cabot), Giovanni da Verrazano, and Giacomo Beltrami.

18. **perennial** (adjective)   pə-rĕn′ē-əl

From Latin: *per-* (through) + *ann* (year)

occurring again and again; constant; lasting for a long time

> The 1946 movie *It's a Wonderful Life* has become a **perennial** favorite for the Christmas holiday season.
>
> Finding good child care is a **perennial** problem for working parents.

NOTE: Something *perennial* has a long life. *Perennial* flowers bloom year after year without having to be replanted.

integer

19. **disintegrate** (verb)   dĭs-ĭn′tĭ-grāt′

From Latin: *dis-* (apart) + *integer* (whole) (When something disintegrates, it becomes "not whole," or falls apart.)

to separate into small parts

> The aspirin **disintegrated** when we put it in a glass of water.

to become worse; to go wrong

> The well-planned attack **disintegrated** into a wild retreat.
>
> The happy family party **disintegrated** into an argument.

▶ *Common Phrase*
   disintegrate into

▶ *Related Word*
   disintegration (noun)   After the *disintegration* of the attack on Russia, Napoleon's army faced a long, cold journey back to France.

In 1990, the almost intact 50-foot fossilized bones of Sue, a *Tyrannosaurus rex* who lived 65 to 70 million years ago, were found in South Dakota. Preserved in sand and mud, which hardened into rock, the bones did not *disintegrate*. Scans of Sue's bones may determine whether dinosaurs were warm-blooded.

  More than 4,600 years ago, a man froze to death in the Alps. His remains were saved from *disintegration* by the cold, and they mummified. Warmed by furs stuffed with grass, the Otzi, as he was named, had tattoos and may have worn an earring.

---

20. **integrity** (noun)   ĭn-tĕg′rĭ-tē

From Latin: *integer* (whole)

honesty; good moral character

> The **integrity** of the government prosecutor was questioned when he was suspected of leaking testimony to the press.

> A person of **integrity** would not cheat on an examination.

wholeness; completeness

> Despite centuries of exposure to severe weather, the Great Wall of China maintains its **integrity.**

Integrity sometimes gets its just reward. In 1992, Allan Fong, a Chinese immigrant working as a busboy in San Francisco, found $250,000 in cash under a restaurant table. Without hesitation, he returned it to its owner. His *integrity* so impressed others that he was featured in the news and was offered the ownership of an excellent business.

---

magn-, mega-

21. **magnanimous** (adjective)   măg-năn′ə-məs

From Latin: *magn-* (great) + *animus* (soul)

noble; above revenge or resentment; forgiving of insults

> Sharon was **magnanimous** toward her defeated tennis rival.

> **Magnanimous** New York detective Stephen MacDonald publicly forgave the man who shot and paralyzed him in 1986.

▶ *Related Word*
> **magnanimity** (noun)   (măg′nə-nĭm′ĭ-tē)   The senator showed his *magnanimity* by congratulating the opponent who had defeated him.

Phan Thi Kim Phuc, victim of the Vietnam War, has shown *magnanimity* in forgiving the Americans who bombed her village, inflicting her

with severe napalm burns. A photo by Nick Ut, flashed around the world, showed Phan, screaming as she ran toward the camera, pulling off fiery clothes in agony. Recovery from her injuries took years and, in fact, she still has symptoms left. Today she lives with her husband and children in Canada.

---

22. **magnitude** (noun)   măg′nĭ-tōōd′

From Latin: *magn-* (great) (*Magnitūdō* meant "greatness.")

greatness of size or importance

It is impossible to imagine the **magnitude** of the universe.

In 1993, a storm of great **magnitude,** combining tornadoes, snow, and thunderstorms, struck the Atlantic coast, causing 270 deaths.

▶ *Common Phrase*
   magnitude of

NOTE: Magnitude can also refer to the brightness of stars.

meter, -meter

23. **metric** (adjective, noun)   mĕt′rĭk

   From Greek: *meter* (measure)

   referring to a measurement system based on grams and meters (adjective)

   The **metric** system is used in scientific measurements.

   For years the United States has been considering changing to the *metric* system. This system is easier to use than the current system of pounds and feet, based on traditional English measures. The metric system is a decimal system; it is based on multiples of ten. Canada uses metric measurements, but the United States has delayed conversion several times.

24. **symmetrical** (adjective)   sĭ-mĕt′rĭ-kəl

   From Greek: *sym* (same) + *meter* (measure) (Things that "measure the same" are balanced, or symmetrical.)

   balanced in physical size or form

   Because there are slight differences between the left and right sides of the human body, it is not perfectly **symmetrical**.

   ▶ *Related Word*
   symmetry (noun)   (sĭm′ə-trē)   Japanese koi fish are bred for the *symmetry* of the patterns decorating their bodies.

Exercises

Part 2

■ *Definitions*

Match each word in the left-hand column with a definition from the right-hand column. Use each choice only once.

1. annals __c__   a. hundred-year anniversary

2. magnanimous __l__   b. existence of mixed feelings

3. integrity __i__   c. written records

4. symmetrical __h__   d. greatness of size or impor-
                                             tance
5. centigrade __f__
                                         e. not clear
6. perennial __j__
                                         f. referring to a temperature
7. metric __g__   scale

8. magnitude __d__   g. referring to a system of mea-
                                             surement
9. centennial __a__
                                         h. balanced
10. ambivalence __b__
                                         i. honesty

                                         j. lasting a long time

                                         k. to fall apart

                                         l. noble

■ Meanings

Match each word element to its meaning. Use each choice only once.

1. meter, -meter __a__   a. measure

2. ann, enn __e__   b. hundred

3. ambi-, amphi- __c__   c. both; around

4. cent- __b__   d. large

5. integer __f__   e. year

6. magn-, mega- __d__   f. whole

■ Words in Context

Complete each sentence with the word that fits best. Use each choice only once.

a. centennial	e. annals	i. magnanimous
b. centigrade	f. perennial	j. magnitude
c. ambiguous	g. disintegrate	k. metric
d. ambivalence	h. integrity	l. symmetrical

1. Traffic control is a(n) **f, perennial**_____ problem in modern cities.

2. The **e, annals**_____ of the scientific society meetings are kept in the library.

3. When it is zero degrees **b, centigrade**_____, it is freezing outside.

4. Because of **c, ambiguous**_____ instructions, we could not tell exactly how to install the software.

5. Nelson Mandela was **i, magnanimous**_____ when he forgave the South Africans who had imprisoned him during the era of apartheid.

6. Paper will **g, disintegrate**_____ into a powder if it becomes too dry.

7. Arizona was admitted to the United States in 1912 and will celebrate its **a, centennial**_____ in 2012.

8. A person of great **h, integrity**_____ can be easily trusted.

9. Because of the **j, magnitude**_____ of his achievements in writing, Polish-American author Czeslaw Milosz won the Nobel Prize for literature in 1980.

10. Many countries use the **k, metric**_____ system of measurement.

■ *Using Related Words*

Complete each sentence by using a word from the group of related words above it. You may need to capitalize a word when you write it in a sentence. Use each choice only once.

1. disintegrate, disintegration

   Meteors are constantly entering the earth's atmosphere from outer space. Most **disintegrate**_____ before reaching the earth's surface. Those that do strike are called meteorites. Scientists estimate that as many as 200 million meteors occur every day. They can be spotted because of the glow caused by their burning and **disintegration**_____ .

2. ambivalent, ambivalence

The public has expressed some **ambivalence**_____ toward fertility treatments for couples who cannot have children. On the one hand, the procedures produce births; on the other, death can result from the low birth weight or immature organs of the infants. Hospital costs can be extremely high. If these risks could be diminished, most people would probably have less **ambivalent**_____ feelings.

3. ambiguity, ambiguous

The use of plants, natural light, and glass walls and ceilings in public spaces, such as hotels and office buildings, creates visual **ambiguity**_____ between the indoors and outdoors. Such **ambiguous**_____ visual clues may create an odd perception, of being both indoors and outdoors at the same time.

4. magnanimous, magnanimity

The great baseball player Lou Gehrig remained **magnanimous**_____ even when illness forced him to retire at age 35. In a farewell speech at Yankee Stadium, he displayed **magnanimity**_____ rather than bitterness when he said, "Today I am the luckiest man in the world." He died two years later of what is now sometimes called Lou Gehrig's disease.

5. symmetry, symmetrically

The ancient Greeks produced some of the greatest architects in the world. In Athens, the Parthenon, a temple dedicated to the goddess Athena, stands as a great architectural achievement. On the temple is a series of decorated columns, which were arranged **symmetrically**_____ . Such **symmetry**_____ was often used in Greek architecture.

■ *True or False?*

Each of the following statements contains one or more words from this section. Read each sentence carefully and then indicate whether you think it is probably true or probably false.

F   1. A meeting between two magnanimous people would disintegrate into bitterness.

T   2. A person who lived to see a birthday centennial would have a life span of great magnitude.

F   3. The centigrade scale uses 212 degrees as the boiling point of water.

T   4. The integrity of a building would be threatened by a strong earthquake.

T   5. Someone with ambivalent feelings has mixed feelings.

F   6. Something perennial has a short life span.

T   7. When the dinner table is set with three people on each side, it is set symmetrically.

F   8. Annals are never written down.

T   9. We can measure something using the metric system.

T   10. Ambiguous statements are not clear.

Chapter Exercises

■ *Practicing Strategies: New Words from Word Elements*

See how your knowledge of word elements can help you understand new words. Complete each sentence with the word that seems to fit best. Use each choice only once.

a. amphibious e. diphosphate i. monorail
b. biannual   f. integrate   j. odometer
c. centimeter g. magnify   k. trimester
d. decapods   h. monodrama   l. uniform

1. A play performed by one person is called a(n) **h, monodrama** .

2. A(n) **b, biannual** meeting is held twice each year.

3. A(n) **a, amphibious** aircraft can land on both land and water.

4. Since lobsters and shrimps have ten legs, they are **d, decapods** .

5. A(n) **k, trimester** system divides the academic year into three terms.

6. A(n) **j, odometer** records the number of miles a car has traveled.

7. If you **g, magnify** something, you make it bigger.

8. Some trains move on a(n) **i, monorail** , or single rail.

9. If you **f, integrate** one thing with another, you form them into a whole.

10. Things that are **l, uniform** all have the same, or one, appearance.

■ *Practicing Strategies: Combining Context Clues and Word Elements*

Combining the strategies of context clues and word elements is a good way to figure out unknown words. In the following sentences, each italicized word contains a word element that you have studied in this chapter. Using the meaning of the word element and the context of the sentence, make an intelligent guess about the meaning of the italicized word. Your instructor may ask you to check the meaning in your dictionary when you have finished.

1. After we counted the sides of the figure, we determined that it was a *decagon*.

   Decagon means **figure with ten sides** .

2. The gracious room, beautiful furniture, and pleasant music all contributed to the *ambience* of the restaurant.

   Ambience means **atmosphere; surroundings** .

3. Using a microscope, we looked at the *unicellular* life forms.

   Unicellular means __**one-celled**_____ .

4. The *tripartite* system of the U.S. government consists of an executive, a legislative, and a judicial branch.

   Tripartite means __**three parts; three branches**_____ .

5. Some people believe that they can prevent illness by taking *megadoses* of vitamin C.

   Megadoses means __**large doses; large amounts**_____ .

■ *Practicing Strategies: Using the Dictionary*

Read the following definition and then answer the questions below it.

> **sham** (shăm) *n.* **1.** Something false or empty that is purported to be genuine; a spurious imitation. **2.** The quality of deceitfulness; empty pretense. **3.** A person who assumes a false character; impostor: *"He a man! Hell! He was a hollow sham!"* (Conrad). **4.** A decorative cover made to simulate an article of household linen and used over or in place of it: *a pillow sham.* —*adj.* Not genuine; fake: *sham modesty.* —*v.* **shammed, sham•ming, shams.** —*tr.* To put on the false appearance of; feign. —*intr.* To assume a false appearance or character; dissemble. [Perh. dial. var. of SHAME.] —**sham′mer** *n.*

1. What four part-of-speech functions does *sham* have?

   noun, adjective, transitive verb, intransitive verb

2. What is another noun form of *sham*? **shammer**

3. Which writer is quoted to give an example of the meaning of *sham*?

   Conrad

4. Give the part of speech and number of the definition that best fits this

   sentence: "His testimony was a sham." **1, as a noun**

5. Give the number and the part of speech of the definition that best fits this sentence: "The *sham* on our sofa protected it from dirt."

   4, as a noun

■ *Companion Words*

Complete each sentence with the word that fits best. Choose your answers from the words below. You may use each word more than once.

Choices: of, toward, into

1. Rival baseball greats Sammy Sosa and Mark McGwire were mag-nanimous **toward** each other off the field.

2. U.S. citizens were shocked by the duplicity **of** the spy.

3. We are amazed by the magnitude **of** the state of Texas.

4. The ambiguity **of** her response left us with many questions.

5. The meeting disintegrated **into** a shouting match.

■ *Writing with Your Words*

This exercise will give you practice in writing effective sentences that use the vocabulary words. Each sentence is started for you. Complete it with an interesting phrase that indicates the meaning of the italicized word.

1. She faced the *dilemma* of _____

   _____ .

2. He showed his *duplicity* by _____

   _____ .

3. A *bilingual* person _____

   _____ .

4. One example of a *trivial* problem is _____

   _____ .

5. I feel *ambivalent* _____

   _____ .

6. During the next *decade*, I hope that _____

_____ .

7. One *perennial* concern of society is _____

_____ .

8. There is *unanimous* agreement that _____

_____ .

9. When another person started to *monopolize* my date's attention, I

_____ .

10. Converting to the *metric* system would _____

_____ .

Passage

Julius Caesar—Hero or Villain?

Was the great Caesar an ambitious monster or an enlightened reformer? In this passage, you can decide for yourself, as you read about the man who left his mark on our calendar, the names of our kings, and even on the way we number our streets.

Although the famous Roman Julius Caesar died over two thousand years ago, his legend lives on in the **annals** of history. Some historians see him as a power-hungry villain. Others feel he was a reformer whose brutal assassination almost destroyed Rome. **(1)** However, there is **unanimity** of opinion on one issue: Caesar was the towering figure of his age.

Born about 100 B.C.E., Caesar came from a poor but noble family. At the time, the rulers of Rome were divided into two parties. The aristocratic party wanted to keep power in its own hands. The radical party wanted the support of the people, many of whom had lost their lands and were living in poverty in Rome. Caesar joined the radical cause.

To be successful, a Roman leader had to conquer new lands and help expand the republic. **(2)** Caesar made conquests of great **magnitude.** **(3)** He **decimated** resisting forces in Gaul (now Belgium and France) and

Julius Caesar was a unique and towering figure.

added this territory to the Roman empire. He invaded England, where he met strange tribes who painted their bodies and worshiped trees.

Caesar was anxious to tell the Romans of his conquests. The books he wrote included a brief statement summarizing his military career: "Veni, vidi, vici." (I came, I saw, I conquered.)

(4) A **decade** of conquest gained Caesar considerable political power. He had formed a ruling "triumvirate" in 60 B.C.E. with Crassus and Pompey. After Crassus's death, Caesar and Pompey became rivals. At first, Caesar felt **ambivalent** about attacking his former friend. **(5)** The fact that Pompey was married to Caesar's daughter deepened the **dilemma.** However, after some thought, Caesar decided to take decisive action.

In the first act of the conflict, Caesar crossed the Rubicon River in 49 B.C.E. to challenge Pompey. (To this day the phrase "crossing the Rubicon" means "taking an irreversible step.") **(6)** Caesar's victory over Pompey is recorded in a **trilogy,** *Commentary on the Civil War.* His triumph gave him a **monopoly** on Roman leadership, and he took the title of "dictator."

Despite his busy career, Caesar took time for several romantic interests, among them the Egyptian queen Cleopatra. Caesar aroused considerable disapproval when, ignoring his own wife, he invited Cleopatra to Rome.

In his short time as dictator, Caesar accomplished many reforms. He extended Roman citizenship to the whole of Italy. **(7)** He improved the **disintegrating** condition of farming by giving land to soldiers who had served under him. His **integrity** in keeping promises to his soldiers gained him the loyalty of poorer citizens. However, Caesar's reform of the calendar had the most long-lasting effects. He replaced an inaccurate calendar with the improved Julian version. In a somewhat more **trivial** action, he named the month of his birth, July, after himself.

(8) Unfortunately, Caesar was a victim of the **perennial** problem of successful people: the jealousy of others. **(9)** Caesar had shown **magnanimity** in not executing old enemies, but they now started to plot against him.

Some senators also feared for the Roman Republic, as Caesar gave signs he might establish a **monarchy**, crowning himself as emperor. One nobleman, Cassius, was particularly angry over his own loss of power. Cassius plotted to assassinate Caesar, and week by week his list of treacherous conspirators grew. The day of Caesar's murder was planned for March 15, 44 B.C.E., called the Ides of March.

Legend records that Caesar was warned to "beware the Ides of March," but decided to face his fate. The assassins gathered on the floor of the Senate building. When Caesar entered, they attacked him with daggers. Caesar resisted until he realized that, **(10)** in a terrible act of **duplicity**, his close friend Brutus had turned against him. "Et tu, Brute?" ("You too, Brutus?") he cried as he submitted to his murderers.

■ *Exercise*

Each numbered sentence below corresponds to a sentence in the Passage. Fill in the letter of the choice that makes the sentence mean the same thing as its corresponding sentence in the Passage.

1. However, there is ___**a**___ of opinion on one issue.
   a. agreement b. evidence c. division d. history

2. Caesar made conquests of great ___**a**___ .
   a. importance b. difficulty c. helpfulness d. violence

3. He ___**b**___ resisting forces in Gaul.
   a. helped b. destroyed c. fought d. greeted

4. A __a__ of conquest gained Caesar considerable political power.
   a. ten-year period   b. three-year period   c. twenty-year period
   d. two-year period

5. The fact that Pompey was married to Caesar's daughter deepened

   the __d__ .
   a. greatness   b. honor   c. danger   d. problem

6. Caesar's victory is recorded in __b__ .
   a. a set of ten books   b. a set of three books   c. a set of two books
   d. one book

7. He improved the __c__ condition of farming.
   a. poverty-stricken   b. unjust   c. worsening   d. terrible

8. Unfortunately, Caesar was a victim of the __c__ problem of successful people: the jealousy of others.
   a. noticeable   b. small   c. constant   d. serious

9. Caesar had shown __c__ in not executing old enemies.
   a. stubbornness   b. pride   c. forgiveness   d. weakness

10. In a terrible act of __b__ , his close friend Brutus had turned against him.
    a. cruelty   b. deceit   c. violence   d. destruction

■ *Discussion Questions*

1. Why was Caesar considered a great soldier?

2. Why do you think Caesar was (or was not) a great leader?

3. Would you have wanted Caesar to become emperor? Why or why not?

◀ **ENGLISH IDIOMS**

Money

Since numbers and measures are often used in relation to money, the idioms for this chapter concern wealth. A person without any money is referred to as *broke*. To lose all your money is to *lose your shirt*. Not to have enough money is to be *caught short*. People who have been cheated out of money have been *taken to the cleaners* or *ripped off*. Such people may be forced to *live from hand to mouth,* meaning that they have only enough to cover their immediate needs, without any savings for the future.

When a person quickly goes from poverty to wealth, he or she goes *from rags to riches*. That person has a lot of money or is *in the money*. A rich person might *live high on the hog*, in great comfort, and with the best of everything. We could say that the person is *on easy street*.

A rich man or woman who refuses to spend money is often called a *cheapskate*. Kate Robinson inherited five million dollars from her parents but spent only about $80 per year. When she died in 1920, her furniture was stuffed with money. Since then, anybody who has money, but will not spend it, has been called *Cheap Kate* or, in more modern English, a *cheapskate*.

Quiz Again

Now that you have finished studying this chapter, here is the brief true-false quiz you took when you began. Take it again.

Unanimity involves agreement.	True	False
To **decimate** something is to improve it.	True	False
Friends generally demonstrate **duplicity** toward each other.	True	False
Something that is **perennial** disappears quickly.	True	False

Answers are on page 406. Did your score improve?

CHAPTER

10

Word Elements: Thought and Belief

Our ability to think and our system of beliefs help to define us as human beings. The importance of thought is apparent when we reason through a difficult problem. The things we believe to be morally correct affect our everyday behavior. Part 1 of this chapter presents word elements dealing with thought and belief. Part 2 presents prefixes we use when we do *not* believe something; these are prefixes of negation. Finally, several idioms will be discussed in this chapter. An idiom carries a different meaning from what we believe it to have when we first hear it.

Chapter Strategy: Word Elements: Thought and Belief

Chapter Words

Part 1

cred	credibility	*ver*	veracity
	creed		verify
	incredulity		veritable
fid	defiant	*-phobia*	acrophobia
	fidelity		claustrophobia
	fiduciary		xenophobia

Part 2

de-	delude	*Idioms*	behind the eight ball
	destitute		get to first base
	deviate		give carte blanche
non-	nonchalant		hold out an olive branch
	nondenominational		star-crossed
	nondescript		tongue-in-cheek

Quiz Yourself

To check your knowledge of some chapter words before you begin to study, identify these statements as true or false.

A person who **holds out an olive branch** wants to fight.   True   False

A **nonchalant** person cares deeply about issues.   True   False

An **acrophobic** person fears heights.   True   False

We usually believe a person who has great **credibility.**   True   False

You will learn the answers as you study this chapter.

Did You Know?

Animal Words of Thought and Belief

For thousands of years, animals have played an important part in human beliefs. Primitive human beings knew and admired many types of animals. Often our ancestors tried to give themselves the powers of the animal world. To acquire the speed of a jaguar or the power of a lion, humans dressed up in the animals' skins and imitated their cries and movements. These customs have contributed words to modern English. The feared ancient warriors of what is now Norway covered themselves in bear *(ber)* skin shirts *(serkr)* and rushed madly into battle, attacking all in sight. From this custom, we derive the phrase *to go berserk,* or crazy.

Many great civilizations worshiped animal gods. In ancient Egypt, the goddess Taurt was thought to have the head of a hippo, the back and tail of a crocodile, and the claws of a lioness. In some parts of Egypt, people worshiped cats, crocodiles, and baboons. All three animals have been found carefully preserved as mummies in special cemeteries.

Some animals retain important places in modern religions. Traditional Hindus hold one type of cow, the East Indian humped zebu, to be sacred. Since these cows symbolize the riches given by the gods to the Earth, Hindus are forbidden to kill these animals or control them in any way. The cow has come to be identified as a national symbol of modern

India. These beliefs have resulted in the English expression *sacred cow,* meaning a belief that is so well established that it cannot be challenged.

Some religions have also involved animals in specific rituals. More than two thousand years ago, the ancient Jews chose one goat to symbolize people's sins against God. This goat was released into the desert wilderness, symbolically carrying sins away with it. Although this custom has vanished, the English word *scapegoat* still means someone who takes the blame for another.

The creation of animal idioms remains a strong trend in modern English. Many of our more current expressions compare human behavior to that of animals. For example, to *parrot* means to repeat, as a parrot repeats familiar words. To *horse around* means to play, as horses do in a field. A man who is nagged by his wife is called *henpecked,* recalling the behavior of female chickens. When we do something wonderful, we may *crow* about it. We may *eat like pigs* (greedily) or disappoint our host by *eating like birds* (eating little). The generally bad reputation of the rat has given us the phrase *to rat on,* meaning to turn someone in or "squeal" on someone. There are hundreds of words and phrases that reflect our human thoughts about animals.

Can you identify the human meanings given to these common animal expressions?

1. catty
2. birdbrain
3. sitting duck
4. pigeonhole
5. a can of worms
6. puppy love
7. hogwash

Answers are on page 406.

Learning Strategy

Word Elements: Thought and Belief

The first part of this chapter concentrates on word elements relating to thought and belief. Three roots are presented: *cred* (believe), *fid* (faith), and *ver* (truth). Part 1 also introduces the suffix *-phobia* (fear of). Part 2 of this chapter presents two important prefixes with negative meanings. We use them when we do *not* believe in something. *Non* means "not." *De-* also has a negative sense, indicating "to remove from" or "down."

Element	Meaning	Origin	Function	Chapter Words
				Part 1
cred	believe	Latin	root	credibility, creed, incredulity
fid	faith	Latin	root	defiant, fidelity, fiduciary
ver	truth	Latin	root	veracity, verify, veritable
-phobia	fear of	Greek	suffix	acrophobia, claustrophobia, xenophobia
				Part 2
de-	to remove from; down	Latin	prefix	delude, destitute, deviate
non-	not	Latin	prefix	nonchalant, nondenominational, nondescript

Word Elements

Part 1

Information on the roots and the suffix for Part 1 is presented below.

cred (believe)

The root *cred* is used in many English words. When we do not **believe** something, we may call it *incredible*. *Credit* is granted to a customer because merchants **believe** that they will be paid. The concept of a *credit card* is also based upon **belief.**

fid (faith)

The English word *faith* is taken from this root. Because dogs are thought to be **faithful** companions to human beings, they have traditionally been given the name of *Fido,* meaning "faithful."

ver (truth)

The root *ver* means "truth." A *verdict,* the judgment of a jury, is made up from the root *ver* (truth) and the root *dict* (say). Even that much-used word *very,* meaning "**truly**" or "really," comes from *ver.*

-phobia (fear of)

As a suffix, *-phobia* describes a strong or illogical **fear** of something and often forms words that are used in psychology. For example, *nyctophobia* is a **fear** of the dark. The base word *phobia* also means "**fear.**"

According to Greek mythology, Phobos was the son of Ares, the god of war who was similar to the Roman god Mars. Greek warriors sometimes painted the likeness of Phobos on their shields, hoping that the enemy would run merely at the terrifying sight of his picture.

Words to Learn

Part 1

cred

1. **credibility** (noun)   krĕd′ə-bĭl′ĭ-tē

From Latin: *cred* (believe)

believability; ability to be trusted

The frequent appearance of Gallup poll results in the media has given these surveys **credibility** with the public.

The witness's **credibility** vanished when he admitted he had not been at the scene of the crime.

She had undermined her **credibility** by lying too often.

▶ *Related Word*
credible (adjective)   (krĕd′ə-bəl)   The police accepted Susan's *credible* account of the accident.

▶ *Common Phrase*
undermine (her/his/our/my/your/their) credibility

Mistakes in movies often reveal that one scene was shot at several different times, undermining the *credibility* of the action. In *The Maltese Falcon,* when a character is hit, he is wearing a striped tie when his head goes one way, and a polka-dot tie when it goes the other. In *The Jagged Edge,* Glenn Close wears three outfits in one courtroom scene.

2. **creed** (noun)   krēd

From Latin: *cred* (believe) (*Crēdo* meant "I believe.")

set of beliefs or principles

The U.S. juror's **creed** states, "I am a seeker of truth."

Five duties, reciting the words of witness, prayer, charity, fasting, and pilgrimage, are central to the **creed** of the Muslim religion.

NOTE: Creed often refers to a formal system of religious or moral beliefs.

3. **incredulity** (noun)   ĭn′krĭ-do͞o′lĭ-tē

From Latin: *in-* (not) + *cred* (believe)

disbelief; amazement

Spanish explorers of the 1500s expressed **incredulity** at the excellent health and sanitation standards of the Incas and Aztecs.

The request to prove that he was over twenty-one was met with **incredulity** by the forty-year-old man.

▶ *Related Word*
  incredulous (adjective) (ĭn-krĕj′ə-ləs) Neighbors were *incredulous* when told that the respected citizen had abused his daughter.

People are often *incredulous* when told that flying in an airplane is safer than driving. However, here are the odds of dying due to various causes (published in Krantz, *What the Odds Are*).

Car crash: 1 in 125
Lightning strike: 1 in 9,100
Skin cancer: 1 in 22,409
Dog attack: 1 in 700,000
Airplane crash: 1 in 4,600,000

---

fid

4. **defiant** (adjective)   dĭ-fī′ənt

From Latin: *dis-* (not) + *fid* (faith)

refusing to follow orders or rules; resisting boldly

Defiant Malaysians ignored bans on protest and gathered in the street.

NOTE: Since this word begins with *de,* we might expect it to have the sense of "down." However, the Latin word had a *dis-* prefix, which became *de-* as the word *defiant* went through the French language.

▶ *Related Words*

defiance (noun)   Political activity in China is often treated as *defiance* of the government and severely punished.

defy (verb)   (dǐ-fī′)   The nine-year-old *defied* his mother's orders and watched a violent TV show at his friend's house.

5. **fidelity** (noun)   fǐ-děl′ǐ-tē

From Latin: *fid* (faith)

faithfulness to obligation or duty

Kock Fee showed his **fidelity** to his family by working for three years to earn the money to bring them from Hong Kong to Canada.

exactness, accuracy

New technology enables scanners to reproduce pictures with great **fidelity.**

Compact disc players reproduce music with excellent **fidelity.**

A 1994 study from the University of Chicago showed that sexual *fidelity* in marriage is common. Of men surveyed over fifty, more than three-quarters reported *fidelity*. Younger men had an even higher *fidelity* rate.

---

6. **fiduciary** (adjective, noun)   fǐ-doo′shē-ěr′ē

From Latin: *fid* (faith) (You need to have faith in the person who handles your money.)

pertaining to money or property held for one person (or several people) by others (adjective)

A condominium board has a **fiduciary** responsibility to manage money in the interest of unit owners.

a person holding money for another (noun)

Under the guidance of the **fiduciary,** the inheritance grew.

ver

7. **veracity** (noun)   və-răs**′**ĭ-tē

From Latin: *ver* (truth)

truth; accuracy

> It is difficult to determine the **veracity** of young children's testimony.
>
> Birth records confirmed the **veracity** of the man's claim to be one hundred years old.

▶ *Common Phrase*
veracity of

8. **verify** (verb)   věr**′**ə-fī

From Latin: *ver* (truth) + *facere* (to make)

to determine the truth or accuracy of; to confirm

> Before Tawio's loan was approved, a bank officer called to **verify** that he was employed.
>
> Long-distance truck drivers must **verify** that they rest four hours for every five hours that they drive.
>
> People often use a dictionary to **verify** a word's meaning.

▶ *Related Word*
verification (noun)   Scientists obtain *verification* of their results by repeating experiments.

9. **veritable** (adjective)   věr**′**ĭ-tə-bəl

From Latin: *ver* (truth)

unquestionable; being truly so

> The city of Columbus, Indiana, is a **veritable** museum of modern architecture.
>
> The food show was a **veritable** gold mine of ideas for the student chefs.

almost; nearly; very similar to

> Our ninety-eight satellite channels provide a **veritable** feast of TV programs.

NOTE: Veritable is usually used in the phrases of "a veritable _____"
or "the veritable _____ ."

-phobia

10. **acrophobia** (noun)   ăk′rə-fō′bē-ə

From Greek: *acros* (highest) + *-phobia* (fear)

fear of heights

> Marek's **acrophobia** prevented him from riding on Ferris
> wheels.

▶ *Related Word*
 acrophobic (adjective)   We warned our *acrophobic* friend not
 to look out the airplane window.

11. **claustrophobia** (noun)   klô′strə-fō′bē-ə

From Latin: *claustrum* (enclosed space) + Greek: *-phobia* (fear)

fear of closed or small spaces

> Mr. Orrington's **claustrophobia** made him nervous in the
> crowded elevator.

▶ *Related Word*
 claustrophobic (adjective)   Denice felt *claustrophobic* in her
 small office.

12. **xenophobia** (noun)   zĕn′ə-fōb′ē-ə

From Greek: *xenos* (stranger) + *-phobia* (fear)

fear or hatred of foreigners or foreign things

> The fear that foreign workers would take away jobs sparked
> **xenophobia** in the eastern European country.

> Because of his **xenophobia,** the senator wanted to pass laws that
> would prohibit immigration into the country.

▶ *Related Word*
 xenophobic (adjective)   The *xenophobic* man refused to travel
 to foreign countries.

What do the following phobias refer to?

1. ailurophobia
2. zoophobia
3. microphobia
4. ergophobia
5. arachnophobia

Answers are on page 406.

Exercises

Part 1

■ *Definitions*

Match each word in the left-hand column with a definition from the right-hand column. Use each choice only once.

1. incredulity __f__	a. set of beliefs
2. creed __a__	b. unquestionable
3. credibility __d__	c. faithfulness
4. fidelity __c__	d. ability to be believed
5. claustrophobia __i__	e. fear of truth
6. fiduciary __k__	f. disbelief
7. xenophobia __g__	g. fear of foreigners
8. veritable __b__	h. to determine truth or accuracy
9. acrophobia __j__	i. fear of small spaces
10. veracity __l__	j. fear of heights
	k. a person holding money for another
	l. truth

■ *Meanings*

Match each word element to its meaning. Use each choice only once.

1. fid ___**a**___

2. -phobia ___**b**___

3. cred ___**d**___

4. ver ___**c**___

a. faith

b. fear

c. truth

d. believe

■ *Words in Context*

Complete each sentence with the word that fits best. Use each choice only once.

a. credible	e. fidelity	i. veritable
b. creed	f. fiduciary	j. acrophobia
c. incredulity	g. veracity	k. claustrophobia
d. defiant	h. verify	l. xenophobia

1. The ___**d, defiant**___ athlete refused to follow the directions of the team captain.

2. The art dealer tried to ___**h, verify**___ that the painting was really the work of the famous artist.

3. The cheap film did not reproduce colors with ___**e, fidelity**___ , so the bride's white dress looked green in the photograph.

4. As people who value diversity in society, we should try to avoid ___**l, xenophobia**___ .

5. People expressed ___**c, incredulity**___ that Maya had named her child Loving Moon Beam.

6. His ___**k, claustrophobia**___ made him panic when he was accidentally locked in the closet.

7. The teacher questioned the ___**g, veracity**___ of the student's report that he had "lost" his homework.

8. The paintings in Irena's attic proved to be a(n) **i, veritable** _____ treasure of old family portraits.

9. Charity and forgiveness are central to the **b, creed** _____ of Christianity.

10. The board of a company has a(n) **f, fiduciary** _____ responsibility to manage the money of stockholders.

■ *Using Related Words*

Complete each sentence by using a word from the group of related words above it. You may need to capitalize a word when you write it in a sentence. Use each choice only once.

1. defied, defiance

A man of great conscience who **defied** _____ his own government, Sempo Sugihara is credited with saving more than 2,000 Jews from murder during the Holocaust. Because he was the Japanese diplomat to Lithuania, people begged him for visas that would allow them to escape the Nazis by going to Japan. In

defiance _____ of government orders and at risk to his own life, Sugihara signed the visas as fast as he could write. His memory is revered by humanitarians everywhere.

2. incredulity, incredulous

People often react with **incredulity** _____ when told of the generosity of some rock stars. For example, in 1998, three band members of the group Smashing Pumpkins gave half a million dollars to the Make-A-Wish foundation. Additionally, they paid their own expenses on a tour that raised two million dollars for

charity. **Incredulous** _____ reactions might be expected from those who feel that rock stars are selfish. Obviously, some performers are truly committed to making the world a better place.

3. acrophobia, acrophobic

The 200-foot-high Mackinac Bridge, in Michigan, inspires

acrophobia _____ in many people, who cannot bear to look down into the water. Some burst into tears or have attacks of dizziness. Fortunately, officials are available to drive the cars of **acrophobic** _____ people, who usually shut their eyes during the journey.

4. verification, verified

Several reports have **verified** _____ that falls from great heights need not be fatal. In 1990, a Russian newspaper reported that a woman survived a three-mile fall after a mid-air plane colli-sion. There has also been **verification** _____ of an incident in which a flight attendant fell six miles to the ground—and lived.

5. credibility, credible

Are some old houses really haunted? The editors of the *Old House Journal* have received twenty-seven case histories of haunting, giving it new **credibility** _____. Reported incidents included ghostly noises, rushes of cold air, and the actual appearance of ghosts. The intelligence and thoughtfulness behind these reports make them quite **credible** _____. By the way, most of these owners are delighted to be sharing their homes with these spirits.

■ *Reading the Headlines*

This exercise presents five headlines that might appear in newspapers. Read each headline and then answer the questions that follow. (Remember that small words, such as *is, are, a,* and *the,* are often left out of newspaper headlines.)

XENOPHOBIC WITNESS NOT CREDIBLE AGAINST ACCUSED IMMIGRANT

1. Does the witness dislike foreigners? **yes** _____

2. Is the witness believable? **no** _____

WEDDING OF FIDUCIARY AGENT AND THIEF A VERITABLE SHOCK

   3. Is the agent responsible for money? **yes**_____

   4. Is the wedding truly a surprise? **yes**_____

DEFIANT GENERAL BREAKS OATH OF FIDELITY TO RULER

   5. Is the general obedient? **no**_____

   6. Is he faithful to the ruler? **no**_____

AFTER INITIAL INCREDULITY, EXPERTS VERIFY THAT PRINCESS WAS MURDERED

   7. At first did experts doubt she was murdered? **yes**_____

   8. Did they try to determine the truth about her death? **yes**_____

VERACITY OF CLAIM TO BE ACROPHOBIC SEEN WHEN MAN PANICS

   9. Was the truth of the claim determined? **yes**_____

   10. Did the man claim to be afraid of small spaces? **no**_____

Prefixes

Part 2

Part 2 of this chapter presents two very common prefixes with negative meanings: *de-* means "to remove from" or "down"; *non-* means "not." Both prefixes are used in thousands of English words.

   This Words to Learn section also presents several idioms. These phrases involve our thoughts and beliefs, for an idiom does not carry the meaning we believe it to have when we first hear it.

de- (removal from; down)

The very common prefix *de-* has several meanings. In some English words it has the sense of "to remove from." For example, when we *decontaminate* something, we **remove** the contamination or impurities **from** it. When people *deforest* land, they **remove** trees **from** it. *De-* can also mean "down." When we *depress* a button, we push it **down.** When something *declines,* it goes **down.**

non- (not)

The prefix *non-* simply means "not." *Nonsense* is something that does **not** make sense. A *nonjudgmental* person is one who does **not** make judgments. *Non-* often combines with base words (roots that can stand alone as English words).

Words to Learn

Part 2

de-

13. **delude** (verb)   dĭ-lōōd′

   From Latin: *de-* (away from) and *lūdere* (to play) (*Delūdere* meant "to deceive, to mock.")

   to mislead; to cause someone to think something that is false

   > The false prophet **deluded** people into thinking the world would end at the new millennium.

   > Some teenagers **delude** themselves into believing that illegal drugs are harmless.

   ▶ *Related Word*
   delusion (noun)   (dĭ-lōō′zhən)   The mentally ill person suffered from the *delusion* that aliens were sending her messages.

   In the days when travel was more difficult, radio sports announcers often could not attend games played in cities away from their homes. Instead, they got news of each play from telegraph wires and "announced" the game over the radio. By providing sound effects such as cheering and the cracking of a baseball bat, announcers *deluded* listeners into thinking that they were hearing eyewitness accounts.

   ---

14. **destitute** (adjective)   děs′tĭ-to͞ot′

From Latin: *de-* (down) + *stat* (placed)

without money; poor

> The **destitute** mother could not afford to feed her baby.

NOTE: Destitute is a very strong word that means "entirely without resources; broke."

▶ *Related Word*
   destitution (noun)   The man's *destitution* reduced him to begging at street corners.

The saintly Mother Teresa, a nun who died in 1998, opened the Nirmal Hriday (Pure Heart) home for the dying and *destitute* in Calcutta, India. Treating the very poorest, those who had been abandoned because they were dying of AIDS or leprosy, Mother Teresa provided help to those who needed it most.

---

15. **deviate** (verb)   dē′vē-āt′

From Latin: *de-* (to remove from) + *via* (road) (*Dēviāre* meant "to go away from the road.")

to vary from a path, course, or norm

> Hikers who **deviate** from the trail risk getting lost in the woods.
>
> The Dixie Chicks **deviated** from a pure country music style to perform rock numbers.

▶ *Common Phrase*
   deviate from

▶ *Related Words*
   deviant (adjective)   (dē′vē-ənt)   Many mentally ill people show *deviant* behavior. (*Deviant* means "odd in a negative way.")

   deviation (noun)   The airline's *deviation* from standard safety procedures resulted in a tragic accident.

non-

16. **nonchalant** (adjective)   nŏn′shə-länt′

From Latin: *non-* (not) + *calēre* (to be warm) (Many people feel physically warm when they get angry. Therefore, someone who is nonchalant, "not warm," does not feel angry or concerned.)

unconcerned; carefree

> With a **nonchalant** toss of the covers, John declared that he had made the bed.

> Maria's **nonchalant** attitude toward paying bills ruined her credit rating.

NOTE: Nonchalant can be a somewhat negative word, indicating that someone should care but does not.

▶ *Related Word*

nonchalance (noun)   The soldier displayed *nonchalance* in the face of danger.

17. **nondenominational** (adjective)   nŏn′dĭ-nŏm′ə-nā′shə-nəl

From Latin: *non* (not) + *nomen* (name) (Something "not named" is not associated with any one "group," or religion.)

not associated with one specific religion

> The **nondenominational** Marketplace Chapel in the West Edmonton Mall holds services at 9:30 and 5:00.

NOTE: Nondenominational can refer to a general category of religion, including all subgroups of the religion. For example, one could attend a nondenominational Christian service.

18. **nondescript** (adjective)   nŏn′dĭ-skrĭpt′

From Latin: *non-* (not) + *de-* (down) + *script* (write) (Something nondescript is hard to describe in writing because it lacks interest.)

not distinct; difficult to describe because it lacks individuality

> In an area of **nondescript** office buildings, the green-tiled library attracted much attention.

> The spy's **nondescript** appearance allowed her to slip into the crowd on the street without detection.

Idioms

19. **behind the eight ball**

at a disadvantage; in a hopeless situation

> Because she missed the first four sessions of the class, Isabella felt that she was **behind the eight ball.**

> With a record of nineteen losses and three wins, the soccer team entered the second half of the season **behind the eight ball.**

In eight ball, a pocket billiards game, the object is to hit all the numbered balls into the pockets at the side of the table before trying to sink the eight ball. If the ball you are shooting at is located *behind the eight ball,* your shot is blocked, and you are likely to lose the game.

20. **get to first base**

do the first thing successfully

The shy and sensitive man could not **get to first base** with women.

If you want to **get to first base** in a job interview, dress neatly.

In baseball, you must run to first base, second base, third base, and then to home plate in order to score. If you cannot even *get to first base,* then you will never score, or get to home plate.

21. **give carte blanche**   kärt blänsh′

From French: a blank document

to give full, unrestricted power

The Secretary of State was **given carte blanche** to negotiate a peace agreement.

Sue Ellen's father **gave** her **carte blanche** to buy clothes.

A *carte blanche* was originally a piece of paper with nothing but a signature on it, used when an army surrendered. The defeated leader would sign his name, and the victor could then write in the terms of surrender.

22. **hold out an olive branch**

make an offer of peace

Colombian leaders **held out an olive branch** to rebel leaders by entering into negotiations with them.

According to the Bible, God punished the wicked world by sending a flood. However, God chose to save one good man, Noah, along with his family and one pair of each type of animal on Earth. Noah floated in an ark for the forty days of the flood. When the waters went down at last, a dove flew from the boat and brought back an *olive branch* as a symbol of God's peace. Today, both the dove and the *olive branch* have come to symbolize peace.

NOTE: The phrase *olive branch* can be used with other words, as in *offer an olive branch* and *serve as an olive branch.*

23. **star-crossed**

doomed to a bad fate; unlucky

> **Star-crossed** ice skater Tania Szewczenko was too ill to compete in one important competition and was struck in the head with a toy before another.

For centuries, people of many cultures have believed that the astrological position, or placement, of the stars at a person's birth determined the person's future. A *star-crossed* person was born under unfavorable astrological influences. Shakespeare described the famous lovers Romeo and Juliet as *star-crossed,* or destined to a bad fate.

24. **tongue-in-cheek**

jokingly; insincerely; without really meaning something

> Mom made a **tongue-in-cheek** threat to force children who left dirty clothes on the floor to do the family wash for the next ten years.
>
> A popular series of computer manuals carries such **tongue-in-cheek** titles as *WordPerfect for Dummies* and *Windows 98 for Dummies.*

At one time, people indicated that they didn't mean what they said by pushing one of their cheeks out with their tongue. Several actions have even longer histories. The "OK" sign, a circle made with the thumb and forefinger, is used as a *mundra,* or sacred sign, by Buddhists and Hindus to indicate perfection. Crossing one's fingers for good luck is thought to be a protective gesture early Christians employed to secretly indicate the cross.

Exercises

Part 2

■ *Definitions*

Match each word or phrase in the left-hand column with a definition from the right-hand column. Use each choice only once.

1. star-crossed ___**a**___

2. tongue in cheek ___**l**___

3. hold out an olive branch

   ___**h**___

4. nondescript ___**b**___

5. get to first base ___**g**___

6. behind the eight ball ___**e**___

7. give carte blanche ___**f**___

8. destitute ___**i**___

9. deviate ___**d**___

10. nondenominational ___**j**___

a. unlucky

b. not distinct

c. to mislead

d. to vary from a path

e. at a disadvantage

f. to give full power

g. to do the first thing successfully

h. to make a peace offer

i. without money

j. not limited to one religion

k. unconcerned

l. jokingly; insincerely

■ *Meanings*

Match each prefix to its meaning. Use each choice only once.

1. non-___**b**___

2. de- ___**a**___

a. to remove from; down

b. not

■ *Words in Context*

Complete each sentence with the word or phrase that fits best. Use each choice only once.

a. delude
b. destitute
c. deviate
d. nonchalant

e. nondenominational
f. nondescript
g. behind the eight ball
h. get to first base

i. give carte blanche
j. held out an olive branch
k. star-crossed
l. tongue-in-cheek

1. "Don't get there first!" was the **l, tongue-in-cheek** _____ comment the driver shouted to the man who was walking.

2. To make peace, the parents finally **j, held out an olive branch** _____ to the son they had not spoken to in years.

3. I'll never **h, get to first base** _____ in a vocabulary course if I don't study.

4. When he lost all his money, the man was **g, behind the eight ball** _____ in his plan to buy a home.

5. Don't **a, delude** _____ yourself into thinking that success is just a matter of luck.

6. If you **c, deviate** _____ even the slightest bit from the recipe for making a soufflé, it may flop.

7. The **e, nondenominational** _____ charity helped people of all faiths.

8. The wealthy owner could **i, give carte blanche** _____ to the decorator to spend whatever money was needed to redo the penthouse.

9. The **d, nonchalant** _____ mother did not seem to care about how her child did in school.

10. The man's **f, nondescript** _____ appearance gave no clue to the fact that he was a billionaire.

■ *Using Related Words*

Complete each sentence by using a word from the group of related words above it. You may need to capitalize a word when you write it in a sentence. Use each choice only once.

1. destitute, destitution

Homeless and **destitute** _____ , Joe Long was spending another lonely day when he spied a car on fire. Rushing to the scene, he heroically pulled two people from the flames, saving their lives.

A grateful public has now saved Joe from **destitution** _____
by gifts of money and the offer of a job.

2. nonchalance, nonchalant

The world was amazed when IBM's Deep Blue computer defeated world chess champion Gary Kasparov. What happened? Both human and computer made errors in logic, but Kasparov

lost some of the "cool," or seeming **nonchalance** _____ , that helps him to win. The computer was able to overcome its errors, while Kasparov seemed to panic over his. Analysts took a

nonchalant _____ attitude toward Deep Blue's victory, pointing out that it was merely the lack of emotion that enabled it to succeed.

3. deviant, deviates

Cultures differ from each other in their social conventions. In the Middle East, people stand close together when they talk. In North America and Europe, a certain distance is expected between speak-

ers. If someone **deviates** _____ from this distance and stands too close, the other speaker becomes uncomfortable. In Japan, one speaker does not look directly at the other. To look

directly is considered **deviant** _____ and offensive.

4. delusions, deluded

In the 1600s, people in Holland started to buy tulip bulbs for investment, causing prices to rise in a fever of "tulipmania." Because

of the bulbs' popularity, people were **deluded** _____
into thinking that prices would rise forever. Some had such

delusions _____ about the value of tulips that they invested everything they had in the flowers. When, after a few years, prices collapsed, many people were financially ruined.

■ *Reading the Headlines*

This exercise presents five headlines that might appear in newspapers. Read each headline and then answer the questions that follow. (Remember that small words, such as *is, are, a,* and *the,* are often left out of newspaper headlines.)

NONCHALANT PILOT DEVIATES FROM FLIGHT PLAN

1. Was the pilot concerned about the flight? **no**

2. Did the pilot follow the flight plan? **no**

NEW CEO GIVEN CARTE BLANCHE WHEN EARNINGS STATEMENT SHOWS THAT COMPANY IS BEHIND THE EIGHT BALL

3. Is the company doing well? **no**

4. Can the CEO do whatever he wants? **yes**

NONDENOMINATIONAL CHRISTIAN MINISTER HOLDS OUT OLIVE BRANCH TO RIVAL

5. Does the minister represent one specific religion? **no**

6. Does the minister want to make peace? **yes**

NONDESCRIPT-LOOKING PERSON, NOW DESTITUTE, WAS ONCE A FAMOUS MOVIE STAR

7. Does the person look different from other people? **no**

8. Is the person poor now? **yes**

STAR-CROSSED MAN MAKES A TONGUE-IN-CHEEK REFERENCE TO HIS "GOOD" FORTUNE

9. Is the man lucky? **no**

10. Does the man mean what he says? **no**

Chapter Exercises

■ *Practicing Strategies: New Words from Word Elements*

See how your knowledge of prefixes, roots, and suffixes can help you understand new words. Complete each sentence with the word that seems to fit best. Use each choice only once.

a. aquaphobia　　e. depopulated　　i. nonstop
b. bona fide　　　f. detour　　　　j. phobic
c. credentials　　g. discredited　　k. verify
d. demote　　　　h. nonprofit　　　l. very

1. Something that is **i, nonstop** keeps going.

2. Somebody who is fearful is **j, phobic** .

3. A(n) **h, nonprofit** organization is not organized to make money.

4. *Bona* means "good," so something that is presented in good faith is **b, bona fide** .

5. When people go away from the plan of a trip, they make a(n) **f, detour** .

6. An *aqueduct* carries water; the fear of water is **a, aquaphobia** .

7. If you can no longer believe in somebody, that person has been **g, discredited** .

8. To promote is to move upward, and to **d, demote**_____ is to move downward.

9. People present **c, credentials**_____ so that you will "believe" in their qualifications.

10. A place becomes **e, depopulated**_____ when people move out.

■ *Practicing Strategies: Combining Context Clues and Word Elements*

Combining the strategies of context clues and word elements is a good way to figure out unknown words. In the following sentences, each italicized word contains a word element that you have studied in this chapter. Using the meaning of the word element and the context of the sentence, make an intelligent guess about the meaning of the italicized word. Your instructor may ask you to check the meaning in your dictionary when you have finished.

1. Because of *cynophobia,* the woman refused to go near any dogs.

   Cynophobia means **fear of dogs**_____ .

2. The *deciduous* trees were bare of leaves in winter.

   Deciduous means **losing leaves in winter**_____ .

3. Truckers carrying *nonflammable* chemicals need not fear fire.

   Nonflammable means **fireproof; not able to burn**_____ .

4. Physicians give *credence* to a new treatment for a disease only after it has been tested.

   Credence means **belief**_____ .

5. Because of the hot sun and lack of water, Moqui's body became *dehydrated*.

   Dehydrated means **dried out; lacking water**_____ .

■ *Companion Words*

Complete each sentence with the word that fits best. Choose your answers from the words below. You may use each word more than once.

Choices: from, into, of, a

1. Because the man had lied before, we doubted the veracity **of** _____ his words.

2. My teacher is **a** _____ veritable treasure trove of information on word origins.

3. The athlete deluded herself **into** _____ thinking she could compete successfully without practicing.

4. The daughter's deviation **from** _____ her parents' traditional beliefs alienated her from them.

5. Creative people often deviate **from** _____ the norm.

■ *Writing with Your Words*

This exercise will give you practice in writing effective sentences that use the vocabulary words. Each sentence is started for you. Complete it with an interesting phrase that also indicates the meaning of the italicized word or words.

1. I would like to have *carte blanche* to _____

   _____ .

2. According to my personal *creed,* _____

   _____ .

3. Because he was *claustrophobic,* _____

   _____ .

4. Despite her *nondescript* appearance, _____

   _____ .

5. The *star-crossed* student _____

_____ .

6. *Fidelity* is _____

_____ .

7. My day became a *veritable* disaster when _____

_____ .

8. I was surprised that he remained *nonchalant* when _____

_____ .

9. It is hard to *verify* that _____

_____ .

10. I would be *incredulous* if _____

_____ .

Passage

The Origins of Superstitions

Just about everyone holds one superstition or another. Read this passage to find out about the origins of your favorites, or should we say your least favorites?

Why is the number thirteen considered unlucky? Why do people who spill salt throw some over their shoulder? Are black cats evil? Can a mirror steal your soul? **(1)** No scientist has **verified** these superstitions, yet people once believed them without question. How did they originate?

The number thirteen has long been considered unlucky. Thirteen was believed to be a central number in the **creed** of witches. These supposedly evil souls were thought to **defy** God and **(2)** to swear **fidelity** to the devil. Thirteen was the ideal number for a witches' coven, or meeting.

Many people considered Friday an unlucky day of the week because it was the day on which Christ was crucified. When Friday coincides with the thirteenth of the month, we get a particularly unlucky day. However, other Fridays have also been known to bring misfortune. On Friday, May 10, 1886, **(3)** a financial panic in London, known as Black Friday, left many people **destitute.**

Unlike the number thirteen and Friday, salt was considered lucky. Because salt was used to preserve food, people believed that it would drive away bad spirits. However, spilling salt was thought to invite evil ones. **(4)** In fact, dropping a salt container could make a **nonchalant** diner suddenly become frantic. There was only one way to avoid disaster: the diner had to take some salt into his right hand (the side for his lucky spirit) and throw it over his left shoulder. **(5)** Any **deviation** from this procedure would invite the invasion of the unlucky spirit, who was always lurking on the left.

Cats have held a special place in our superstitions. Their mysterious ability to survive falls from high places led the Egyptians to believe that they had nine lives. In fact, the Egyptians worshiped cats. **(6)** In contrast, cats have had a rather **star-crossed** fate in Europe. The fact that cats' eyes reflect light in the dark caused Europeans of the Middle Ages to think they were evil spirits. Cats were often pictured as witches' companions, and some people believed that, after seven years' service, a cat might even become a witch. Since black was the color of the devil, black cats inspired especially intense fear. God-fearing people walking at night might see a black cat cross their path. **(7)** Certain that they had met the devil, they would break into a **veritable** panic. A cat that crossed from left to right was particularly frightening.

People often made ridiculous claims about cats. For example, in 1718 a man named William Montgomery claimed that two elderly women had been found dead in their beds on the morning after he had killed two noisy cats. **(8)** Montgomery **deluded** himself into thinking that the cats had been these women in disguise.

A less harmful, though no less silly, superstition revolved around mirrors, which many people believed had magical powers. Perhaps you remember Snow White's stepmother asking her magical mirror: "Mirror, mirror, on the wall. Who's the fairest one of all?" The ancients believed that breaking a mirror would bring seven years of bad luck, avoidable only if the pieces were quickly buried. The seven-year figure was given by the Romans, who thought that the human body renewed itself every seven years. Others believed that a mirror broke because bad spirits appeared in it. Throughout history, people have feared that a mirror would steal the weak soul of a sick person or a newborn. Of course, this idea had no **veracity,** yet some people would not allow infants to see a mirror until they reached one year of age.

(9) Most modern people are **incredulous** when told of these superstitions. Yet some of us still believe that they have **credibility.** An occasional high-rise lacks a thirteenth floor; the numbers simply skip from twelve to fourteen. **(10)** Some people throw salt over their left shoulders, even if it is a **tongue-in-cheek** gesture or they no longer know why they

Cats have a special place in our superstitions.

are doing it. Perhaps you know somebody who shivers with fright when a black cat crosses a path at night and flashes its fiery eyes. Whatever the origin of superstitions, it's clear that some haunt us, even today.

■ *Exercise*

Each numbered sentence below corresponds to a sentence in the Passage. Fill in the letter of the choice that makes the sentence mean the same thing as its corresponding sentence in the Passage.

1. No scientist has ___**c**___ these superstitions.
   a. established the belief of   b. experimented with
   c. established the truth of   d. established the trust of

2. Witches were thought to swear ___**a**___ to the devil.
   a. faithfulness   b. belief   c. truthfulness   d. luck

3. A financial panic known as Black Friday left many people ___**c**___ .
   a. unhappy   b. insane   c. poor   d. fearful

4. In fact, dropping a salt container could make a __a__ diner suddenly become frantic.
   a. calm   b. horrified   c. hungry   d. pleasant

5. Any __d__ from this procedure would invite the invasion of the unlucky spirit.
   a. noise   b. benefit   c. rumor   d. change

6. In contrast, cats have had a rather __d__ fate in Europe.
   a. religious   b. fortunate   c. unusual   d. unlucky

7. Certain that they had seen a devil, they would break into a __d__ panic.
   a. dreadful   b. sudden   c. slight   d. true

8. Montgomery __c__ himself into thinking that the cats had been these women in disguise.
   a. frightened   b. helped   c. fooled   d. advised

9. Most modern people are __a__ when told of these superstitions.
   a. unbelieving   b. amused   c. fooled   d. horrified

10. Some people throw salt over their left shoulders, even if it is a __d__ gesture.
    a. foolish   b. frightened   c. believing   d. joking

■ Discussion Questions

1. Why were infants not allowed to see mirrors?

2. Why did so many people think cats have supernatural powers?

3. Would you be comfortable living on a thirteenth floor? Why or why not?

> ◄ **ENGLISH IDIOMS**
>
> ### *Animals*
>
> This section adds more animal idioms to those in the **Did You Know?** section. An *ugly duckling* is a child who is physically unappealing. The phrase comes from a Hans Christian Andersen fairy tale, in which an ugly duckling becomes a beautiful swan. A *lame duck* is a political official who is completing a term after someone else has been elected.
>
> People who are nervous often *have butterflies in their stomach,* perhaps because of the movement they feel there. When we tell people to *hold your horses,* we want them to slow down. An unknown or unfavored political candidate is called a *dark horse.*
>
> Dogs appear in other idioms. People who are out of favor because of wrongdoing are *in the doghouse.* When a situation gets very bad, we say it has *gone to the dogs.* When we refer to the brutality of our world, we say, "*It's a dog-eat-dog world.*" A *wolf in sheep's clothing* is a bad person who pretends to be good. To *keep the wolf from the door* is to keep out hunger.
>
> In the 1890s, cartoonist Francis "Red" Tulane, a radical, wrote a comic strip featuring overworked, exploited mice and a fat, unsympathetic cat who was their boss. Today a rich, unsympathetic person is known as a *fat cat.*

Quiz Again

Now that you have finished studying this chapter, here is the brief true-false quiz you took when you began. Take it again.

A person who **holds out an olive branch** wants to fight.	True	False
A **nonchalant** person cares deeply about issues.	True	False
An **acrophobic** person fears heights.	True	False
We usually believe a person who has great **credibility.**	True	False

Answers are on page 407. Did your score improve?

CHAPTER

11

Word Elements: The Body and Health

In the past hundred years, medical scientists have learned much about how the human body works. This has led to new methods to prevent and treat health problems. Children can be immunized against once-dreaded diseases, including polio, measles, chickenpox, smallpox, and tetanus. Since 1900, life expectancy in the United States has risen from 47 years to almost 80. The word elements in this chapter deal with the human body and health. Part 1 presents four roots; Part 2 presents four prefixes. Although these word elements are commonly used in the sciences and health professions, they also form words that you will meet in your general reading.

Chapter Strategy: Word Elements: The Body and Health

Chapter Words

Part 1

audi	audit	*ped*	expedite
	auditory		impede
	inaudible		pedigree
patho, -pathy	empathy	*spec, spic*	auspicious
	pathetic		conspicuous
	pathology		introspection

Part 2

a-, an-	anarchy	*bio-, bio*	biodegradable
	anonymous		biopsy
	apathy		symbiotic
bene-	benefactor	*mal*	malady
	beneficial		malevolent
	benign		malpractice

339

Quiz Yourself

To check your knowledge of some chapter words before you begin to study, identify these statements as true or false.

Inaudible sounds are loud.	True	False
Something **beneficial** is helpful.	True	False
Something **conspicuous** is easily noticed.	True	False
A **malevolent** person is evil.	True	False

You will learn the answers as you study this chapter.

Did You Know?

How Did Snacks Originate?

Health specialists constantly advise us to eat spinach, broccoli, and carrots. Yet modern life is filled with food that may not be as healthy as spinach but tastes better and is easily available in packaged form. Such snacks are sometimes called "junk food." Despite this negative label, most of us are far more likely to snack on a package of potato chips or nachos than on a raw carrot. The popularity of junk food shows that it is likely to be with us for a long time, so let's see how some of the names originated.

The potato chip was invented in the 1860s. According to one story, Chef George Crum once had an annoying customer who kept complaining that his french fries were too thick. Finally, Mr. Crum cut the potatoes into very thin slices, and the potato chip was born. According to another account, the potato chip was invented by settlers of Spanish descent who lived on large haciendas in California. In any event, the first potato chip factory was founded in 1925.

In 1896, Leo Hirschfield, an Austrian immigrant, invented a chewy candy and gave it the nickname of his childhood sweetheart, Tootsie. This was the Tootsie Roll. In the 1940s, the daughter of Charles Lubin gave her name to Sara Lee cakes and desserts.

The ice cream cone was invented in 1904 at the St. Louis World's Fair. Ernest A. Hamwi, a Syrian immigrant, was selling *zalabias*, wafers that could be rolled up. When a person at the ice cream booth next to

him ran out of plates, Hamwi substituted his rolled-up wafers, and the ice cream cone was born.

In the early 1900s, eleven-year-old Frank Epperson accidentally invented a snack food by leaving a sweet drink out overnight in the cold. The liquid froze around the stick that had been used to stir it. Epperson originally called his invention the Epsicle, but the name was later changed to the more appealing "popsicle."

Loved by children and adults throughout the world, the Twinkie was named for the Twinkle Toe shoe. In 1930, the inventor, Jimmy Dewar, passed a billboard advertising the shoe, and decided it would be a fitting name for an inexpensive snack. How do they get the filling into the Twinkie? The manufacturers bake the surrounding cake, and then inject the cream. The famous snack has formed another English expression: "Twinkie defense." In 1978, San Francisco Mayor George Moscone and City Supervisor Harvey Milk were shot to death by a former supervisor. The supervisor later claimed that he committed the act because the artificial ingredients in the many Twinkies he ate caused "diminished mental capacity."

M & M's got their name from the initial letters of the last names of inventors Forrest Mars and Bruce Murrie. The candies first became popular during World War II among soldiers, who could eat them without making their trigger fingers sticky. Fifty years later, M & M's remain a popular snack.

Match the food to the origin of its name.

1. Pez	a. the Chinese word for pickled fish
2. Baby Ruth bar	b. a plant with a sticky root
3. marshmallow	c. the first, middle, and last letters of the word for *peppermint* in German
4. ketchup	d. the daughter of President Grover Cleveland

Answers are on page 407.

Learning Strategy

Word Elements: The Body and Health

With the many advances in medicine and the life sciences during the past century, more and more scientific words have been made from the word elements in this chapter. Part 1 presents four common roots; Part 2 presents four common prefixes.

Element	Meaning	Origin	Function	Chapter Words
				Part 1
audi	hear	Latin	root	audit, auditory, inaudible
patho, -pathy	feeling, suffering; disease	Greek	root; suffix	empathy, pathetic, pathology
ped	foot	Latin	root	expedite, impede, pedigree
spec, spic	look	Latin	root	auspicious, conspicuous, introspection

				Part 2
a-, an-	without	Greek	prefix	anarchy, anonymous, apathy
bene-	good, well	Latin	prefix	benefactor, beneficial, benign
bio-, bio	life	Greek	prefix; root	biodegradable, biopsy, symbiotic
mal-	bad, harmful	Latin	prefix	malady, malevolent, malpractice

Word Elements

Part 1

The four roots in Part 1 are explained in more detail below.

audi (hear)

Our *auditory* nerves enable us to **hear.** The word root *audi* is used also in such words as *audience,* a group of people who **hear** a performance, and *auditorium,* a place where crowds gather to **hear** something.

patho, -pathy (feeling, suffering; disease)

The root *patho* has two meanings, both stemming from ancient Greek. First, *patho* can mean "feeling, suffering," as in the word *pathos,* meaning "a **feeling** of pity." A second meaning of *patho* is "disease," as in *pathologist,* a doctor who diagnoses **disease,** and *psychopath,* a person with a **diseased** mind. The spelling *-pathy* is used for the suffix form. For example, *sympathy* means "**suffering** along with the sorrows of another."

ped (foot)

Ped is found in such words as *pedal,* a control operated by the **foot,** and *quadruped,* an animal with four **feet.** Some words made from *ped* reflect society's scorn for the lowly foot. *Pedestrian,* which refers to people who travel by **foot,** is also used to describe something that is dull or ordinary.

spec, spic (look)

The root *spec* is used in such words as *inspect,* "to **look** at carefully," and *despise,* to "**look** down on" or "scorn" someone. Glasses used to improve vision are called *spectacles.* Finally, the word *spy,* a person who secretly **looks** at the actions of others, may also be derived from *spec.*

Words to Learn

Part 1

audi

1. **audit** (noun, verb)   ô′dĭt

   From Latin: *audit* (hear)

   examination of financial accounts by an outside agency (noun)

   > Companies registered on public stock exchanges must submit their accounts for a yearly **audit.**

   > An **audit** revealed that the company was financially sound.

   to examine accounts (verb)

   > The accountant **audited** the records of several small businesses.

   to attend a class without receiving credit (verb)

   > I **audited** Spanish 103 so that I could practice the language.

   ▶ *Related Word*
   auditor (noun)   The *auditor's* report revealed that the company had made a large profit. (*Auditor* means a person who is a financial analyst.)

   NOTE: At one time, official examinations of financial accounts were held in public so that all could hear. In modern times, however, such examinations are done in written form.

2. **auditory** (adjective)   ô′dĭ-tôr′ē

   From Latin: *audi* (hear)

   referring to hearing

   > The ear is the outermost part of the body's **auditory** system.

   Animals often have well-developed and sensitive *auditory* systems. In 1994, an okapi (a relative of the giraffe) collapsed and died from stress caused by unusual noise. Three hundred yards away, an opera company was rehearsing Wagner's heroically loud *Tannhäuser*.

   ---

3. **inaudible** (adjective)   ĭn-ô′də-bəl

From Latin: *in-* (not) + *audi* (hear)

not able to be heard

> Pigeons can hear low-frequency tones that are **inaudible** to human beings.

NOTE: The opposite of *inaudible* is *audible,* meaning "capable of being heard."

patho, -pathy

4. **empathy** (noun)   ĕm′pə-thē

From Greek: *em-* (in) + *-pathy* (feeling, suffering)

understanding of or identification with another person's feelings

> After raising her own disabled child, the woman baby-sat for autistic children out of **empathy** for their parents.

> When children identify with characters in books, they develop **empathy** for others.

▶ *Common Phrase*
empathy for

▶ *Related Words*
empathic/empathetic (adjective)   (ĕm-păth′ĭk)   (ĕm′pa-thĕt′ĭc)
People who have lost loved ones in airplane crashes can join support groups where *empathic* (or *empathetic*) members help each other deal with grief.

empathize (verb)   Northwestern University students laughed and groaned as they *empathized* with *University Place,* a student-produced TV soap opera about student life.

NOTE: How does *empathy* differ from *sympathy*? Sympathy means feeling sorry for another person. However, if we have empathy, we can actually identify with or experience the feelings of another human being.

5. **pathetic** (adjective)   pə-thĕt′ĭk

From Greek: *patho* (feeling, suffering)

pitiful; arousing pity

> The injured bird made a **pathetic** attempt to fly.

6. **pathology** (noun)   pă-thŏl′ə-jē

From Greek: *patho* (disease) + *-logy* (study of)

the study of disease

> The science of **pathology** was greatly advanced when the microscope came into general use.

> Progress in genetic mapping is helping to explain the **pathology** of colon and breast cancer.

▶ *Related Words*
pathological (adjective)   (păth′ə-lŏj′ĭ-kəl)   He was a *pathological* liar. (*Pathological* can mean mentally ill.)

pathologist (noun)   The *pathologist* examined the murder victim, hoping to find clues about the crime.

NOTE: A pathologist is a medical doctor who investigates body tissue samples (biopsies) for disease. Pathologists also do autopsies, or examinations of bodies, to determine the cause of death. Forensic pathologists help establish clues to criminal activities.

ped

7. **expedite** (verb)   ĕk′spĭ-dīt′

From Latin: *ex-* (out) + *ped* (foot) (*Expedīre* meant "to free a person's feet from fetters or chains.")

to speed up; to accomplish quickly

> E-mail has **expedited** communication so much that a traditional letter is sometimes referred to as "snail mail."

> Our trip home was **expedited** when three stops were dropped from the bus route.

▶ *Related Word*
expedition (noun)   (ĕk′spĭ-dĭsh′ən)   Charles Darwin formed his theory of evolution after an *expedition* to the Galapagos Islands. (*Expedition* means "journey.")

expeditious   (adjective)   (ĕk′spĭ-dĭsh′əs)   Special services promise *expeditious* delivery of packages.

NOTE: Do not confuse *expedite* with *expedient* (which means "convenient").

8. **impede** (verb)   ĭm-pēd′

From Latin: *im-* (in) + *ped* (foot) (*Impedīre* meant "to entangle.")

to hinder; to block

> The ice on the road **impeded** our progress.
>
> Fear of failure **impedes** success.

▶ *Related Word*
   impediment (noun) (ĭm-pĕd′ə-mənt) Because stairs are an *impediment* to wheelchairs, ramps are required outside many public buildings.

9. **pedigree** (noun)   pĕd′ĭ-grē′

From Latin (*ped*) through Old French: *pie* (foot) + *de* (of) + *grue* (crane) (In a pedigree, or family tree, an outline shaped like a crane's foot was used to show the different generations.)

ancestry; certificate of ancestry

> The **pedigree** of English royalty includes many German ancestors.

Zoos that need to purchase a lion look carefully at the animal's *pedigree.* Because zoo scientists hope to bring new genes into the breeding pool, they search for animals that are not related to other lions held in the zoo. Most valuable are lions whose *pedigrees* show that they are only a few generations removed from the wild.

---

spec, spic

10. **auspicious** (adjective)   ô-spĭsh′əs

From Latin: *avis* (bird) + *spic* (look, watch)

favorable; promising success

> Increased employment is an **auspicious** sign for our economy.
>
> Suleyma's **auspicious** first concert promised a great singing career.

The ancient Romans believed that since the flight of birds was close to the heavens, it could easily be guided by the gods. Thus, birds were watched as signs or omens. A man who was trained to observe flight patterns was called an *auspex*. When any matter of importance was being considered, the *auspex* decided whether the signs given by birds were *auspicious*.

11. **conspicuous** (adjective)   kən-spĭk′yoo-əs

From Latin: *con-* (closely) + *spec* (look)

easy to notice; attracting attention

> The important announcement was posted on doors, in hallways, and in other **conspicuous** places.

> Pam's flaming red hair made her **conspicuous** among her brown-haired cousins.

▶ *Related Word*
   conspicuousness (noun)   I was embarrassed by the *conspicuousness* of my sister's low-cut dress.

12. **introspection** (noun)   ĭn′trə-spĕk′shən

From Latin: *intro-* (within) + *spec* (look)

self-examination of one's thoughts and feelings

> After a near-death experience, we often engage in **introspection** about our life goals.

▶ *Related Words*
   introspect (verb)   People should *introspect* about their feelings before they marry.

   introspective (adjective)   In *introspective* moments, the man realized he, alone, was responsible for the problems in his life.

Exercises

Part 1

■ *Definitions*

Match each word in the left-hand column with a definition from the right-hand column. Use each choice only once.

1. pedigree ___l___   a. identification with another
                                          person's feelings
2. introspection ___j___
                                      b. to hinder
3. auditory ___e___
                                      c. noticeable
4. inaudible ___i___
                                      d. favorable
5. audit ___h___
                                      e. referring to hearing
6. auspicious ___d___
                                      f. pitiful
7. empathy ___a___
                                      g. to speed up
8. pathology ___k___
                                      h. examination of financial
9. conspicuous ___c___   accounts

10. pathetic ___f___   i. not able to be heard

                                      j. self-examination of one's
                                          thoughts

                                      k. study of disease

                                      l. record of ancestry

■ Meanings

Match each word element to its meaning. Use each choice only once.

1. ped ___a___   a. foot

2. spec, spic ___b___   b. look

3. audi ___d___   c. feeling, suffering; illness

4. patho, -pathy ___c___   d. hear

■ Words in Context

Complete each sentence with the word that fits best. Use each choice only
once.

a. audit   e. pathetic   i. pedigree
b. auditory   f. pathology   j. auspicious
c. inaudible   g. expedite   k. conspicuous
d. empathy   h. impede   l. introspection

1. I would like to **a, audit** _____ the course, rather than take it for credit.

2. Because the **i, pedigree** _____ of the racehorse showed it was descended from many champions, the owners had high hopes for it.

3. The perfect score on Anne's first test was a(n) **j, auspicious** _____ sign for her performance in the course.

4. Consuelo's **l, introspection** _____ helped her understand her own feelings.

5. To **g, expedite** _____ answers to consumer questions, the company has installed a "hot line" that operates 24 hours a day.

6. Deaf people have problems in their **b, auditory** _____ systems.

7. Because I took the engineering course last semester, I have **d, empathy** _____ for the students who are now finding it difficult.

8. We nearly wept at the **e, pathetic** _____ sight of starving people begging on the street.

9. Carrying a heavy load will **h, impede** _____ your ability to run.

10. The bell was so far away that its ringing was nearly **c, inaudible** _____ to us.

■ *Using Related Words*

Complete each sentence by using a word from the group of related words above it. You may need to capitalize a word when you write it in a sentence. Use each choice only once.

1. conspicuous, conspicuousness

Concerns about both ethics and the quality of life have become **conspicuous** _____ in today's undergraduates. Colleges report an increasing number of courses dealing with ethical, spiritual, and personal issues. The **conspicuousness** of this issue is shown by the popularity of courses with such titles as "Quest for Human Destiny," "The Good Life," and "Interpersonal Communications."

2. pathological, pathologist

Physicians are now able to freeze cancerous tumors that cannot be removed by surgery. After a **pathologist** has determined that a tumor is malignant, it is located through ultrasound techniques. Then liquid nitrogen is injected to freeze the tumor. This process destroys the **pathological** tissue without harming healthy organs.

3. impeded, impediments

There are many **impediments** to government approval of new foods in the United States. Recently, scientists developed the Flavr-Savr, a tomato that can be shipped without spoiling. This genetically altered food had to be approved by the Food and Drug Administration. The thoroughness of the testing **impeded** release of the product for several months, but helped to ensure consumer safety.

4. expedite, expedition, expeditious

In 1911, two teams set out to be the first to reach the South Pole. Battling through the freezing, unknown land, each tried hard to **expedite** its progress. Norwegian Roald Amundsen's **expedition** reached the pole first and made a reasonably **expeditious** return. The British explorer Robert Falcon Scott reached it a month afterward, but on the return journey perished in the cold.

■ *True or False?*

Each of the following statements contains one or more words from this section. Read each sentence carefully and then decide if it is probably true or probably false.

__T__   1. A laughing, happy person would be conspicuous in a room full of pathetic children.

__T__   2. A prince or princess in your pedigree would be an auspicious sign for social success.

__T__   3. You would want to expedite your progress in a race.

__F__   4. An audit is a musical recording that you can hear.

__T__   5. Introspection is thought.

__T__   6. A person born in a foreign country is in a position to have empathy with new immigrants.

__F__   7. Loud noises are inaudible at close distances.

__F__   8. A pathology report examines a company's finances.

__T__   9. A nearby waterfall would be noticed by our auditory system.

__F__   10. When we are impeded, we go faster.

Word Elements

Part 2

Part 2 concentrates on four prefixes that are often used in words about the body and in the health sciences.

a-, an- (without)

The words *amoral* and *immoral* help us understand the prefix *a-, an-* by contrasting it with *im-* (meaning "not"). An *immoral* person is *not* moral: this person has a sense of right and wrong, yet chooses to do wrong. An *amoral* person is **without** morals: such a person has no sense of right or wrong. The prefix *a-* is used in many medical words, such as *aphasia* (loss of speech) and *anesthetic* ("**without** feeling," referring to chemicals that make patients unconscious or unable to experience pain during a medical procedure).

bene- (good; well; helpful)

Bene- is used in such words as *benefit* (something that is **helpful**) and *beneficiary* (one who receives **help** or money from another).

bio-, bio (life)

The prefix *bio-* is used in the word *biology,* "the study of **living** things." You may have taken a biology course in school. *Biochemistry* deals with the chemistry of **living** things. A word you have already studied in this book, *autobiography,* includes *bio* as a root.

mal- (bad; badly; harmful)

The prefixes *mal-* and *bene-* are opposites. *Mal-* is seen in the word *malpractice,* or "**bad** practice." Doctors and lawyers may be sued for malpractice. In 1775, the playwright Richard Sheridan coined the word *malaprop* as a name for his character, Mrs. Malaprop, who used words that were not appropriate (or **badly** appropriate). One of her malapropisms is "He's the very pineapple of politeness." (She should have used the word *pinnacle.*)

Words to Learn

Part 2

a-, an-

13. **anarchy** (noun)   ăn′ər-kē

From Greek: *an-* (without) + *arkhos* (ruler)

political confusion; disorder; lack of government

Anarchy resulted when the ruler fled the country.

The rioting and looting were a sign that the country was in a state of **anarchy.**

Without an adult present, the fourth-grade class was soon in a state of **anarchy.**

▶ *Related Word*
anarchist (noun)   The *anarchist* hoped to bring about the fall of the government.

14. **anonymous** (adjective)   ə-nŏn′ə-məs

From Greek: *an-* (without) + *onoma* (name)

not revealing one's name; of unknown identity

> The famous tune "Greensleeves" was written by a composer who is now **anonymous.**

> Iris wondered who was sending her the **anonymous** love letters.

▶ *Related Word*
> **anonymity** (noun)   To protect the *anonymity* of their best source in the Watergate investigation, reporters Woodward and Bernstein referred to the person as "Deep Throat."

15. **apathy** (noun)   ăp′ə-thē

From Greek: *a-* (without) + *-pathy* (feeling)

lack of emotion, feeling, or interest

> Public **apathy** resulted in a low voter turnout at the election.

> The city's **apathy** toward soccer turned to enthusiasm when its team started winning.

▶ *Related Word*
> **apathetic** (adjective)   (ăp′ə-thĕt′ĭk)   The teenager was interested in rock music but *apathetic* toward schoolwork.

bene-

16. **benefactor** (noun)   bĕn′ə-făk′tər

From Latin: *bene-* (well) + *facere* (to do)

a person who gives financial or other aid; a donor

> A campus building was named for the **benefactor** who donated a million dollars.

17. **beneficial** (adjective)   bĕn′ə-fĭsh′əl

From Latin: *bene-* (well) + *facere* (to do)

helpful; producing benefits

> Employment with a major firm is often **beneficial** to an accountant's career.

> Moderate exercise is **beneficial** to health.

18. **benign** (adjective)   bĭ-nīn′

From Latin: *bene-* (well) + *genus* (birth) (*Benignus* meant "well-born, gentle.")

kind; gentle

Santa Claus is a **benign,** fatherly figure.

not containing cancer cells

Fortunately, my grandfather's tumor was **benign.**

NOTE: The antonym, or opposite, of *benign* is *malignant.*

bio-, bio

19. **biodegradable** (adjective)   bī′ō-dĭ-grā′də-bəl

From Greek: *bio-* (life) + Latin: *de-* (down) + *gradus* (step)

capable of being chemically broken down by natural biological processes

Biodegradable golf tees are now being made of cornstarch.

NOTE: Biodegradable substances break down into natural elements.

As our society becomes increasingly concerned about excessive waste, the word *biodegradable* has become more popular. Many companies now claim that their products are *biodegradable.* However, the word, strictly interpreted, should mean "not harmful to the environment." Paper, for example, is *biodegradable* in small amounts, but if too much is thrown away, the excess will not be broken down as quickly and may harm the environment. Food may be *biodegradable,* but if it is buried in a landfill, it will take much longer to decay. Claims are made by companies that certain plastics are *biodegradable.* However, many of these plastics simply break down into smaller particles rather than into naturally occurring elements. The best way to ensure a healthy environment is to produce less garbage by recycling and reusing products.

---

20. **biopsy** (noun)   bī′ŏp′sē

From Greek: *bio-* (life) + *opsis* (sight)

the study of living tissue to diagnose disease

A **biopsy** of the brain tumor showed that it was not cancerous.

NOTE: To diagnose disease with a *biopsy,* a doctor will cut away a small piece of living tissue and inspect it under a microscope.

The words *biopsy, benign,* and *pathology* are often used in the diagnosis of cancer. If cancer is suspected, a doctor will take a *biopsy* of cell tissue, which is then examined for the presence of *pathology* (by a *pathologist*). If the biopsy shows the tumor to be *benign,* it is harmless. If the tumor is *malignant* (note the *mal-* prefix), it is harmful and must be treated.

---

21. **symbiotic** (adjective)   sĭm′bē-ŏt′ĭk

From Greek: *sym-* (together) + *bio* (life)

living interdependently; referring to a relationship where two organisms live in a dependent state

> In one **symbiotic** relationship, shrimp live protected within the stinging tentacles of sea anemones.

> The **symbiotic** relationship between the sisters was so strong that when one died, the other soon followed.

NOTE: Symbiotic relationships can be either biological or social. If they are social, *symbiotic* can be a negative word.

▶ *Related Word*
> **symbiosis** (noun)   (sĭm′bē-ō′sĭs)   Peanut plants live in *symbiosis* with nitrogen-fixing bacteria on their roots.

mal-

22. **malady** (noun)   măl′ə-dē

From Latin: *mal-* (badly) + *habēre* (to keep) (*Mal habitus* meant "ill-kept, in bad condition.")

disease; bad condition

> The common cold is a **malady** that affects everyone at one time or another.

> The **malady** of discontent spread throughout the land.

Some genetically caused *maladies* have affected American history. The inherited madness of King George III weakened him and encouraged the American colonies to revolt in 1776. George Washington may have suffered from a genetic defect that prevented him from having children. Washington's lack of a son may have been a factor in his refusal to become "king of America," as his soldiers wanted him to do. His *malady* may also have accounted for his hot temper and hatred of authority, traits that made him difficult to live with but an excellent general.

23. **malevolent** (adjective)   mə-lĕv′ə-lənt

From Latin: *mal-* (bad) + *volens* (wishing)

ill-willed; evil; filled with hate

> **Malevolent** ruler Pol Pot's government killed over a million Cambodians.

▶ *Related Word*
   malevolence (noun)   The aunt in the novel *Jane Eyre* shows her *malevolence* by hiding the fact that Jane has inherited money.

24. **malpractice** (noun)   măl-prăk′tĭs

From Latin: *mal-* (bad) + *practice*

failure of a professional to give proper services

> After the physician left surgical pins inside her arm, the woman accused him of **malpractice.**

> The lawyer was accused of **malpractice** when she missed a client's important court date.

Exercises

Part 2

■ Definitions

Match each word in the left-hand column with a definition from the right-hand column. Use each choice only once.

1. malevolent __k__

2. malpractice __a__

3. benign __d__

4. apathy __f__

a. failure to give proper services

b. capable of being broken down by natural processes

c. political confusion

d. not containing cancer cells

e. study of living tissue

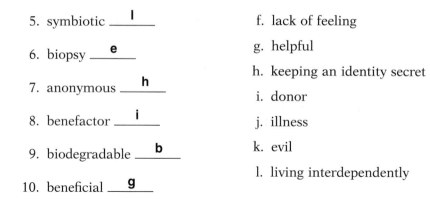

5. symbiotic ___l___

6. biopsy ___e___

7. anonymous ___h___

8. benefactor ___i___

9. biodegradable ___b___

10. beneficial ___g___

f. lack of feeling

g. helpful

h. keeping an identity secret

i. donor

j. illness

k. evil

l. living interdependently

■ *Meanings*

Match each word element to its meaning. Use each choice only once.

1. bene- ___b___

2. mal- ___a___

3. bio-, bio ___c___

4. a-, an- ___d___

a. bad

b. good

c. life

d. without

■ *Words in Context*

Complete each sentence with the word that fits best. Use each choice only once. You may need to capitalize some words.

a. anarchy	e. beneficial	i. symbiotic
b. anonymous	f. benign	j. malady
c. apathy	g. biodegradable	k. malevolent
d. benefactor	h. biopsy	l. malpractice

1. The ruler's death led to __a, anarchy__ in the country until a strong leader took control of the government and reestablished order.

2. The __h, biopsy__ determined that the mole on my shoulder was not cancerous.

3. Because the person wanted to remain __b, anonymous__ , her face was hidden and her voice was mechanically changed in the TV interview.

4. A careful physician is rarely accused of **l, malpractice** .

5. We were happy to learn that my mother's tumor was **f, benign** .

6. In many action-thriller movies, some **k, malevolent** criminal wants to destroy the world.

7. Studying is **e, beneficial** to a student's grade.

8. In past centuries, a wealthy **d, benefactor** would often support an artist or musician.

9. Many people try to use **g, biodegradable** containers that will not cause harm to rivers and streams.

10. Recently, a vaccine was developed to protect children from the **j, malady** of chickenpox.

■ Using Related Words

Complete each sentence by using a word from the group of related words above it. You may need to capitalize a word when you write it in a sentence. Use each choice only once.

1. apathy, apathetic

There are many complaints about the political **apathy** of citizens who do not vote. But 83-year-old Myun Ja Chang, a recent U.S. citizen who was born in Seoul, is attending a voter workshop to prepare for exercising her rights. In contrast to the often **apathetic** attitude of native-born citizens, she believes strongly in the power of citizen choice.

2. symbiotic, symbiosis

Human beings live in **symbiosis** with the bacteria that line their digestive tracts. In a **symbiotic** arrangement, humans supply a home for the bacteria, and the bacteria help to digest food. When people take antibiotics, they can destroy these bacteria and cause temporary indigestion.

3. malevolence, malevolent

If you slice into a tomato, are you a __**malevolent**_____ person?

Do we show __**malevolence**_____ when we forget to water plants? Malcolm Wilkins, an English botanist, claims that plants have feelings and produce crackling noises inaudible to the human ear when they are hurt.

4. anarchy, anarchists

In a famous case, Nicola Sacco and Bartolomeo Vanzetti, who were __**anarchists**_____ , were found guilty of murder. Their supporters charged that the two men were convicted because of their belief that all forms of government oppress people and __**anarchy**_____ is, therefore, desirable. Even though evidence surfaced that other people had committed the murder, the men were executed in 1927.

5. anonymous, anonymity

In former years, mothers who gave up children for adoption often preserved their __**anonymity**_____ . In addition, parents who adopted children were unknown to the birth mother. Today, however, there is a trend toward open adoption and away from closed, or __**anonymous**_____ , adoption.

■ *True or False?*

Each of the following statements contains one or more words from this section. Read each sentence carefully and then decide if it is probably true or probably false.

__F__   1. Beneficial treatment results in many malpractice suits.

__F__   2. A benign person would probably try to harm others.

__T__   3. Symbiotic relationships are dependent.

_F_   4. Apathy is enthusiastic interest.

_F_   5. Biodegradable waste will stay in landfills because it cannot be broken down.

_F_   6. An anonymous benefactor would want to be thanked publicly.

_T_   7. Anarchy is a state of disorder.

_F_   8. Lawyers perform biopsies.

_F_   9. We honor the intentions of malevolent people.

_F_   10. A malady can be played on a musical instrument.

Chapter Exercises

■ *Practicing Strategies: New Words from Word Elements*

See how your knowledge of word elements can help you understand new words. Complete each sentence with the word that fits best. Use each choice only once. You may need to capitalize some words.

a. antipathy	e. audition	i. malaria
b. asocial	f. benediction	j. malodorous
c. atypical	g. biorhythms	k. pedicure
d. audiovisual	h. centipede	l. spectator

1. **d, Audiovisual** _____ aids are instructional supports that students look at and hear.

2. At a(n) **e, audition** _____ , people hear you in order to determine if you should be hired for a performance.

3. People once thought that bad air caused the disease of **i, malaria** _____ .

4. People or things that are not like most others are **c, atypical** _____ .

5. **a, Antipathy** _____ describes feelings "against" others, or hatred.

6. Your __g, biorhythms__ control the timing of life functions, such as sleeping.

7. A(n) __h, centipede__ is an insect said to have one hundred feet.

8. A(n) __f, benediction__ is a blessing, or "good words."

9. A(n) __l, spectator__ looks at a performance or display.

10. In a(n) __k, pedicure__ , one's feet and toenails receive cosmetic care.

■ *Practicing Strategies: Combining Context Clues and Word Elements*

Combining the strategies of context clues and word elements is a good way to figure out unknown words. In the following sentences, each italicized word contains a word element that you have studied in this chapter. Using the meaning of the word element and the context of the sentence, make an intelligent guess about the meaning of the italicized word. Your instructor may ask you to check the meaning in your dictionary when you have finished.

1. Under the microscope, the *amorphous* amoeba changed its shape many times.

    Amorphous means __without permanent shape; changing shape__ .

2. A virus is the *pathogen* of polio.

    Pathogen means __something that causes a disease__ .

3. A *maladroit* person often drops items and bumps into things.

    Maladroit means __clumsy__ .

4. The *audiometer* revealed that the child had a hearing loss.

    Audiometer means __machine to measure hearing__ .

5. No bacteria can infect a patient in an *aseptic* operating room.

    Aseptic means __clean; sterilized; without germs__ .

■ *Practicing Strategies: Using the Dictionary*

Read the following definition. Then answer the questions below it.

> **ridge** (rĭj) *n.* **1.** A long narrow upper section or crest. **2.** A long narrow chain of hills or mountains. **3.** A long narrow elevation on the ocean floor. **4.** *Meteorol.* An elongated zone of relatively high atmospheric pressure. **5.** A long, narrow, or crested part of the body. **6.** The horizontal line formed by the juncture of two sloping planes, esp. the line formed by the surfaces at the top of a roof. **7.** A narrow raised strip, as in cloth or on plowed ground. —*v.* **ridged, ridg•ing, ridg•es.** —*tr.* To mark with, form into, or provide with ridges. —*intr.* To form ridges. [ME *rigge* < OE *hrycg.* See **sker-²**.]

1. What was the first language in which *ridge* was recorded?

   Old English

2. Give the number and the part of speech of the definition of *ridge* most used in meteorology. **4, as a noun**

3. What is the third-person-singular form of *ridge* when used as a verb?

   ridges

4. Give the number and the part of speech of the definition that best fits this sentence: "The baker *ridged* the edge of the pie crust."

   transitive verb (only definition)

5. Which common word in the dictionary key contains a vowel pronounced like the *i* in *ridge?* **pit**

■ *Companion Words*

Complete each sentence with the word that fits best. Choose your answers from the words below. You may use each word more than once.

Choices: of, for, toward, about, with, by, to

1. Because of the poverty of his childhood, the rock star felt empathy

   for, toward the poor.

2. The pathology **of** lung cancer often involves behavior such as smoking.

3. We will expedite the research process __by____ using the Internet.

4. Aphids live in symbiosis __with____ bacteria that enable them to grow and reproduce.

5. The pathologist did a biopsy __of____ the intestinal tissue.

6. We had to respect the anonymity __of____ the benefactor.

7. Vegetables are beneficial __to____ your health.

8. Unfortunately, the mother showed only apathy __toward____ her children.

9. The cardiologist was falsely accused __of____ malpractice.

10. I often introspect __about____ my feelings.

■ *Writing with Your Words*

This exercise will give you practice in writing effective sentences that use the vocabulary words. Each sentence is started for you. Complete it with an interesting phrase that also indicates the meaning of the italicized word.

1. Relaxation is *beneficial* because _____

_____ .

2. The *malevolent* person _____

_____ .

3. I want to remain *anonymous* when _____

_____ .

4. People are too *apathetic* about _____

_____ .

5. If your intentions are *benign,* _____

_____ .

6. The *auspicious* sign meant _____

_____ .

7. The *pathologist* _____

_____ .

8. The *conspicuous* rock star _____

_____ .

9. *Introspective* people _____

_____ .

10. Traffic on the freeway was *impeded* because _____

_____ .

Passage

The Disease That Science Eliminated

It started with a fever and developed into a rash. Soon, sores appeared all over the body. Many sufferers died from damage to their hearts, livers, and lungs. This was smallpox, the most destructive disease in human history. Here is the story of its defeat.

Today, when so many diseases can be prevented or cured, it may be difficult for modern people to feel **empathy** for the people that smallpox attacked. There was no cure, and one in four who got the disease died from it. Those who survived were forever marked, for **(1)** smallpox left **conspicuous** scars called "pocks." Smallpox was also highly contagious; everything a sick person touched could carry the disease. Often, sick people were "quarantined," or separated, from healthy ones. This meant that **pathetically** ill people were sometimes left alone with no one to care for them.

(2) Smallpox struck people of all classes, including those with royal **pedigrees.** Two princes died of it in 1700 and 1711, ruining the alliances that depended upon their marriages. It killed King Louis XV of France in 1774.

In the 1600s and 1700s, smallpox changed history in the Americas by wiping out much of the Native American population. Since the disease had been newly introduced by Europeans, Native Americans had little resistance to it. When first exposed, they died in great numbers. In at least one shameful incident, a smallpox epidemic was started deliberately when **(3) malevolent** Jeffrey Amherst, an English soldier, sent infected blankets to Native Americans.

The defeat of this deadly disease is one of medical science's great triumphs. First steps were taken in China over a thousand years ago, when **(4) anonymous** physicians protected people by giving them the disease deliberately. To do this, material from a pox sore of an infected person was introduced into a healthy person. If this procedure was done carefully, **(5)** the receiver usually developed a **benign** version of the **malady,** but would then be protected from smallpox for life. By 1700, this practice had spread throughout Asia and the Middle East. It was brought from Turkey to England in the early 1700s. Although the method protected many people, it was not always safe, for some receivers developed severe smallpox and died.

Then, in 1796, Edward Jenner, an English doctor, made an important discovery. Jenner had noticed that milkmaids never seemed to get smallpox. He reasoned that through their contact with cows, they got a related but relatively **benign** disease, called "cowpox," which protected them from smallpox. To test this theory, on May 14, 1796, Jenner took a small sample of a cowpox sore from the finger of Sarah Nelmes, a milkmaid, and applied it to a sore on eight-year-old James Phipps. James developed a very slight infection—and never contracted smallpox. Because cowpox came from cows, which were named *vacca* in Latin, Jenner called this procedure a "vaccination."

As Jenner treated more people, **(6)** he became certain of the **beneficial** effects of vaccination. He was eager to publish his findings, but **(7)** the Royal Society **impeded** his efforts by rejecting his paper. **(8)** Finally, to **expedite** publication, Jenner printed the results himself.

Even after the publication of Jenner's findings, public reaction remained **apathetic,** especially in large cities. Jenner located no volunteers for vaccination in a three-month search of the London area. Although the method was soon endorsed by physicians and used often in the English countryside, Londoners did not commonly undergo vaccination until the middle of the next century. **(9)** In fact, an **audit** of the "Bills of Mortality," or record of deaths in London, shows smallpox to be a common cause of death until the 1840s.

Resistance to vaccination lasted even longer in France and Germany, where opponents accused physicians of **malpractice** for deliberately introducing disease into a healthy person. Ministers objected to doctors interfering with "God's will" by preventing disease. However, others in these countries trusted Jenner's method. The French emperor Napoleon had his entire army vaccinated in 1805.

In the Americas, rapid adoption of vaccination was an important factor in the population growth of the New World. People in both English and Spanish colonies made wide use of the method.

Jenner lived to see honors and awards, as well as attacks and betrayals. Through it all, he remained dedicated to the cause of vaccination. He worked so hard on its behalf that he had no time to earn money practicing medicine. Although he died a poor man, this **benefactor** left a great legacy to the world.

A century after Jenner's death, smallpox vaccination was practiced almost universally, and fewer and fewer people contracted the disease. In the second half of the twentieth century, the number of cases decreased every year, **(10)** an **auspicious** sign for world health. The last case was reported in 1977.

Today, all that remains of the smallpox virus are two small samples—one in the United States and one in Russia. The samples are being kept alive in case they are needed for scientific study. Otherwise, this once-deadly killer of mankind has vanished from the earth.

■ *Exercise*

Each numbered sentence below corresponds to a sentence in the Passage. Fill in the letter of the choice that makes this sentence mean the same thing as the corresponding sentence in the Passage.

1. Smallpox left ___**a**___ scars.
   a. noticeable   b. sick   c. huge   d. harmless

2. Smallpox struck those with royal ___**b**___ .
   a. wealth   b. ancestries   c. powers   d. dependence

3. ___**d**___ Jeffrey Amherst sent infected blankets to Native Americans.
   a. Careless   b. Ill   c. Thoughtful   d. Evil

4. ___**a**___ physicians protected people.
   a. Unknown   b. Kind   c. Helpful   d. Intelligent

5. The receiver usually developed a ___**b**___ form of the malady.
   a. severe   b. harmless   c. long-term   d. helpful

6. Jenner became certain of the ___**a**___ effects of vaccination.
   a. helpful   b. noticeable   c. sad   d. fast

7. The Royal Society ___**d**___ his efforts.
   a. ignored   b. speeded   c. inspected   d. blocked

8. Finally, to __c__ publication, Jenner printed the results himself.
   a. enable   b. demand   c. speed   d. help

9. A(n) __a__ of the "Bills of Mortality" shows smallpox to be a common cause of death.
   a. examination   b. publication   c. official record   d. accusation

10. This was a __d__ sign for world health.
    a. reasonable   b. bad   c. noticeable   d. favorable

■ *Discussion Questions*

1. Why was the word *vaccination* taken from a word meaning "cow"?

2. What were some of the ways that smallpox changed history?

3. Name three other diseases that can now be prevented by vaccination.

> ◀ **ENGLISH IDIOMS**
>
> ### *Food*
>
> Perhaps because of the importance of food to our health, many widely used English idioms contain references to cooking and things we eat. A sensitive, difficult issue is called a *hot potato*. When we are in difficulty, we are *in hot water*. Ideas that are not fully thought out are often called *half-baked*.
>
> People who feel strong and energetic are *feeling their oats*. However, when we are disgusted with something, we are *fed up* with it, and when we lose our tempers, we *boil over*.
>
> Other expressions refer to the birds we eat. To ruin or destroy one's hopes or plans is to *cook one's goose*. *Duck soup* refers to something easily done, and "That test was duck soup" refers to an easy test.
>
> Idioms also refer to fruits and vegetables. To *go bananas* and to *go nuts* both mean to go crazy. One's *salad days* refer to the days of one's youth.
>
> To *take with a grain of salt* means not to take seriously. To *cry over spilt milk* means to complain about something that can no longer be prevented.
>
> The butter of the yak, a relative of the ox, had great value to the people of Tibet. When they wanted to please someone, they presented tubs of the butter as a present. Today, to *butter up* means to flatter.

Quiz Again

Now that you have finished this chapter, here is the brief true-false quiz you took when you began. Take it again.

Inaudible sounds are loud.	True	False
Something **beneficial** is helpful.	True	False
Something **conspicuous** is easily noticed.	True	False
A **malevolent** person is evil.	True	False

Answers are on page 407. Did your score improve?

Word Elements: Speech and Writing

This chapter presents word elements of speech and writing, the two major forms of human communication. The first part of the chapter contains three elements related to speech; the second part gives two elements related to writing. Part 2 also presents three pairs of words that people often confuse in speech and writing and helps you learn to use these confusing words correctly.

Chapter Strategy: Word Elements: Speech and Writing

Chapter Words:

Part 1

dict	contradict	*voc, vok*	advocate
	dictator		invoke
	edict		revoke
log, -logy, loq	colloquial		vociferous
	ecology		
	loquacious		
	monologue		
	prologue		

Part 2

-gram, -graph,	demographic	*Confusable Words*	affect
-graphy,	epigram		effect
graph	graphic		conscience
scrib, script	inscription		conscious
	manuscript		imply
	transcribe		infer

Quiz Yourself

To check your knowledge of some chapter words before you begin to study, identify these statements as true or false.

A **loquacious** person rarely talks.   True   False

An **inscription** may be carved.   True   False

An **epigram** is long.   True   False

Colloquial speech is formal.   True   False

You will learn the answers as you study this chapter.

Did You Know?

Shortening English

English speakers seem to like short words. The most widely used English words all have four or fewer letters. Listed from number one to ten, they are *the, of, and, a, to, in, is, you, that,* and *it.*

In fact, when an English word is used frequently, it is often shortened, or *clipped.* Many people now refer to *television* as *TV* and *telephone* as *phone.* Most students use the word *exam* to refer to an *examination. Fax,* as in *fax machine,* has been shortened from *facsimile.*

Some words were clipped over fifty years ago, and people may not know the original words. The word for a common malady, *flu,* was clipped from *influenza.* A *bus* was once called an *autobus,* and signs for *autobuses* can still be seen in Scotland. The word *caravan* has been replaced by *van.*

Some clippings date back even longer than words like *flu, bus,* and *van*—several hundred years longer, in fact. In the 1500s, Italian comedies featured a foolish character named *Pantaloon* who wore an unfashionable, loose-fitting garment to cover his legs. This piece of clothing became known as *pantaloons,* a word shortened to *pants* in the 1800s. For centuries, when people parted, they said, "God be with you," to each other. Four hundred years ago, this was shortened to "good-bye."

A relatively modern way to shorten expressions is to form an *acro-*

nym, a series of words that are replaced by their initial letters. For example, *laser* stands for *l*ight *a*mplification by *s*imulated *e*mission of *r*adiation. *Radar* was created from the initials of *r*adio *d*etection *a*nd *r*anging.

Acronyms have been coined to describe many aspects of American life. In business, a *c*ertified *p*ublic *a*ccountant is called a *CPA.* *BASIC* is a computer acronym for *b*eginner's *a*ll-purpose *s*ymbolic *i*nstruction *c*ode. In sports, a *scuba* diver uses a *s*elf-*c*ontained *u*nderwater *b*reathing *a*pparatus. If an athlete sprains a muscle, *"rice,"* meaning *r*est, *i*ce, *c*ompression, and *e*levation, is often prescribed.

Acronyms have also been devised for lifestyles. *Dinks* are *d*ouble *in*comes, *no* *k*ids—that is, childless couples who both work outside the home. The U.S. census now counts the number of *POSSLQs,* or unmarried *p*ersons of the *o*pposite *s*ex *s*haring *l*iving *q*uarters. Even political views have acronyms. People who favor reforms, until they are personally affected, are referred to as *nimbys,* or *n*ot *i*n *m*y *b*ack *y*ard.

Although most acronyms are designed to shorten expressions, at least one organization using an acronym takes a long view of things. The project *Longstop* (*Long*-term gravitational *s*tability *t*est *o*f the *o*uter *p*lanets) has charted the movements of our solar system one million years into the future.

Not all English words are short, of course. What is the longest word in English? According to the *Oxford English Dictionary,* it is "pneumono-ultramicroscopicsilcovolcanoconiosis," a disease of the lungs. Hints to meaning are often found inside very long words. In this case, you may know that *pneumono* refers to the lungs, as in the word *pneumonia,* a disease of the lungs. This root is taken from the ancient Greek word for "lung." *Microscopic,* as in *microscope,* means "small" and describes the organisms causing the disease. The ancient-Greek-derived *micro* means "small," and *scope* means "to look." Finally, *osis* means "disease" or "abnormality," as in *psychosis,* a mental disorder. Thus, even the longest word in the dictionary has some clues to meaning.

Learning Strategy

Word Elements: Speech and Writing

Human beings are skilled communicators. Not surprisingly, English has many word elements that deal with communication in oral and written form. Part 1 of this chapter concentrates on speech, and Part 2 deals with writing.

Element	Meaning	Origin	Function	Chapter Words
				Part 1
dict	speak	Latin	root	contradict, dictator, edict
log, -logy, loq	word; study of; speak	Greek; Latin	root; suffix	colloquial, ecology, loquacious, monologue, prologue
voc, vok	voice; call	Latin	root	advocate, invoke, revoke, vociferate
				Part 2
-gram, -graph, -graphy, graph	write	Latin; Greek	suffix; root	demographic, epigram, graphic
scrib, script	write	Latin	root	inscription, manuscript, transcribe

Word Elements

Part 1

The word roots for Part 1 are explained below in more detail.

dict (speak)

This root appears in several common words. *Dictation* is something **spoken** by one person and copied down by another. *Diction* is the clearness and quality of one's **speech.**

Speech is now a key element of popular music. Rap, which uses speaking instead of singing, is one of the most creative and important developments in current music. Its roots come from African chanting, spoken blues, the performances of James Brown, and the toasts of Jamaican disk jockeys. Rhythm and beat are important to rap and hip-hop. Lyrics often deal with current social issues, and some rap groups are extremely controversial. Popular performers include Dr. Dre and Snoop Doggy Dog.

---

log, -logy, loq (word; study of; speak)

To be *eloquent* is to **speak** well. A *dialogue* is **speech,** or a conversation, between two or more people. However, the suffix *-logy* means "study of." You may have taken courses in *biology* (the **study of** living things), *psychology* (the **study of** the mind), or *anthropology* (the **study of** human beings).

voc, vok (voice; call)

A record that contains the human **voice** speaking or singing is called a *vocal* recording. *Vocabulary,* meaning "things spoken by the **voice,**" or "words," also comes from *voc.* You will not confuse this root with the other word roots in this chapter if you remember to associate it with the word *voice.*

Words to Learn

Part 1

dict

1. **contradict** (verb)   kŏn′trə-dĭkt′

   From Latin: *contra-* (against) + *dict* (speak)

   to say or put forth the opposite of something

   > It is not wise to **contradict** your boss in front of coworkers.

   > A report by a private firm **contradicted** the government agency's findings that airport noise was decreasing.

   ▶ *Related Words*

   contradiction (noun)   *Contradictions* between the versions of the crime given by two different witnesses left jurors confused.

   contradictory (adjective)   Research into the benefits of vitamins has yielded *contradictory* results.

   Oxymorons are *contradictions* of language, or statements in which one word seems to contradict another. A few examples are *definite maybe, sweet sorrow, exact estimate, jumbo shrimp, killing with kindness, dull shine,* and *whole half.*

   ---

2. **dictator** (noun)   dĭk′tā-tər

   From Latin: *dict* (speak) (A dictator is a ruler who speaks with power; whatever the ruler says is done.)

   a ruler with total authority

   > Joseph Stalin, **dictator** of the former Soviet Union, ordered several million people into gulags, or prison camps.

▶ *Related Word*
dictatorial (adjective) (dĭk′tə-tôr′ē-əl) The club president's *dictatorial* manner ensured that he lost the next election.

3. **edict** (noun) ē′dĭkt′

From Latin: *e-* (out) + *dict* (speak)

an order or decree

King Henry IV of France signed the **Edict** of Nantes in 1598, becoming the first ruler to decree religious toleration.

In 1998, the White House published an **edict** requiring that government regulations be written in plain English.

Edicts may not always be followed. On May 4, 1493, Pope Alexander VI issued an edict dividing the "New World," or the Americas, between Spain and Portugal. Today these two European countries rule not one square inch of land in the Americas. However, their legacy is seen in the many countries whose inhabitants speak Spanish and the large country (Brazil) where Portuguese is spoken.

---

log, -logy, loq

4. **colloquial** (adjective) kə-lō′kwē-əl

From Latin: *com-* (together) + *loq* (speak) (When we "speak together" with friends, our speech is colloquial.)

informal conversation or expression

The word "yeah" is a **colloquial** way of saying "yes."

▶ *Related Word*
colloquialism (noun) The word "frosted" is a *colloquialism* for "angry."

5. **ecology** (noun) ĭ-kŏl′ə-jē

From Greek: *oikos* (house) + *-logy* (study of) (Ecology is concerned with the environment, the "home" or "house" in which we all live.)

the relationship of living things and their environment; the study of this relationship

A hole in the earth's ozone layer, caused by pollution, might threaten the **ecology** by allowing harmful solar radiation to reach the earth.

A study in **ecology,** which showed the effects of cutting trees on animal life, helped lead to controls on logging in the province of Sichuan, China.

▶ *Related Words*

ecological (adjective) (ĕk′ə-lŏj′ĭ-kəl) Acid rain has ruined the *ecological* balance of many lakes and ponds.

ecologist (noun) The *ecologist* investigated the effect of traffic noise on nearby wildlife.

The science of *ecology* is increasingly needed to protect plant and animal life. The rain forests of the world are being cleared to obtain lumber and provide farmland. Ecologists have demonstrated how this practice may lead to the extinction of forest animals and plants. Plants that may have great value to medicine would be lost forever. Even human life would be affected because the leaves of rain forest trees release oxygen into the atmosphere. The study of *ecology* is having some positive effects, however. In 1998, Suriname, in South America, announced that a valuable rain forest covering 12 percent of its land would be declared a nature reserve.

---

6. **loquacious** (adjective)   lō-kwā′shəs

From Greek: *loq-* (speak)

very talkative

My **loquacious** sister kept me on the telephone for over an hour.

The TV talk show host had to cut off the **loquacious** actor by calling for a commercial.

▶ *Related Words*

loquaciousness (noun) Because of his *loquaciousness,* the politician loved to grant interviews to reporters.

7. **monologue** (noun)   mŏn′ə-lôg′

From Greek: *monos* (one) + *log* (speak)

a speech or performance by one person

Comedian Bill Cosby is a master of amusing **monologues.**

In Hamlet's **monologue** "To be or not to be," Shakespeare examines the mind of a person who cannot make a decision.

8. **prologue** (noun)   prō′lôg′

From Greek: *pro-* (before) + *log* (speak)

the introduction to a literary or artistic work

> In the **prologue** of the movie *Titanic,* a ship's crew searches for a valuable jewel.

> The author described the historical background of the book in the **prologue.**

an introductory event

> Social changes in the 1960s were the **prologue** for the greater freedoms of the 1970s and 1980s.

> The stock market crash of 1929 was a **prologue** to the Great Depression.

The *prologues* to many TV programs and movies have become famous. Can you identify what these introduce?

1. Faster than a speeding bullet, more powerful than a locomotive. . . .

2. Space, the final frontier. . . .

3. A long time ago, in a galaxy far, far away. . . .

Answers are on page 407.

---

voc, vok

9. **advocate** (verb)   ăd′və-kāt′;   (noun)   ăd′və-kĭt

From Latin: *ad-* (toward) + *voc* (to voice, call)

to urge publicly; to recommend (verb)

> Members of Amnesty International **advocate** the protection of human rights and the elimination of torture.

a person who publicly urges a cause (noun)

> Economist Milton Friedman is an **advocate** of the free market system.

▶ *Common Phrase*
advocate of

10. **invoke** (verb)   ĭn-vōk′

From Latin: *in-* (in) + *voc* (to call) (*Invocāre* means "to call upon.")

to call in assistance; to call upon

> The minister **invoked** the help of God in troubled times.
>
> The social worker **invoked** the aid of the police to remove the child from the abusive home.

▶ *Related Word*
invocation (noun)   (ĭn′və-kā′shən)   The rabbi gave an *invocation*. (*Invocation* means "prayer.")

The Fifth Amendment of the U.S. Constitution states that those accused of a crime cannot be forced to testify against themselves. Thus, when asked to explain something that may injure their case or make them appear guilty, accused people may "*invoke* the Fifth Amendment" and refuse to answer.

---

11. **revoke** (verb)   rĭ-vōk′

From Latin: *re-* (back) + *vok* (to call)

to cancel or withdraw

> Judges often **revoke** the licenses of people convicted of driving drunk.

▶ *Related Word*
revocation (noun)   (rĕv′ə-kā′shən)   A country that violates human rights risks *revocation* of trade agreements with the United States.

12. **vociferous** (adjective)   vō-sĭf′ər-əs

From Latin: *voc* (voice) + *ferre* (carry)

crying out noisily; speaking loudly

> The **vociferous** Salt Lake City crowd whistled, cheered, and shouted encouragement to the Utah Jazz basketball team.
>
> At a city hearing, **vociferous** neighborhood residents forcefully protested the replacement of low-cost housing with expensive condominiums.

Exercises

Part 1

■ *Definitions*

Match each word in the left-hand column with a definition from the right-hand column. Use each choice only once.

1. monologue ___h___   a. to cancel

2. invoke ___g___   b. informal

3. ecology ___e___   c. very talkative

4. vociferous ___k___   d. order; decree

5. loquacious ___c___   e. the relationship of living
                                          things and their environment
6. edict ___d___
                                       f. helpless
7. colloquial ___b___
                                       g. to call in for assistance
8. prologue ___i___
                                       h. speech by one person
9. revoke ___a___
                                       i. introduction to book or play
10. advocate ___j___
                                       j. to recommend

                                       k. crying out noisily; speaking
                                          loudly

                                       l. to say something opposite

■ *Meanings*

Match each word element to its definition. Use each choice only once.

1. voc, vok ___c___   a. speak; study of; word

2. log, -logy, loq ___a___   b. speak

3. dict ___b___   c. voice; call

■ *Words in Context*

Complete each sentence with the word that fits best. Use each choice only once.

a. contradict   e. ecology   i. advocate
b. dictator   f. loquacious   j. invoke
c. edict   g. monologue   k. revoke
d. colloquial   h. prologue   l. vociferous

1. The __l, vociferous__ man shouted slogans at the political rally.

2. The small, poor country tried to __j, invoke__ the aid of its rich neighbor during the famine.

3. Students should use formal rather than __d, colloquial__ English when they write term papers.

4. The __b, dictator__ had total control over the country.

5. When a mother and father __a, contradict__ each other, a child may not know whose directions to follow.

6. Standing alone on a stage, the actor delivered a powerful __g, monologue__ .

7. Clouds are usually a(n) __h, prologue__ to rain.

8. The __f, loquacious__ woman talked on and on throughout our card game.

9. I am a(n) __i, advocate__ of women's rights.

10. The government issued a(n) __c, edict__ declaring that all citizens must be off the streets by 10 P.M.

■ *Using Related Words*

Complete each sentence by using a word from the group of related words above it. You may need to capitalize a word when you write it in a sentence. Use each choice only once.

1. colloquial, colloquialism

Teenagers and young adults are often active inventors of __colloquial__ expressions. In the 1920s, they employed the word *peachy* to describe something wonderful; this changed to *groovy* in the 1960s, and the 1990s' **colloquialism** _____ was *awesome.*

2. dictator, dictatorial

Was Napoleon a **dictator** _____ or an enlightened ruler? He savagely slaughtered those who resisted his **dictatorial** _____ actions in Italy. Yet he extended the rights of citizens and created a series of laws called the Napoleonic Code.

3. contradicted, contradictory, contradiction

The great architect Frank Lloyd Wright was a study in **contradiction** _____. His great artistic achievements were **contradicted** _____ by his disturbing private behavior. He left his wife and his children to run off with the wife of a client. He left unfulfilled contracts and debts as well. Wright's example shows that public achievements and private behavior may be **contradictory** _____.

4. revoked, revocation

At one time, plastic tubing for plumbing, or PVC, was banned from use in many cities. Recently, the ban has been **revoked** _____ in various areas. However, this **revocation** _____ often does not cover high-rise buildings. Copper tubing for plumbing must still be used in many of these taller structures.

5. ecology, ecological

Even a few degrees of global warming would have a major effect on world **ecology** _____. Melting ice would cause higher sea levels, and the wildlife that occupies shorelines and shallow water would have difficulty surviving. Areas that once supported crops might turn into deserts. As the earth warmed, the **ecological** _____ balance would be upset.

■ *Reading the Headlines*

This exercise presents five headlines that might appear in newspapers. Read each headline and then answer the questions that follow. (Remember that small words, such as *is, are, a,* and *the,* are often left out of newspaper headlines.)

PROLOGUE TO PLAY CONSISTS OF A MONOLOGUE

1. Is the monologue given after the play? __no__

2. Does one person give the prologue? __yes__

DICTATOR ISSUES EDICT THAT REVOKES GAMBLING

3. Does the person have complete control? __yes__

4. Is gambling allowed? __no__

GOVERNOR TAKES CONTRADICTORY STANDS ON ECOLOGY

5. Is the governor taking one clear position? __no__

6. Is the environment being discussed? __yes__

IN VOCIFEROUS DEMONSTRATION, CROWD MEMBERS ADVOCATE BAN ON DEATH SENTENCE

7. Is the demonstration quiet? __no__

8. Do crowd members want a ban on the death sentence? __yes__

LOQUACIOUS PROFESSOR USES MANY COLLOQUIALISMS

9. Does the professor talk a lot? __yes__

10. Does the professor talk very formally? __no__

Word Elements

Part 2

The second part of this chapter presents two word elements that deal with the concept of writing. Then three pairs of easily confused words, which college students often have trouble distinguishing, are introduced.

-gram, -graph, -graphy, graph (write)

This suffix has three spellings. It is spelled *-gram*, as in *telegram*, a **written** message sent by wires. (*Tele-* means "far.") The spelling *-graph* is used in *autograph*, a person's signature, or "self-**writing**." (*Auto* means "self.") Finally, the suffix can be spelled *-graphy*, as in *photography* (literally, "**writing** in light"). *Graph* can also function as a base word.

Graffiti, that often illegal writing that appears in elevators, on overpasses and walls, and, of course, in bathrooms, has plagued us throughout history. Archaeologists have discovered the name of Padihorpakhered, who, identifying himself as a powerful Egyptian priest, carved his name on the sandstone sides of a monument in Thebes 2,700 years ago. Thus, like *graffiti* writers of today, he assured himself notice. The word *graffiti* comes, through Italian, from the word element *graph.*

---

scrib, script (write)

This root is found in many common words. A *script* is the **written** form of a television program, movie, or play. When small children make **written** marks, they often *scribble*. A *scribe* **writes** down the words of other people.

Words to Learn

Part 2

-gram, -graph, -graphy, graph

13. **demographic** (adjective)   děm′ə-grăf′ĭk

    From Greek: *demos* (people) + *-graph* (write)

    referring to the study of population characteristics

Demographic studies showed that the number of children living with single fathers increased by 25 percent from 1995 to 1998.

Demographic trends show a rise in the elderly population of the United States.

▶ *Related Words*

demographics (noun, plural)   U.S. *demographics* reveal that more people are choosing to remain single.

demography (noun) (dĭ-mŏg′rə-fē)   The United States is working to update data on *demography* every year, rather than every ten years.

demographer (noun, person)   One *demographer* reported that in the early 1990s, people tended to move from California to other western states.

14. **epigram** (noun)   ĕp′ĭ-grăm′

From Greek: *epi-* (on) + *-gram* (write)

a short, clever saying, often in rhyme

Benjamin Franklin's **epigram** on the value of consistent work was "Little strokes fell great oaks."

15. **graphic** (adjective)   grăf′ĭk

From Greek: *graph* (write) (*Graphe* meant "drawing, writing.")

referring to drawings or artistic writing

My computer software can create charts, drawings, and other **graphic** displays.

described vividly or clearly

Steven Spielberg's movie *Saving Private Ryan* depicts the bloody 1944 invasion of Normandy in **graphic** detail.

Charles Dickens's **graphic** description of abused and neglected children shocked the English public of the 1800s.

▶ *Related Word*

graphics (noun)   The Hyatt hotel chain had its *graphics* professionally designed.

scrib, script

16. **inscription** (noun)   ĭn-skrĭp′shən

From Latin: *in-* (in) + *script* (write)

carving or writing on a surface

> Many U.S. coins bear the **inscription** *E pluribus unum,* meaning "one from many."

> The Saudi Arabian flag bears an **inscription** from the Koran.

a signed message on a picture or in a book

> "Don't forget me, M. Goldberg" was the **inscription** the teacher wrote in her yearbook.

▶ *Related Word*
inscribe (verb)   (ĭn-skrīb′)   A granite memorial to police slain in the line of duty was *inscribed* with the name of each officer.

> Atif, an excellent student who died in a car accident, is *inscribed* in teacher Judy McDonald's memory. (In this sentence, *inscribe* is used in a nonphysical sense.)

17. **manuscript** (noun, adjective)   măn′yə-skrĭpt′

From Latin: *manu* (by hand) + *script* (write)

the original text of a book or article before publication (noun)

> Long after his death, Robert Hale Strong's **manuscript** about his battle experiences was published as *A Yankee Private's Civil War.*

> The **manuscript** of *The Life and Times of Frederick Douglass* sold for several thousand dollars at a recent auction.

referring to writing done by hand (adjective)

> It took many years to master the beautiful **manuscript** lettering that was once used to write books.

Before printing was invented, scribes laboriously copied whole books. The *manuscripts* they created were often beautiful works of art, and they were quite expensive.

Johann Gutenberg invented modern printing in about 1450. The famous *Gutenberg Bible* was his first production. The printing process brought about a social revolution because it made books, and therefore knowledge, less expensive and more widely available.

NOTE: Manuscript writing (done with disconnected letters) is often distinguished from cursive writing (done with connected letters).

18. **transcribe** (verb)   trăn-skrīb**′**

From Latin: *trans-* (across) + *scrib* (write)

to make a complete written copy

> Court reporters **transcribe** every word of a legal proceeding.

to copy something into another form

> The piano concert was **transcribed** onto an audiotape.

▶ *Related Words*
> **transcriber** (noun)   The *transcriber* turned the dictation into a letter.

> **transcription** (noun)   The government made a *transcription* of the tapes recorded by former President Richard Nixon.

Confusable Words

19. **affect** (verb)   ə-fĕkt**′**

to have an influence on; to change

> According to studies, pets **affect** people's happiness positively.

20. **effect** (noun)   ĭ-fĕkt**′**

a result

> Pets have positive **effects** on people's happiness.

NOTE ON POSSIBLE CONFUSION: Try to remember that *affect* is usually a verb and *effect* is usually a noun, as in the following two sentences.

The great teacher *affected* my life.

The great teacher had an *effect* on my life.

21. **conscience** (noun)   kŏn**′**shəns

sense of right and wrong; moral sense

> The child's guilty **conscience** made her return the candy bar she had shoplifted.

► *Related Word*

conscientious (adjective) (kŏn′shē-ĕn′shəs) *Conscientious* jury members listened attentively throughout the long trial.

22. **conscious** (adjective)   kŏn′shəs

aware; awake

> We are not **conscious** when we sleep.
>
> The jury members were **conscious** of the importance of their decision.

► *Related Word*

consciousness (noun)   The boy lost *consciousness* after his head struck the car window.

NOTE ON POSSIBLE CONFUSION: Remember that *conscience* is a noun and *conscious* is an adjective, as in the following two sentences.

My *conscience* was bothering me.

I am *conscious* of my responsibility.

23. **imply** (verb)   ĭm-plī′

to suggest; to say something indirectly

> A soft smile and kindly voice **imply** that a person is pleased.

► *Related Word*

implication (noun) (ĭm′plĭ-kā′shən)   Professor Lois Daly feels that the TV series *Star Trek* contains many religious *implications*.

24. **infer** (verb)   ĭn-fûr′

to conclude; to guess

> I **infer** from your soft smile that you are pleased.

► *Related Words*

inference (noun) (ĭn′fər-əns)   The chemistry student made an *inference* from the results of her experiment.

inferential (adjective) (ĭn′fə-rĕn′shəl)   This difficult problem requires *inferential* thinking.

NOTE ON POSSIBLE CONFUSION: A speaker or writer *implies;* a listener or reader *infers.*

Recently, James Joyce's book *Ulysses* was voted the most important book of the twentieth century. However, about the same time, it was reported that many original copies of the book, given by Joyce to publishers and friends, had uncut pages. These pages, joined at the edges, would have needed to be separated to be read. This strongly *implies* that, indeed, the great masterpiece was not read. From the location of the uncut pages, we can *infer* that some people started the book, but never finished.

Exercises

Part 2

■ Definitions

Match each word in the left-hand column with a definition from the right-hand column. Use each choice only once.

1. effect __**j**__

2. graphic __**l**__

3. inscription __**g**__

4. epigram __**f**__

5. affect __**d**__

6. transcribe __**c**__

7. conscious __**a**__

8. imply __**e**__

9. infer __**i**__

10. manuscript __**h**__

a. aware

b. a sense of right and wrong

c. to make a complete written copy

d. to influence

e. to hint

f. short, witty saying

g. carving on a surface

h. text of a book before publication

i. to draw a conclusion

j. a result

k. referring to population statistics

l. referring to drawings or charts

■ *Words in Context*

Complete each sentence with the word that fits best. Use each choice only once, and capitalize when necessary.

a. demographic	e. manuscript	i. conscience
b. epigram	f. transcribe	j. conscious
c. graphic	g. affect	k. imply
d. inscription	h. effect	l. infer

1. The rare **e, manuscript** _____ of a Jane Austen book was on display at the cultural center.

2. **a, Demographic** _____ surveys reveal that about one-fourth of Canadians speak mainly French at home.

3. The executive asked the secretary to **f, transcribe** _____ her dictation into written form.

4. I have a clear **i, conscience** _____ because I did no wrong.

5. The description of the cold weather was so **c, graphic** _____ that we began to shiver.

6. I try not to let my mood **g, affect** _____ how I interact with my family.

7. I was not **j, conscious** _____ of the fact that I had broken any rules.

8. In her speech, the governor will **k, imply** _____, but not directly state, that there should be no more high-rise buildings on the ocean front.

9. The mayor was concerned about the **h, effect** _____ of increasing the number of flights at the city airport.

10. "Man proposes, God disposes" is an example of a(n) **b, epigram** _____ .

■ *Using Related Words*

Complete each sentence by using a word from the group of related words above it. You may need to capitalize a word when you write it in a sentence. Use each choice only once.

1. infer, imply

   When a plane crashes, the Federal Aviation Administration tries

   to **infer** _____ the cause. An accident may be due to
   human or mechanical failure, and loss of life can be great. How-

   ever, statistics **imply** _____ that you are still safer riding
   in a plane than driving a car.

2. inscriptions, inscribed

   Designed by Yale architectural student Maya Lin, the memorial for

   the Vietnam War is a long slab of black granite. **Inscribed** _____
   in the surface are the names of all U.S. soldiers who died in
   battle. People throughout the United States come to see the

   inscriptions _____ honoring those who have fallen. Many visitors are moved to tears.

3. demographics, demographic

   Demographics _____ show that an increasing number of moth-

   ers of young children are working. This **demographic** _____
   trend points to a need for high-quality and widely available child-
   care facilities.

4. affect, effect

   Which has a greater **effect** _____ on a person, heredity
   or environment? In the 1800s and early 1900s, scientists believed
   that heredity had a far greater influence. Since then, environment

   has been shown to **affect** _____ people strongly. For example, in a study done by Skeels in the 1930s, when children placed
   in an orphanage were given loving attention, their IQs increased
   dramatically.

5. consciences, conscientious

   Many consider serving their country in the armed forces to be
   an honor. However, others have felt they cannot. Some young
   men refused to serve because they did not believe that war is

justified. Their __**consciences**_____ would have bothered them if they had killed another. These young men were called __**conscientious**_____ objectors.

■ *Reading the Headlines*

This exercise presents five headlines that might appear in newspapers. Read each headline and then answer the questions that follow. (Remember that small words, such as *is, are, a,* and *the,* are often left out of newspaper headlines.)

DEMOGRAPHICS SHOW WOMEN ARE CONSCIOUS OF DELAYING CHILDBEARING

1. Is the population being studied? __**yes**____

2. Are women aware of the delay? __**yes**____

ANCIENT EPIGRAM FOUND INSCRIBED IN RUINED WALL

3. Was a long piece of writing found? __**no**____

4. Was the epigram carved? __**yes**____

STUDIES SHOW NOTICEABLE EFFECT OF GRAPHIC DESCRIPTION ON VIOLENT BEHAVIOR

5. Does the description change anything? __**yes**____

6. Is the description vivid? __**yes**____

SCIENTIFIC PROJECT TRANSCRIBES ANCIENT MANUSCRIPT

7. Is the form of the manuscript staying the same? __**no**____

8. Is the project dealing with something written? __**yes**____

INFERENCE THAT CONSCIENCE AFFECTS APPETITE IS DRAWN FROM STUDY

9. Is the conclusion directly stated? **no**

10. Does conscience have anything to do with appetite? **yes**

Chapter Exercises

■ *Practicing Strategies: New Words from Word Elements*

See how your knowledge of word elements can help you understand new words. Complete each sentence with the word that seems to fit best. Use each choice only once.

a. biography	e. hologram	i. scriptorium
b. cardiogram	f. interlocution	j. seismograph
c. dermatology	g. prescription	k. sociology
d. graphite	h. revocalize	l. travelogue

1. The study of society is called **k, sociology** .

2. A(n) **g, prescription** is something that must be written out before you can get medicine. (*Pre-* means "before.")

3. A book written about someone's life is a(n) **a, biography** .

4. Since *seismo* means "earthquake," a **j, seismograph** is a recorded (or "written") record of an earthquake.

5. The substance of **d, graphite** was named for its use as a writing material.

6. A spoken account of a trip might be called a(n) **l, travelogue** .

7. A(n) **e, hologram** is a three-dimensional picture in which a whole object seems to appear.

8. Since *cardio* means "heart," the picture of heartbeats is called a(n) **b, cardiogram** .

9. When we "voice something again," we **h, revocalize** it.

10. Books were once written by hand in a(n) **i, scriptorium** .

■ *Practicing Strategies: Combining Context Clues and Word Elements*

Combining the strategies of context clues and word elements is a good way to figure out unknown words. In the following sentences, each italicized word contains a word element that you have studied in this chapter. Using the meaning of the word element and the context of the sentence, make an intelligent guess about the meaning of the italicized word. Your instructor may ask you to check the meaning in your dictionary when you have finished.

1. The *entomologist* specialized in ants, bees, and wasps.

   Entomologist means **scientist who studies insects** .

2. Delivering a *eulogy* in his brother's honor, Winston said many wonderful things about him.

   Eulogy means **praising speech** .

3. *Pictographs* were used by ancient civilizations.

   Pictographs means **pictures carrying words or ideas; pictures carrying the meaning of writing** .

4. At the *colloquium,* many people gave talks about the economy.

   Colloquium means **conference; meeting at which people come together to talk** .

5. The written word *toy* has three *graphemes*.

   Graphemes means **letters** .

■ *Companion Words*

Complete each sentence with the word that fits best. Choose your answers from the words below. You may use each word more than once.

Choices: of, on, from

1. After the revocation **of** _____ civil liberties, people fled the country.

2. We can make an inference **from** _____ a speaker's implications.

3. A mother is often conscious **of** _____ her baby's every movement.

4. I am an advocate **of** _____ equal pay for equal work.

5. Weather often has an effect **on** _____ people's decisions to travel.

■ *Writing with Your Words*

This exercise will give you practice in writing effective sentences that use the vocabulary words. Each sentence is started for you. Complete it with an interesting phrase that also indicates the meaning of the italicized word.

1. I am a *vociferous* opponent of _____

   _____ .

2. My favorite *colloquial* expression is _____

   _____ .

3. The *loquacious* employee _____

   _____ .

4. I have *contradictory* feelings about _____

   _____ .

5. According to the *edict,* _____

   _____ .

6. When the publisher read the *manuscript* of the book, _____

   _____ .

7. If I gave a *monologue,* I _____

   _____ .

8. We *inferred* from the speech that _____

_____ .

9. I am *affected* by _____

_____ .

10. A *conscientious* worker _____

_____ .

Passage

The Man Who Did Not Cry Wolf

Are wolves as evil as they are portrayed in fairy tales and folklore? After you read this passage, you, like Farley Mowat, may never think of these animals in the same way.

Centuries of folklore and tradition have revealed humans' distrust and fear of wolves. We speak of starvation as "having the wolf at the door." It is the wolf who tricks the folktale figure Little Red Riding Hood. Finally, an evil person who appears to be innocent is called a "wolf in sheep's clothing."

Only a few brave people have ever tested these legends by observing wolves at close range. Farley Mowat was one such person. **(1)** The Canadian government was concerned that wolves were damaging the **ecology** of the Arctic by eating so many caribou that the animal was disappearing. Therefore, officials sent Mowat to see what **effect** hungry northern wolves were having on caribou herds. **(2)** In his book *Never Cry Wolf*, Mowat's description of a year living close to wolves **contradicts** the traditional image of the "big, bad wolf."

From the beginning, Mowat's encounters with wolves surprised him. Weaponless, he found himself at their mercy three times; although they could have killed him, they simply walked away. Even when he went into their territory, the wolves did not attack. **(3)** The **implication** was clear: the senseless viciousness of the wolf was largely in the human imagination.

Fascinated, Mowat was determined to observe the wolves at close range. He defined his own territory, lived in a tent, and watched them through a telescope. Mowat's wolf family consisted of a couple, "Georgie" and "Angeline," their wolf pups, and "Uncle Albert," a single male. They

Mowat's description contradicts the image of the "big, bad wolf."

were affectionate and caring. The entire wolf den was organized around feeding the pups. Each afternoon, George and Uncle Albert went off to hunt, returning the next morning. **(4)** However, Angeline, apparently **conscious** of her responsibilities as a mother, stayed home to watch her youngsters.

During family play, sometimes a pup's lively nipping and licking wore Angeline out, but the good-natured Uncle Albert was always ready to take her place. **(5)** Mowat gives a **graphic** description of wolf games of "tag," with Uncle Albert playing "it." Uncle Albert was also an effective, if unwilling, baby sitter. All three adults carefully instructed the puppies in hunting.

At first, wolf calls disturbed Mowat. The animals would come together and cry in high-pitched howls for several minutes, sending chills of fear down Mowat's spine. Gradually, he began to realize that wolves could communicate different messages. After listening to howls one day, Ooteck, Mowat's Eskimo companion, became greatly excited and rushed off. A few hours later, he returned with a host of visitors. How had Ooteck known where to find them? He had gotten the information from the wolves' howls. Another time, Ooteck claimed that two wolf packs, separated by many miles, announced the presence of caribou herds to each other.

As he continued to watch the wolves, Mowat began to wonder what they ate. For most of the year, the caribou were far away. How did the den support itself during this time? One day he watched Angeline trap twenty-three mice in one afternoon. Could it be that the great beast of the north could support itself by eating the lowly mouse?

To test the ability of a large animal to live on mice, Mowat used himself as a subject. For several months, he ate only mice, developing several recipes! He reported that this diet did not **affect** his health, and he remained as vigorous as ever. **(6)** He made the **inference** that wolves could also live on a diet of mice.

Did wolves ever hunt caribou? Mowat found that the wolves hunted a few, mainly weak or old, caribou. By removing the animals that would find it hard to survive, the wolves actually strengthened the caribou herd. But if wolves were not killing the caribou, who was? Mowat decided that most were hunted by human beings.

(7) Mowat's experience with Arctic wolves was a **prologue** to efforts that aroused the public's **conscience** about the treatment of the animals. Soon after he returned from the wild, he began work on a **manuscript** to make people more aware of wolves. The resulting book, *Never Cry Wolf,* played an important part in saving the northern wolf, which, he estimated, numbered fewer than 3,000. **(8)** Mowat **invoked** the aid of wildlife organizations in preserving and increasing the wolf population. **(9)** He urged the government to **revoke** rewards for dead wolves. **(10)** In response to the pleas of Mowat and other wildlife **advocates,** people are now taking steps to protect this valuable animal.

■ Exercise

Each numbered sentence below corresponds to a sentence in the Passage. Fill in the letter of the choice that makes the sentence mean the same thing as its corresponding sentence in the Passage.

1. The Canadian government was concerned that wolves were damaging the ___**b**___ of the Arctic.
   a. balance of fur trapping   b. environmental balance
   c. balance of power   d. weather balance

2. Mowat's description of a year living close to the wolves ___**a**___ the traditional image of the "big, bad wolf."
   a. denies   b. draws on   c. shows   d. supports

3. The ___**a**___ was clear.
   a. suggestion   b. moral   c. talk   d. singing

4. However, Angeline, apparently __b__ of her responsibilities as a mother, stayed home to watch her youngsters.
   a. because   b. aware   c. forgetful   d. resentful

5. Mowat gives a(n) __d__ description of wolf games of "tag."
   a. long   b. accurate   c. scientific   d. vivid

6. He __b__ that wolves could also live on a diet of mice.
   a. noted   b. drew the conclusion   c. drew the picture
   d. gave the explanation

7. Mowat's experience with Arctic wolves was a(n) __d__ to efforts to make people more aware of wolves.
   a. climax   b. answer   c. resistance   d. introduction

8. He __d__ the aid of wildlife organizations.
   a. hoped for   b. refused   c. dreamed about   d. called for

9. He urged the government to __c__ rewards for dead wolves.
   a. offer   b. support   c. withdraw   d. increase

10. In response to the pleas of Mowat and other wildlife __c__, people are now taking steps to protect this animal.
    a. donors   b. models   c. supporters   d. leaders

■ Discussion Questions

1. What events first made Mowat suspect that wolves were not as vicious as people believed?

2. How do the wolves compare with human parents?

3. Killing wolves and selling their skins is one way for people who live in the Arctic to support themselves. Do you think the Canadian government should allow this? Why or why not?

◀ ENGLISH IDIOMS

Speech and Writing

Since language is used to express ideas, many English idioms contain concepts of speech and writing. To *talk back* means to answer rudely. To *talk down to* is to speak to somebody as if he or she were stupid. However, to *talk up* something means to make something appear to be good. When we *talk big*, we boast, or brag, possibly about something that is not true. When we *talk over* a problem, we discuss that problem for quite a while. To *talk* people *out of* something is to persuade them not to do it. A person might *talk a friend out of* quitting college.

When we *talk through our hats*, we don't know the facts but make unsupported or untrue statements anyway. When a person *sweet talks* someone else, he falsely flatters that person. On the other hand, when he *talks turkey* he speaks the truth frankly, or *tells it like it is*.

Writing also plays a part in our idioms. To do something *to the letter* is to do it exactly. When we say *"It's nothing to write home about,"* we mean we are not enthusiastic about something.

To see the *handwriting on the wall* is to realize that disaster is coming. In the Bible, Belshazzar, king of Babylon, saw a hand appear at a feast and write on the wall a cryptic message that only the Jewish prophet Daniel could understand. The message predicted the destruction of Belshazzar's kingdom.

Quiz Again

Now that you have finished studying this chapter, here is the brief true-false quiz you took when you began. Take it again.

A **loquacious** person rarely talks.	True	False
An **inscription** may be carved.	True	False
An **epigram** is long.	True	False
Colloquial speech is formal.	True	False

Answers are on page 407. Did your score improve?

REVIEW

Chapters 9–12

■ Reviewing Words in Context

Complete each sentence with the word or term that fits best.

AN ETHIOPIAN'S JOURNEY TO THE UNITED STATES

a. ambivalence	e. conscious	i. destitute	m. incredulous
b. benefactors	f. creed	j. edict	n. introspect
c. beneficial	g. decades	k. empathy	o. malady
d. bilingual	h. defiant	l. expedite	p. nonchalant

Background: Semir, a student in the author's class, tells the story of his family's journey from Ethiopia to Saudi Arabia and the United States.

1. Ethiopia, my home, is not like the United States. It is an under-developed country, with many **i, destitute** people who live in poverty.

2. For three **g, decades** , almost thirty years, there was civil war in my homeland.

3. A(n) **j, edict** ordered all young men into the army and, to avoid this, my father escaped to Saudi Arabia.

4. As a teenager, my mother must have been **h, defiant** to some authority, for she spent some time in prison.

5. My aunt was **e, conscious** that my mother was in danger when she left prison, so she worked to get her out of Ethiopia.

6. My aunt tried hard to **l, expedite** her departure to the Sudan. My mother then went to Saudi Arabia to marry my father.

7. I was raised in Saudi Arabia and so I was **d, bilingual** , since I spoke Tigrinya and Arabic.

8. Originally, my mother was a Christian, but she now follows the Muslim **f, creed** .

9. When we came to the United States, I was surprised and delighted

   by the __k, empathy_____ that other Ethiopian immigrants
   showed us.

10. We had many __b, benefactors_____ who gave us things to make
    our lives easier.

11. Watching TV shows like *Sesame Street* was __c, beneficial_____
    to my English.

12. People are often __m, incredulous_____ when I tell them that I spent
    only two weeks in English as a Second Language classes in high
    school!

13. In more thoughtful moods, I __n, introspect_____ about my life
    in the United States.

14. Although people are richer here, I feel some __a, ambivalence_____
    toward all of the freedom in the United States and the lifestyle of the
    people.

15. At times, people in the United States seem __p, nonchalant_____
    about family life; but in Ethiopia people care deeply about
    family.

■ *Passage for Word Review*

Complete each blank in the Passage with the word or phrase that makes
the best sense. The choices include words from the vocabulary lists along
with related words. Use each choice only once.

WHY MY STEPFATHER WAS COURT-MARTIALED

a. affect	e. conspicuous	i. given carte blanche
b. audit	f. destitute	j. incredulous
c. beneficial	g. deviation	k. malevolent
d. centigrade	h. effect	l. verify

Background: This is a memorial tribute to the author's stepfather, Milton
Markman. A few hours after this story was told to the author's vocabulary
class, Mr. Markman collapsed and died.

In 1941, when my stepfather was drafted into the United States Army,
he had no interest or experience in cooking. Therefore, he was

(1) j, incredulous _____ when he was told that, on a written test, he had displayed a talent for preparing food. Army officials offered him a six-week course in becoming a chef. My stepfather accepted because he was sure he would be able to eat lots of leftovers.

As things turned out, he got good grades in cooking school. He be-

came head chef of an army kitchen and was **(2) i, given carte blanche** _____ to run things as he wanted to. All went well until he had to deal with spinach. Because spinach contains several vitamins that are

(3) c, beneficial _____ to human health, the army supplied it several times a week. Unfortunately, the soldiers simply refused to eat it. Even seeing spinach on their plates put them in a bad mood. After many hours spent cooking spinach, my stepfather realized that, at the end of the meal, he was throwing all of it away. To save time and effort, he decided simply to dispose of the hated vegetable before it was cooked.

Unfortunately, one day a visiting army officer, passing through the

camp, noticed a large, **(4) e, conspicuous** _____ pile of raw spinach in

the garbage. Another officer was sent out to **(5) l, verify** _____ that the first officer had seen everything correctly. Then an army accoun-

tant made an official **(6) b, audit** _____ of the amount that was missing from the raw spinach supply. At the end of this investigation, the army accused my stepfather of destroying government property.

At his court-martial trial my stepfather told the army officers that

his intentions had not been **(7) k, malevolent** _____. Instead, he was simply trying to save the army the trouble of cooking the unwanted vegetable. Nevertheless, the army officers found him guilty and deducted five dollars from his pay for the next three months. Because he did not have much money, this loss of pay was enough to leave him

(8) f, destitute _____ for quite a while.

After the trial, however, one officer talked to my stepfather privately

and told him that cooking spinach would **(9) a, affect** _____ the way that the army thought about the vegetable. Raw spinach was govern-ment property, but cooked spinach was considered garbage. In other words, if the spinach was cooked, it could be thrown out.

From then on, my stepfather cooked all the spinach and then imme-diately put it into a garbage can. By following this procedure without any

(10) g, deviation _____, he kept everyone happy. The government did not have its property thrown out, and the soldiers did not have spin-ach on their plates.

■ *Reviewing Learning Strategies*

New Words from Word Elements　Below are some words you have not studied that are formed from classical word elements. Using your knowledge of these elements, write in the letter of the word that best completes each sentence. Use each choice only once.

a. accredited   e. dictaphone   i. pedometer
b. audiologist   f. galvanometer   j. telepathy
c. biometrics   g. hippophobia   k. uniped
d. binary   h. malcontent   l. verdict

1. Named after Luigi Galvani, a pioneer in electricity, a(n) **f, galvanometer** measures electrical current.

2. Sensing or feeling from far away is **j, telepathy** because *tele-* means "far."

3. A(n) **k, uniped** is an animal that walks on one foot.

4. A(n) **b, audiologist** is a specialist in the study of measuring hearing.

5. If you are not content, you are **h, malcontent** .

6. If you want to measure how far your feet walk, you can use a(n) **i, pedometer** .

7. A jury is said to "speak the truth" when it gives a(n) **l, verdict** .

8. Something **d, binary** consists of two parts.

9. **c, Biometrics** is the branch of science that takes statistical data, or measurements, on living things.

10. We can believe in the skill of a doctor or dentist who is **a, accredited** .

Answers to Quizzes

Page 16 1. noun, transitive verb, intransitive verb 2. 2, as a noun 3. Old French

Page 41 gullible—true; ascetic—false; frugal—true; stoic—false

Pages 44–45 1. The Bruins were losing 3–1, but, to the Rangers' surprise, the Bruins ended up winning the ice hockey game 4–3. 2. Minnesota, not Iowa State, was expected to win. The game was tied at the end, so it went into overtime. Iowa State won. 3. The Bulls had been playing away from their home town and had been losing games. Surprisingly, they won this game, which was also away from home.

Pages 45–46 a. 3 b. 2 c. 1

Page 46 a. 2 b. 1

Page 47 1. overloaded, flooded 2. begged

Page 48 1. replaced 2. delay 3. agreement

Page 74 attrition—false; ominous—true; radical—false; ludicrous—true

Page 79 1. having indent curves 2. severe 3. a city in Greece
1. noisy 2. copy; imitate 3. doubting

Page 89 1. c 2. e 3. d 4. a 5. f 6. b

Page 103 emulate—true; chagrin—false; enigma—false; contemplate—false

Page 107 1. c 2. a 3. d 4. e 5. b

Page 109 1. careful 2. puzzling 3. required

Page 120 1. painful 2. lied 3. rerun 4. buried 5. used

Page 133 chivalrous—false; zealous—true; mitigating—false; euphemism—false

Page 141 Reaction—prefix "re-"; root "act"; suffix "-tion."
Unlikely—prefix "un-"; root "like"; suffix "-ly."
Exchanges—prefix "ex-"; root "change"; suffix "-s."

Reviewing—prefix "re-"; root "view"; suffix "-ing."
Invisibly—prefix "-in"; root "visible"; suffix "-ly."

Page 146   1. c   2. d   3. a

Page 147   equidistant—equal in distance;   indirect—not direct;   reappear—appear again

Page 148   revive—to live again, to become healthy again;   incredulous—not believing

Page 159   1. e   2. c   3. d   4. f   5. a   6. b

Page 176   incongruous—false;   eccentric—true;   equivocate—false; antipathy—true

Page 179   1. b   2. f   3. a   4. d   5. c   6. e

Page 186   1. d   2. a   3. e   4. c   5. f   6. b

Page 208   vivacious—false;   congenital—true;   maverick—false; psychosomatic—false

Page 225   1. c   2. h   3. f   4. b   5. g   6. a   7. e   8. d

Page 240   jettison—true;   staunch—false;   status quo—false;   perverse—false

Page 259   1. f   2. b   3. d   4. e   5. c   6. a

Page 271   disparity—true;   charisma—true;   gregarious—false;   disreputable—false

Page 279   a. two   b. three   c. four   d. five   e. six   f. seven

Page 307   unanimity—true;   decimate—false;   duplicity—false;   perennial—false

Page 310   catty—mean;   birdbrain—stupid or foolish person;   sitting duck—an easy target to hit;   pigeonhole—to identify as something very specific, to limit to one thing;   a can of worms—having lots of problems; puppy love—childish, youthful love;   hogwash—nonsense, silly talk

Page 317   1. fear of cats   2. fear of animals   3. fear of germs   4. fear of work   5. fear of spiders

Page 338   holds out an olive branch—false;   nonchalant—false;   acrophobic—true;   credibility—true

Page 342   1. c   2. d   3. b   4. a

Page 369   inaudible—false;   beneficial—true;   conspicuous—true;   malevolent—true

Page 377   1. Superman, as a television series;   2. Star Trek   3. Star Wars (movie)

Page 399   loquacious—false;   inscription—true;   epigram—false;   colloquial—false

Index of Words and Word Elements

Word elements are printed in italics.

Index of Key Terms